HARVARD HISTORICAL STUDIES

PUBLISHED UNDER THE DIRECTION OF
THE DEPARTMENT OF HISTORY

FROM THE INCOME OF
THE HENRY WARREN TORREY FUND

VOLUME XLVII

CONSTITUTIONAL THOUGHT IN SIXTEENTH-CENTURY FRANCE

A STUDY IN THE EVOLUTION OF IDEAS

BY

WILLIAM FARR CHURCH

1969

OCTAGON BOOKS

New York

PREFACE

THE necessary acknowledgements of aid rendered to the author in the preparation of this study may be quickly made. The work was originally undertaken at the suggestion of Professor Charles Howard McIlwain of Harvard University, and to him I owe a great debt, both for his constant encouragement and for his many fruitful suggestions. Those who are familiar with Professor McIlwain's writings will recognize at once the extent to which I have utilized his many and masterly contributions in the field of political thought. Throughout the preparation of this volume, he has given abundant guidance coupled with unflagging enthusiasm, the finest things in teaching. At most, I may hope that the following pages will take their place among the many valuable studies resulting from his inspiration.

W. F. C.

ST. JOSEPH, MICHIGAN
October, 1940

CONTENTS

CONSTITUTIONAL THOUGHT IN
SIXTEENTH–CENTURY FRANCE

INTRODUCTION

THE present study is an attempt to trace the evolution of French constitutional thought through the sixteenth century as it is revealed in a specific body of writings. The two concepts upon which we have constructed our treatment are those which formed the fundamentals of contemporary theory of the constitution: the royal authority and the rights of the subjects. Through their manifestation in fundamental and customary law, these portions of the constitution formed the primary divisions of right and property in the social structure; they will be treated in their details and variants, together with their relations to the more important institutions of government. The period considered in this study was one of the most important in the evolution of these vital concepts, since at that time there occurred the significant change from essentially medieval constitutional theories. The deviation was effected in general by the centering of political thought about the newly formed national state, and as concomitant developments there appeared interpretations recognizing the royal authority of legislation and the direct subjection of all persons to the monarch. Parallel with the rapid changes in the social structure, there occurred a definite development of political concepts which corresponded roughly to the evolution within society. Yet this alteration of accepted constitutional doctrine was not caused exclusively by factual considerations; intellectual currents, philosophical as well as legal, exercised marked influence upon theories of state. Simple elaboration, development, and recombination of accepted ideas provided thinkers with many new interpretations which were often decisive in changing the older modes of thought. By analyzing these aspects of a complex and interesting movement, we shall attempt to present the essential features of the evolution of French constitutional thought in the sixteenth century.

The written sources through which we propose to trace these developments may be classed as the works of three groups of men: the legists, the historians, and the officers in the royal administration. Although differing in the exact nature of their literary efforts, these men formed a single, distinct unit through their presence in a common social class, the similarity of their legal training, and the resulting correspondence of their ideas concerning the organization and fundamentals of the state. Among them, the legists were by far the most important and constituted in themselves a great school of writers, the finest of their profession to be found in Europe during the century. The activity of this large body of able practitioners reflects the great intellectual ferment characteristic of the age; but as a school they may be regarded as carrying on the long tradition of the profession which centered about the courts, the royal administration, and the schools of law. Their formal treatises dealt with a multitude of legal considerations, ample subjects of investigation being found not only in the questions studied by their predecessors during centuries of legal practice but also in the newly codified customary law. Their works are a mine of information concerning the constitutional thought prevailing throughout the period.

The writings of contemporary historians are of similar value in presenting theories of state held by men with legal background. Although these works were written as histories of earlier periods, they embody treatment of constitutional problems confronting men in the sixteenth century, both through direct statement and through implication concerning the continued value of modes of life prevailing in the past. During the century there appeared in France for the first time historians worthy of the name, and it was invariably their intention not only to instruct their contemporaries concerning the lives of men in earlier periods but also to aid in coping with present difficulties through an understanding of those solutions found to be successful in previous human experience. This approach was permitted by the prevailing lack of any sense of historical relativity and rested upon the all-important idea of the state as a permanent, unchanging entity. Men conceived of the social structure in this fashion both because the law upon which it rested was thought necessarily to be fixed and because the ideals which the law embodied were likewise considered to be permanent. The constitution prevailing in earlier periods was believed to be the same as that rightly forming the foundation of the sixteenth-century state, and this permitted writers to outline their legal theory in terms of the usage prevailing in previous centuries. Argument from historical precedent had immense weight in the eyes of men imbued with this approach to political questions and caused thinkers frequently to formulate their interpretations concerning immediate problems in terms of older regulations. For this reason, the histories of France written during the century take their place beside the formal treatises on constitutional problems as major sources of contemporary legal thought.

Finally, the writings left by members of the central administration contain interpretations of vital importance because they embody the ideas of men who handled practical matters of government and thus reflect the impact of factual considerations which shaped in part the prevailing constitutional thought. The statements of these men are of especial importance in regard to the major institutions because they represent the ideas held by active members of those bodies. Analysis of the writings of the councillors and magistrates is the most accurate means of understanding both the historical activity of those institutions and contemporary theory of their place in the constitution. Like the other groups of writers whose works we shall consider, these men were necessarily trained in the law and approached political problems through its medium. Thus, although the legists, historians, and administrators varied slightly in the exact nature of their written works, together they form a single group of men whose writings embody the major portions of contemporary constitutional thought as it was propounded in terms of accepted law. Because of these common qualities, the three groups may be classed together for purposes of discussion under the single heading of "legists." [1]

The place of the legists in the intellectual life of the period was such that they were peculiarly fitted to reveal in their works not only the prevailing political thought but also the factors making for its evolution. The vital characteristic of their position was that they stood midway between those writers whose concern was limited to the facts of social organization and those whose works were purely speculative in nature. On the one hand, the legists were grounded through their training and immediate practice in the facts of accepted law and could not deviate appreciably from such; they were bound to incorporate into their intellectual systems the traditional bases of society. But this did not preclude an understanding of, and an emphasis upon, the more abstract and ideal qualities inherent in contemporary political thought; on the contrary, such was required both by their approach to problems of a general nature and by their system of education. It was this fundamental quality of their thought — unerring acceptance of the substantive law at the basis of the social structure and yet keen perception of the intangible principles held universally to govern society — that admirably fitted them to present the theory of state accepted during the century, both in terms of its content at any given moment and the forces making for the evolution of concepts. The state was identified with law, both in terms of established law of the constitution and the universal principles over society, to such a point that the most penetrating and influential evaluation of political problems was necessarily through legal considerations. The legists approached constitutional questions through such media and thus dealt with the fundamentals at the basis of society. Their study became a discipline in terms of accepted legal values provided by the framework of the social structure and by the ideals which it was

---

[1] It will be noted that our use of the term "legist" is much more inclusive than the connotation carried by the French *légiste*, which, for students of the sixteenth century and earlier, usually means simply Roman lawyer.

held partially to embody. Thus their work avoided the danger of becoming a series of facile descriptions without basis. Because of this quality of the legists' thought, their works form a most representative source for the political theory prevailing during the period. When the doctrines of the legists underwent significant alteration, the accepted constitutional thought may be regarded as having changed in the same direction.

The intellectual systems of the legists included cognizance not only of the details of constitutional law but also of more abstract values, and this fact exercised very important influence upon the nature of their thought. In a very real sense all learning was one in the sixteenth century. Although the legists had received their specialized training in the schools of law, they were frequently educated in the entire body of Renaissance learning and thus tended to treat constitutional problems in terms of criteria broader than strictly legal concepts. In considering questions essentially political in nature, they enriched — and often encumbered — their discussions with material from philosophy, history, religion, classical literature, astrology, and many other "sciences" of the period. Their idea, that all fields of learning constituted but various portions of universal knowledge, permitted, and even required this utilization of all available materials in the treatment of constitutional problems. One very important influence of this approach in the field of political thought was that it caused the legists to give great weight to natural and divine law. Although the immediate concern of the majority of the profession was the detailed law of the constitution, they were highly conscious of abstract ideals as definite criteria in the light of which to evaluate lesser considerations. Throughout the century they maintained unbroken the great scale of legal values which was an inheritance from medieval thought and which extended from eternal law to earthly custom. Although they varied considerably in the degree of completeness with which they incorporated the abstract qualities of the scale into their constitutional systems, they never questioned the fundamental unity of all legal values in a great, single whole. This quality of their thought renders it impossible to evaluate their interpretation of given political problems strictly through their ideas of fundamental and customary law. In the thought of a given legist, his emphasis upon the laws of God and nature must be taken into consideration because it often exercised decisive influence upon his interpretation of questions pertaining to the law of the constitution. Furthermore, the weight attributed by the legists to these universal values was a significant factor in the evolution of constitutional thought. As the century progressed, the tendency became more and more to interpret legal problems in terms of natural and divine law rather than the customary law of the land. This increased emphasis upon the upper brackets of the scale appeared in the works of such men as Charondas Le Caron and exercised an unmistakably devitalizing influence upon the older constitutionalism; for when many of its crucial aspects, such as the essence of customary law and the legal limitations upon the king, were interpreted purely in terms of abstract values, there was certain to occur a change in the qualities ascribed to the legal foundations of the state. Emphasis upon the immediate applicability of natural and divine law to constitutional questions arose from the conception, accepted by the legists without question, that those universals formed an inherent part of the scale of legal values and served as criteria for judging the lower portions of the whole. Nevertheless, to interpret the major portions of the accepted constitution in terms of abstract principles struck at the roots of the traditional constitutionalism because it changed the nature of the law of the land. Such a use of universal principles by the legists served as a vital factor in the rise of absolutism.

It is necessary to indicate the relation of these men of the law to the other schools of thought during the period, both to establish their position in the intellectual life of the century and to define the limits of the present study. Always keeping in mind the undifferentiated and extremely fluid character of sixteenth-century intellectual activity, we have adopted the

following working categories. The majority of the men whose
works we propose to examine are those who may be classed as
French constitutional legists, that is, those who approached
problems of legal theory and practice through French law in
contrast to those whose interpretations were based upon Roman
law. We recognize at once that this distinction is arbitrary
and involves distortion of the facts of French legal history;
every student of the period is well aware of the great influence
exercised by Roman conceptions in the political thought of the
age. Yet the history of Roman law in the century is a study in
itself which we cannot undertake within the compass of the
present treatment. It is our conviction that, at least for purposes of study, a rough distinction between French and Roman
may be made and that in a single monograph on the subject the
dominant emphasis may be placed upon the French. This does
not necessitate a complete isolation of treatment; in dealing
with specific problems of law upon which Roman concepts
definitely impinged, the fact and significance of this Roman
influence will be indicated, although without elaboration.
Furthermore, the broad lines of the history of Roman law in
the century render this distinction impossible of application in
our second chapter which deals with political thought during
the first half of the century. Although the writers of that period
disowned much that characterized the work of Bartolus, they
did not hesitate to follow his example in applying Roman conceptions to contemporary questions of law; in their works there
was a deliberate and well-nigh complete fusion of Roman and
French interpretations causing the practical identification of
the French king and the Roman *princeps*. We have necessarily
given attention to Roman legal conceptions in studying the
works of that period. But with the advent of Cujas and his
school, Roman law came increasingly to be regarded as a body
of legal precepts to be established with historical accuracy
according to their variation in the periods of the classic state.
Humanism tended to dissociate the system from practical affairs
and to make it rather a subject for historical research. The

Bartolist approach continued to exercise strong influence throughout the century, but the establishment of the historicity of Roman law caused a divergence of currents lessening the immediate applicability of the system and thereby allowing the emphasis followed in this study.

The relation of the legists to the great religious movements of the century — the Reformation and the Counter-Reformation — will be dealt with only as these affected the former's interpretations of points of law and thus influenced the evolution of their concepts. Although the political thought of the Huguenots was very important during the second half of the century, its influence upon the thought of the legists was but slight as concerned specific interpretations. Certain Catholic historians indulged in a very limited borrowing from the ideas presented by the opponents of the monarchy, but the concepts which the latter set forth were, in the main, a distinct variation from those of the great body of legists and thus had small weight in affecting accepted constitutional thought. The only exception was that of causing the legists, as defenders of monarchy, to harden their lines of interpretation in opposition to the variations introduced by those questioning the older theory. Of greater immediate effect, although not of comparable intrinsic value, were the doctrines put forward by the Leaguers, but again their influence upon the thought of the legists — Gallicans and *politiques* almost without exception — was that of causing a reaction in opposition to the ideas put forward rather than a borrowing of them by the men of the law. Moreover, the hostility and open opposition of the legists to the pretensions of the Leaguers was of very important consequence upon accepted constitutional thought: the nature and great strength of the League's challenge to legitimate monarchy was such that it caused the defenders of secular government to put forward a complete theory of the divine right of kings. Thus it appears that if the two great religious movements in the sixteenth century influenced the evolution of legal concepts as they appeared in the writings of the legists, this was largely through external pressure causing a hardening of lines of interpretation rather than through the borrowing of ideas from one school by another. The legists throughout represent a central party from which there appeared deviation first in the works of the Huguenots and later in those of the Leaguers, and although these variations caused the jurists to exercise greater precision in their details of interpretation, they arrived at their conclusions essentially by developing concepts long accepted by members of their own ranks. It is by showing these definite but limited points of contact that we have attempted to outline the relationship of the legists with the major religious movements of the century.

It must be emphasized that the present study is concerned primarily with legal theory and not with the facts of legal practice. The two form in any given period parallel elements and exercise definite influence the one upon the other, yet each is distinct within itself. Certain materials from legal practice and procedure — the royal ordinances, details of customary law, decisions of the courts, and the actions and administrative processes of the various institutions of government — have been utilized as they were related to vital questions of constitutional thought, particularly in regard to those of public law; but the emphasis is necessarily upon the theoretical element. This approach involves a limitation of treatment according to the thought content to be found in the written works of the legists and a corresponding variation from the facts of legal history. Thus, if it is stated that the corporations and legal communities of various types held their rights entirely subject to the discretion of the king, this is but a representation of the statements in the treatise under consideration; it is not intended to convey the facts of the situation, which, in this case as in many others, were at variance with the statements of the theorists. This difference between the developed concepts of the legists and the facts of legal practice appeared in the most important works of the century: Du Moulin's approach would have reduced great portions of the legal system stemming from the Middle Ages to a mere shadow of its former self and would have substituted a theory of state based essentially upon the primary concepts of king and subjects. Again, if it is stated that subsequent to Du Moulin such was the accepted theory of state, this is intended to be understood merely as representing the interpretation of a group of writers and not as a statement of the prevailing situation in terms of law. This distinction does not deny the influence of legal concepts upon the evolution of the law of the constitution. Again the case of Du Moulin is instructive, for it is certain that his many treatises were of immense weight in influencing the ideas of men in the profession, the judgments of the courts, the opinions of royal commissioners carrying out the codification of custom, and hence the law itself. Yet this consideration does not deny the essential identity of the theoretical element, and it is that which has received greatest stress in the present discussion.

The question whether the subject of this study is political theory is answered largely by one's definition of that field. Professor Barker in a brilliant chapter has shown the necessity of legal materials in any well-rounded political theory, whether one's initial approach be through the legal or the sociological facet of human society. He likewise makes the generalization, subject to exception, that the legal approach has characterized the major portion of political writing produced on the continent of Europe throughout the centuries.[2] The validity of this generalization relative to the thought of certain periods may well be challenged, but there is no doubt of its accuracy concerning the political theory of sixteenth-century France. At that time probably more than at any other, the legal approach dominated political speculation. With the decline of universal papacy and Empire and the emergence of the sovereign, national state as the primary consideration in political life, theorists withdrew their attention from the formal organization of universal

[2] Ernest Barker, editor, Otto von Gierke, *Natural Law and the Theory of Society* (Cambridge University Press, 1934), Introduction, § 2, "Law and Political Theory."

Christendom and placed their dominant emphasis upon the national unit, the realm. Political treatises lost their theological coloring and reflected rather the laicization of concepts generally and the breakup of Europe into independent kingdoms. In seeking a solid foundation upon which to build a political theory reflecting primarily the life of the national unit, writers turned inevitably to the law at its basis. The constitution of each sovereign state provided the most readily available basis for theoretical speculation concerning the same, and throughout the sixteenth century political thought was invariably grounded in the legal organization of one or more national units. This was particularly true of France where the national consciousness was in advance of that obtaining in the great majority of European kingdoms. If we recall to mind the three types of political thinkers mentioned above — those approaching the field through the facts of society, through the law, and through pure speculation — and attempt to find illustrative examples from among the political treatises produced in sixteenth-century France, it is at once apparent that the legal approach dominated the field to the practical exclusion of all others. Purely speculative treatises, so characteristic of the eighteenth century, were all but non-existent and at their rare appearances seem oddly out of place.[3] The approach through sociological factors, after the manner of Machiavelli, characterized incidentally the work of certain historians and was of greater significance than the purely speculative,[4] but for reasons given above, the historians were much closer to the legists of the period than to our modern writers of history who propound social philosophies. The only major group of political writers not included in these categories were those who wrote coinci-

---

[3] A possible example is the *Discours de la servitude volontaire* of Etienne de La Boétie.

[4] It is customary to recall in this connection the similarity between the method of Bodin, especially in his *Methodus*, and that of Machiavelli. See Pierre Mesnard, *L'Essor de la philosophie politique au seizième siècle* (Paris, 1936), pp. 538–541. This is undoubtedly true to a certain extent. However, there is little doubt that in Bodin's *Republic*, the pattern of his thought is that of a jurist and not that of a sociologist or even an historian.

dentally with the Reformation and the Counter-Reformation, but even in the works of those authors legal constructions abound. The political theories of Beza and Hotman were without doubt conditioned by, and incidental to, their religious beliefs; yet when they constructed their systems of state they betook themselves to the law. Even the author of a more heavily religious and philosophical work such as the *Vindiciae contra tyrannos* relied upon legal interpretations for the framework of his political conceptions; while in the opposite camp a zealot like Boucher attempted to convince his hearers with arguments concerning the authority of the Estates General and the legal justification of tyrannicide. The inescapable conclusion is that political thought during the sixteenth century, even when presented by authors with a non-political cause to support, was invariably approached after the manner of the jurists. In a very real sense, the history of political theory during the period is all but indistinguishable from the history of legal philosophy.

The written sources through which we propose to study the thought of the men under consideration are their formal treatises, their speeches in the courts and in the Estates General, and certain portions of the immense pamphlet literature produced by the social upheavals of the period. These works are the only available guides to the concepts held by this group of men who lived some four centuries ago, and as such they must be studied with great care if an appreciable perception of the intellectual life of an age long past is to be achieved. Often the emphasis lent by an individual writer to an important concept is apparent not from the specific details of his statement but rather from the fine shades of interpretation caused by his subtly stressing certain aspects of the question. This is especially characteristic of the writings of the legists who as a body dealt essentially with like materials and whose originality lay not in innovation but rather in the elucidation of concepts accepted by the profession as a whole. For this reason, it has been necessary to illustrate the thought of given men through quotations of considerable length taken from their writings. For the same reason, we have left the majority of these passages untranslated, presenting in the text merely the substance and implications of the passages utilized.

There are many problems of organization which must be taken into account in outlining the legal thought extending over a considerable period of time and covering a relatively large number of very important concepts. Even among the legists, every man's thought presents in itself a distinct system and must be evaluated as such, yet it is impossible to present the history of legal thought in terms of a series of such systems without endless repetition of ideas. The alternative is to present the variations and specific contributions of individual men, thus incurring the risk of distorting a given man's doctrine through false emphasis upon one small portion of his thought. However, the works of the legists are peculiarly adapted to this latter type of treatment. Because of their common educational background and roughly similar professional experience, they approached political questions through a body of precepts generally accepted by the members of the profession. Their thought falls into a single, general framework or pattern, the essentials of which were common to all. Thus, after grouping the legists of the period among individual schools of thought, the student may trace important concepts through the general body of writings of each school with tolerable accuracy and establish the position of each component member in terms of his variation and contribution. When approaching the evolution of ideas through this type of source material, it is permissible to stress certain aspects of a man's thought beyond the place which they occupied in his system as a whole. Only occasionally does there appear a Du Moulin or a Bodin whose intellectual vigor and breadth of interpretation enabled him to reevaluate great sections of accepted law in terms of certain fundamental criteria and thus to create a unique intellectual system. Such figures necessitate special treatment, but the great majority of writers did little more than add miscellaneous emphases and annotations to the accepted body of law and thus may be dealt with as component parts of a given school. It is by seeking out the contributions made by the greater men in terms of their systems as distinct units and by the lesser men as members of specific schools that we propose to examine the flow of constitutional thought.

Among the legists, the greater and lesser men alike were careful to avoid in their writings all innovations of a radical character. Their approach to political problems through the law precluded in itself any drastic change in concepts, and thus the evolution of legal thought often resolves itself into a series of fine shades of emphasis and interpretation. Nevertheless, the period witnessed many important and far-reaching alterations in constitutional doctrine, and these seem to have been effected at the hands of those legists whose contributions, either because of intrinsic merit or timeliness or both, were taken up by a large body of followers. The most significant innovations in political thought were set forth in the writings of the ablest thinkers who had reevaluated much accepted law in the light of certain criteria and had drawn conclusions which were sufficiently close to current ideas to permit of their receiving wide recognition, but which nevertheless constituted specific innovation. But in the process of winning widespread acceptance, such a contribution was necessarily altered and vulgarized according to the lesser abilities of the men who adopted it. In the mind of the one setting forth the new interpretation, it stood as a single portion of a complete intellectual system, but when torn from its original milieu by those making it their own, it was very frequently distorted, often causing it to imply something quite different from the meaning intended by its originator. Yet in the evolution of ideas, this distortion is often of greater importance than the exact sense of the original concept. For this reason, the second- and third-rate men may be ascribed a position in the history of ideas as important, if not as immediately influential, as those of highest calibre. It is for this reason that we have considered in this study the works written by numbers of lesser men of the profession, both as indices to the flow of ideas and as guides to the increasing acceptance of earlier contributions during any given period.

We are quite sensible of the incompleteness of the present study in proportion to the great body of relevant legal theories and the mass of writings in which they were presented during the sixteenth century. Treatment has been limited to consideration of certain fundamental concepts as they were set forth in the works of the men susceptible of classification in the groups indicated above. In the first chapter, we have attempted to outline the general setting of French constitutionalism through the medium of the thought of Claude de Seyssel. His system provides an excellent point of departure in tracing the growth of ideas, both because it embodied the major elements of legal thought in their traditional form, and because it represented the theory of state widely held at the opening of the century. The second chapter is concerned with the thought of the extremely absolutist school which flourished under the strong rule of Francis I and Henry II. This body of writers included Grassaille, Rebuffi, Chasseneuz, Budé, and many lesser figures. As an illustration of the implications of their concepts upon immediate legal practice, we have included a short consideration of the writings of Tiraqueau. In analyzing the thought of these writers, we have considered only those salient features which were important as general developments of constitutional interpretation. This is in order to place especial stress upon those intellectual currents which were concomitant then and later with a theory of absolutism.

Following the first two chapters which are essentially introductory in character, we have presented in the third the theory of the French constitution as it was revealed in the writings of that great school of legists which flourished in the capital from the mid-century throughout the Wars of Religion. Including such men as Du Moulin, Du Tillet, Pasquier, Du Haillan, Choppin, de Harlay, and a host of lesser figures, this group represented the great body of constitutionalists *par excellence* in the century. Their works may be regarded as presenting in developed form those legal concepts which the majority of the profession believed to form the foundations of the state and which comprised the essentials of sixteenth-century constitutional thought. Their interpretations have been analyzed in their elements and variations and have been treated topically according to the major divisions of constitutional organization: the fundamental and customary law and the major institutions of government. The greater portions of this constitutional doctrine stemmed from theories accepted in the Middle Ages and represent the traditional conceptions in matured form. Although the system contained elements making for its own destruction, in the round it may be regarded as representing the theory of state most widely accepted during the sixteenth century.

Following this outline of the traditional constitutional system, we have attempted to present in the fourth chapter the major features of the evolution of legal thought making for a deviation from the older concepts and the substitution of a theory of absolutism. The most important innovations causing that change appear to have been made by certain thinkers of greatest ability, and subsequently to have won general acceptance among the legists because of their natural position as defenders of the monarchy throughout the Wars of Religion. We have attempted to trace the manner in which each of these developments tended increasingly toward a theory of absolutism. The chapter comprises treatment of three divisions of thought which gave rise to the new theory. All were similar in placing increased stress upon the position of the people as essentially equal subjects directly under the rule of the king. The first division of the chapter is devoted to the thought of Charles Du Moulin, with especial emphasis upon the manner in which he attempted through devious means to undermine the hierarchical system of society stemming from the Middle Ages and to bring all men into immediate subordination under the king. The second division deals with the thought of Jean

Bodin and certain of his more important contemporaries whose
systems provide the current interpretations in the light of which
it is necessary to evaluate Bodin's contribution. In this section
we have laid special stress upon the theory of royal sovereignty
and legislation, utilizing the political systems of Bodin and
Charondas Le Caron as most representative of the two contemporary theories of kingship. Emphasis has also been placed
upon the concomitant subjection of the customary law to the
authority of the king and upon the tendency toward royal
domination over the rights of the subjects. In the third portion
of the chapter, we have attempted to trace the expansion and
distortion of Bodin's thought among subsequent writers, first
among the major legists of the time, Jean Duret, François
Grimaudet, Pierre Grégoire, and Adam Blackwood, and secondly in the works of the royalist pamphleteers who defended
legitimate monarchy against the attacks of the League. The
latter included such figures as Pierre de Belloy, François Le
Jay, and Jacques Hurault. The chief importance of this school
was in their amalgamation of Bodin's theory of sovereignty
with the divine right of kings, thus developing an interpretation
fundamental to the later theory of absolutism.

In the fifth chapter, we have considered as a unit the constitutional thought of Guy Coquille. Although this chapter may
appear to be out of place in the general body of this study, it
has been inserted at this point because of the unusual character
of Coquille's ideas. Writing the majority of his works in the
last fifteen years of the sixteenth century, Coquille presented a
constitutional system of such extreme conservatism that it
stood apart from the major currents of legal ideas in the century
and contrasted not only with the doctrines of the royalists but
with those of the Parisian constitutionalists as well. Coquille
was essentially a man of the provinces rather than of the school
of legists in the capital, and he passed the greater portion of his
active career in the service of one of the few remaining feudal
dignitaries. His thought evinced the feudal and provincial
point of view to such an extent that he upheld conceptions

which, although logical in constitutional thought and widely
accepted during the Middle Ages, had long been discarded by
the Parisian jurists. Thus although a very important evidence
of intellectual currents during the century, his system stands
apart from the major lines of development and must be treated
as a third division of constitutional thought prevailing in France
at the close of the Religious Wars.

In the final chapter we have considered the elements of
seventeenth-century absolutism as they were embodied in certain writings published during the reign of Henry IV. It has
been emphasized that the conceptions fundamental to the new
theory had been presented in works written previously during
the Wars of Religion, and that those thinkers who upheld royal
absolutism during Henry's rule had but to utilize earlier contributions as they would. The increasing acceptance of the
new theory has been illustrated through the medium of three
types of sources. First, the increasing veneration for discipline,
strict control from above, and the various elements of seventeenth-century classicism relative to political theory have been
examined as they appeared in the thought of Pierre Charron.
Secondly, the series of pamphlets written by such men as Du
Rivault, Constant, Poisson, and Regnault Dorleans. These
broadsides appeared during the short interval, 1596–98, and
reflect the widespread desire for peace and strong rule and a
willingness to attribute authority to the king almost without
limits in order that he might bring order to the land. The ideas
of the pamphleteers were likewise upheld by the major contemporary legists who presented the theory of absolutism in
that more rigid form lent by its incorporation into complete
legal systems. These jurists included Loisel, Du Vair, L'Hommeau, Barclay, and Loyseau; they comprise the final group
whose writings have been considered. Although many of the
concepts contained in these works had been presented earlier,
the manner in which they were upheld by writers under the
rule of the first Bourbon king reveals that they were passing
through a process of crystallization concomitant with their

rapid achievement of general acceptance. The establishment of royal absolutism as the dominant consideration in accepted theory of state brings to a close that period in the evolution of French constitutional thought which is the subject of the present study.

CHAPTER I

CLAUDE DE SEYSSEL AND THE CORPORATE STATE

EVERY discussion of an evolutionary process must necessarily consist of a statement of the three stages included therein: the original position from which the development proceeded, the details of the process of change, and finally the position achieved at the conclusion. In a field as complex and inclusive as the history of political thought, the two termini must of necessity be chosen arbitrarily, yet it is impossible to study a given development without such delimitations. Students of French political thought in the sixteenth century are fortunate in having their point of departure well defined in the work of one man, the *Grande Monarchie* of Claude de Seyssel;[1] for it is generally agreed that his ideas were representative of the conception of state held generally by Frenchmen early in the century. It has well been said that the later evolution of French constitutional thought may be interpreted as little more than a series of varying emphases upon one or more aspects of his system.[2] For this reason, it is fitting that we initiate our study with an outline of the thought of Seyssel, together with illustrations from that of a few parallel theorists.

As a member of the royal administration and an ardent admirer of Louis XII, Seyssel was admirably fitted to summarize the political thought current in his day, yet it should be noted that he intended his book not as a treatment of theory but as a vehicle for the instruction of the young Francis I concerning the laudable policies of his predecessor. Furthermore, if his constitutional doctrine emphasized the limitations upon the ruler, the bulk of his effort was concerned solely with the prince,

---

[1] *La Grande Monarchie de France*, first published in 1519. Our references are to the edition of Paris, 1558.

[2] J. W. Allen, *A History of Political Thought in the Sixteenth Century* (London, 1928), p. 275.

his policy and his authority. The impression derived from the book is a complete confidence in a comfortable paternal rule. Throughout his writing, Seyssel's dominant aim was to counsel and guide his sovereign, for, as he said, in this monarchical state, everything depends upon the monarch.[3]

Later in the century, Seyssel's book was regarded as a model of constitutional thought, but in his day he did little but present a theory which, in its main outlines, had long been accepted. Briefly stated, the traditional, medieval theory of kingship held the ruler to be absolute within his sphere — the mosaic of rights accruing to him by virtue of his authorities as *rex* and *dominus* — but limited by divine, natural, and customary law which served as the guarantee of the rights enjoyed by the various categories of men.[4] This was definitely the theory of Seyssel. If his emphasis was upon the factors limiting the discretion of the king, it is nevertheless clear that he regarded the royal authority as *puissance absolue* suffering neither the control of any constituted organ nor any legal restriction as long as the ruler concerned himself solely with the exercise of the prerogative. Matters pertaining strictly to government were his to handle as he chose. Within the limitations set by law, the king, as Seyssel said, enjoyed an absolute authority to command and do what he would.[5] Only when he crossed its constituted bounds did his discretion suffer limitation.

In strict accord with Gallican tradition of long standing, Seyssel found the ultimate source of the royal prerogative in

---

[3] *Grande Monarchie*, p. 19b. Recto and verso of pages will be indicated by "a" and "b."

[4] Charles H. McIlwain, *The Growth of Political Thought in the West* (New York, 1932), chapter VII.

[5] The absolute character of the royal authority, in combination with specific legal limitations, is illustrated by the following passages. "Lequel iaçoit qu'il ayt toute puissance et authorité de commander et faire ce qu'il veut, toutesfois ceste grande et souueraine liberté est si bien reiglee, et limitee par bonnes loix et ordonnances. . . ." Seyssel, translator, *Appian Alexandrin, historian grec, des guerres des romains liures XI* (Paris, 1573), dedicatory epistle, no pagination. "Il y a plusieurs remedes pour refrener leur auctorité absolue, s'ilz sont deprauez et voluntaires. . . . Et pour parler desdictz freins par lesquelz la puissance absolue des Roys de France est reglée, i'en treuue trois principaux. . . ." *Grande Monarchie*, pp. 9b, 10a.

direct authorization by the Divinity without the aid of any communicating intermediary.[6] Although he never outlined in detail the exact content of the prerogative, it is clear that he was at one with the great majority of his predecessors in regarding it as essentially the authority to dispense justice and to carry out necessary acts of administration. The king was divinely instituted, he held, principally in order that he might administer justice to his subjects.[7] In his all-important capacity of supreme judge, he carried out his vital function of giving each man his due, of maintaining all legal rights within the social structure, and of preserving at once the legal bases and harmonious inner life of the state.

Seyssel summarized the limitations upon the exercise of the royal prerogative in his famous doctrine of the three checks. The first of these he found in the religious life of the state. But for Seyssel, a cleric, the political significance of religion was but one of its minor manifestations; in its essence it was the most precious possession of the realm.[8] Religion provided a definite way of life, a criterion of justice and right, an attitude dominating all persons from the king to the lowest subject. It was the primary element in the life of the state whose aims and ends were defined in terms of it. Consequently, a king who was true to his mission of just government should always be guided by this ideal in the exercise of the royal authority. A religious tyrant was an impossibility.[9] Although this check was entirely

[6] *Grande Monarchie*, pp. 29a, 29b, 33a. See Wera R. Lewin, *Claude de Seyssel* (Heidelberg, 1933), pp. 57–60. It is to be noted that Seyssel distinguished between the king and the crown and placed greatest stress upon the divine authorization of the latter.

[7] "Et d'autant est plus tenu le Prince et monarque de l'entretenir et garder [i.e. justice], qu'il est esleu et deputé par la diuine prouidence à ceste dignité si grande et si honorable principalement pour maintenir et faire iustice, qui est le vray office des princes." *Grande Monarchie*, pp. 33a–33b.

[8] *Grande Monarchie*, p. 33a. General discussion: pp. 29a–33a.

[9] "Or viuant le Roy (à tout le moins par apparence) selon la loy et religion Chrestienne, ne peult gueres faire choses tyranniques, et s'il en faict quelqu'vne, il est loisible à vn chascun prelat ou à autre homme religieux bien viuant: et ayant estime enuers le peuple, le luy remonstrer et increper, et à vn simple prescheur le reprendre et arguer publicquement, et en sa barbe." *Grande Monarchie*, pp. 10b–11a.

intangible, even when in the form of remonstrance by clerics, it had great weight in an age which derived its greatest motivating forces from religious concepts and values.

The second check upon the exercise of the royal prerogative Seyssel found in *la justice*. In effect, this limitation represented merely the application by the courts of the legal qualities inherent in kingship. The royal authority of administering justice was the essence of the prerogative, but if the king held title to supreme jurisdiction, he was nevertheless limited by it. This was necessarily the case, since the dispensing of justice involved the application of values binding upon ruler and subject alike because of the nature of the constitution. The established law provided the bases for the two primary spheres of right in the social structure — those of king and people respectively — and it was the duty of the Parlements, as guardians of the law, to give redress whenever the king went beyond the established bonds of accepted law by encroaching upon the rights of his subjects. The Parlements, wrote Seyssel, have been established for the purpose of administering justice and limiting the absolute authority of the monarch; thus, in carrying out their function, they not only provide judicial recourse of subject against subject but also of subject against king.[10] Such a statement leaves no doubt that Seyssel's concept of jurisdiction, the highest royal prerogative, involved effective limitation of the ruler in terms of law. His permission of judicial decision even against the monarch who held title to all authority of jurisdiction reveals strikingly the legal limitations inherent in his definition of kingship.

Unlike many writers later in the century, Seyssel did not

---

[10] "Le second frein est la iustice, laquelle sans point de difficulté est plus auctorisée en France qu'en nul autre pais du monde que lon sçache, mesmement à cause des parlemens qui ont esté instituez principalement pour ceste cause, et à ceste fin de refrener la puissance absolue dont vouldroient vser les Roys. Et si furent des le commencement establiz de si grans personnages, en tel nombre et auec telle puissance et pouuoir, que les Roys y ont, quant à la iustice distributiue, tousiours esté subiectz: tellement que lon a iustice et raison à l'encontre d'iceulx, aussi bien qu'à l'encontre des subiectz, es matieres ciuiles." *Grande Monarchie*, pp. 11b–12a.

believe that the sovereign authority of the king was sufficiently superior to private rights to permit him to encroach upon them through acts of government. On the contrary, the duty of the ruler was the maintenance of those rights, and his discretion suffered consequent limitations. These appear in Seyssel's thought in exact correspondence with the nature of the royal authorities in question. The prerogative of *jurisdiction* contained, as we have seen, inherent limitations of law. Likewise, the king held supreme right over matters of *government* or administration *per se*. These took the form simply of acts of authority and included no inherent limitations but suffered exterior limits of law whenever acts of the king encroached upon popular rights. If an officer carried out an unjust royal order, Seyssel said, it was not sufficient protection for him to plead command of the king, for eventually, when the jurisdiction of the courts enjoyed full sway, he would be punished according to the tenets of law and justice regardless of the command initiating his act.[11] Furthermore, it was an undoubted royal prerogative to give out letters in answer to individual petitions, yet Seyssel insisted that in doing so, the king had no authority to prejudice a man's legal right. In order to prevent this, royal letters were judged in the Parlement of Paris not only on the basis of obreption and subreption but also according to their consonance with the customary law of the land.[12]

---

[11] "Dont il aduient que bien peu de gens, mesmes ayans à perdre, soient si osez de faire, par le commandement precipité d'vn Prince volontaire, chose digne de punition, par ce que celuy commandement ne les excuseroit pas d'estre apres tost, ou tard, punis, quand l'exercice de la iustice seroit en pleine liberté, ainsi qu'on a veu, et voit lon iournellement de vostre temps, Sire, estre aduenu à plusieurs qui ont porté la peine des violences qu'eux ou leurs predecesseurs auoient faictes en temps de guerre ou autre, que la iustice n'auoit pas eu entierement son cours." Seyssel, *Appian Alexandrin*, dedicatory epistle, no pagination.

[12] "Et entre les parties priuées, leur auctorité ne peult preiudicier au droict d'autruy: Ains sont leurs lettres et rescris subiectz au iugement desdictz parlemens en tel cas, non pas touchant obreption et subreption seulement, comme ceulx des autres princes selon les loix Romaines: Mais touchant la ciuilité et inciuilité." *Grande Monarchie*, p. 12a. We have rendered the word *civilité* as consonance with custom. Godefroy, *Dictionnaire de l'ancienne langue française*, IX, 103, gives the definition: "observation des convenances, des égards usités

It is clear that Seyssel was entirely uncompromising in his insistence that the court might limit the action of the king when, even in his official capacity, he infringed the rights of his subjects. This was not a division of governmental authority nor a control of one constituted organ over another; it was simply the declaration by the court of the rights of a given party according to law. The law provided the basis and the limits of the rights of king and people respectively, and the court merely applied the law in preventing encroachment of one party upon another. For effective limitation of the king in this manner, Seyssel perceived that permanent tenure of judges was indispensable. Thus the magistrates, he said, were and ought to be perpetual officers. It was not within the authority of the king to remove them; they should be deprived of office only on the basis of forfeiture which should be judged by the court, and not by the king.[13] The circle was complete: strictly defined spheres of legal right enjoyed by king and people respectively, with the irremovable court as the body to maintain the legal bases and distinction.

The third check upon the exercise of the royal authority Seyssel called *la police*. This limitation was the most complex and likewise the most revealing concerning his constitutional system, since it included both the organized structure of the state and the established law at its basis. The royal authority constituted one important sphere of right in the social organism, and a specific body of law, known as the fundamental laws, was recognized as pertaining exclusively to the exercise and transmission of the prerogative. These were the inalienability of the royal domain and the law of succession to the crown, usually called the Salic Law. Regarding the inalienability of the domain, Seyssel maintained that this law not only limited the king but was put into effect by the Parlement and the *chambre*

<hr>

entre les hommes qui vivent en société." Charondas Le Caron defined *lettres inciviles* as those "obtenues contre le droict commun, coustume, ordonnance et equité." *Pandectes ou digestes du droict françois* (Paris, 1637), p. 100.

[13] *Grande Monarchie*, pp. 12a, 34b.

des comptes which debated royal letters ordering alienations
and often refused to allow their application.[14] This was but one
of Seyssel's statements revealing the manner in which he believed the constituted administrative bodies to provide effective
limitation of the royal discretion in terms of law. Even more
important was the law providing for the royal succession.
Seyssel described the Salic Law as a special law regulating the
succession to the French crown in a manner superior to that
followed in any other state because it automatically eliminated
all female claimants.[15] Unfortunately, he did not elaborate his
theory of the royal succession beyond the inherent advantages
and the actual working of the system, but he doubtless accepted
the more detailed theory of Jean de Terre Rouge who wrote a
century earlier against the pretensions of the Duke of Burgundy.[16] Terre Rouge was concerned with establishing the
legal qualities of the royal succession rather than the specific
elimination of heiresses, and in his work he developed a complete legal theory of the transmission of the royal authority.
Succession to the crown, he said, was according to fixed law;
the legal regulations being permanent, the present holder of
the crown could not dispose of it by will or in any other manner alter the succession.[17] Thus the heir to the crown did not
succeed in virtue of any hereditary or patrimonial right comparable to that followed in inheritance according to private
law; he simply received the royal authority as a dignity con-

[14] *Grande Monarchie*, pp. 12b–13a; *Appian Alexandrin*, dedicatory epistle.
[15] *Grande Monarchie*, pp. 8a–8b.
[16] *Contra rebelles suorum regum* (Lyon, 1526). André Lemaire shows that
Terre Rouge elaborated the theory of the royal succession which was accepted
throughout the *ancien régime*. *Les Lois fondamentales de la monarchie française
d'après les théoriciens de l'ancien régime* (Paris, 1907), pp. 54–62. Concerning
the theories of the royal succession held by Terre Rouge and other writers of the
fifteenth century, see John Milton Potter, "The Development and Significance
of the Salic Law of the French," *English Historical Review*, LII (1937), 235–253.
[17] "Quod reges Franciae non potuerunt vnquam neque posset rex modernus
facere testamentum de regno: nec primogenitum: aut alterum heredem facere in
illo. Probatur conclusio: quia ex quo vt praedicitur per consuetudinem non est
obtentum de regno testari statur super hoc iuri communi secundum quod
facultas de regis testari non competit: nec est locus hereditariae succes-
sioni. . . ." *Contra rebelles*, p. xiib.

ferred upon him by established legal usage pertaining specifically to the transmission of the prerogative.[18] The royal
authority was a body of right independent of the person of the
king who received it merely in trust for the duration of his
reign. Having no personal claim to the prerogative, much less
to the realm as a whole, it was the duty of the king to preserve
these in their entirety, avoiding all division through alienations.[19] His function as governor was simply the exercise of the
royal authority during his reign to the best of his ability.

The great contribution of Terre Rouge was that he presented
in very sharp focus a theory of king and crown and a detailed
statement of the law regulating the royal succession. It is clear
that his interpretation rested upon a concept wherein the king
was administrator of an authority not his, an authority which
devolved upon him through law and which thus found its basis
in established legal usage. The exact quality of this fundamental law pertaining to the royal authority Terre Rouge found
in its character as established custom, or, more specifically,
legal regulation which had been introduced by the consent of
the three estates and the entire civil or mystical body of the
realm. Consequently, it was beyond the authority of the ruler
to alter that law which had been established in this fashion for
the ordering of the state.[20] Like Terre Rouge, Seyssel regarded
the rules of succession to the crown as binding upon the king

---

[18] "Duodecima conclusio: que sequitur ex praemissis: quod primogenitus:
aut alius in regno Franciae succedens non est: nec proprie dici potest heres eius
cui succedit: nec patrimonialiter successor: sed successor solum quadam simplici
et non hereditaria successione in vim consuetudinis: quae (vt praedicitur) ei
confert successionem. . . ." *Contra rebelles*, p. xiiib.

[19] "Caeterum successor in patrimonialibus dominiis habet multo plenius ius
quam rex in regno. nam .ille potest vendere: alienare: diminuere: et etiam per
alienationes patrimonialia in alios transferre: sic quod consequenter liberi aliqui
nihil ex eis vendicabunt quae tamen rex agere non potest: nec per aliquas
alienationes ad alios regimen transferre. . . ." *Contra rebelles*, pp. xiiib–xiva.

[20] ". . . quod rex Franciae non posset constitutionem: aut legem facere per
quam patrimonali iure: aut hereditario (quam consuetudine iuerit obtentum) in
regno succederetur. Probatur conclusio: quia consuetudo quae est iam in actu
super hoc fuit: et est introducta ex consensu trium statuum: et totius ciuilis siue
mystici corporis regni ad quos spectabant de iure communi regis institutio: et
electio. . . . Regi non licet immutare ea quae ad statum publicum regni sunt
ordinata." *Contra rebelles*, p. xviib.

and transmitting to him the royal authority as a dignity in trust
for a period, but his idea of the exact nature of fundamental
law marked a notable departure from the interpretation given
by his predecessor. Seyssel's writings included the idea that
fundamental law — and indeed all law of the constitution —
had originally been instituted by act of the king. These legal
regulations had received additional weight through long usage
and continuous application, but Seyssel was definite that they
had originated in acts of the ruler.[21] This interpretation, tending to attribute the beginnings of the constitution to the action
of an original legislator, had expanded in the political writings
of the late fifteenth century [22] and reflected the effort of men to
group their concepts so as to take account of the newly formed
national state. Seyssel found no inherent contradiction in his
idea that laws which had originated in acts of the king now
limited the exercise of the royal discretion and were beyond
his authority to touch, but such was not the case with all later
proponents of the idea. It was to be expected that thinkers
upholding a doctrine of royal absolutism would utilize this interpretation to give the monarch continued authority over the laws
of which he was, in Seyssel's eyes, merely the originator.

Fundamental law constituted but one portion of Seyssel's
check of *la police*. It included in addition the legal rights and
privileges of the many social groups which formed the structure
of the state. Seyssel's classification of the social estates was
unusual: the nobility constituted the first estate; the upper

---

[21] Seyssel's definition of the *police* was that it consisted of "plusieurs ordonnances qui ont esté faictes par les Roys mesmes, et apres confirmées et approuuées de temps en temps: lesquelles tendent à la conservation du royaume
en vniuersel et particulier." *Grande Monarchie*, p. 12b. Also: "Dont s'ensuit
ce qui a esté dict cy dessus, que la puissance souueraine monarchique des Roys
est reglee et moderee par honnestes et raisonnables moyens, qu'iceux Roys ont
introduicts et gardez le plus souuent." *Appian Alexandrin*, dedicatory epistle.

[22] In presenting this interpretation concerning the origins of the Salic Law,
Seyssel was doubtless influenced by the anonymous treatise, *La Loy salicque,
premiere loy des françois*, which was read widely during the late fifteenth century and provided the account, invariably repeated later, of the creation of that
law by Pharamond. This treatise is included in the edition of Seyssel's *Grande
Monarchie* followed in this study. On this treatise, see Potter, *op. cit.*, pp. 249–
252.

bourgeoisie, office holders and merchants formed the second, and the cultivators of the land the third, while the clergy were common to all, being drawn from all. Seyssel regarded the nobility as enjoying the highest "prerogatives and preeminences"; they were the defenders of the king and the realm, and in consequence of their favored position enjoyed the privilege of carrying arms and immunity from the tailles and other levies. As means of living nobly, they were given preference in appointments to certain offices in the royal government according to their rank within the estate: princes of the blood and peers of the realm might enter the highest offices, while others might serve in the king's army, become governors of provinces, *baillis* or *sénéchaux* or receive the great household offices of constable, marshal and admiral. Seyssel regarded the nobility as the most favored of any estate, a fact rightly commensurate with their heaviest obligations in the preservation of the state and their inherent superiority over other men.[23] The sphere of the second estate, which Seyssel defined in very realistic terms as comprising the major portions of the rising bourgeoisie, consisted of business and professional pursuits generally, including the holding of financial and judicial offices in the government. The men of the judiciary he found to be of especial importance, making the cryptic remark that there were more of them in France than in all the rest of Christendom.[24] The third estate or population on the land devoted itself to agriculture and handicrafts. As it was the greatest in number, so it should not become versed in the use of arms but should be made content with its sphere, yet there should be opportunity for deserving members to rise to the second estate.[25] The clergy, being drawn from all others, constituted no well defined estate within the social structure.[26]

This enumeration by Seyssel was much more than a mere classification of the groupings of men in the realm; it provided the basis of his theory concerning a great portion of the consti-

[23] *Grande Monarchie*, pp. 14a–15a.
[24] *Grande Monarchie*, pp. 15b–16a.
[25] *Grande Monarchie*, pp. 16a–16b.
[26] *Grande Monarchie*, pp. 14a–17b.

tution. Seyssel regarded the state as a composite society of pyramided social groups, each occupying a given position in the hierarchical structure and performing a specific function necessary to the life of the whole. The interpretation pictured the state as composed of many interlocking and mutually dependent social units, and thus definitely corporate in composition. This complex structure was capped at the summit by the prince, and together the king and people formed a mystical body whose exact content was the subject of considerable speculation. A favorite figure used by the writers of the period was the comparison of this social organism with the human body composed of many individual but mutually dependent members and guided by a single head; another illustration found the likeness of the state in the universe ruled by God. Such figures of speech were frequently used to illustrate the superiority of monarchy to any other form of government, not only for reasons of efficiency of administration but also because of the consonance of that type of government with the divinely instituted order of things.[27]

More important for our immediate purpose, however, is the constitutional interpretation which Seyssel gave to this concept of the state. From the emphasis of his treatment, it is clear that he regarded each social unit not only as contributing its share to the life of the state but as enjoying corresponding rights and privileges in proportion to the dignity of its sphere. Each of the said estates, he said, has its rights and preeminences according to its quality.[28] The great body of law which at once reflected and protected the rights of those social groups constituting the body of the state was quite beyond the authority of the king to touch. It formed a major portion of the *police* and thus not only placed distinct limitations upon the king's discretion but also provided the basis of organized society which it was his duty to preserve.

Later in the century, this theory of the social organism was

---

[27] E.g., *Grande Monarchie*, p. 6b.
[28] *Grande Monarchie*, p. 13b.

presented in more elaborate form by Guillaume de La Perriere whose book has not received due consideration.[29] The work is chiefly an elaboration of this interpretation in all its aspects; La Perriere used it as a basis upon which to treat every element in the state. Society was composed, he held, of a complex synthesis of individuals, families, corporations, and estates, each occupying a specified position and performing a distinct function necessary to the life of the whole.[30] The king stood at the summit of the hierarchy, and his primary duty was that of preserving the social structure. One very important aspect of his rule was the preventing of sedition, and here La Perriere voiced the idea, repeated so frequently throughout the century, that social unrest was a major cause of the disruption of states because it broke down their internal order, disorganizing the delicate balance of relations between the many component parts.[31] In his effort to preserve the state, said La Perriere, the king could do no better than to maintain the established law, since legal usage and the internal ordering of the realm were largely synonymous.[32] Sedition was a danger not only to the order of the state but also to the law at its basis; in this connection La Perriere insisted that there was great danger in any change, however slight, in the law of the constitution.[33] For him, as for almost all other thinkers of his day, the state and the law were essentially unchanging and sufficient as they stood.

---

[29] *Le Miroir politique* (Lyon, 1555).

[30] "Premierement toute bonne cité et social ciuilité doit estre necessairement fournie et accomplie en six choses: à scauoir est, Sacrifices, Iugements, Armes, Richesses, Arts et Aliments: Ausquelles six choses et œuures faut que soyent respondans six manieres de gens, lesquelz sont Prestres, Magistrats, Nobles, Bourgeois, Artisans et Laboureurs. Les prestres fournissent à la Republicque et cité les sacrifices. Les magistrats fournissent les iugements. Les nobles fournissent les armes. Les bourgeois les richesses. Les artisans les artifices. Et les laboureurs fournissent les aliments." *Le Miroir*, p. 164. This occurs in his introduction to the section on social classes.

[31] *Le Miroir*, chapter V, which outlines methods of preventing sedition.

[32] The conclusion of the pertinent section reads: "Bref, la loy est en la cité, comme l'esprit au corps, et tout ainsi que le corps sans l'esprit vient infaillible- ment à putrefaction, semblement tout cité et Republique sans loy vient en ruyne et perdition." *Le Miroir*, p. 90.

[33] *Le Miroir*, p. 89.

These ideas had been presented earlier in the writings of Seyssel. It was a primary duty of the ruler, he said, to preserve the internal harmony of the state by preventing the encroachment of one estate upon another. The king should not permit the nobles to oppress the third estate through force of arms; the bourgeoisie should not impoverish the nobility by forcing lawsuits upon them and by exploiting their penchant for luxuries, and neither should be allowed to oppress unduly the common people.[34] The same idea was applicable to the king himself: he should never encroach upon the rights and privileges of the feudal lords but should content himself with jealously guarding his sovereign authority.[35] As the best means of maintaining this established order of society, Seyssel urged simply that the king preserve the *libertez, privileges et louables coustumes* of each social division.[36] In the legal practice of the age, by far the greater portion of popular rights found their guarantee in the customary law, and Seyssel clearly regarded that part of the constitution as normally beyond the authority of the king to touch. He pointed to the fact that the oath which the king had taken at his coronation bound him to preserve the established laws and customs of the state.[37] It followed logically that that body of law formed one of the major limitations upon

[34] *Grande Monarchie*, pp. 38a–40b, 43b–44a.

[35] *Grande Monarchie*, p. 38b.

[36] "Et pour acheuer cest article de la police . . . fault venir au second poinct que i'ay touché en la premiere partie, de la conseruation de ceste monarchie de France, causée par l'entretenement des subiectz de tous estatz en bon accord, et au contentement d'vn chascun: car puis que cela est la cause principale de la conseruation et augmentation d'icelle monarchie, comme lon void par experience, est moult requis de l'entretenir et garder qu'elle ne vienne à roture et discord, pourtant que facilement s'en ensuyuroit la ruine de la monarchie, et la dissolution de ce corps mistique. . . . Et pour ne venir à cest inconuenient, ne fault autre chose fors entretenir lesdictz estatz vn chascun en ses libertez, priuileges et louables coustumes." *Grande Monarchie*, p. 36b.

[37] "Quant au tiers point de la police, pour tant que tout ce que ie diray cy apres depend d'icelle, n'en diray sur ce propos autre chose, fors que le Roy et monarque, cognoissant que par le moyen des loix et ordonnances et louables coustumes de France concernans la police, le royaume est paruenu à telle gloire, grandeur et puissance que lon void, et se conserue et entretient en paix, prosperité et reputation: les doit garder et faire obseruer le plus qu'il peult, attendu mesmement qu'il est astrainct par le serment qu'il faict à son couronnement de ce faire." *Grande Monarchie*, p. 36a.

the exercise of the royal authority.[38] It was the combined effects of those restraints provided by law, religion, and justice, which reduced the king's policy to *civilité*.[39]

The unqualified independence of the customary law from regulation and control by the sovereign was a concept almost never presented by writers during the sixteenth century, for reasons which we shall examine in a subsequent chapter. At this point, we should note that Seyssel made certain reservations in his statement that the king should be bound by custom. His idea that the laws of the state had originally been fashioned by the ruler tended to weaken his position. Furthermore, he recognized the fact that certain customs might be outworn or iniquitous, and it was clear that only the king had sufficient authority to abolish such regulations. Combining these ideas, Seyssel wrote that while the prince ought to preserve the *good* customs and laws of the realm, he should correct or annul those no longer of value and substitute others according to need.[40] The ideas contained in this statement went far toward subordinating customary law to the royal discretion and were so used by many later writers; thus we find the dilemma of the constitutionalists already illustrated in the writings of Seyssel. But in his thought, this interpretation was present only in its incipient stages. In spite of this necessary qualification, he invariably urged that the king should normally be bound by custom.

Seyssel's ideas concerning customary law marked no essential break from theories which had been accepted for centuries, but certain other details of his thought throw into relief the fact

[38] "Et neantmoins demeure tousiours la dignité et auctorité royalle en son entier, non pas totalement absolue, ne aussy restraincte par trop, mais reglée et refrenée par bonnes loix, ordonnances et coustumes, lesquelles sont establies de telle sorte qu'à peine se peuuent rompre et adnichiler, iaçoit qu'en quelque temps et en quelque endroit, il y aduienne quelque infraction et violence." *Grande Monarchie*, pp. 9b–10a. Cf. *Appian Alexandrin*, dedicatory epistle.

[39] *Grande Monarchie*, p. 28b.

[40] "Car ayant l'obeissance entiere des subiectz, il peult sans difficulté faire obseruer et garder les bonnes ordonnances et coustumes, corriger et anuller celles qui ne sont vtiles ou assez accomplies, et en faire des nouuelles s'il est expedient." *Grande Monarchie*, p. 19b.

that he was a man of the Renaissance and not of the Middle Ages. Among these was his attitude toward the royal authority to tax. Seyssel's theory of state was based upon a concept of two independent and mutually exclusive spheres of legal right as forming the major elements of the constitution. Property rights were the essence of those enjoyed by the people and were excepted from those things subject to the prince. Thus, logically, taxation by the king, with the exception of those levies established by customary usage, was a violation of the rights of one element of the state by another through an illegal extension of authority. Non-customary taxes should require the consent of the people. But at this point the theorists hesitated. Faced with the fact that the king was collecting the great majority of his levies without the consent of the populace, they were unwilling to uphold an interpretation requiring popular consent to all extraordinary levies. Seyssel expressed marked disapproval of heavy taxation: it was displeasing in the sight of God; it fomented sedition and unrest, and it even forced subjects to quit the realm.[41] He recalled that the *chambre des comptes* might examine the royal expenses, ordinary and extraordinary, and restrain the king's extravagance,[42] and he urged his young sovereign to follow the example of Louis XII who, in spite of his many campaigns, found it possible to reduce taxation by a third.[43] However, this was no more than counsel for moderation; it constituted no specific check upon the ruler. Seyssel's thinking on this point seems dominated by another consideration, as traditional in constitutional thought as ideas of property, but tending to obscure the strictly legal issue. This was the concept, so important in feudal society, of reciprocal duties and mutual obligations of king and people: the duty of the king to give justice and protection, while the subjects owed service

[41] *Grande Monarchie*, pp. 42b–43b.

[42] *Grande Monarchie*, p. 13a.

[43] *Grande Monarchie*, p. 43a. See Seyssel, *Les Louenges du bon roy de France, Louis XII. de ce nom, dict pere du peuple, et de la felicité de son regne*, pp. 13, 135. This was first published in 1508; we have used the edition of Paris, 1615.

with their persons and goods for the maintenance of the state. The exact details of law regulating these reciprocal relationships were sufficiently obscure, and the mentality of an age which knew the rule of a benevolent monarch was sufficiently conditioned, to permit the extension of the principle to cover a multitude of specific details. In the thought of Seyssel, these factors were sufficiently strong to cause him to deny explicitly the necessity of popular consent to royal taxation. In case of need, he said, the king might resort to new levies;[44] it was the established order of things that the populace owed service with arms and the necessary tailles and aids.[45] Thus it might not be claimed that Louis XII's benevolence in not increasing taxation was forced upon him by legal considerations because, said Seyssel with brutal directness, the tailles which are levied from the people are arbitrary.[46] It is apparent that the benevolent paternalism of which Seyssel so approved had caused him to develop from one aspect of medieval thought a concept of almost unlimited popular obligation toward the maintenance of the realm. The application of this theory to the relations of king and subjects in a rapidly crystallizing national state was to have disastrous effects upon the traditional constitutionalism.

Seyssel defined his check of *la police* so as to include not only the limitations of law provided by the constitution but also the counsel tendered by the many officers and organized bodies having a part in the work of administration. Although he regarded the king as holding unshared all authority in public matters, he nevertheless insisted heavily that the ruler should

---

[44] *Grande Monarchie*, p. 13a.

[45] "Dont par ce moyen [royal justice], ne pensent fors à viure en bonne police et en bons accords les vns auec les autres, et sur tout en obeissance du Roy, lequel pour raison de ce, tous les subiectz ont en amour et reuerence singuliere: Dont il aduient qu'ilz sont tousiours prestz à eulx mettre en armes quand il est requis, et à contribuer aux tailles et aides necessaires: et si est en toutes autres choses le Roy obei et serui de bon cueur et sans contredire, mieux et plus promptement que nul autre prince qui soit sur terre." *Grande Monarchie*, p. 18b.

[46] "Et si ne peut l'on dire, qu'il [Louis XII] n'eust loy de croistre son reuenu, et de mectre nouuelle creue sur son peuple, pourtant que le reuenu du Royaume est si grand que le Roy veult. Car la taille qui se leue sur le peuple, est arbitraire." *Les Louenges*, p. 135.

be guided by the advice of his aids in making all decisions of weight. In addition to the great officers, Seyssel listed as constituted counsellors the Parlement, *grand conseil, conseil général, conseil ordinaire*, and the *conseil secret*. The first two were judicial bodies, the third and fourth large groups of officers who handled important matters of administration, while the *conseil secret* he regarded as a key instrument of government, since it was the small, select body which formulated policies of state and handled weighty problems necessitating secrecy and quick action.[47] These bodies, Seyssel made it clear, had no authority of government independent of that held by the king, and thus their representations to the monarch had no more weight than that of advice. The responsibility for making the final decision and the authority necessary for putting it into effect rested entirely with the monarch; Seyssel gave elaborate instructions for his young sovereign to follow in evaluating men and their opinions.[48] Nevertheless, he maintained that free and unrestrained discussion was necessary in the formulation of an enlightened policy and was thus a factor hedging the discretion of the ruler.

The detailed work of administration was necessarily carried out by a great body of officials subordinate to the ruler. Seyssel sketched a picture of the multitude of officers, feudal as well as royal, fulfilling the varied tasks of government not only in the capital but throughout the provinces.[49] Yet he did not assign to these administrators any title to governmental authority independent of that held by the king. The monarch, he said, was the source from which flowed all public authority exercised by others.[50] A great officer such as a prince of the blood might

[47] *Grande Monarchie*, pp. 22b–25b. Seyssel also mentioned an *assemblée casuelle* which included, in addition to the members of the *conseil général*, deputies sent from the major cities. This was his only reference to the Estates General; in making it, he doubtless had in mind the assembly of 1506 at Tours. See Seyssel, *La Proposition et harangue faicte et proposée par messire Claude de Seyssel . . . au roy d'Angleterre Henry VII*, printed with *Les Louenges*.

[48] *Grande Monarchie*, pp. 25b–28a.

[49] *Appian Alexandrin*, dedicatory epistle.

[50] "Et d'autant vont plus les affaires du Royaume prosperans, que les Rois,

have jurisdiction over many men, but the authority which he wielded was not separated from that held by the king; rather, he acted as a "member and collateral" of the king, merely putting into effect a portion of the royal jurisdiction in place of the king himself and always subordinate to the ruler to whom appeal might be made.[51] All feudal and royal officers were but royal agents who exercised a portion of the prerogative to which the king retained unbroken right. Although Seyssel thus upheld the typical Renaissance doctrine denying any independent authority to the magistrates, he nevertheless approved of the diversified exercise of it by innumerable types of office-holders. He recalled that the men holding positions in the courts, the great offices of the crown, the posts of local jurisdiction and administration, and even the feudal dignities, were recruited from the clergy, the nobility, and the professional classes according to their especial abilities and positions within the social structure.[52] In this circumstance, he found not only a stabilizing factor of vital importance but also a parallel and supporting illustration of his theory of the corporate social structure: the wealth, honors, offices and administration of the state were divided and allotted among the various social estates according to their quality, and there resulted from this a harmony within society acting as an important factor in preserving the monarchy.[53] Thus the work of government was but one among many duties and contributions provided by the several social

qui sont la fontaine et la source de laquelle fluent et descendent tous les ruisseaux de bonne police et de iustice, sont plus attentifs à faire entretenir ceste vnion et correspondance. . . ." *Appian Alexandrin*, dedicatory epistle.

[51] "Entre lesquels les principaux sont les grans Princes tant du sang Royal qu'autres, qui sont de tous les Regnicoles honorez et reuerez, tout ainsi que membres et collateraux des Roys, et si ont obeissance et iustice sur grans pays, peuples, et contrees, dependante toutesfois du monarque, et respondent en dernier ressort à ses cours souueraines." *Appian Alexandrin*, dedicatory epistle.

[52] *Appian Alexandrin*, dedicatory epistle, *passim*.

[53] "Et par ainsi estans les biens et les honneurs, les charges, et administration de la chose publique diuisez et departis entre tous les estats proportionnablement selon leur condition, et vn chacun d'iceux gardé en sa preeminence et equalité, s'ensuit vne harmonie et consonance qui est cause de la conseruation et augmentation d'icelle Monarchie." *Appian Alexandrin*, dedicatory epistle.

entities constituting the state. Seyssel carried this interpretation to the point of asserting that the French kingdom partook of the three forms of government, monarchy, aristocracy, and democracy,[54] an idea which suffered varied fortune throughout the century. But it is clear that by this he meant merely the cooperation of diverse social elements in the work of administration, and not a division of authority.

Thus it appears that Seyssel's theory of the constitution was dominated by a concept of corporate and functional unity, not only as concerned the rights of the various social units but also the processes of government. At the summit of the social structure, but not far above other men, stood the king who governed with the close cooperation of his counsellors and whose chief duty was the preservation of the state according to the tenets of established law. His right, different in substance from that of the individuals and groups below him, was nevertheless similar to theirs in finding its basis and limitations in the law. The emphasis was upon a series of unequal and legally defined spheres of right; such was the basis of the theory of dominium which continued dominant early in the century. Each member of the social organism, from the king to the lowest artisan, enjoyed certain constituted rights and fulfilled corresponding duties; the whole was preserved by bonds of law and ties of mutual obligation and respect between ruler and people. As each legal authority in the state was a unit within itself and suffered no restraint as long as the person or group holding that authority remained within its legally defined limits, likewise there was no control of one unit by another save through declaration of the law. In the final analysis, the state rested upon reverence for law. Such was implicitly required from every true sovereign, for the king, although subject to the pronouncements of the

---

[54] "Car à bien prendre le total de cest Empire François, il participe de toutes les trois voyes du gouuernement politique. Premierement il y a Roy qui est Monarque, aymé, obey, et reueré ensemble. . . ." *Appian Alexandrin*, dedicatory epistle. See *Grande Monarchie*, p. 13b. La Perriere criticized Seyssel for this statement, saying that his reasons had little weight and that France was a pure monarchy. See below, ch. II, n. 78.

courts, suffered a control largely self-imposed.[55] For this reason, Seyssel addressed his admonitions to the prince and believed an enlightened monarch to be a prime necessity. Also for this reason, his system was to prove insufficient when there arose a ruler lacking respect for the delicately traced bonds of law and the network of intangible rights animating the entire structure.

Such a political system appears highly precarious through the eyes of the twentieth century, but it was entirely sufficient for Seyssel. For a moment in the history of France, a state of this type had actually existed, and Seyssel, while not necessarily believing it to be perpetual, made no allowance for the possibility of change. This disregard for any evolution of the social structure was characteristic of the thought of the age and reflected an attitude quite without appreciation of disruptive forces. True, Seyssel held ideas, doubtless derived from classical sources through Renaissance learning, of the cyclical rise and fall of states caused by occult influences and the necessary impermanence of all earthly things,[56] but he did not integrate these with his constitutional theory. The only immediate change which he thought possible was that of decay, and the remedy was to be found simply in the duty of the king to maintain the state through preserving established law.[57] Innovations were to be checked at the outset, being dangerous to the permanence of the social structure. At most, the king might use his authority to abolish outworn customs and replace them with better ones, according to the dictates of necessity. But the ideal

---

[55] "Et sont les Roys beaucoup plus à louer et priser de ce qu'ilz veulent en si grande auctorité et puissance estre subiectz à leurs propres loix et viure selon icelles, que s'ilz pouoient à leur volunté vser de puissance absolue." *Grande Monarchie*, p. 13b. Cf. *Les Louenges*, p. 16.

[56] *Grande Monarchie*, pp. 4b–5a, 9a–9b.

[57] "Quant au premier [the maintenance of the *police*], ie faiz vne maxime que toutes choses naturelles, se conseruent par les mesmes causes et moyens, qu'elles ont esté faictes et introduictes. Parquoy à bien considerer ce que i'ay dict au commencement de ce traicté, parlant des formes et moyens, par lesquelz ceste monarchie a esté introduicte, conseruée et augmentée par le passé, aisée chose seroit la conseruer et accroistre de plus en plus, tenant les mesmes moyens." *Grande Monarchie*, p. 28b.

was permanent, and the greatest freedom allowed to the ruler was slight reformation of the law in terms of that ideal. This was far from constituting a theory of state admitting of real change and allowing for such in the life of the social structure. This factor alone was sufficient to cause the eventual repudiation of Seyssel's system during an age of rapid transition.

CHAPTER II

THE APOLOGIES FOR ABSOLUTISM

THE reigns of Francis I and Henry II witnessed a period of French history during which, in spite of the undoubted break from much that was considered traditional, the policies of the central administration and current expressions of political thought formed a remarkably homogeneous unit. If the kingdom of Louis XII had been pictured in idealized form by Seyssel, Francis I and his son were also favored by theorists who provided the intellectual counterpart of the policies of their royal masters in well-rounded theories of state. These strongest of the Valois rulers were fortunate in receiving the services of many able administrators, and the government of king and councillors, largely through the councils of state, foreshadowed the type of monarchy to achieve greater importance in the seventeenth century. The officials in the central administration often set the tone of royal policy and formed a very uniform group, both in the character of their active service and their political opinions. Many were imbued with the principles of Roman law as taught in the University of Toulouse; the regime under Francis I has been characterized as the rule of legists trained in that school.[1] Whether the Roman law was responsible for their absolutist opinions, or whether the fact of strong personal rule by the monarch was of prior importance in shaping their modes of thought is not for us to determine; but it is certain that there was entire harmony between the expressions of opinion and the policies of the government. Such was necessarily the case, since the bulk of contemporary political theory was propounded by men very close to the royal administration.

[1] Gabriel Hanotaux, *Etudes historiques sur le XVIe et le XVIIe siècle en France* (Paris, 1886), pp. 8–18.

It is fortunate that the political thought of these Romanists has been preserved in a series of formal treatises. The most important were written by such men as Grassaille, Chasseneuz, Rebuffi, and Tiraqueau,[2] and all were either jurisconsults or members of the royal administration, in close touch with practical affairs. The writings of the humanists, among whom Budé was the most important, evinced theories quite in harmony with those of the legists. In fact, the men of the new learning often went to greater lengths than the legists in their glorification of the ruler. This circumstance was certainly occasioned in part by the humanists' position as hangers-on at court and by their closer acquaintance with the heroic deeds and virtues of the past than with the more prosaic limits of law inherent in contemporary political thought. The most striking characteristic of the writing produced during this period is its complete unanimity in glorification of the monarch; throughout, there was not a discordant note in the chorus of praise for personal rule and enlightened monarchy as the most perfect form of government.[3] The second- and third-rate writers of the period — Breche, Ferrault, Heluis, La Perriere, and de Bourg — accepted without question the ideas of the greater authorities and even developed their concepts toward conclusions which the latter had feared. It may be said without major qualification that in the concordance of governmental policies and theoretical speculation concerning the same, this period represents one of the most homogeneous in the entire history of France. However, it is not to be assumed that the more traditional and constitutional view represented by Seyssel had disappeared; toward the close of the period it was again expressed in complete form by a new school including such men as Du Tillet. The powerful combination of aggressive royal policy and elaborate theoretical justification for the same had not succeeded in eliminating the older constitutional thought. Thus, we may regard the earlier

---

[2] Du Moulin, although contemporary, stood somewhat apart; we have reserved his works for consideration in a later chapter.

[3] The *Discours de la servitude volontaire* of La Boétie dealt with intellectual problems only and met no response until the Wars of Religion.

theory of state as continuing as a vital force throughout the period, although its adherents were not vocal. Furthermore, the ease with which the more constitutional position was revived later in the century indicates that the ideas of the Romanists were not as complete a break from the traditional interpretations as might be inferred. Although the emphasis upon absolutism was dominant and alone in being expressed during the period, it rested upon bases equally venerable with those of the theory later to be revived. That it was but an exaggerated emphasis upon much that was permanent in French thought is illustrated by its great influence upon the vital work of synthesis by Jean Bodin.

In the political thought of the legists and humanists alike, the central point and ultimate consideration was the king. Treatises very often took the form of an *Institution du prince* or an elaboration of the royal authority as in the book of Grassaille. The aim and end of all political speculation was seen in the king; all aspects of the state — private rights, the authority of administrative bodies, and details of law — were discussed in terms of their relation to the prerogative. When considering the foundation upon which the royal authority was held to rest, these thinkers did not turn to the fundamental law but instead interpreted kingship as originating through a direct gift of authority to the prince by God. This theory of the direct divine authorization of kingship was a primary tenet of Gallicanism and was accepted all but universally among writers of the period as the most satisfactory basis upon which to establish the legitimate character of the political power.[4] Yet it should be noted that there was at this time no effort to formulate a complete theory of the divine right of kings such as appeared at the close of the Wars of Religion. The theory presented by the Romanists earlier in the century was composed largely by compiling interpretations deduced from the direct divine authorization of

---

[4] E.g., Barthélemi de Chasseneuz, *Catalogus gloriae mundi* (Lyon, 1546), pp. 105b, col. 2, to 106a, col. 2, where he develops the proposition: "Unde non est potestas nisi a deo. . . . Prouisum etiam est a deo dominium siue considerata natura entis, siue motus, siue finis."

kingship, as far as there was any fundamental concept. Thus the theory represents a multiplication of statements magnifying the dignity and quasi-divine qualities of the ruler rather than the closely knit interpretation fashioned, albeit painfully, toward the close of the century.

The immediate purpose of this emphasis upon the institution of kingship by direct act of God was the refutation of doctrines attributing to the Emperor and the pope positions as communicating intermediaries between the Deity and all lesser secular rulers. Theories of universal papacy and Empire retained widespread adherence on the continent of Europe generally and were sufficiently strong to oblige those writers supporting the independence of the Valois rulers to stress again and again the direct contact between God and their sovereign. On every occasion, they insisted that their ruler was king by the grace of God alone and that he consequently held his authority from no earthly superior.[5] In answer to the claims of the papalists, the monarchists considered it sufficient to recall the Gallican doctrines of long standing. These were built upon the Gelasian concept of independent but cooperating king and papacy, and were interpreted so as to attribute to the king all rights of a marginal character, thus restricting the pope to purely spiritual matters.[6] Secondly, these writers countered the claims of those maintaining the superiority of the Emperor over the King of France by reiterating the venerable but controversial principle that the king was Emperor within his realm, entirely independent from the successors of the Caesars.[7] From this, they drew the inference that Roman law was not binding in France, although they opened the path for its general application by regarding it as written reason. More important, this doctrine permitted the investing of the French king with that authority given by the Roman system to the Emperor.

---

[5] Charles de Grassaille, *Regalium Franciae, libri duo: jura omnia et dignitates christianissimi Galliae regis continentes* (Lyon, 1538), pp. 71, 77; Chasseneuz, *Consuetudines ducatus Burgundiae* (Paris, 1547), pp. 3a, 287a–287b, and many other works of the period.   [6] Grassaille, *op. cit.*, Book II.

[7] Grassaille, *op. cit.*, pp. 71–90; Chasseneuz, *Consuetudines*, pp. 3a, 287a.

Having thus established direct contact between God and their king, incidentally attributing to the latter the twin authorities of medieval king and Roman Emperor, the groundwork was laid for the glorification of the monarch almost without limit. The political writers of the period invariably regarded their ruler as God's appointed agent in temporal government, and they often utilized this all-important capacity of the king as a basis for describing him as little less than a divinity on earth. The primary purpose of divinely instituted kingship they believed to be government of the people according to God's will; thus Budé could assert that the heart of the king received its impetus from God who guided the ruler toward good or bad enterprises according to the merit or sinfulness of himself and his people.[8] Rebuffi maintained that the divine grant of authority demonstrated the familiarity of the king with God and caused the royal will to conform with that of the Deity.[9] Thus Grassaille was quite in accordance with the ideas of his contemporaries when he asserted that the King of France was a fleshly god in his realm, for whatever he did was not wrought by himself but by God through him; God spoke through the mouth of the king, and whatever he did was inspired by God. Thus the king was at once a minister of God on earth and a living law.[10] And Chasseneuz, even when consider-

---

[8] ". . . le cueur du roy tient son mouuement par instinct et impulsion de dieu qui le tourne et attrait selon son plaisir a entreprises faire louables et honnestes et vtiles a son peuple et a luy, ou autrement selon que luy et ses subiectz ont merite." Guillaume Budé, "De l'institution du prince." *Bibliothèque de l'arsenal*, Paris, MS. 5103. Dated 1519. 31ᵛ.

[9] "Alia vtilitas quae patet ex tali donatione est, summa Dei nostri erga reges Franciae familiaritas. . . ." Pierre Rebuffi, *De christianissimi atque invictissimi regis Franciae muneribus et eius tractatus*, in *Tractatus varii* (Lyon, 1600), p. 3, col. 1. "Quarta autem vtilitas, proueniens ex ea iam praedicta consecratione diuina est, conformis Dei nostri voluntas, cum Regis nostri Franciae voluntate." *Ibid.*, p. 11, col. 2.

[10] "Rex Franciae est in regno suo tanquam quidam corporalis Deus. . . . Nam quod Rex facit, non tanquam ipse, sed vt Deus facit . . . per Principis os, Deus loquitur; et quae facit, Deo inspirante facit. . . . Et est lex animata in terris. . . . Item minister Dei in terris. . . . Item Rex, est Delegatus Dei. . . ." Grassaille, *op. cit.*, pp. 63–64. Chasseneuz was equally explicit; see *Consuetudines*, pp. 287a–287b.

ing specific details of law, did not hesitate to clinch an interpretation with the blunt statement: the king is God on earth.[11]
It is readily apparent that these Romanists had extended the
idea of divinely authorized dominion to the extravagant lengths
of regarding the king as little less than the earthly incarnation
of the Deity Himself. The concept colored, and even predetermined, innumerable details of constitutional thought, in particular the exact nature of the king's authority as judge and the
legal limitations upon his discretion.

A king who was placed on earth by God for the rule of the
people and the guidance of them according to His dictates
should logically personify the ideal of virtue and human aspiration. It was a favorite statement of these writers that the king
set the standard and the tone for the life of his subjects, and
that all men could do no better than to follow his leadership
and example.[12] In the writings of the humanists, and to a lesser
extent the legists, this ideal of super-human kingship was given
additional coherence by their reverence for discipline, con-
trolled strength, and military glory which were later to characterize seventeenth-century classicism.[13] Although Seyssel had
likewise advocated strong, paternal rule from above, his emphasis was entirely different. In the works of the Romanists,
there was a glorification of the majesty of kingship to such a
point that the monarch was placed at great heights above his
subjects, often resembling a *potestas legibus soluta* in action
rather than the closely hedged ruler pictured by Seyssel.[14]

In such an interpretation of kingship, any fundamental law
regulating the succession to, and exercise of, the royal preroga-

[11] *Consuetudines*, p. 62a.

[12] E.g., Chasseneuz, *Catalogus*, p. 106a.

[13] The works of Budé, and to a lesser extent Grassaille, cited above are full
of it.

[14] The lesser writers of the period followed without exception this absolutist
conception of kingship. E.g., Etienne de Bourg, *Solium regis christianissimi
Franciae in suprema curia parlamenti Parisiensis, tribunal iudicium et cathedra
doctorum* (Lyon, 1550); Jean Breche, *Manuel royal* (Tours, 1541); Jean
Ferrault, *Tractatus jura seu privilegia aliqua regni Franciae continens*, in Du
Moulin, *Opera* (Paris, 1681), II; Jean Heluis, *Le Mirouer du prince chretien*
(Paris, 1566).

tive might seem at first sight quite out of place; yet the tradition of that law in juxtaposition with the royal authority was
too strong for the Romanists to break, even if they had wished
to do so. Without exception they maintained the two fundamental laws which were undeniable — the Salic Law and the
inalienability of the domain [15] — although they upheld the
royalist interpretation concerning the origin of those laws. If
we found Seyssel attributing the institution of the Salic Law,
binding upon the king, to the act of an earlier sovereign, it is
not surprising to find the same idea in the works of the Romanists. Grassaille did not hesitate to place side by side the statements that the Salic Law had originally been introduced by the
king through his authority to give out laws and ordinances
binding generally through the realm, and that that law obtained
force through long usage and observance.[16] Chasseneuz was
similar in regarding such law as customary usage originally
instituted by the king.[17] This insistence upon the royal origin
of the Salic Law reflects a conscious effort of these writers to
group their concepts about a national monarch who could make
law as well as preserve it. But they never drew the conclusion
that since the king had originated the law, he was now above it;
its quality of regulating succession to the crown necessarily
limited the king who had acceded according to its terms. Even
more important, the Romanists maintained unaltered the vital
interpretation concomitant with fundamental law, that the royal
authority was conferred upon the reigning prince by law alone
and was consequently a dignity which he was called to fill for a
period and in which he held no personal, hereditary right. Jean
d'Angleberme, in outlining the qualities of the Salic Law, gave

---

[15] E.g., Grassaille, *op. cit.*, pp. 148, 234 ff., Chasseneuz, *Catalogus*, p. 111b,
and *Consuetudines*, pp. 112–114.

[16] ". . . obtentum est istud ius altum ex longaeua consuetudine tenaciter in
regno Francorum obseruata." ". . . potuit hanc legem Saliquam authoritate
sua, non alterius superioris roborare: sicut et alias leges siue ordinationes generales
in regno suo facere." Grassaille, *op. cit.*, pp. 237, 252. See Jean d'Angleberme,
De lege salica et regni successione, in *Opuscula*, printed with his *Consuetudines
Aurelianenses* (Paris, 1543).

[17] *Consuetudines*, pp. 112b–114a.

as one reason for its validity the fact that women might fittingly succeed only to property (*bonis*) and not to honors, and he classed the royal authority as belonging strictly to the latter category.[18] In this classification, d'Angleberme merely reiterated that set forth by Philippe Pot in the Estates General of 1484 when he said that the kingship was a dignity and not an heredity;[19] the major importance of fundamental law is summed up in his statement. Although the Romanists occasionally said that the heir to the crown succeeded *iure haereditario*, they used this phrase chiefly in order to distinguish between hereditary and elective monarchy.[20] There was no concerted effort to establish a personal, hereditary right of the king to the crown such as appeared later in the century. In spite of the superabundant glorification of the monarch in the works of this period, the king remained according to legal tradition merely the administrator of an authority devolving upon him strictly through fundamental law.[21]

The legists of the Renaissance outlined the exact content of the royal prerogative, which was thus bestowed upon the king by the joint action of fundamental law and divine authorization, in their favorite manner of listing various "marks of sover-

---

[18] "Decimoseptimo, quia foeminae licet in bonis succedant, non tamen in honoribus. . . . Sed regnum est ius quoddam consistens in dignitate, et honore, praeeminentia, potestate, consilio, administratione reipublicae." D'Angleberme, *op. cit.*, p. 158a, col. 1. D'Angleberme, or Pyrrhus, was the teacher of Du Moulin and did his major work prior to the period considered in this chapter. Chasseneuz criticised this interpretation of d'Angleberme by showing that, strictly speaking, succession to all honors was not limited to men; he recalled that many great dignities such as peerages and dukedoms were acceded to by women. However, he did not deny the especial law of succession to the crown and the character of the latter as a trust committed by law. *Consuetudines*, pp. 112b–113b.

[19] Jean Masselin, *Journal des états généraux de France tenus à Tours en 1484 sous le règne de Charles VIII*, edited by A. Bernier (Paris, 1835), p. 146.

[20] E.g., Chasseneuz, *Consuetudines*, p. 112b; Rebuffi, *op. cit.*, p. 26, col. 1.

[21] The generally accepted concept was that of Charles Du Moulin: "Rex nouus non est haeres decessoris, nec ei per obitum succedit in acquisitus vel patrimonialibus, nec in haereditate ab eo derelicta in seculo nisi sit proximior haeres; sed . . . succedit in corona iure sanguinis ad normam legis Salicae." *Commentarii in consuetudines Parisienses* (Paris, 1681), Tit. I, *proemium*, no. 62. Cf. Tit. I, § XIII, glo. I, no. 26, and glo. III, no. 8.

eignty." This was doubtless the best method as long as the crown continued to be regarded as a mosaic of rights accruing to the monarch because of his headship of the state and reflecting his multitudinous duties, largely judicial and administrative. Lists of these regalian rights or marks of sovereignty are to be found in the major contemporary treatises; the value of a given book may often be measured in terms of the completeness with which each of these marks is treated. The outline given by Grassaille was one of the best. One of the most important marks, he found, was the quality of the king as being Most Christian; in consequence, he might demand written evidence of faith from the pope, control the existence of Jews in the realm, punish usurers, act as supreme judge, and exterminate heretics.[22] The king possessed the power to work miracles; his agents enjoyed ten days' indulgences.[23] He recognized no temporal superior and was Emperor within his realm; consequently he might revoke all inferior jurisdictions, make laws and ordinances binding throughout the realm, coin money, and create new taxes.[24] The king alone had and held a Parlement; from him were derived all offices and dignities; his officers exercised exclusive jurisdiction over the *cas royaux*.[25] He had *droit d'aubain* and *droit de bâtardise*.[26] These and many other rights the king was regarded as holding absolutely through his complete and unshared title to the crown. A glance at the full list, of which this is but a part, reveals that the royal authority was truly an agglomeration of miscellaneous rights bound together only by the general and closely related capacities of the king in dispensing justice and authorizing the necessary acts of administration.

Although the king alone held title to the crown, it was physically impossible that he carry out all acts of justice and administration in person; these were necessarily effected by the

[22] *Op. cit.*, pp. 41–61.
[23] *Op. cit.*, pp. 63–64, 66–67.
[24] *Op. cit.*, pp. 71–90, 146–152.
[25] *Op. cit.*, pp. 159–181, 301–303, 205–219.
[26] *Op. cit.*, pp. 220–226.

multitude of royal and feudal officers scattered about the realm. Often the specific function exercised by a given officer devolved upon him through his inheritance of the ancestral domains or through his purchase of an office in the royal administration. The question whether these officers held title to the authority which they exercised, or whether they were mere agents of the king who retained unbroken right to all governmental authority, had long troubled the professional jurists and had been answered in varying fashions at different periods. The Bartolists, immediate predecessors of the Renaissance legists, had very closely approximated the situation obtaining in feudal society simply by attributing to each baron, officer, corporation, or city a proprietary right in that authority which each had traditionally exercised within its sphere. But during the Renaissance, there was developed a contrary interpretation which was to dominate the entire sixteenth century. The jurists of the period revived the older concept that the king held the crown completely and unshared, and that if certain prerogatives were exercised by feudal or royal officers, this was simply in virtue of their capacity as agents of the ruler. The king retained strictly all right in the authority necessarily wielded by others. True, the older idea of the Bartolists was slow in dying and was preserved, at least in its essentials, in the works of Rebuffi.[27] But all other writers considered in this chapter upheld the interpretation, rapidly achieving general acceptance, attributing to the king alone all right in authority of government.[28]

It was in relation to the mark of sovereignty permitting the king to create magistrates and to hold his Parlement that the

---

[27] The works of Rebuffi present a curious mixture of Bartolist and Renaissance interpretations regarding this question, but he was a Bartolist concerning the crucial detail, the ownership of authority. See his *Explicatio ad quatuor primos pandectarum libros* (Lyon, 1589), pp. 195–214. His concept is summed up in the statement: "Rex aut princeps non potest sine causa officiales ordinarios remouere, et eos eorum iurisdictione priuare: cum iurisdictionem quam habent tales officiales dicantur habere tanquam suam, et ad eos pertinentem iure proprio." *De christianissimi*, p. 21, col. 2.

[28] For the history of this concept and the closely related theory of office, see Myron P. Gilmore, *Argument from Roman Law in Political Thought: 1200–1600* (Harvard University Press, 1941).

question of the officers' right to their authority appeared in sharpest focus. The interpretation given by Chasseneuz concerning the authority of the court was built upon the doctrine of the Renaissance jurists attributing ownership of jurisdiction to the king alone; and being an able statement of the accepted solution to the problem, it was repeated without significant alteration by several later writers of the school.[29] All jurisdiction, said Chasseneuz, pertains to the supreme authority of the prince; no man may have jurisdiction except through the ruler's concession and permission. The authority to create magistrates thus belongs to the prince alone; all offices and dignities flow and are derived from him as from a fountain.[30] And as he may create officers and grant jurisdiction, thus also he may revoke the same even without cause;[31] if he does this, things revert simply to their original nature which is easily permitted.[32] Thus the Renaissance jurists, through denying to any man but the king a right in governmental authority, reached the logical conclusion of regarding all officers, feudal and royal, merely as agents of the king and holding office largely at his discretion. Nevertheless, these writers were able to take into account in their theory the existence of the great, permanent judicial

[29] The treatment of this question in the works of Grassaille and de Bourg is little more than a repetition of Chasseneuz. Grassaille, *op. cit.*, pp. 148, 159–181, 301–302; de Bourg, *op. cit.*, pp. 21a–29b.

[30] ". . . omnes iurisditiones pertinent ad supremam potestatem supremi principis. . . . Vnde nemo potest iurisditionem habere nisi ex eius concessione vel permissione: loquendo de iure Romanorum, quoniam iurisdi. non possunt exerceri nisi per magistratus, qui diuersis nominibus nuncupantur: quorum creatio ad authoritatem Principis pertinet." *Consuetudines*, p. 21a. "Omnes magistratus et dignitates a principe profluunt et deriuantur tanquam a fonte, quia in eo sunt omnes dignitates, et in eo sunt omnes dignitatum thesauri reconditi." *Catalogus*, p. 113a, col. 2.

[31] Chasseneuz hesitated to permit the king to revoke officers appointed in perpetuity without first establishing just cause. See *Consuetudines*, p. 58a. But he included that point in his statement of general concepts. See below, n. 32. Unlike Rebuffi, he did not deny this authority to the ruler because of the officers' right in their jurisdiction. See above, n. 27.

[32] "Et ideo non mirum si possit aliquid statuere super iurisdictione in aliquibus casibus, cum illam in totum tollere possit. et hoc casu res reuertitur ad suam primitiuam naturam. quod de facili permittendum est, inspiciendo primum statum, qui attendi potius debet, et maxime quando est status originis." *Consuetudines*, p. 81b.

bodies, such as the Parlement of Paris. This they accomplished by representing the courts as participating in the exercise of the prerogative with the king at the same time that the latter retained entire title to that authority. In this interpretation, the magistrates, because of their cooperation with the ruler in wielding the rights of highest jurisdiction, were held to represent the person of the prince; or more exactly, they were a part of the royal person. The writers of the period summarized the position of the Parlement as *pars corporis principis*.[33] This concept likewise went far toward approximating the judicial authority of the court with that ordinarily exercised by the ruler; Chasseneuz stated that the power and preeminence of the court were equal to that of the king who was consequently unable, by act of ordinary authority, to quash a decision of the court.[34] Grassaille added that the Parlement pronounced its decisions in its name and not in that of the king; like the king, it was not bound by the letter of the law but judged according to its conscience.[35] And since the Parlement was thus all but identified with the person of the king, it enjoyed correspondingly regal dignities. Persons resisting the magistrates in their official capacity, Chasseneuz said, were punished as rebels against the realm; those offending the councillors of the prince committed leze-majesty.[36] This curious chain of reasoning followed logically from the current theory attributing to the king all title to jurisdiction. It represents the conclusion of that movement long supported by the Parisian legists, namely, the grouping of all rights of a governmental character under the authority of the king to make or break. The specific details

---

[33] Chasseneuz, *Catalogus*, p. 148a, col. 2; Grassaille, *op. cit.*, pp. 161, 174; de Bourg, *op. cit.*, p. 24a.

[34] "De eius potestate et praeeminentia in iurisditione, quod est aequalis cum rege, ita quod Rex ex sua ordinaria potestate non potest tollere ex quae acta sunt per eius parlamenta: imo etiam de plenitudine potestatis ordinata." *Catalogus*, p. 148a.

[35] *Op. cit.*, pp. 161, 174.

[36] "Et rebellantes, iniuste in his quae ad eorum officium spectat, vt rebelles regni puniuntur . . . offendentes tales consiliarios principis committunt laesae maiestatis." *Catalogus*, pp. 148–149.

of the concept preserved, and even enhanced, the dignity of the court through attributing to it truly regal qualities. But at a later period, many thinkers found that the legists of the Renaissance had overshot the mark, for there was inevitably in their interpretation a lessening of the limitations which the court might place upon the royal discretion.

In their theorizing concerning the exact place and ownership of governmental authority, the legists thought particularly in terms of the *merum imperium*. This concept, borrowed from Roman law, was of vital importance in their idea of kingship. Although the *merum imperium* in their systems did not embrace all the marks of sovereignty listed by Grassaille, it did include the twin authorities of supreme jurisdiction and the promulgation of laws binding throughout the realm (*condere legem generalem*). This union of legislation and adjudication in the concept of rulership was one of the most important characteristics of the political thought of the age, and it was brought about largely by the preoccupation of the Renaissance legists with concepts drawn from Roman law. The attribution of these prerogatives to the ruler was of vital significance in the evolution of the concept of kingship from the medieval idea of the monarch as primarily a judge to the later conception of the law-making sovereign.[37] However, the interpretation set forth by the legists of the early sixteenth century represented but one step in that development. Their discussions of the exact content of the *merum imperium* show that they placed by far their greatest stress upon the element of jurisdiction.[38] The emphasis of Chasseneuz was representative when he identified *merum imperium* with *haute justice*, adding that the authority incidentally included additional rights such as the giving of laws.[39] Throughout the period, political writers were dominated by the medieval tradition of rulership as essentially adjudica-

[37] McIlwain, *op. cit.*, p. 392.
[38] Chasseneuz, *Consuetudines*, pp. 12–20; Rebuffi, *Explicatio*, pp. 195–214. The preoccupation of Grassaille with jurisdiction is evident from the discussions beginning on pages 57 and 292 of the work cited.
[39] *Consuetudines*, p. 12b.

tion. In fact, this preoccupation with jurisdiction as the major element in the prerogative caused a curious lack of precision in dealing with the authority to give law, and a consequent willingness of the Renaissance thinkers to accept details from the Bartolist concept of legislation while discarding the concurrent interpretation concerning the judicial authority. The Bartolists' position concerning the prerogative of giving law was in exact conformity with their idea of jurisdiction, namely, that each social unit — individual or corporate — which held high judicial authority (*merum imperium*) in its circumscription likewise had the right to make laws and ordinances binding within the same sphere. Jurisdiction and legislation were divided among, and owned by, the many civil and governmental units scattered throughout the state.[40] It is readily apparent that such an interpretation constituted the complete negation of any theory of legislative sovereignty, that is, it rendered impossible the attribution to the sovereign of the single and undivided authority to make law binding upon all men.[41] We have seen how the jurists of the Renaissance broke with the Bartolist interpretation concerning jurisdiction by attributing title to it solely to the prince. But their preoccupation with the judicial prerogative caused a lag in their breaking from the Bartolists in similar fashion concerning the authority to give law. Thus, in certain writings of the period there appears the curious combination of strictly Renaissance ideas regarding jurisdiction side by side with the Bartolist concept of the right to give law. The best example of this is found in the thought of Chasseneuz who thus represents a stage of transition between the Bartolists and the developed ideas of the sixteenth century. We have seen how he insisted that the king alone held title to jurisdiction. But he also said that not only the king but likewise dukes,

---

[40] This interpretation is preserved in the works of Rebuffi. See above, n. 27. Also: "Rex, Dux, Marchio potest condere legem in territorio suo." *De regum et principum muneribus ac praerogativis*, in *Tractatus varii* (Lyon, 1600), p. 10, no. 140.

[41] Cecil N. Sidney Woolf, *Bartolus of Sassoferrato* (Cambridge University Press, 1913), pp. 144–161, especially the concluding paragraph.

barons, and castellans might make edicts and statutes binding within their jurisdictions.[42] The same statement had been made earlier by Ferrault.[43] Among the authors considered in this chapter, only Grassaille found occasion to doubt the validity of this interpretation. In commenting upon the statement of Ferrault, Grassaille said that such was not, strictly speaking, the case, because constitutions and edicts were rightly those which only the king or the Emperor had established.[44] Thus the later Renaissance legists finally broke completely with the Bartolist ideas and attributed to the king alone the twin authorities of legislation and adjudication. The concept was to achieve general, if belated, acceptance among legal writers of the century. It marks a very important step toward the later theory of legislative sovereignty.

The political system outlined by Grassaille might at first sight appear to contain all the elements needed to establish a theory of sovereignty as it was defined by later writers, but such was far from being the case. True, he attributed to the king alone the important authorities of legislation and adjudication, but the exact sense in which he used those concepts shows that there remained many barriers yet to be crossed before political thinkers could outline a concept of legislative sovereignty. In the thought of Grassaille and others of his

---

[42] "Item etiam quando dicitur quod solus rex potest facere leges et constitutiones in regno, est verum, et intelligendum complexiue, non autem distributiue, quia per eius distributionem et feudorum concessionem, possunt duces, et barones, et alii domini castellani, non excendendo metas iurisdictionis concessae, facere edicta et statuta." *Consuetudines,* p. 381a. This was parallel with his idea: "Reges, Duces, Marchiones, et Comites, perpetuo constitui in terris eorum sunt principes, et possunt omnia (quo ad subditos eorum) quae potest Imperator in toto orbe, in consequentiam illarum dignitatum perpetuo concessarum." *Ibid.,* p. 62b.

[43] *Op. cit.,* p. 547, col. 2.

[44] "Hinc est quinto, quod sicut soli Imperatori conuenit leges condere . . . ita ad solum Regem Franciae leges (quae ex communi vsu loquendi ordinationes vocantur) facere pertinet et spectat: secundum . . . Ioan. Ferran. in tract. de insig. peculi. Reg. Fran. in xii. iure. vbi dicit, istud esse intelligendum de legibus generalibus: secus de particularibus aedictis: quia Duces, Comites et Barones regni, intra territoria eorum edicta et leges faciunt . . . sed improprie: quia proprie constitutio vel edictum est quod tantum Rex vel Imperator constituit." *Op. cit.,* p. 149.

type, legislation continued subordinate to adjudication; or more exactly, legislation was but a minor manifestation of the function represented by adjudication. This was necessarily the interpretation given by these writers because of their concepts of kingship and the legal foundations of the state. It will be recalled that the Romanists regarded the king as God's representative on earth, ruling the people according to His plan and dictates — a fact permitted by the divine authorization of kingship and the close contact of the king with God.[45] From this premise, the Renaissance legists without exception drew the conclusion that the justice administered by the king was divinely inspired and represented, however imperfectly, the super-earthly ideal according to which it was the duty of the king to govern.[46] It was in this sense that they regarded the king as holding all law *in scrinio pectoris* and as representing *lex animata in terris*.[47] The law of the constitution was believed to embody, although imperfectly, the principles contained in that abstract ideal, and the greatest freedom of action allowed to the king was the reformation of the law in terms of that criterion. Thus, if the interpretation placed the king above the law of the land, it likewise restricted his freedom of action within the categories fixed by the principles according to which he was bound to govern. This theory allowed the giving of law within very narrow limitations, but it is clear that

---

[45] Above, pp. 47–48.

[46] "Cum iustitia sit maior ex quatuor virtutibus cardinalibus, ex quibus principes magis laudantur, cum inter omnes virtutes cardinales iustitia teneat principatum . . . iustitia coelestis virtus esse demonstratur: et hoc satis ostendit Homerus, cum ait. Reges, discipulos summi Regis Iouis esse, a quo iustitiam imprimis ediscant, quam deinde inter mortales obseruent, et eam omni studio omnique diligentia tueantur. Plato etiam philosophorum summus, Iustitiam bonorum omnium maximum esse ait, a deo hominibus datum: proinde deum ipsum iustitiae authorem, causam ac principium multis in locis asserit." Chasseneuz, *Catalogus*, pp. 106b–107a. See Rebuffi, *De christianissimi*, pp. 3, 5–6. De Bourg went to the lengths of saying: ". . . leges diuinitus per ora Regum promulgatae sunt, et Reges diuinitus consequuti sunt priuilegium condendarum legum. . . . Rex facit legem nutu diuino cum propter hoc fecit Deus Regem." *Op. cit.*, pp. 18a–18b.

[47] Chasseneuz, *Catalogus*, p. 108a, col. 1; *Consuetudines*, p. 47b; Rebuffi, *De regum*, nos. 29, 103, 344, and many others.

in doing so, the prince could do little more than amend or enforce existing regulations. In a very exact sense, his duty was one of preservation and not of innovation. In such a concept of rulership, legislation could but remain subordinate to adjudication. Strictly, legislation was but a different manifestation of the preservative function effected by adjudication. It was for this reason that Grassaille discussed the making of laws and ordinances under the heading of adjudication and said that they were created for the defense of the good and the punishment of the wicked.[48] As long as political thinkers believed the chief function of the prince to be the preservation of the state in terms of fixed law and ideals, jurisdiction necessarily remained the primary royal prerogative.

In the framing of these laws and ordinances, it was needful that the king take counsel. Although the Romanists exalted the king to great heights above other men, they nevertheless were unanimous that the ruler ought to consult his officers concerning major questions of policy, particularly when making laws and ordinances.[49] The contradictory elements in contemporary thought on this point were well presented by Rebuffi when he said that the great and natural wisdom of the king caused him necessarily to do all things according to law and reason, but that it was better for him to act with the counsel of his advisers.[50] This was necessitated by the current idea

---

[48] "Ideo ad tuitionem bonorum, et punitionem malorum, factae sunt leges regiae quas ordinationes Galli vocant, vt earum metu, humana coerceatur audacia tutaque sit inter improbos innocentia, et in ipsis improbis formidato supplicio refrenetur audacia et nocendi facultas." Grassaille, *op. cit.*, p. 60. See Rebuffi, *Commentarii in constitutiones seu ordinationes regias* (1613), I. No place of publication.

[49] E.g., Grassaille, *op. cit.*, p. 60; Budé, *Annotationes in quatuor et viginti pandectarum libros* (Basel, 1557), pp. 96–98; Chasseneuz, *Consuetudines*, p. 5, and many others.

[50] "Vnum tamen non omitto, quod tanta aliquando in regibus soleat esse solertia ingenii, et naturalis sapientia (praesertim in nostro Rege praesenti) vt quae constituunt, non nisi iure et ratione efficere possint. Quod quasi sufficit, quia tales sufficientem videntur habere scientiam. . . . Vnde tamen verum est, quod longe melius fieret, si cum consilio, dico sapientum, id fiat. quia dubium non est omnia omnino, quae consilio recte geruntur, iureque meritoque effectu et firmitate niti." *De christianissimi*, p. 7, col. 2.

that government should be conducted according to a fixed ideal, and it was believed that the justice of a given measure might be evaluated and established in terms of the set criteria only through the exercise of reason. Thus de Bourg maintained that although the prince had all law *in scrinio pectoris*, he was not alone; his counsellors were at his side and were said to hold the conscience of the king. God illuminated the mind of the king for just rule and the giving of laws; yet his constitutions, promulgated under his authority alone, were assumed to have been framed after the deliberation of his counsellors.[51] In this fashion, the writers of the period preserved a place for counsel even in their theory founded upon the concept of greatly exalted kingship. However, the tendencies inherent in their thought went far toward the denial of the necessity of counsel; it was but a step from the concept of divinely inspired monarchy to assert that whatever the king did was *ipso facto* just. The place of counsel in the framing of laws and ordinances was reduced to an intellectual function of facilitating the establishment of justice through the exercise of reason, and as such it had a definite though limited place in government. But the practical effect of the doctrine which exalted the king to great heights even above his counsellors was to eliminate the necessity of them and to justify in large measure the personal rule of the divinely instituted monarch.

The question at once arises concerning the legal limitations upon kingship in the sense that Seyssel interpreted them. All admitted that the king was subject to natural and divine law

[51] "Respondeo propter patricios sapientes et consiliarios regios regi assistentes dicitur habere Princeps omnia iura in scrinio pectoris . . . nec unquam princeps solus est, vt quod sit presentia eius sine dubio valet et conscientiam regis tenet inter tot nobiles probatasque personas quae semper sunt ad latus regis . . . alias vbi eueniret quod absit regem repellere scientiam non posset facere legem, quia careret iure et ratione. . . . Rexque sequens Deum regere valet populum, Rex quandoque debet alloqui subiectos quos Deus sibi donauit, quia Deus tunc illuminat regem iuste sancientem et dantem legem. . . . Rex debet offerre legem Deo, et quod est ordinatum cum consilio, et cum consensu plurium redundat in gloriam Regis . . . licet constitutio dicatur ea, quam facit Rex proprio motu tamen illud intelligitur habita prius deliberatione sapientum doctorum et consiliariorum suorum quibus est credendum." *Op. cit.*, pp. 19b–20a.

and the general dictates of reason; also the Romanists maintained the two fundamental laws. But these were far from
constituting Seyssel's checks of *la justice* and *la police*. It was
in this department of political thought that the different tendencies of the legists and the humanists were revealed most
clearly. The two groups of writers were usually agreed concerning the exact content of the prerogative, but they often ran
counter to each other regarding the exterior limitations upon
the exercise of that authority. This appeared very sharply in
the commentaries of the two bodies of thinkers upon the text
princeps legibus solutus est. For Budé, the essentials of the
question were simple. By repeating a passage from Aristotle's
Politics and applying it strictly to the king, Budé developed the
idea that the ruler, as a quasi-divine individual, was necessarily superior to all other men and that laws binding men
equally could not apply to him. Laws were for the average and
the equal; they could not touch the prince who among men
approached most closely to perfection. On the contrary, he
was a god among men and a law unto himself.[52] Drawing upon
other passages from Aristotle, Budé compared the authority of
the king with the philosopher's absolute royalty and identified

[52] "Aristoteles lib. tertio Politic. huius dicti rationem memorabilem affere
mihi uidetur. . . . Is igitur in eo libro in hanc propemodum sententiam inquit,
si tamen recte uertimus, in repub. autem optime constituta is demum ciuis esse
dici debet, qui et regere et regi, et uoluntate et aptitudine ad uitam paratus est
secundum uirtutem agendam. Agedum sit aliquis unus, aut uno etiam plures
(pauciores tamen quam ut ciuitatis numerum implere possint) tanto caeteris
uirtutis exuperantia praestantes si plures sint, aut praestans si unus sit, reliquorum
ut uniuersorum uirtus cum illius aut illorum non sit comparabilis: dico, inquit,
huiusmodi uiros non iam ciuitatis partem existimandos esse, quippe iniuriam illis
haud dubie factum iri credendum est, si aequas ferre partes digni ipsi uidebuntur,
tanto caeteris inaequales uirtute, ciuilique facultate. Huiusmodi enim quasi
deum quendam censeri inter homines par est. Proinde legum quoque lationem
inter aequaleis necesse est esse et genere et facultate ciuili. In illos autem
huiuscemodi nulla est prorsus legislatio: quippe qui ipsi lex sint, quodque enim
ridiculum fore putemus eum, qui legem de huiusmodi ferre aggrediatur?"
Annotationes, p. 67. This was a favorite statement of Budé: ". . . et ne sont
point subiectz aux loix et aux ordonnances de leur royaume comme les autres
se bon ne leur semble. car il est a presumer quilz sont si parfaictz en prudence et
noblesse et equite quil ne leur fault point de reigle et forme escripte pour les
astraindre par craincte et par necessite dobeissance comme il faut aux autres."
"De l'institution du prince," 7ᵛ–8ʳ.

this with his economical regime wherein there were no legal qualifications between ruler and people as between father and son. Such could hardly be the case, since the king was a human Jove.[53] This super-human monarch he would place above all law and make in himself a source and criterion of justice. Repeating the statement later to become popular with the more absolutistic legists, he said that justice was the end of law, law the work of the prince, and the prince the image of God.[54] True, said Budé, the *digna vox* requires voluntary submission to established law on the part of the ruler. But by nature it is impossible that he submit to positive law; the only law which is superior to him is found in the abstract concepts of natural justice and reason.[55] Thus Budé regarded the royal authority as lacking entirely any limitations except the eternal principles binding all men. The latter constituted important factors in his concept of kingship, but they were entirely intangible. And when combined, as in Budé's system, with a monarch vastly superior to other men, these concepts presented but small effective limitations in the practical affairs of government. Hence Budé's insistence upon the great dimensions of the

[53] "Age cum quinque sint genera regni, quintum genus est quod παμβασιλεία dicitur, quasi dicas regnum numeris omnibus dominationis absolutum: cuiusmodi erant Reges, Principes Romani Vlpiani tempore, nihil iam priscae ciuilitatis retinentes, omnia arbitrio suo statuentes: ut et nunc Reges nostri sunt, qui omnia in potestate habent, quique (ut Homericus ille Iupiter) quoque sese uerterint, omnia circumagunt, nutu etiam solo omnia quatientes: denique humani Ioues, ut inquit Plautus in Casina, sed qui tamen hominum more emoriantur. Hoc autem regni genus est, inquit Aristoteles, cum unus omnium potestatem habet tum communium tum publicarum rerum, non aliter atque ciuitas una, aut populus unus habent. Haec autem species quinta oeconomica est ratione instituta. Vt etiam oeconomia regnum est domesticum, sic regnum oeconomia est ciuitatis aut populi unius aut plurium, id est domestica dispensatio. . . . Ad haec cum nullum ius ciuile inter patrem et liberos, et inter dominum et familiam intercedat, ut Aristoteles docet lib. 5. Ethicor . . . sit autem eadem ratio inter Principem et populum." *Annotationes*, p. 68.

[54] "Iustitia igitur finis est legis, lex autem officium est principis. At princeps ipse imago est dei, qui omnia recte ordineque constituit." *Annotationes*, p. 69. It is evident that Budé came very close to saying that whatever the king did was *ipso facto* just.

[55] Budé quoted Plutarch: "Lex, inquit, principis imperatrix erit: non illa quidem aut in libris extrinsecus scripta, aut in tabulis, sed animata intus in ipso ratio, semper cum eo conuersans, eiusdemque obseruatrix, quaeque eius animam nunquam sinit tutela sui esse uacuam." *Annotationes*, p. 69.

legitimate royal discretion and his willingness at times even to draw a parallel between the French king and the Roman dictator.[56]

Few legists were willing to go to such lengths in attributing to their ruler an authority without effective limitations. On occasion, they even denied Budé's idea that the king was free from law because inherently superior to other men. Rebuffi said that if the king were *legibus solutus*, it was not because of natural reasons; the king was mortal like all other men. Rather, it was because he was thus better able to act in the best interests of the state.[57] In elaborating this idea, he reiterated Saint Thomas' distinction, frequently found in the works of this period, between the coactive and the directive force of law. The prince, he said, was free from the coactive or coercive force of his laws simply because he recognized no earthly superior capable of enforcing his submission to those laws. His obedience to laws was thus necessarily voluntary. But the prince should be bound by the directive or instructive force of law, for the reason that he was the founder of the law and because it embodied that which he represented.[58] Thus, if the Romanists believed that the submission of the prince to law was purely voluntary, they nevertheless held that he ought to abide by the principles which it contained. From this they developed the idea that in all ordinary matters, the prince was *assumed* to restrain his discretion within the limits of estab-

[56] "Cestuy sylla se feist dictateur a rome pour six vingts ans, combien que loffice ne durast par lordonnance ancienne que six moys pour le plus. car au moyen de la grande puissance que auoit ung dictateur, qui estoit telle comme est celle du roy en france, on ordonna quelle ne dureroit que vng peu de temps." "De l'institution du prince," 82r.

[57] "Tamen solutus non est ratione naturali, quia est animal rationale, mortale, et tanquam homo damnibitur, si quid contra Deum, et ius diuinum faciat. . . . Princeps tamen legis nexibus dicitur absolutus, non quia ei iniqua liceant, sed quia is esse debet, qui non timore poenae, sed amore iustitiae aequitatem colat, Reipublicae procuret vtilitatem, et in omnibus, aliorum commoda, priuatae praeferat voluntati." *Explicatio*, p. 34.

[58] ". . . princeps est solutus legibus . . . intelligitur quoad vim coactiuam, quia non cogitur a seipso ad obseruandum legem, nec ab alio quidem, cum non habeat superiorem. . . . Sed in quantum lex habet vim directiuam, princeps est suae legi subditus: quia pater legum est princeps . . . ideo propria voluntate eas debet seruare." *Commentarii in constitutiones*, I, p. 11, no. 54.

lished law. The prince, wrote Chasseneuz, has a double authority, to wit, the ordinary and the absolute; according to the
absolute he may undoubtedly break all positive laws.[59] But
this latter authority was to be used only in unusual circumstances. As a general rule Chasseneuz insisted that the will of
the prince was assumed to be that which it should be according
to law; even if his orders were given out *motu proprio*, his
intention was not assumed to be such that it injured another.[60]
In this fashion, the Romanists attempted to insure a respect
for law even when attributing to the king the authority to
dispense with the same.

It is evident at once from the tenor of these statements that
the ideas of the Romanists marked a drastic diminution of
Seyssel's check of *la police*. The fundamental law these
writers retained in its essentials, but they subordinated the
customary law — by far the greater portion of the constitution — to the royal authority. Their hesitance concerning this
interpretation is illustrated by the statements of Chasseneuz
who, as has been noted, urged that the king ought ordinarily
to be assumed to abide by law. The medieval tradition of
respect for custom was strong in his thought. In one passage
he outlined an apparently iron-clad argument derived from the
older concepts and binding the king to observe customary law.
The customs of Burgundy, he said, have been approved by the
king; he has sworn to observe them as laws. They were ordered in the assembly of the three estates of the province and
with their consent, and after approval by the prince they ought
not to be broken by him, even with a *non obstante*.[61] But at

---

[59] "Habet nam princeps duplicem potestatem, ordinariam, scilicet et absolutam,
et secundum absolutam potest omnia iura tollere." Chasseneuz, *Consilia* (Lyon,
1588), p. 168b, col. 2.

[60] ". . . voluntas principis talis esse praesumitur, qualis de iure esse debet
. . . etiam si princeps scribat cum clausula, motu proprio, eius intentio non
praesumitur, quod quis grauetur." *Consilia*, p. 29b, col. 1. ". . . voluntas principis praesumitur esse talis, qualis est iuris dispositio, seu talis, qualis esse debet
de iure." *Ibid.*, p. 161b, col. 1.

[61] "Primo eo quod consuetudines nostrae ducatus Burgundiae sunt approbatae
a Christianissimo rege nostro, et illas iurauit obseruare pro legibus, et fuerunt

that point, Chasseneuz brought in the king's *plenitudo potestatis* which, as we have seen, permitted the ruler to quash all positive law. As a general rule, Chasseneuz was forced to admit that the king held undoubted authority to override customary law, and all others of the school presented a like interpretation.[62] Chasseneuz might urge that the king ought to use this authority but rarely,[63] but he was definite in attributing it to the king. In the final analysis, the king he believed to be subordinate to custom only if it embodied principles of natural or divine law. Pushing the ideas of this school to their logical conclusions, Rebuffi wrote that the prince was bound to observe custom only if it contained natural law and reason.[64] Thus the legists, like the humanists, came to the point of believing the king to be bound only by intangibles. Any rights which the people might possess were consequently beyond the authority of the prince to touch only if they were grounded in natural or divine law; the specific details of local custom offered in themselves no such guarantee because they were subjected to the royal discretion. Rebuffi drew from his statement, just cited, the conclusion that the prince might not divest

---

factae in conuocatione trium statuum patriae, et de consensu illorum, et sic transierunt in vim pragmaticae, ex quo non potest illis derogari, per quamcunque clausulam quae apponi possit. . . . Et ex quo etiam sunt confirmatae per principem, non possunt tolli, nec illis derogari, cum clausula, non obstante." *Consuetudines*, p. 332a.

[62] "Nam non est dubium, quod in his quae sunt positiui iuris princeps supremus prout est Rex Franciae, in regno habet liberam potestatem disponendi et immutandi." *Consilia*, p. 168b, col. 2. Also, *Consuetudines*, pp. 287b, 377a, 381a; *Catalogus*, p. 117a. Grassaille, *op. cit.*, p. 307; Rebuffi, *Tractatus de consuetudine, usu, et stylo in iudiciis valde frequens, et utilis*, in *Commentarii in constitutiones*, III, pp. 592–593.

[63] " . . . tamen plenitudo potestatis nunquam praesumitur nisi expresse dicatur . . . princeps debet raro vti hac clausula." *Consuetudines*, p. 332a.

[64] " . . . princeps tenetur consuetudines obseruare, et ius consuetudinarium ligat ipsum . . . quod est verum si rationem contineat naturalem: vt dicit Bal. . . . quia fortius est ius naturale, quam principatus, secundum eum. Ideo non poterit diuestire vassalum sine causa, vel officialem suum officio priuare." *Tractatus de consuetudine*, p. 589, no. 35. In similar vein, Chasseneuz wrote: " . . . princeps possit tollere etiam sine causa ea quae non sunt inducta de iure diuino naturali vel gentium cum clausula, non obstante. etiam si agatur de alterius graui praeiudicio." *Consilia*, p. 168b, col. 2.

a vassal of his fief without cause or deny a man his office, but it is clear that the only limitations placed upon the discretion of the king to do those things were provided by abstract concepts. This shift of the basis of a man's legal right from the specific details of custom to general ideas of justice acted as a vital influence in undermining the limits traditionally placed upon the action of the ruler.

That this approach to customary law was not mere speculation but might be applied by jurisconsults to considerations turning on details of positive law was illustrated in the writings of André Tiraqueau.[65] His works dealt entirely with that portion of law which today would be called private; thus they are valid illustrations of the ideas of the Romanists concerning the effective weight of custom. His emphasis may be appreciated only by stating the points of law involved. Tiraqueau considered the question of a woman who contracts with the prince without the consent of her husband, thereby acting contrary to customary law. Is the contract valid? The first answer Tiraqueau gave in the affirmative on the ground that the prince was not limited by the customs and laws of his subjects. But in this case, the act was not valid because it involved the right of a third person, the husband, whose right the prince might not violate without just cause. And although this regulation was recorded in customary law, it was also according to *jus gentium* and was founded in natural and divine law which gave authority over the wife to the husband.[66] In this passage there

---

[65] See Jacques Brejon, *André Tiraqueau* (Paris, 1937).

[66] "Decimono quaero, Quid si mulier cum fisco, aut principe contraxit, sine autorite mariti, an valeat contractus? videtur quod sic, per id quod voluit Iac. Aret. . . . quod stante statuto, quod filiusfam, non possit obligare, poterit tamen obligari fisco. . . . Et confirmari potest, quoniam Princeps non subest statutis, et legibus subditorum. . . . Contrarium tamen videtur in hoc casu, quoniam hic agitur de iure alterius, videlicet mariti, quod Princeps ipse sine causa tollere non potest. . . . Et licet hoc ius sit ex statuto aut consuetudine introductum, non potest tamen negari, quin sit Iurisgentium. . . . Praeterea huiusmodi consuetudo fundatur ratione naturali et diuina. Nam vt supra . . . ostendimus, mulier est in potestate viri, iure divino et naturali. . . . At consuetudo, siue statutum, quod ratione naturali nititur, ligat Principem. . . ." *De legibus connubialibus*, gl. 8, nos. 175-176, in *Opera* (Frankfort, 1616), I.

is an interesting combination of ideas. The prince was not bound by custom unless that custom was based upon divine or natural law or *jus gentium*. But also the prince ought not to infringe a man's legal right without just cause. Thus, while making the prince subject to customary law only if it were based upon a higher type of law, thus changing its traditional basis, Tiraqueau refused to push his theory to the conclusion of allowing the king to quash a man's legal right without cause, merely through exercise of the royal authority. Although his interpretation was a half-measure and a compromise, he maintained it throughout his writings.[67] It clearly represented a stage in the transition from the medieval identification of law as custom to the later concepts subordinating both law and popular rights to the prince.

A similar hesitation is visible, although to a lesser extent, in the Romanists' idea of the royal authority to tax. The majority of the school followed the emphasis given by Seyssel, namely the attribution of the taxing power to the king apparently without limits, although urging moderation in his use of that prerogative.[68] Yet the theoretical bases of popular consent to taxation were not dead. Rebuffi repeated the interpretation, long a vital point in constitutional thought, that the prince did not hold title to all wealth in the state and was lord over private property only in matters pertaining to protection and jurisdiction. Thus he could not deprive any man of his possessions and could not take taxes at will from the people. Taxes were, on the contrary, given to him by his subjects simply in order that he might better defend them.[69] This

---

[67] E.g., *De iure primigeniorum*, quaestio xxii, in *Opera*, I; *De retraict lignagier*, § 1, gl. xiii, nos. 38, 39, in *Opera*, II.

[68] Grassaille, *op. cit.*, p. 151; Ferrault, *op. cit.*, p. 548, col. 2; Budé, *De asse et partibus eius, libri V* (Lyon, 1550), pp. 296–299.

[69] "Princeps non est dominus rerum singularium personarum, nisi quoad protectionem et iurisdictionem. . . . Princeps sine iusta causa non potest priuare quem domino rerum suarum. . . ." *De regum*, p. 5, no. 52. "Princeps non potest tributum auffere a subditis suis, quia non est dominus singulorum . . . quia tributum ei datur, vt suos defendat subditos, quod si non defendat, ei denegandum est. . . ." *Ibid.*, p. 7, no. 92. See *Explicatio*, p. 99.

reasoning followed logically from the all-important concept of the two categories of legal right comprising the constitution, and its reaffirmation by a theorist writing during the period of successful absolutism bears witness to the continued strength of that tradition. More representative, however, were the ideas of Chasseneuz. As in his consideration of the customary law, he began with principles very medieval but ended with ideas highly absolutistic. In outlining the mutual obligations of king and people, he showed that the monarch owed justice and protection to his subjects while the latter should contribute to the needs of the state with their services and goods. Under the heading of monetary contributions by the people, he listed first those levies granted by the local estates for a limited period (specifically, the *fouage* granted for three years by the Estates of Burgundy), and secondly those taken by the king according to custom.[70] His initial approach to the problem was thus through strictly medieval concepts. But at this point, he brought in the absolute authority of the king in matters pertaining to government. For the defense of the realm, he said, the king might levy taxes at will, and he cited Ferrault to the effect that the king held that authority over all men, clerics as well as laymen.[71] Thus he arrived at the idea that the justice of a particular levy was not to be determined according to its consonance with customary law but rather according to its necessity in terms of the immediate situation. He preserved the traditional categories of ordinary and extraordinary levies, but instead of defining the latter as those accorded by popular consent, he stated simply that they were taken by the ruler as demanded by unusual circumstances. And he made it clear that both types fell under the royal authority to take as needed.[72] Thus the absolute authority of the king absolved

---

[70] *Consuetudines*, pp. 28b–29a.

[71] *Consuetudines*, pp. 29b–30b. ". . . dominus pro defensione sua et suae patriae, potest cogere subditos vt ei contribuant et eos cogere, vt ei inseruiant." *Ibid.*, p. 29b.

[72] "Est ergo munus ordinarium quod et indictum appellatur . . . quando procedit lex vel prouisio generalis, quod singulis mensibus vel annis, quisque

him from effective restrictions of law in taking taxes necessary for the functions of government. Summing up his doctrine, Chasseneuz wrote that the prince ought first to draw upon the funds in his own purse, but if those were insufficient he might levy taxes for the defense of the realm not only from his immediate vassals but from all his subjects. The prince might take such levies even without the consent of the people. The only qualification was that they should be taken for just cause, that is, for the defense of the realm or public necessity; otherwise he sinned.[73] In this fashion the Renaissance thinkers developed a theory without effective limitations upon the authority of the king to tax, for they attributed to him at once the right to take necessary taxes and to judge of their necessity. The details of Chasseneuz' treatment reveal in striking manner the method in which the legists, by modifying the medieval concept of mutual obligations of king and populace, evolved a theory placing greatest stress upon the prerogative rights of the prince and the almost unlimited obligations of the people.

If the traditional limitations of law upon the royal prerogative suffered a lessening at the hands of the Renaissance jurists, such was also the fate of Seyssel's check of *la justice*. Yet to a degree surprising in view of their major emphases, these writers maintained the structure of this check intact. We have seen how Chasseneuz insisted that the king ought to abide by the law and was assumed to do so in all cases not explicitly

---

allibratus soluat vnum solidum pro libra: tunc quia habet tractum successiuum et regulatum: et non concernit tempus praesens, dicitur ordinarium. . . . Extraordinarium vero munus est quando eius impositio non sit prouisione vel lege generali seu regulari: nec ob causam ordinariam et successiuam, sed ob causam extraordinariam occurrentem: vt pro hastiludiis: vel pro latrunculis, ne damna inferant, vel ob aliam similem causam momentaneam quae reiterationem non expectat. . . . Ad vnum tamen aduerte, quod princeps, lex, vel statutum, potest facere munera quae sunt extraordinaria, ordinaria." *Consuetudines*, p. 31b.

[73] ". . . principes debent se primo praemunire de eorum marsupio, et si marsupium eorum non sufficiat possunt subditis imponere collectam . . . nedum principes a vasallis feuda tenentibus, sed etiam ab aliis suis subditis possunt exigere collectam pro defensione suae patriae . . . princeps seu habens alia iura regalia propter necessitates publicas patriae, potest a subditis suis etiam inuitis exigere praestantias . . . sed debent fieri pro defensione patriae, et publicae necessitate, et sic cum causa, alias princeps peccat." *Consuetudines*, p. 327a.

otherwise. Thus, although maintaining that the king was *lex animata*, that he might quash positive law, that he might judge his own case, and that his judgments should be based upon equity rather than the letter of the law, he nevertheless stated that the Kings of France submitted to the judgment of their officers, not only those in the Parlement but also the *bailli* and *sénéchaux*. And if the judgment went against the king, he permitted it to be carried out and submitted to it, even ordering its execution through royal letters.[74] Almost in the words of Seyssel, he asserted that royal letters were often given out on impulse without due consideration, and for that reason they might be judged according to their *incivilité* and iniquity.[75] Budé, even to a greater extent than Chasseneuz, had presented a theory of monarchy above law, yet he maintained the basic outlines of the judicial check upon the king. He compared the Parlement with the Areopagus and the Roman Senate, asserting that the three bodies alike enjoyed the double capacity of judging and sharing in acts of administration. For this reason, the Kings of France submit their ordinances to the Parlement for that publication which gives them their sanction. Likewise, although the king is *legibus solutus*, he submits to the judgments of the court.[76] Budé found no contradiction in his ex-

---

[74] ". . . reges Franciae iudicio suorum officiariorum nedum curiarum parlamenti, sed etiam senescallorum seu balliuorum suorum sponte se submiserunt, et quod iudicatum est contra se, efficaciter exequi permittunt et patiuntur, iudicatoque obediunt, imo illud propriis patentibus literis exequi mandant. . . ." *Catalogus*, p. 107a, col. 2.

[75] "Plerunque . . . regis voluntates vt vehementes, sic mobiles saepe ipsae sibi aduersae, vnde opus fuit moderatione, quae tanta extitit apud reges Franciae: vt ex ordinatione plurium regum ac verbali praecepto officiariis Franciae saepius fuisse iniunctum literas regias iudicialiter et publice posse impugnari de nullitate ac subreptione, et vt tales per iudices quibus diriguntur posse declari, etiam de inciuilitate et iniquitate, et ita in omnibus curiis Franciae seruatur." *Catalogus*, p. 107a, col. 2.

[76] "Ut enim Areopagitae criminibus primum diiudicandis instituti, et caedibus uindicandis, regendisque Atheniensium moribus, ad rem tamen publicam administrandam interdum aduocabantur: sic curia haec nostra utrunque munus amplectitur cum opus est . . . ita Principum constitutionibus, ut uim sanctionum habeant, et huiusmodi actis ad remp. pertinentibus, autorem curiam fieri hodie necesse est, eaque in curia promulgari. . . . In ea igitur curia in qua summa iurisdictionis Gallicae, atque etiam iuridicialis imperii sita est, omnia inesse mihi

altation of kingship to a point above all earthly law and his maintenance of the judicial check upon the ruler in terms of that law. His interpretation fitted well with the concept — held generally during the period — of the absolute royal authority which found no control but was limited merely through the declaration of the law to which there could be but voluntary submission. Much in his system was similar to that of Seyssel, but the final emphasis of his thought was entirely different. He may have maintained the details of the check of *la justice* in their entirety as concerned the verification of royal acts in court and the submission of the king to its judgments, but his exaltation of kingship to a point above the law and earthly society generally was a major step toward the complete devitalizing of the judicial check upon the king. For when this conception of kingship was combined with the idea — accepted by the great majority of Renaissance jurists — that the king alone held title to all jurisdiction exercised in the state, there was provided ample basis for reducing the Parlement to the position of a mere tribunal administering justice among the people and lacking entirely any authority to check the king. Grassaille, while attributing to the court truly regal qualities, presented essentially this interpretation.[77] And La Perriere, by developing the idea that the king alone held all governmental authority, denied Seyssel's statement that the Parlements formed an aristocratic element in the constitution capable of binding the king. On the contrary, he said, France is a pure monarchy; all jurisdiction exercised by the courts is derived from the king as from a fountain. Thus, although the Parle-

---

videntur, quae et in Senatu, et in Centumuiratu, et in Areopago erant, duntaxat quod ad iurisdictionem imperiumque iuridiciale attinet. . . . In huius acta referri diplomata regiaque beneficia solent, ut perpetua esse possint, ac nunquam antiquabilia. Huius auctoritate rata irritaue Principum acta, ne ipsis quidem recusantibus fiunt. Vna haec curia est, a qua sibi ius dici Principes legibus soluti ciuili animo ferant: quam autorem fieri sacrandis promulgandisque sanctionibus suis velint: Cuius consilii censurae, constitutiones suas eximi, edictaque sua nolint, imo cuius decretis huiusmodi sua acta consecrari aeternitati velint." *Annotationes*, pp. 95–96.

[77] *Op. cit.*, pp. 159–181.

ment may administer supreme justice among the people, it may
never check the ruler; rather, it is the king who binds, reforms,
regulates, and punishes the court, even quashing its decisions
if he so desires.[78] The statement was extreme, even among
writers of the early sixteenth century, yet it represented but
the logical extension of concepts common to all. Seyssel's
checks of *la justice* and *la police* were fast disappearing.

In conclusion, it should be emphasized that although the
jurists of the Renaissance brought about definite and very
important developments in political thought, they evolved these
largely through adopting and reinterpreting ideas which had
long been accepted. The divine authorization of kingship, the
concept of fundamental law, and the all-important idea of the
king as primarily a judge were the stock in trade of political
writers. The specific alterations in constitutional thought
effected by these jurists are in the main traceable to the influence of Roman law and to their effort to group their concepts
so as to account increasingly for the rapidly crystallizing
national state. These mutations were many and far-reaching,
yet it should be noted that the legists abhorred on principle the
idea of change. As emphatically as Seyssel, they urged that the
law ought to be altered only in case of urgent necessity, be-

[78] "Aucuns [Seyssel] ont voulu dire, que le Royaume de France n'est pas
seulement gouuerné par monarchie d'vn seul Roy, ains est aussi gouuerné par
l'Aristocratie de Parlemens, lesquelz ils comparent aux Ephores des Lacede-
moniens: mais ceste comparaison est mal proportionée. . . . Mais quant à ce
que lesditz Ephores bridoyent leurs Roys, la comparaison d'eux à noz parlemens
cloche de ce pied, et n'est pas bonne: car les Parlemens ne brident pas nos Roys,
ains nos Roys les brident, reforment, et en cas de coulpe punissent, cassent et
annullent leurs arrestz quand bon leur semble, et par leurs edictz et ordonnances
les reglent. . . . Mais (quand i'ay bien tout calculé) considerant que les Parlemens, voire tous sieges de iudicature de France, sont comme ruysseaux procedens
de la fontaine de Royauté, et le Roy est chief vnique sur tous, et que de luy seul
procede toute leur autorité comme arteres du coeur, toutes veines du foye, et
tous nerfz du cerueau: ie conclus, que nous viuons en ce florissant Royaume,
souz vne seulle espece de Republicque, c'est souz la monarchie d'vn treschrestien
et trespuissant Roy, auquel Dieu par sa grace doint prosperer de bien en mieux.
Ie n'ignore pas que le tradecteur de l'hystoire d'Appian Alexandrin en François
[i.e. Seyssel], en son epistre liminaire dirigee au Roy Lois douzieme, n'ait faict
ses effors de prouuer que la Republique des François est en partie, Monarchique:
en partie, Aristocratique: et en partie Democratique: mais les raisons desquelles
il se sert, ne sont certaines ny bien fondees, voire sont si froides, qu'elles ne
peuuent eschauffer son opinion. . . ." *Op. cit.*, pp. 22–25.

cause any change in accepted law tended to disrupt the foundations of the state. Thus appears the curious fact that although the Romanists placed the king over all law of the constitution, except the fundamental laws, to make or break, their primary convictions were opposed to the ruler's freely using that prerogative. The interpretation given by Rebuffi was representative when he urged that before new laws were made, the old ones should be examined for any possible utility before being discarded. Would that the Chancellor and the counsellors of the prince, he said, might keep this before their eyes and not fashion so many laws, especially for France. When the laws are barbaric and iniquitous, it is necessary to change them, but this ought to be done sparingly. Laws obtain force only through long usage; while they may easily be altered, they may be established in force only with difficulty. Even when the signs of the times require changes in the law, such alterations are dangerous.[79] Although the Romanists paved the way for later theories of royal legislation by attributing the rudiments of that authority to the king, they were unwilling to include the free exercise of that prerogative in their constitutional systems because they regarded the state as resting upon legal foundations rightly unchanging. The Renaissance jurists may have differed from Seyssel regarding the position occupied by customary law relative to the royal authority, but they were at one with him in holding to an essentially static theory of state.

[79] "Vlpianus statuit ius nouum non esse statuendum ad corrigendum ius antiquum, quod iamdiu visum est aequum: quia antequam istud nouum sit tantopere obseruatum, non ita aequum inuenietur, sicut antiquum, sed multae amaritudines in eo reperientur. Ideo antequam constituatur ius nouum, recedens ab antiquo debet esse vtilitas, et non solum vtilitas apparens, sed etiam euidens, id est, aperta et manifesta, quae videri ex inspectione legis constitutae possit. Et vtinam Cancellarii et Consiliarii Principum ob oculos ista haberent, et non fingerent tot leges, maxime nostri Galli, quos a leuitate vix excusare possumus. . . . Itaque cum leges antiquae sunt rudes et iniquae, tunc mutandas esse censet in lib. Politic. Arist. sed raro hanc immutationem faciendam, dicens: neque enim simile est mutare artem, atque legem. Nam lex vim habet, vt ipsi pareatur, nullam, nisi ex more: Mos autem non sit, nisi temporis longitudine, quare faciliter mutare leges ex praesentibus in alias nouas, infirmam est facere vim legis, sed quandoque variantibus temporibus expedit iura mutare . . . immutationes esse periculosas." *Explicatio*, p. 38, cols. 1, 2.

CHAPTER III

THE THEORY OF THE FRENCH CONSTITUTION

THE sixteenth century was one of the most fascinating periods of European history in stirring action and the free play of human emotions. A period of rapid development and transition, it witnessed the appearance of much that has characterized European civilization until the present time. In France, the revival of learning brought new intellectual horizons and disturbing changes in social codes and ways of life. The Reformation broke the religious unity which had been a fundamental basis of society since time immemorial. A complex series of social changes permanently altered the position and mutual relations of the classes constituting society: the rising bourgeoisie, hitherto despised as following a profession definitely degrading, took its place as a major and almost respectable social entity, while the nobility suffered a sharp decline through the undermining of their economic position and the decimation of their ranks during the Wars of Religion. The royal authority, strong to the point of absolutism during the first half of the century, was held after 1559 by feeble hands permitting it to be challenged by a series of parties and factions and to be reduced practically to their level. The baronage and the host of local units whose jealously guarded franchises had suffered steady encroachment under the strong rule from Paris seized the opportunity to reassert their traditional quasi-independence. The state rapidly disintegrated into a composite of local seigneuries, city states, and factions which warred with royalty itself and did not hesitate to utilize the assistance of foreign invaders. To the apparent collapse of the central government was added the break in religious unity, and since this found root in the fundamental motivating principles of the age, it was regarded by contemporaries as of even more serious consequences than the decline of the secular authority. The more traditionally conditioned thinkers of the period feared, and with reason, the collapse of all that they had held fundamental to the state and sacred to the life of the people.

In the midst of such currents, there was inevitably much speculation concerning that which had heretofore been taken for granted, and in place of the unbroken praise for strong monarchy which had characterized the period of Francis I, there appeared a thorough questioning and evaluation of the very bases of social and political existence. Thinkers became excited concerning great things and wrote with an earnestness which reveals at once a sincerity of purpose and a conviction which frequently arose from the heat of combat. If much political speculation, particularly that of the religious factions at war, was little more than interested apology for the means adopted for the furtherance of the faith, there nevertheless appeared many treatises, especially those of the legists, which were concerned primarily with political problems and which took their places among the best theoretical treatments produced in France during the entire *ancien régime.*

France was fortunate in possessing during the sixteenth century a great body of jurists such as appeared in no other country in Europe. If the freedom with which they wrote may be ascribed in part to the relaxation of the royal authority and the widespread concern for the fundamental bases of the social organism, their appearance at this critical juncture was not the result of fortuitous circumstance but the flowering of centuries of legal study and practice centered about the schools of law, the Parlements, the court and the royal administration generally. If there were few among them who reached the heights of a Jean Bodin, there was produced — as has happened so frequently in the intellectual life of France — a host of very able men falling just short of greatness. Such figures as Du Moulin, Du Tillet, Pasquier, Du Haillan, Choppin, Du Vair, Loisel, and de Harlay, to mention but a few of the better known, were sufficient to place the constitutional thought of the period on a very high level and to form the nucleus of a distinct school. True, there were wide variations among the approaches evinced by the works of these men: Du Moulin was a Bartolist, while Du Haillan avoided the major implications of the Roman law. Furthermore, the works of Du Moulin were important in the evolution of constitutional thought chiefly through their subtle undermining of the traditional system rather than their preservation of it; for this reason we have postponed our major treatment of his ideas until a later chapter. For the same reason, we have largely eliminated from the present discussion Louis Le Roy, Jean Bodin, and to a lesser extent Charondas Le Caron, for if much that these men held was in line with the older modes of thought, their influence during the century lay rather in their emphases tending toward a newer theory of state. The purpose of the present chapter is to set forth in detail the theory of the French constitution as it was revealed in the works of those legists whose interpretations embodied in matured form the traditional constitutionalism stemming from the Middle Ages and representing the true legal heritage. Those aspects of contemporary thought making for a disruption of, and an evolution away from, that theory will be considered in the following chapter. Admittedly, there were elements of both in the majority of works to be considered, and consequently any discussion of this type must be a partial distortion of contemporary thought in the sense that it isolates one portion from the whole. Yet, such a division is necessary in a study in which it is obviously impossible to present the parallel chronology of all currents involved.

We may regard this theory of the French constitution as that which was widely supported during the first years of the century only to go underground during the period of successful absolutism and to reappear again in full form as the age waned. With the decline of effective royal power, there appeared once more an interpretation of political life centered not upon the majesty of the king but upon the legal bases of the state. However, if the weakening of the royal control and the disruption of the traditional bases of political existence brought opportunity for careful evaluation of those things, the chaos of the land soon forced men once more to seek a strengthening of the royal authority if only in order to preserve the state. With the apparent collapse of the two traditional pillars of society — religious unity and royal government — men could but allow increased discretion to the ruler as the last agent which might restore order to the land. Thus, if the chaotic second half of the century witnessed a revival of the traditional theory of the constitution, it also gave rise to intellectual currents making for the destruction of that theory because of the growing consciousness that the older concepts would no longer suffice. This intellectual reaction, in part the child of desperation, followed much that had characterized the absolutist thought current during the two strong reigns, but it differed from the earlier movement both in the hesitance of its concessions to royalty and in the reception which it found in the state. For at the close of the century, popular attitude was of a type to welcome absolutism. It was this counter-reaction in political thought which finally sealed the fate of the traditional constitutionalism.

A. The Law of the Commonwealth

One of the ablest among modern students of French constitutional thought has concluded, after elaborate inquiry into the subject, that the strictly traditional doctrine, and that which was most widely accepted throughout the *ancien régime*, represented the realm as simply a union of social structure and rulership. The latter was held to animate the otherwise inert body of the state, and the two together formed the primary component parts of the living social unit, yet each remained distinct within itself.[1] When translated into legal terminology,

---

[1] "L'Etat, alors, *respublica*, c'était la chose publique: c'était une *chose*, et non pas une personne. . . . La *respublica* n'est plus une personne morale, la personnification de la nation elle-même; elle est, si l'on veut, une sorte de corps, mais un corps sans âme. L'âme qui anime ce corps, c'est la souveraineté, et la souveraineté est considerée comme quelque chose de *personnel*, d'intelligent et

this statement appears as the exact counterpart of the all-important doctrine noted above, namely, the existence in the realm of two primary spheres of legal right, those of ruler and people respectively. The sum-total of the fundamental and customary laws giving basis to those rights formed the constitution or legal framework of the state. This concept of dual spheres of right and law was the basis of Seyssel's thought and was maintained in the works of the Romanists, who, however, tended to obscure the line of division and to assert the mastery of one sphere over the other. This theory appears constantly throughout the works of the constitutionalists of the century; it was the basis of their approach to political problems and to the legal quality which they ascribed to every portion of the state. Furthermore, the evolution of constitutional thought throughout the period may very nearly be summed up as a series of varying emphases ascribed by successive writers to this theory. The changes were often slight and difficult to evaluate, but they constituted a major and highly significant portion of the evolution of sixteenth-century political thought.

There were certain higher values which all political theorists accepted as bonds within, and ultimates over, the state, however greatly they might vary in the actual incorporation of these concepts into their intellectual systems. Of these, religion was of greatest influence, while natural and divine law were placed as undoubted principles over all men and things. The definitions of the laws of God and nature ranged from the early Christian identification of the two [2] to the more frequent interpretation of the latter as natural instinct implanted in all animals; but there is no doubt of their importance in the legal thought of the day. All legists who expressed themselves on the question preserved the medieval hierarchy of legal values

---

de libre, qui ne peut appartenir qu'à la personne humaine, dans la monarchie au prince. . . . La souveraineté est essentiellement distincte de l'Etat (*respublica*)." André Lemaire, *Les Lois fondamentales de la monarchie française d'après les théoriciens de l'ancien régime* (Paris, 1907), pp. 283–284.

[2] E.g., Tiraqueau. Cf. Brejon, *op. cit.*, p. 70.

ranging from eternal law to earthly custom. The latter was regarded as an integral part of that great system and could be at most a body of additions to the higher principles contained therein. Charondas wrote that all human laws should be fashioned after the model of natural and divine law.[3] Laws, said L'Alouette, might be classed as fundamental or civil, but they necessarily had their origin in reason and justice and as such were rendered legitimate by their consonance with divine truth.[4] Because of their intimate association with political concepts, these higher principles were not simply remote ideals serving as aims and ends but were directly fused into every important political problem. Seyssel had listed *la religion* as a major check upon the king, and Pasquier said that religion was the basis of every *république bien ordonnée*.[5] In an age when religion provided the strongest motive forces, the importance of religious concepts and values in the field of political thought is quite evident. Again we may refer to a major conclusion of Lemaire: the French monarchy, throughout its entire duration and because such was its essence, was an absolute monarchy tempered by tradition and by religion.[6] Not only the ancient form of the state but its fundamental bases and meaning were summarized by the adage: *un roi, une foi, une loi.* It was this important and undifferentiated approach which caused legal writers to be influenced by religious concepts and to view the break in unity of religion as fraught with peril not only to religious values but also to the state itself.

But there was also the element of tradition which was, in the

---

[3] *Pandectes ou digestes du droict françois* (Paris, 1637), p. 12.

[4] "Mais il y a diuerses sortes de Lois: les vnes concernent l'etablissement et disposition de l'Etat vniuersel, comme sont les fondamentales. . . . Les autres regardent la societé publique. . . . Toutes lesquelles Lois pour les faire valoir et receuoir pour bonnes et iustes, il faut qu'elles ayent leur mouuement et origine de la raison et droiture, de plus haut qu'en la fantasie humaine, passant par les cercles de la droiture et iustice Diuine, qui les rende valables et legitimes." François de L'Alouette, *Des affaires d'état: des finances, du prince, de la noblesse* (Metz, 1597), p. 10.

[5] Etienne Pasquier, *Lettres*, Liv. VI, no. 1, pp. 147, 390. Our references are to the *Œuvres* published at Amsterdam, 1723.

[3] *Op. cit.*, p. 327.

eyes of the legists, specifically the law of the land. It is difficult
to overestimate the importance of that body of law, the established constitution, in sixteenth-century political thought. Du
Haillan merely reiterated the ideas of his contemporaries when
he wrote that law provided the pattern for the life of the state
and the vital element without which no body politic, large or
small, could exist.[7] Although his statements make it clear
that he regarded the constitution as forming a portion of the
traditional scale of legal values, throughout his works his emphasis was upon the specific details of customary legal usage.
The typical mind of the legist, dealing with the multitudinous
details of substantive law and close to practical affairs, was
inherently distrustful of natural and divine law as the sole basis
of a man's legal right. Occasionally they even called attention
to the variation between the law of the constitution and pure
natural law, and showed the inapplicability of the latter in
many departments of legal practice.[8] The practitioners placed
greater reliance upon tradition or substantive customary law
and approached the details of constitutional theory through
that medium. Tradition, in this sense, was the immediate ob-
ject of their inquiry and was established by man and quite
earthly. Although they did not always elaborate upon the
point, the distinction between fundamental and private law in
the constitution was usually present in their thought, and the
essence of each was the same: the custom of the land. The

[7] "Et pource les longues guerres et leur suite recente, auoient porté son
peuple à vne grande licence de faire ce qu'il vouloit, il [Pharamond] delibera de
faire de nouuelles loix pour faire viure les siens soubs certaine reigle et police,
considerant qu'aussi peu peut vn peuple viure sans loix, qu'vn corps sans
membres, sang et nerfs et qu'il n'y a rien si conuenable à la condition de la
nature, que la loy, sans laquelle ny aucune maison, ny aucune ville, ny nation
ny tout le genre humain ne peut subsister, ny demeurer, ny mesmes la nature
des choses, ny le monde mesme: et que le fondement de la liberté, la fontaine
d'equité, et l'entendement, le coeur, le conseil, et les volontez et aduis d'vn estat
sont plantez et establis sur les loix." Bernard de Girard Du Haillan, *Histoire de
France* (Paris, 1585), I, 16a. This work was first published in 1576 and appears
under various titles.

[8] E.g., Pasquier, *Dialogue de la loy*, in *Œuvres*, I, 1045–1050, where he shows
the great variation between natural and constitutional law in regard to property
rights. Cf. *Lettres*, Liv. XIX, no. 7, pp. 551–554.

basis of the distinction, clearly recognized, was in the sphere of right to which each division applied. Although the jurists did not consciously break down the traditional hierarchy of legal values, their immediate concern was with the law of the land.

The theory that fundamental law regulated the accession to, and exercise of, the royal prerogative was completely developed, as we have seen, by the time of Seyssel. Although the Romanists early in the century denied certain limitations heretofore restricting the monarch's freedom of action, they nevertheless maintained the idea of fundamental law untouched. The traditional school here under consideration preserved this theory not only regarding specific regulations, such as the Salic Law and the inalienability of the domain, but also as concerned the legal basis of the crown and the consequent limits upon the royal discretion. The interpretation pictured the crown as that body of right or authority specifically pertaining to public matters and thus forming one vital portion of the state structure. The Salic Law regulated the succession to the crown, while its non-division and proper preservation were insured by the law prohibiting the alienation of the royal domain.[9] Together, these regulations provided a modicum of legality which was ever-present in sixteenth-century thought concerning the prerogative. These ideas were stated with vigor by Simon Marion when pleading a royal case in 1572.[10] Here was reiterated the theory

---

[9] The fundamental law prohibiting the alienation of the royal domain was ascribed various meanings according to the subject at hand. The "domain," meaning simply the lands and financial income of the crown was the more frequent meaning and was, of course, the subject of the Ordinance of Moulins, 1566, by which L'Hospital codified the rules of long standing in regard to the domain. But this fundamental law was also held to refer to the entire body of the prerogative and to prohibit its division by the ruler; it was used in this sense by Simon Marion in the passage quoted in the following footnote. See also Esmein, *Histoire du droit français* (Paris, 1910), p. 328.

[10] "Tous ceux qui ont escript de la maiesté des Roys et de leurs droits, mesme des Roys de France et de leur couronne, de leur royaume et de leur domaine et de leur souveraineté, encores que ce discours soit passé par la plume de plusieurs estrangers, voire ennemis de cest Estat, toutesfois la force de la verité les a tous contraints de confesser que c'est le plus grand, le plus noble et le plus splendide royaume de la terre. La conseruation de sa grandeur est fondée sur deux principales loix: l'vne est celle qui règle la succession du royaume par ligne masculine

of fundamental law as regulating the transmission of the prerogative through the members of a legally chosen family, whose right was in terms of law rather than a proprietary right in the thing itself. Being beyond the capacity of its holder, the royal authority was not in the king's possession and consequently not subject to his discretion. The concept provided basis for a complete theory of king and crown, with the former as that especially constituted individual whose duty was simply the exercise of the authority thus conferred upon him as a trust for the duration of his reign. The resulting theory, picturing the royal authority as a constituted entity which was regulated by a special type of law limiting at once the capacity and discretion of the prince, was accepted so generally among the constitutionalists that it is hardly necessary to elaborate upon the point. Choppin wrote that the king was not permitted to communicate honors or authority to the queen because he was simply the guide and governor of the state and the "mystical spouse" of the crown.[11] This theory of fundamental law, as constituting the legal basis and limitation of the royal authority which, as a body of right, was distinct from the rights of the subjects, was accepted generally by men of all camps during the century. The most extreme absolutists did not deny the force of at least the two essential fundamental laws. The legal quality of kingship may be regarded as part of the political mentality of the century.

If men were agreed that fundamental law regulated the position of the royal authority in the state, they were far from

---

tant seulement, et en exclut perpetuellement les femmes; l'autre est la loy qui rend le domaine de la couronne sainct et sacré, hors de tout commerce, inséparable du corps du royaume, et du tout inaliénable, mesme en ce qui dépend de la souveraineté. Car ceste souveraineté est la vraye marque de la royauté, et partant, elle doibt tousiours perpétuellement, absolument et solidairement résider en la personne du prince, qui ne la peut séparer de soy, ne en communiquer aucune portion à autre quelconque. Tant c'est vne chose saincte, sacrée, adherante et conioncte inséparablement à la couronne et à la personne du Roy!" Quoted in Edme Cougny, *Un Procès en matière de droits régaliens au XVIe siècle* (Paris, 1864), pp. 10-11.

[11] René Choppin, *Traité du domaine*, p. 382, in *Œuvres* (Paris, 1643), II.

agreed concerning the exact nature of that law. Writers early in the century had regarded that body of law as originating in act of the king, although they maintained unaltered its basic quality as custom of the land. With the increasing questioning and evaluation of all aspects of the constitution, fundamental law was subjected to rational and historical analysis which rendered the theory of it increasingly complex. This inquiry took the form of research into its historical origins. Du Tillet was the first to investigate the history of the Salic Law to any extent and concluded that it had always been binding simply because of its character as custom of the realm. If it was first put into writing at the order of Pharamond, such represented merely the codification of extant law similar to the redaction of provincial customs effected in the local estates.[12] The *lex salica* was a compiled body of customary law of succession for a given territory; it was merely private law. The exclusion of heiresses from the French crown was, moreover, in virtue of a custom and particular law of the House of France, founded upon the magnanimity of the French who could not endure to be ruled by women and in order to prevent their transferring the crown to foreigners by marriage.[13] Thus, although Du Tillet's research caused him to doubt the generally accepted identification of the Salic Law with the law of the Salian Franks, he retained the idea that fundamental law was essentially custom.

[12] "Les François ont deux anciennes loix celebrees par tout: l'vne est la Salique, redigee par escrit regnant Pharamond, l'an de grace quatre cens vingt-deux: non qu'auparauant ils eussent vescu sans loix. Car celles des Germains dont ils estoient auoyent au precedent esté declarrees par Tacite. . . . Mais pour l'interpretation, reformation et amplification des coustumes et polices des François encores non escrites, furent lors deputez Vvisogast, Bodogast, Salogast et Vvidogast, qui n'estoyent noms propres d'hommes, ains d'Officiers, Gouuerneurs, Baillifs, ou Iuges de quatre prouinces, lesquels . . . assemblerent les estats, et par l'aduis d'iceux arresterent, et firent escrire ladite loy, comme de nos iours a esté obserué, pour reformer et rediger en preuue litteratoire les coustumes de France." Jean Du Tillet, *Recueil des roys de France, leur couronne et maison* (Paris, 1607), pp. 9–10. This work was first published in 1577.

[13] ". . . par coustume et loy particuliere de la maison de France, fondee sur la magnanimité des François, ne pouvans souffrir estre dominee par femmes de par elles: aussi qu'elles eussent par mariage peu transferer la couronne aux estrangers. . . ." *Recueil des roys*, p. 308.

Subsequent historians carried their investigations further and drew conclusions of greater significance in constitutional thought. The intellectual ferment of the time was forcing men increasingly to inquire into the historical origins of fundamental law and to account for its existence in more elaborate fashion than simply by pointing to its character as customary usage. This appearance of historical consciousness was one of the most important intellectual developments of the mid-sixteenth century, and it often caused men to present ideas at variance with those of their predecessors. Pasquier and Du Haillan were among the most important writers to investigate the origins of the Salic Law, and both ascribed it to an original act of the king.[14] This interpretation had been presented by earlier writers in the century, as we have seen, but the investigations of these historians not only gave the concept greater solidity through "historical" accounts of the origins of fundamental law, but also permitted writers to draw far-reaching conclusions lacking heretofore. Du Haillan was particularly thoroughgoing in ascribing the origins of the constitution, not only as a whole but in each of its parts, to acts of the various French kings. He recounted the work of the three races of rulers and found that each, particularly the Capetian, had contributed toward the establishment of the French state as it was known in the sixteenth century.[15] In regard to the Salic

---

[14] Pasquier, *Les Recherches de la France*, pp. 141–148; Du Haillan, *De l'estat et succez des affaires de France* (Paris, 1571), p. 101b. Unless otherwise indicated, our references are to this edition of Du Haillan. On this question, see Lemaire, *op. cit.*, p. 87.

[15] "La race de Merouée . . . fut la premiere qui passa le Rhin, et vint en France, qui y establit sa demeure, qui y planta la religion Chrestienne, et qui donna le nom, le commencement et la naissance à cest Empire. La race de Pepin fut grande en France et en Allemagne, et eust plusieurs Rois, qui furent pareillement Empereurs, mais il semble que tous ces Empereurs ne furent si amateurs de la France que de leur Empire. De façon que la France doit la grandeur qu'elle a, à la race de Hues Capet. C'est celle là, qui luy a donné les loix ciuiles et politiques, qui a ordonné et establly le solide estat de la France, qui a fait les Parlemens sedentaires pour la iustice, qui a dressé le reglement des finances pour les frais de toutes les choses necessaires à vn royaume, qui a institué le domaine, les aides, et les tailles, qui a mis en ordre certain les bans et arrierebans, qui a institué la gendarmerie ordinaire, qui a creé les conseils de diuers noms, et bref

Law, he carried this idea to the point of asserting that that law had been originated by Philip V, the first French king to accede in virtue of its elimination of heiresses![16] His attempt, to find the origins of accepted laws in specific royal acts represents an effort to give additional coherence to a political theory reflecting primarily the national state, by representing the constitution as the work of the monarch who had become synonymous with the life of the national unit.

The idea that the king was the originator of the constitution contained highly explosive potentialities when placed in the framework of sixteenth-century political thought. In the intellectual system of Pasquier, who was one of the most circumspect constitutionalists of the period, the concept seems to have had little influence except to support his ideas, drawn from other sources, that the king was a continual source of law and that he was consequently superior to at least a portion of the constitution. However, Pasquier did not exaggerate these far-reaching interpretations, and his system remained, in the round, quite traditional.[17] Much more pointed were the conclusions drawn from this premise by Du Haillan. Since the king, the interested party, had originated the Salic Law, it seemed that law itself was but a means of legitimating acts which in reality were little more than forceful usurpation. Du Haillan made this the basis of his statement that the bulk of established law was founded simply on force.[18] Such an inter-

---

qui a fait toutes ces belles ordonnances, edicts, et autres excellentes constitutions, qui decorent et soustiennent cest estat, et qui le rendent en soy fort, et admirable aux estrangers." *Estat et succez*, pp. 78a–78b.

[16] "Car il ne se treuue en aucun monument antique, qu'il s'en soit iamais auparauant parlé. [I.e. before 1314.] Ie ne veux pas, estant François, m'opposer à si honorable constitution, qui est assez ancienne, et assez emologuee et receue, et se peult dire vraye loy, puis qu'il y a trois cens ans qu'elle est faicte, car les loix ne sont receues, ny authorisees que par le temps, et quand vne fois vne loy a esté mis à effect, elle sert de preiugé pour l'aduenir: mais ie diray, qu'il ne s'en parla iamais que depuis la mort de Loys Hutin, et fut bien fort debattu apres la mort de Charles le Bel. . . . Philippes le Long, second fils du Roy Philippes le Bel, et frere de Loys Hutin Rois de France, fut le premier qui à la verité l'inuenta." *Estat et succez*, p. 101b.

[17] See below, pp. 116–117.

[18] "Et bien que ce soit vne des plus belles loix qui ait iamais esté faicte en

pretation went far toward denying entirely the element of right
in law, since in such a system the origins as well as the final
meaning of law could be little more than successful violation of
another's right. It is manifest that a rule of law is incompatible
with such fundamentals. This emphasis, derived from inquiry
into the historical antecedents of fundamental law, we believe
to be peculiar to Du Haillan in the century, yet he was sufficiently logical to apply it to other considerations equally
important.[19]

As the century progressed, there appeared a second theory
of fundamental law, which, although of venerable age, had
rarely been expressed in France earlier in the century. This
was the theory, strong throughout the Middle Ages, that the
people were prior to the state in the sense that they had created
it by setting up the king over themselves and instituting the
laws which regulated the life of the state and limited the discretion of the ruler. This interpretation may be regarded as the
ultra-constitutional position concerning the origins of fundamental law, and was diametrically opposed to the more widespread idea, quite royalist in character, that such law had
originally been instituted by the king. These two concepts
were often utilized as initial bases of argument in the erection
of highly divergent theories of state, yet neither was supported
exclusively by any political faction during the Wars of Religion. The idea that the ancient predecessors of sixteenth-
century Frenchmen had chosen their king and had fashioned
their laws according to their pleasure was elaborately set forth
by Marion in 1570.[20] Marion was no enemy of the traditional

---

royaume quelconque, si est-ce qu'elle n'a vigueur en France, que par la force,
comme la plus part des loix du droict des royaumes et estats, ne sont fondees
que sur la force. . . ." *Estat et succez*, p. 101b.

[19] See below, pp. 170–171.

[20] "Mais noz majeurs eseleuans leur pensee chacun par dessus soy, pour la
referer au bien commun de tous, et au repos de leur posterité, se sont souzmis
d'eux-mesmes à la Monarchie, comme au plus tranquille et durable Estat.
D'autres ont retenu l'authorité d'eslire, ou confirmer leurs princes, à chasque
mutation: mais les François s'en sont du tout remis au vouloir de Dieu, par
l'ordre qu'il luy plaist donner à la nature. Et comme ils n'ont faict leur Royaume

theory of state which contained highly absolutistic elements, and his support of the popular origin of the constitution in one of his speeches bears witness to the widespread acceptance of that idea even among members of the royal administration. However, the implications of this theory offered ample opportunity of argument to the opponents of the central government. When it was once admitted that the people had set up the king and fashioned the laws binding him, it was but a step to assert that the monarch was continually responsible to the people who retained final authority in all matters affecting the fortunes of the realm. It was the thesis of Hotman's *Francogallia* [21] that since the original *francsgaulois* had set up the state and instituted the laws, their descendants retained the right to control royal policies and all matters of general import through the action of their representatives in the Estates General. In the case of Hotman, this theory was utilized to justify acts of the Huguenots who were motivated by forces other than political ideas, but his treatment was sufficiently expert and in accordance with current ideas to force certain Catholic historians to reevaluate their concepts in terms of his contribution. Du Haillan, who, however, borrowed from a great variety of sources, accepted in part Hotman's ideas concerning the early history of the French state. In his *Histoire de France*, he

---

electif en faueur d'eux-mesmes, aussi ils ne l'ont pas voulu rendre proprietaire en faueur du Roy, ny le luy commetre si absolument, qu'il peust, comme ont peu quelques autres, y faire vn heritier, le donner, le leguer et tout ou en partie, à son plaisir, et à qui bon luy semble: au contraire, ils l'ont rendu inalienable, et indiuisible: et en tout et part tout successible par le seul droict du sang, selon la loy de France: à celle fin que le prince qui regne, viuement époinct enuers son successeur des mesmes aiguillons d'amitié naturelle, qu'il a senty de son predecesseur, luy laisse la couronne aussi pleine et entiere qu'elle luy est escheue." Simon Marion, *Plaidoyez* (Paris, 1609), pp. 131–132. This statement was made in court in 1570.

[21] François Hotman, *Francogallia.* This work was first published in 1573; our citations are to the edition of Frankfort, 1586. This interpretation we have borrowed, with modifications, from Lemaire. *Op. cit.*, pp. 101–102. Lemaire asserts that Hotman was the first in the century to formulate a theory of the constitution on the basis of this principle. This is accurate as concerns formal treatises, but the idea was present earlier and in other camps, as is evidenced by the statement of Marion given in the previous footnote.

changed visibly the emphasis previously set forth in his *Estat et succez*, and represented the institution of the state by the Franks under Pharamond as effected through the election of the king and the deliberate placing of legal bonds upon his discretion.[22] And Hotman's treatment of the question was to affect the ideas of even such an exacting jurist as Charles Loyseau.[23]

As if to run the gamut of all possible interpretations, there appeared during the second half of the century a third theory which represented fundamental law as created by the king and the people in concert. Representing a hybrid product combining the two older ideas supporting the royal and the popular origins of those laws respectively, this theory recognized that the king and people together might create fundamental law because they represented the two primary portions of the state. This idea found expression on numerous occasions during the century. Specifically, it was utilized in connection with efforts to establish new fundamental laws by the united action of the king and the representatives of the people in the Estates General. As early as 1577, Pierre d'Epinac asked in the Estates of Blois that there be established a fundamental law by joint action of king and deputies for the curbing of leagues and associations which were habitually challenging the royal authority and exhibiting great disloyalty in their negotiations with foreign rulers.[24] This was a remarkably clear statement of the authority of the king and deputies jointly to create an

---

[22] ". . . nous le briderons si bien par les loix, qu'il ne pourra faire mal, quand bien il voudroit." *Histoire de France*, I, 7b.

[23] See below, ch. VI, n. 34.

[24] "Et puis ayant ainsi doucement ordonné pour le passé, vostre Majesté sera tres-humblement suppliée de faire pour l'aduenir, vne loy generale du consentement des estats, et qui aura mesme auctorité que la Salique: par laquelle sera deffendu tresexpressement à toutes sortes et manieres de gens, de dresser aucunes pars, associations, ou ligues, de traitter des affaires du Royaume auec les estrangiers, les soliciter de venir en France, ou faire leuée de gens, soient estrangiers, soit François, sans le consentement et expres commandement de vostre Majesté." Pierre d'Epinac, *Harengue prononcée deuant le roy, seant en ses estats generaulx à Bloys . . . au nom de l'estat ecclesiastique de France* (Paris, 1577), p. 34.

additional fundamental law, and it is the more noteworthy in that the question in hand — the control of leagues and factions — was an undoubted royal prerogative. Epinac apparently held that that portion of the royal authority might be changed into fundamental law by formal action of king and deputies as representatives of the entire body of legal authority within the realm.

More complex were the currents surrounding the elevation of the Edict of Union to the level of fundamental law in the Estates of Blois, 1588, in an effort to exclude Henry of Navarre from the throne. The basis of that edict was the religious unity of the state, a conception which was accepted in varying fashions by men of all camps. In 1577, the instructions carried by the emissaries from the Estates of Blois to Henry of Navarre had declared that Catholicism was the principal and fundamental law of the realm, more fundamental and inviolable than the Salic Law, and that religious unity was fundamental to the constitution not only because of long observance but also because it had originally been instituted by king and people in the Estates General.[25] Here was reiterated the idea that the

---

[25] "Si ledit sieur Roy de Nauarre veult pretendre au contraire de ce que dessus la parole et serment du Roy pour l'entretenement dudit édit: lesdits sieurs remonstreront qu'à la verité il n'y a plus precieux thresor et gage que la foy et parole d'vn Roy mais aussi comme il n'est en ce degré que pour le bien de ses subiects, ce seroit chose de trop dangereuse consequence, qu'il peut donner sa foy au preiudice de tout son estat, et contre les anciennes et louables loix et coustumes du royaume, et de chasque pais. que la profession de la religion Catholique, Apostolique, Romaine, n'a point esté seulement d'ancienne coustume mais la principale et fondamentale loy du Royaume, et forme essencielle, qui donne le nom et tiltre de Tres-Crestiens à noz Roys: qu'il y a difference entre les loix du Roy et du Royaume, les loix de l'Empereur et de l'Empire: que celles cy comme elles ne peuuent estre faictes qu'en generale assemblee de tout le Royaume, ou en diette Imperiale, auec le commun accord et consentement des gens des trois estats, et de ceux qui peuuent assister et auoir voix aux dites diettes, aussi depuis ne peuuent estre changees n'y en façon quelconque alterees. Estant d'ailleurs assez connu à vn chacun comme la religion Catholique Apostolique Romaine soit en son essence du temps de Clouis, ou en ses ceremonies du regne de Charlemagne, na esté receue à la seule volonté des Roys mais consentie et approuuée en generale assemblee des trois estats, auec serment et promesse reciproquement faicte, tant par les Roys que les subiects de n'en auctoriser, permettre n'y tollerer autre. . . . il est trop certain qu'ils ne peuuent apres varier pour quelque occasion ou pretexte que ce soit, non plus que de la

king and people held authority to make such laws. The Leaguers of 1588 would have been wiser had they adopted the theory which this earlier statement had outlined, namely, that the Catholicism of realm and ruler was an ancient fundamental law, rather than attempting to establish it as a new law. True, they were far from unanimous on the point; many pamphlets of the League represented religious uniformity as a legal regulation of long standing,[26] while many persons within the Estates of 1588 held the same view.[27] However, the institution of a new fundamental law establishing unity of religion seems to have been the dominant idea in the Estates of the League. If Henry III had hoped to create such a law through unilateral action in issuing the Edict of Union,[28] he quickly dropped that idea in the sessions of the Estates. In his speech opening the assembly, he said that the proposed fundamental law would be made by joint action of himself and the deputies.[29] This was carried out in a subsequent session by the swearing of the king and all deputies to observe the Edict of Union, requiring religious unity, as fundamental law of the realm. The only historical example of the creation of a new fundamental law by the king and the Estates in concert had been consummated, at least in outward form. The incident is an interesting appli-

---

Loy Salique, estant ladite loy de religion beaucoup plus fondamentale que n'est celle-la et beaucoup plus inuiolable." *Instruction des gens des troys estats . . . à . . . leurs deputez vers le roy de Nauarre* (Blois, 1577), no pagination.

[26] See Lemaire, *op. cit.*, p. 138.

[27] "Premierement, Qu'il vous plaise ordoner et declarer que la Religion Catholique, et Apostolique Romaine, sera (comme elle a esté Iadis) teneue, et mainteneue en ce Royaume, pour la premiere loy fondamentale d'icelle. . . ." *Extraict des registres du premier chapitre du caier des trois estatz . . . à Blois en janvier, 1589* (Lyon), p. 9. No date of publication.

[28] The Edict of Union, 1588, contained the clause: ". . . voulons, statuons, ordonnons, et nous plaist, que les articles suyvans soyent tenuz pour loy inviolable et fondamentale de cestuy nostre royaume." Isambert, *Recueil général des anciennes lois françaises* (Paris, 1829), XIV, 618.

[29] ". . . ie suis d'advis pour le rendre plus stable, que nous en facions une des loix fondamentales du Royaume, et qu'à ce prochain iour de Mardy, en ce mesme lieu et en ceste mesme et notable assemblée de tous mes Estats, nous la iurions tous, à ce que iamais nul n'en pretendent cause d'ignorance." *Sommaire de toutes les harangues, edits et ordonnances . . . en ses estats tenus à Bloys* (1588), p. 808. No place of publication.

cation of the idea that the king and the representatives of the three estates held authority to create new fundamental law because they represented the two major portions of legal right in the state. The fact that the League made this concept its basis of action in 1588 places beyond a doubt the widespread acceptance of the idea.

The controversy concerning the Salic Law carried on in the pamphlet literature from 1587 to 1593 illustrates well the lack of precision in thought regarding that law but unfortunately contributes little else. The battle of pamphlets was carried on largely by Pierre de Belloy, representing the legitimist cause, and several anonymous writers for the League. Unfortunately, Belloy's method of composition consisted merely in the multiplication of arguments from any source, rather than the construction of a logical system upon a few fundamentals. His first work in the controversy was his *Examen du discours publié contra la maison royalle de France, et particulièrement contre la branche de Bourbon*, published in 1587 in answer to an attack upon the legitimate heir.[30] In this work, Belloy's theory appeared in one of its weakest manifestations. In establishing the claim of the Bourbon to the throne, he asserted that the Salic Law was custom of the realm, that it was according to nature since women were inherently inferior beings, that it had been established by the Estates General, that there had been similar laws among other races, that it was according to Scripture, and that it found its basis in natural reason.[31] If there was any contribution in that type of argument, it was merely to illustrate the fact that the Salic Law was regarded as an integral portion of a great body of values and that consequently theorists could find a basis for any given item, such as the Salic Law, in its consonance with a miscellany of other principles. The answer of the Leaguers appeared in the same year under

---

[30] This work of Belloy was in answer to the anonymous pamphlet, *Discours sur la maison royale de France, et particulièrement contre la branche de Bourbon* (1587). As far as we have been able to discover, this work no longer exists.

[31] Belloy, *Examen*, pp. 176–180, 56–65, 183–203, 331, 206–207.

the title *Sommaire Responce à l'examen d'un heretique, sur un discours de la loy salique, faussement pretendu contre la maison de France.* This work was one of the weakest of the controversy. Its author contented himself with detecting faults in Belloy's facts and ridiculing him as a self-styled prophet of all types of law. In answer to this work, there appeared the anonymous *Replique faicte à la responce* [32] which contained little more than a summary of the statements made earlier by Belloy. In addition, there appeared a host of pamphlets, which, however, were similarly weak in presenting any theory of fundamental law and are worthless today except as expressions of a series of attitudes. [33] The truth is that at no time during the controversy was the issue directly engaged. The Leaguers had the argument all in their favor when they based their assertions upon the fundamental religious unity of the state, while the proponents of legitimacy easily carried the day when the details of fundamental law and the succession were alone considered. When the Leaguers attempted to undermine Henry of Navarre's claim to the throne through arguments in terms of law, they failed at once. The ablest of the pamphleteers for the League perceived this and based their arguments squarely upon the necessity of religious unity in the state. [34] The writers for neither camp would undertake a well-rounded consideration of the fundamentals supporting the case of the other, and thus the expressions of opinion concerning the succession were usually little more than the elaboration of positions already assumed. But it is noteworthy that it was in the heat of this controversy

[32] *Replique faicte à la responce, que ceux de la ligue ont publiee, contre l'examen qui avoit esté dressé sur leur precedent discours, touchant la loy salique de France* (1587). No place of publication.

[33] E.g., Jean Guyart, *De l'origine verité et usance de la loy salique fondamentale et conseruatrice de la monarchie françoise* (Tours, 1590). This work merely repeats in less able fashion the ideas of Belloy. Also: *Traicté de la succession à la couronne de France* (1588). No place of publication. This pamphlet merely argues that since the Salic Law had served the state well, it ought to be preserved regardless of theoretical considerations.

[34] E.g., *De la puissance des roys, et droict de succession aux royaumes, contre l'vsurpation du tiltre qualité de roy de France, faicte par le roy de Navarre* (Paris, 1590). This was one of the ablest pamphlets written by the Leaguers.

that Belloy put forward, as a means of counterbalancing the claims of the League, the doctrine of the divine right of kings.

In 1593, Antoine Hotman wrote a short but able work which may be regarded as closing the controversy.[35] He stated his theory of the Salic Law in straightforward terms: although he did not hesitate to bring in the natural superiority of men in matters of government,[36] he placed that law strictly upon a basis of customary usage.[37] The movement of historical criticism and controversy between factions had done its work, and theorists came back to the traditional concept of fundamental law as simply established custom of the land. Ideas of its historical origins and of the ability of king and people to create fundamental law had been upheld in widely separated quarters and must be regarded as important portions of contemporary thought, but the legists finally returned to the customary basis of that law as the most secure. Such was the meaning of Du Vair in the same year when he made his historic oration in the Parlement calling for an *arrêt* nullifying the action of the Estates General in breaking the Salic Law.[38] The resulting *arrêt* given out by the Parlement was at once a victory for the Salic Law and a recognition of its character as customary law of the land.

Although the theory of the royal prerogative held by the

---

[35] *Traicté de la loy salique*, in *Opuscules françoises des Hotmans* (Paris, 1616), pp. 267–288.

[36] *Traicté*, pp. 268–269.

[37] "Non que ce droict de succeder à la Couronne soit compris en ces termes qui se treuuent entre les loix Saliques: *De terra Salica nulla portio ad foeminam etc.* Car en toutes ces loix là qui furent redigees par escrit du temps de Charles Magne, il n'est pas question de la succession du Royaume de France, ains seulement du reglement qui doit estre entre les François. Les loix de la succession des Rois dependent plus de l'ancienne obseruance, que non pas de l'establissement par escrit, et cette antiquité est de plus grand poids et authorité; comme estant son origine incertaine plus auguste et venerable pour estre colligee par vne immemoriale obseruance inuiolable gardee et sans aucune interruption." *Traicté*, pp. 267–268.

[38] "Car c'est aujourd'huy que lon entreprend de les renverser toutes et d'un coup; c'est à la loy Salique que lon en veut . . . et neantmoins c'est celle-la qui depuis douze cens ans a conservé ce Royaume entier. . . ." Guillaume Du Vair, "Pour la manutention de la loy salique," p. 128, in René Radouant, ed., *Actions et traictez oratoires* (Paris, 1911). Cf. Lemaire, *op. cit.*, p. 143.

legists was based upon considerations of law, it was neverthe-less impossible for them to avoid treating the person of the king who was called upon to fill the crown. The current concept of the inequality of individuals placing the king at the summit of the hierarchy of virtue, and the mentality of the age making for abundant optimism toward enlightened paternal rule, ren-dered such considerations inevitable. Seyssel had regarded the king as merely the superior among many cooperating units, but his successors during the period of absolutism had exalted to great heights the person and majesty of the ruler. The latter attitude was fraught with dangers for the traditional limita-tions of law upon kingship, for the combination of direct divine authorization and the mystical exaltation of the royal person tended inevitably to relax the bonds of law upon the king's discretion. Elements of the attitudes held by Seyssel and the Romanists respectively are visible in the works of the consti-tutionalists, yet their emphasis tended frequently toward that of their more absolutistic predecessors. They constantly reiter-ated the primary tenet of Gallicanism — they were Gallicans almost to a man — upholding the direct divine institution of the secular power and its consequent divine basis. Almost to the same extent as the earlier Romanists, they asserted that the king somehow represented God on earth.[39] Furthermore, the idea that the king was necessarily a superior human being was quite widespread.[40] It was constantly maintained, perhaps in desperation, that he should set the standard and the tone of society.[41] Theorists could hardly state the contrary, since they

[39] Statements in this vein were legion. "Et d'aultant que tous les humains sont souz le gouuernement de Dieu, ils ont creu que la domination qui est baillée aux Roys est vn vray don de Dieu, lequel comme pere des hommes adopte peculierement pour ses enfans ceulx ausquels il donne puissance de regner, lesquels representent l'auctorité et maiesté de Dieu en la terre." Jean de La Madeleine, *Discours de l'estat et office d'vn bon roy, prince ou monarque* (Paris, 1575), p. 3b.

[40] E.g., Du Haillan, *Histoire de France*, I, p. 3a.

[41] "Car puis que ce Prince doit estre le patron, le mirouer, l'exemple, et la guide de la vie et des actions des autres hommes qui seront soubs luy, et que les yeux et les oreilles de ses subiects visent droit à luy, comme à leur but vnique, ie souhaite qu'il soit non seulement bon mais aussi que son exemple nous rende

believed the meaning of kingship to be government of the people according to highest principles.[42] Far from mere flattery of the monarch, these statements embodied important characteristics of contemporary political thought which was completely infused with an ideal of strong paternal rule as the best possible type of government. But this exaltation of the royal majesty was often found in uncomfortable juxtaposition with constitutional considerations in the works of those legists whose emphasis was upon the bonds of law rather than the glories of strong personal rule. Certain of the ablest apparently realized that exaggeration of idealized paternalism would eventually give rise to a mode of rule little different from enlightened despotism. Pasquier asserted that constant emphasis upon the glories of military might and the irresponsibility of the ruler went far to justify much that was both unethical and illegal and consequently extremely dangerous to the continued existence of the constitution.[43] The majority of legists in the capital did not express themselves so definitely in regard to that delicate subject, usually contenting themselves with decrying the encroachments of royal agents upon legal liberties while continuing to praise the ruler. But the appearance of this questioning of a very popular and rising doctrine in the works of one of the ablest legists in the century illustrates well the fact that constitutionalism and hero-worship made strange bedfellows.

The legists elaborated carefully the exact content of the royal prerogative which the king was called upon by law to

---

tous bons. L'estat d'vn Prince se compose à son exemple, et ses subiets au modelle de ses actions: et sa vie a plus de force au reglement de celle des siens, que tous les Edicts et ordonnances qu'il pourroit faire sur la reformation des moeurs." Du Haillan, *Histoire de France*, I, p. 6b.

[42] "Les Princes, comme dit le Sage, ont esté Diuinement ordonnés pour chacun peuple, ausquels des leurs commencement, Dieu les a departis et par sa Prouidence formé en eus, l'etat de souueraine puissance et domination, auec vn instine et mouuement emeu et produit de l'Esprit d'enhaut, de reigler et policer leurs sujets, et les conduire et gouuerner par l'adresse et inuention de bonnes et saintes Lois, dont il donna premierement l'exemple à Moyse, pour formulaire des autres qui en ont par conformité tiré les leurs. . . ." L'Alouette, *op. cit.*, p. 6.

[43] *Pourparler du prince*, pp. 1036–1038.

exercise. The attributes which they assigned to the crown were completely in harmony with those maintained by earlier schools: kingship was regarded essentially as the authority to dispense justice and to carry out necessary acts of administration. Pasquier gave one of the most precise definitions. Justice, he said, was the single vital element, the essence of rulership. To this were appended a host of subordinate attributes: feudal dues, coinage, salt works, tailles, remission of guilt, *gabelles*, *amortissement*, *aubain*, *espaves*, and many other lesser prerogative rights.[44] This conception of the royal authority was entirely in keeping with earlier theories and stemmed from the recesses of the Middle Ages. The essence of kingship was the royal capacity to judge, and as such, the ruler's primary duty was the preservation and enforcement of the law. Definitions of tyranny as rule contrary to law continued to be abundant.[45] If the element of legislation was present, it was invariably subordinated to adjudication; Du Haillan went to the lengths of reiterating the Bartolist idea of the law-giving function.[46] This was an interpretation which precluded, as we have seen, any idea of legislative sovereignty, and was set forth only by those who placed their primary emphasis upon the role of the king as judge.

However, the judicial capacity of the king was much more complex than that of highest judge according to customary law; the ideas of divine institution and the capacity of the king as God's vicar on earth were exercising influence even upon the constitutionalists. L'Alouette upheld the idea that had appeared earlier in the works of the Romanists, namely,

---

[44] *Plaidoyé*, in *Œuvres*, I, pp. 1083–1084. Cf. L'Alouette, *op. cit.*, pp. 65–69; Choppin, *Traité du domaine*, p. 254.

[45] E.g., Pasquier, *Pourparler du prince*, pp. 1037–1038, 1041; Charondas, *Questions diverses et discours* (Paris, 1579), pp. 8b–12b.

[46] "En France le Roy seul fait Constitutions, Loix, et Ordonnances, et toute la puissance souueraine est entre ses mains, laquelle toutesfois . . . il ne recognoist en la Temporalité aucun superieur. Bien est vray que les Ducs, Barons, et autres Seigneurs peuuent faire ordonnances en leurs terres moyennant que ce soit sans exceder les bornes de la iurisdiction qui leur est attribuee, et encore ceste puissance leur est donnee par la distribution et concession des fiefz que les Roys leur ont donnez." *Estat et succez* (Paris, 1595), pp. 312b–313a.

that the king was God's representative on earth and that the
judicial function of the ruler was to be interpreted simply as his
establishing upon earth of higher principles, thereby acting as
a channel for their transmission.[47] For Du Moulin, the king
was *lex animata a Deo hominibus demissa*.[48] Justice was held
to be resident in the person of the prince;[49] he was frequently
attributed the authority to judge his own case.[50] This interpretation of the capacity of the king as judge fitted entirely with
the current idea that rulership was authorized by God and thus
necessarily took the form of enlightened paternalism. The
constitutionalists combined their ideas of legal limitations upon
kingship with concepts of the divine right and quasi-divine
qualities of the ruler, thus producing a theory of monarchy at
once legal and enlightened by factors higher than constitutional
law. Throughout the writings of the jurists, there appears this
double conception of kingship; no outline of the theory held
during the period may be complete without both aspects. If
few writers were conscious of any inherent contradiction in
their attitude, that was because they accepted the major tenets
of current political doctrine without question. The prevailing
constitutional thought formed a well-balanced whole, but it
contained elements drawn from different sources and presenting highly divergent implications. As a body of doctrine, it was
complex to the point of permitting innumerable variations of
emphasis within the great, single framework, and thus it was of
such nature to permit that repeated emphasis upon certain component parts which ultimately brought about its destruction.

As the prerogative constituted the public authority in matters of government, so the rights and privileges of the populace

[47] ". . . la bonne et iuste loi ne doit proceder d'ailleurs, que d'vn don de
Dieu decoulé en l'esprit du Prince, qui par la main des Officiers l'exerce et depart
à tous: Aiant fait vne demande et dispute en ses politiques, si la loy n'est pas
meilleur et n'a pas plus d'efficace que l'homme. . . . Conclud que celui qui veut
que la loi commande et tiene la superieure autorité, veut aussi que Dieu de qui
elle vient commande; et la Loy auec lui." L'Alouette, *op. cit.*, p. 9.
[48] *Commentarii in consuetudines Parisienses*, Tit. I, § III, glo. III, no. 6. Our
references are to the *Opera* of Paris, 1681.
[49] L'Alouette, *op. cit.*, pp. 65–66.   [50] Du Tillet, *op. cit.*, p. 252.

formed the second major portion of legal authority in the state. If the legal right vested in the crown was regarded as animating the realm and bringing life to it as a unit, the body or structure of the state was provided by the various social groups composing the whole. The jurists viewed society as a great, complex hierarchy of social entities — individuals, corporations, classes, and estates — each of which enjoyed rights and privileges according to its status. Those rights had their foundation in the law of the land, and together they constituted a major portion of the *police* of the realm. Equally with Seyssel, these legists regarded the state as a corporate structure composed of interlocking and mutually dependent parts, each with its sphere, rights, and duties in the life of the whole.[51] Reflecting the general acceptance of this theory, Jean Lange, the speaker for the third estate at the Estates of Orleans, 1560, said in remonstrance that since the social organism was but the union of many cooperating members, the encroachment of one portion upon the sphere and rights of another was a false profit which would eventually bring about the disintegration of the state. The king, like any other member of the realm, should be content with his sphere, for if he sought to increase his grandeur at the expense of the people, there would eventually occur the destruction of king and people alike.[52] This was but

[51] Du Haillan repeated without significant change Seyssel's statements concerning the rights and mutual dependence of the social estates and the duty of the king to prevent the encroachment of one upon another. *Estat et succez*, pp. 81b–82a.

[52] "Qu'est que aux administrations des Royaulmes, bien souuent on fault soubs le pretexte d'vn faulx proffit et d'vne faulce utilité. Par laquelle plusieurs ont esté retirez de ce que la vertu et la raison leur commande, car rapportant ce corps mystique dont vous estes le chef, et vostre peuple les membres, à vn corps naturel comme font les anciens saiges. Tout ainsi que si vn chascun membre du corps naturel cuidoit preualoir prenant pour soy la nourriture du prochain membre, il fauldroit dans peu de temps que tout le corps fust debilité et mourust. Aussi en ce corps mystique vous, sire, qui en estes le chef, si tombez en pareil erreur et cuidiez que l'affoiblissement de vostre peuple fust augmentation de vostre grandeur, dans peu de temps sensuyuroit que tant que vous que vostre peuple, seriez à neant et auriez prins fin." Jean Lange, *La Harangue du peuple et tiers estat de toute la France* (Orleans, 1560), no pagination. The most telling argument in Du Tillet's *Aduertissement à la noblesse, tant du party du roy, que des rebelles et coniurez* (Lyon, 1558) was his warning that the rebellious

another way of saying that it was the primary duty of the king to maintain these social groups in their rights and privileges; to do so was at once to enforce the law and to preserve the structure of the state. To remonstrate with the monarch for seeking personal benefit at the expense of the general body of his subjects, as did Jean Lange, was to criticize him as willfully neglecting a main purpose of his existence.

Although the legists very frequently set forth this theory of the state organization, they were curiously silent concerning the legal position held by one major category of social groups. These were the guilds, academies, universities, and various professional organizations which may be classed together as corporations. The corporate structure of society during the sixteenth century has long been accepted by students of the period, yet theoretical treatises concerning those bodies were extremely rare among contemporary legal writings.[53] The exact nature of the corporations seems to have been examined only by those theorists who tended to subordinate them to the will of the ruler. Thus, Bodin described a corporation as an intermediary body standing between the family and the sovereign, but strictly subordinate to control by the latter.[54] The family and the monarch were the two fundamental entities within the state, but the corporation partook in no manner of their natural qualities and was but a civil community which had originated through royal grant and was therefore under the authority of the sovereign. The king might regulate its policies, make ordinances controlling it, and coerce its members, although such should be carried out according to the

nobility were destroying the structure of the state and thereby jeopardizing their own favored position. Criticisms of sedition in this vein were legion throughout the century.

[53] On this question, see François Olivier-Martin, *L'Organization corporative de la France d'ancien régime* (Paris, 1938), esp. ch. 8, "Esquisse d'une théorie des corps professionnels." Olivier-Martin notes (pp. 473–474) the remarkable absence of theoretical treatments of the corporations during the entire *ancien régime*.

[54] Jean Bodin, *Les Six Livres de la république* (Paris, 1576), p. 381. Bodin was one of the few to examine the corporations.

terms of the original royal authorization and the laws of the state.[55] The corporations were continually subordinate to the authority of the prince; he might abolish them if they committed offense.[56] Thus, these intermediary bodies were regarded by Bodin as distinctly subordinate to the royal prerogative to make or break; unlike other social units, they could claim no rights against the ruler on the basis of customary law. They existed at the suffrance of the king who permitted them to continue only if their acts conformed with the best interests of the state, but he might abolish them if such were required by public necessity or if they committed offense. Bodin's theory of the corporations represents a hardening of several trends and was consequently a departure from the meaning of much contemporary constitutional thought, but he was almost alone in formulating precise statements concerning the matter.

If many jurists regarded the corporations as enjoying no independent legal rights which might be defended against the monarch, such was not their idea concerning the juridical position occupied by the social estates and their component members. Writers on constitutional subjects outlined the rights and privileges of the social classes with distinctly legal implications. To be a noble or a cleric automatically conferred certain privileges generally recognized; these were the rights accruing to the individual through class status, and, in spite of their variation in degree, they were the same in kind for all members of that estate. In outlining the privileges of the nobility, Du Haillan found it sufficient to repeat, in amplified form, the statements on that subject made earlier by Seyssel.[57] But even more important in constitutional thought were the rights held by each individual in virtue of his specific place in society. To give each man justice was to give him his due according to his legal position, and that position was determined

---

[55] *République*, p. 390.
[56] *République*, pp. 397, 400.
[57] *Estat et succez*, pp. 80b–81a.

not only by his presence in a given social estate but also by those rights which he enjoyed through legal relationships with other individuals. This latter type of legal authority constituted the greater portion of those private privileges which contemporaries regarded as the inviolable rights of the subjects. Together, they constituted the legal counterpart of the organized state structure and thus formed a major portion of the constitution.

In the legal practice of the period, private rights rested almost without exception upon customary law. The individual proved his legal position by establishing his relations with other individuals, both in terms of personal ties and proprietary rights, and even the most cursory examination of sixteenth-century legal procedure reveals that those rights and relationships were based upon customary law of the land. Judicial proof of a legal right turned upon the establishment of the relevant custom, written or unwritten, guaranteeing the particular claim in question. Long usage constituted sufficient legal basis for any right not specifically regalian; prescription established for a period of thirty years was sufficient to prove a man's claim in private affairs, while even the title to certain regalian rights might be vindicated by a baron on the basis of one hundred years' prescription.[58] The customary law provided at once the manifestation and the guarantee of those rights enjoyed by the complex hierarchy of individuals and estates which constituted the body of the realm. It was the essence of the rights of that portion of the state and provided authorities which might be defended even against the prince.

With the rights of the subjects and the social estates generally resting upon customary law, it becomes vitally important to examine the theories set forth by the constitutionalists concerning that body of law. The usual definition of custom represented it as embodying those usages of legal weight which had been introduced into the juridical life of a given territory with

[58] Jean Bacquet, Œuvres (Geneva, 1625), p. 339; Pasquier, Plaidoyé, pp. 1085–1086; Chasseneuz, Consuetudines, p. 62a.

the tacit or express consent of the populace. It received its authority through acceptance 'and observation for a period, and rested essentially upon the common consent. This quality of custom as a popular act, or legal regulation introduced by the people for the preservation of their rights and practically synonymous with them, was recognized by the majority of jurists as a primary tenet of legal thought.[59] It was in the customary law that the people made manifest their *droit des intéressés*. The legal authority which it represented was entirely separate and distinct from that of the ruler who had, in theory, nothing to do with the establishment of custom: Du Tillet wrote that customs were accorded by the subjects, not instituted by the kings.[60] The great body of customary law formed a portion of the constitution outside the competence of the ruler and thus necessarily limiting his discretion. Such had been the major significance of Seyssel's check of *la police*, and the essentials of the concept were preserved in the major constitutional writings of the century. Likewise, when writers outlined the rights of the various social estates which it was the duty of the king to maintain, they necessarily thought in terms of the customary law.[61] The preservation of established law and right was the essence of the king's all-important capacity as judge. In illustration of the duty of the king to give justice to his subjects according to local custom, Pasquier wrote that the evocation of cases from a local to a central court constituted an abuse approaching the denial of justice, because the change of court brought a corresponding change in the law applied. On the contrary, justice should be administered in that locality where the persons and things under consideration were situated, in order to insure decision according to local usage.[62] And if

---

[59] E.g., Pasquier, *Plaidoyé*, p. 1092; Choppin, *Coûtume d'Anjou*, p. 3; Jean de La Madeleine, *op. cit.*, p. 36a, and countless others of the period.

[60] ". . . les coustumes sont accordees par lesdits subjets, non ordonnees par lesdits Roys." *Recueil des roys*, p. 252.

[61] E.g., Du Haillan, *Estat et succez*, pp. 79a–82a.

[62] The essence of his argument is contained in the statement: ". . . il [the king] nous est debiteur de la Justice, et nous la doit administrer és lieux où

there is needed any additional illustration of the fact that customary law and popular rights were normally beyond the discretion of the ruler, this may be found in the doctrine, accepted throughout the entire period, permitting judicial decision even against the monarch whenever he or his agents violated the rights of the people through acts of government.[63] The theory of customary law as the basis of the independent legal authority of the people was the cornerstone of the constitutionalism set forth by the French legists.

Although the major tenets and ultimate meaning of sixteenth-century constitutional thought required that customary law remain independent of the royal prerogative, there were nevertheless several intellectual currents tending to place that body of law under the royal discretion and consequently to lessen drastically the independence of popular rights. First, the doctrines borrowed from Roman law had definite influence in that direction. Certain texts contained in that body of law were regarded as attributing to the Emperor the authority to abolish local customs, and the legists, true to their practice of ascribing to their monarch all imperial prerogatives, were all but unanimous in conceding to the king a similar authority on the basis of Roman principles.[64] This influence of the Roman system in the legal practice of the century was clearly recognized by the major contemporary writers.[65] The more circumspect constitutionalists frequently decried the interpretation as

---

nous residons, où là ou nos biens sont assis. C'est une charge fonciere, qui est annexée à sa Couronne: et ce n'est pas proprement nous la rendre, quand on intervertit nostre bon droit, par un changement de Juges, et Parlemens." *Lettres*, Liv. VI, no. 2, p. 157. The treatment of this question extends through pages 155 to 158.

[63] See below, pp. 131–133.

[64] The texts most frequently cited in support of this point were: Dig. Lib. XLVII, Tit. XII, law 3 (de sepulcro violato); Code, Lib. VIII, Tit. LIII, law 2 (quae sit longa consuetudo); and the passage from canon law, Sexti Decretalium, Lib. I, de constitutionibus, cap. 1.

[65] E.g., Charondas. "On peut donc icy demander si par les Edicts du Roy publiez depuis les coustumes est derogé à icelles: par le droict Romain il est sans doute que si les rescrits et Edicts des Princes sont generaux, ils doiuent auoir auctorité en tous lieux et valoir par dessus les coustumes: tellement que par iceux y est derogé." *Pandectes*, p. 169.

arising from an extraneous body of doctrine and containing unacceptable implications,[66] but they never denied its validity in contemporary legal practice and frequently made it the basis of their statements attributing authority to the king over custom.[67] Secondly, all were agreed that customary law was not valid if iniquitous,[68] and the legists upheld without exception the tradition stemming from the Middle Ages that it was the duty of the king to abolish such customs.[69] This provision resulted from the generally accepted idea that constitutional law formed but a part of the complete scale of legal values, the higher portions of which served as criteria for evaluating the lower and less perfect portions such as custom. This doctrine was entirely traditional and quite compatible with a rule of law, but when combined with ideas of exalted and quasi-divine monarchy, it went far toward placing the ruler over all customary law. The theory that the king was God's representative on earth, transmitting true justice to his subjects, and that his decisions were and ought to be enlightened by higher ideals than the letter of the law, was very widely accepted among the

[66] "O aveugle opinion de tout le monde, de penser que les Roys mesmes, se pensent par dessus la loy! Mais ainsi l'ont escrit (diras-tu) les loix anciennes de Rome? Je t'accorde que ces Empereurs, qui jadis par le trenchant de leurs espées firent vouer au peuple Romain une perpetuelle servitude, prindrent cette prerogative, comme leur voulurent faire accroire quelques flatteraux de Legistes. . . . Or, voy, je te prie, combien plus debonnairement nos Roys: Car le peuple Romain (ainsi que ont voulu dire quelques Courtisans, qui se sont meslez de la Loy) de tout temps accoustumé à vivre librement, se despouilla de son ancienne liberté pour en vestir les Empereurs, ausquels il donna tout commandement sur la Loy. Et au contraire, nos Roys, combien que le peuple de Gaule, de toute memoire fust coustumier d'estre regy sous puissance Royale, toutes-fois s'emparans du Royaume, despouillans tout passion, se voulurent soubmettre à la Loy, et ne faire par ce moyen chose qui ne fust juste et raisonnable. . . ." Pasquier, *Pourparler du prince*, pp. 1041–1042.

[67] E.g., Pasquier. See below, pp. 116–117.

[68] Pasquier, *L'Interprétation des Institutes de Justinian* (Paris, 1847), p. 35. Among the countless statements illustrating this idea, we may select that of Antoine Hotman: "La longue et immemorial possession ont cela de semblable, qu'elles doivent estre accompagnées de justice." *Traité des droits ecclésiastiques*, in Jean Louis Brunet, *Traitez des droits et libertez de l'église gallicane* (Paris, 1731), I, 155.

[69] On this question, see Olivier-Martin, "Le Roi de France et les mauvaises coutumes au moyen âge," *Zeitschrift der Savigny-Stiftung für Rechtsgeschichte. Germanistische Abteilung*, LVIII (1938), 108–137.

jurists and had definite, though elusive, influence toward placing custom under the royal discretion. Through this interpretation, the king became *lex animata*; his judgments based upon
reason had force of law, and since custom represented a type of
law inferior to that enlightening the mind of the ruler, his
dictates were necessarily superior to custom. These several
factors, accepted without question by the great majority of
professional jurists, went far toward the formulation of a political doctrine wherein the king was the undoubted master of
customary law. Together they explain the willingness of even
the most circumspect constitutionalists to admit to the monarch
a modicum of discretionary power over this great portion of
the constitution.

Although the evaluation of custom according to criteria of
justice higher than those embodied in that law was permitted
by concepts which had been accepted for centuries, the legists
had found no extensive opportunity for the application of that
principle until the redaction and codification of the customary
law. Initiated by the Ordinance of Montilz-les-Tours in 1454,
this movement was carried to completion largely during the
sixteenth century.[70] Its primary purpose was to clarify many
obscure details of local usage and thus to permit the better
administration of justice, but the resulting body of written
custom incidentally gave rise to a school of commentators which
included the greatest legists of the century. Through elucidation and simplification of these readily available volumes of
local custom, many writers sought eventually to create a great
body of *droit commun coutumier* which would have force
throughout the realm. Du Moulin was by far the most influential single writer among those seeking that end; through a
series of commentaries and subsequent compilations, he hoped
to reduce the amorphous mass of local custom to a state-wide

---

[70] In addition to the older works on this movement, see J. van Kan, *Les
Efforts de codification en France* (Paris, 1929), Auguste Lebrun, *La Coutume*
(Paris, 1932), and René Filhol, *Le Premier Président Christofle de Thou et la
réformation des coutumes* (Paris, 1937).

body of common law.[71] This super-human program he carried remarkably near to completion, for after commenting a large number of the provincial *coutumiers*, he issued toward the close of his career his *Grand Coustumier général* [72] bringing together all customs accepted throughout the realm and listing as sub-divisions the local regulations modifying the generally accepted provisions.

As a legist, Du Moulin perceived that the only means of unifying the customary law of France was through the suppression of many troublesome local variations and the recasting of the whole about certain general concepts to be drawn from custom and from other legal systems as well. The latter meant for him the application of tenets of Roman law after the fashion of the Bartolists. Furthermore, he did not hesitate to judge customary usage in the light of natural justice and equity, and this resulted in his advocating, to a limited extent, the abolition of certain portions of customary law. In the general body of his writings, these emphases were but reflections of his all-embracing attitude favoring the extension of the royal authority at the expense of customary law and the authority of the barons. To unify was to judge, and the process of judging tended to subordinate the thing evaluated to the discretion of the enlightened monarch who was inspired by the criteria applied. His approach to the customary law was nothing new, but it was carried out with such ability and determination of purpose that its product was regarded by contemporaries as something quite new in French jurisprudence. His contribution and its relation to current theories of custom may best be examined in the light of his controversy with Bertrand d'Argentré, the Breton legist who wrote somewhat later in the century and whose works were largely a defense of the customary law of Brittany against the policies of the central government

---

[71] He outlined his program in his *Oratio de concordia et unione consuetudinum Franciae. Opera*, II. His aim was the creation of a "libellus . . . juri communi et aequitati naturali consonantissimus, publicae et singulorum omnium utilitati accommodatissimus." *Ibid.*, p. 691, col. 1.

[72] *Le Grand Coustumier général, contenant toutes les coustumes generalles et particulieres du royaume de France et des Gaulles* (Paris, 1567), 2 vols.

and the theorizing of Du Moulin. For if the latter's writings, reflecting a very pro-royal bias, received great praise in the capital, they did not go unchallenged in the provinces among which Brittany was one of the most ardent in preserving her ancient liberties. D'Argentré realized that the major defense of those traditional rights, and especially those of the local nobility, lay in the customary law, and he consequently became an apostle of particularism, criticizing Du Moulin's criteria as well as his interpretations. The clearest example of their variation appeared in connection with feudal dues and the rights of the barons over their serfs. Du Moulin, utilizing to the full the generally accepted doctrine that law should be the embodiment of justice, asserted that customary law should be interpreted according to that which was good and equitable, even suffering restriction if necessary, in order to insure that it was in no manner iniquitous.[73] Such an approach, if carried to extremes, would open the way for restrictions and abolitions of customary law almost without end, for it was certain that the critic acting in the light of higher principles could find much in the chaotic customary law contrary to his ideals. Du Moulin proceeded to apply this criterion to feudal dues and services, and concluded quite logically that they could be regarded as little more than base servitudes.[74] Before this general condemnation of a very important portion of the feudal system, d'Argentré expressed a sincere astonishment. Such obligations could hardly be degrading, because they were founded upon the contractual relations of lord and serf. They were based upon customary law and were the rights of lordship.[75]

---

[73] *Commentarii*, Tit. I, § XIII, glo. IV, no. 8; § LI, glo. II, nos. 86, 87.

[74] "Et generaliter huiusmodi releuia, quinta, subquinta, et duodecimae pretiorum, tam in feudalibus quam in censuariis praediis, sunt graues et odiosae ne dicam sordidae seruitutes, et experientia docente prouocant et inducunt homines ad multas fraudes, simulationes, tricas, mendicia, suspiciones, lites, odia, et alia conscientiae onera contra legem Dei, sincerum amorem, et legalitatem proximis debitam, et quam inter homines crescere, coalescere, et quam minus fieri possit laedi summopere curare debent legumlatores et iudices." *Commentarii*, Tit. I, § XXXIII, glo. 2, no. 3. Cf. Tit. I, § XXXV, glo. II, no. 18.

[75] "Quare mirari non desinam, quid in mentem Molinaeo venerit, homini caetera considerato et prudenti, quod baillium, releuia, rachatus, laudimia, cateraque talia dominorum iura, identidem odiosa scribit, et restringenda

As a further means of weakening the position of the feudal lords, Du Moulin classed feudal dues and duties into two categories: those arising from general custom of the province and those originating in the specific contract between the lord and his vassal. The first he called ordinary, the second extraordinary, and the distinction was of great practical importance because forfeiture of a fief by the vassal might be enforced legally only because of his failure to give ordinary dues.[76] In answer to this statement, d'Argentré maintained that both types were based in law, equally binding, and that seizure of the fief might be carried out upon the vassal's failure to render either type of due. In his response, he accused Du Moulin not unreasonably of inciting the barons' natural subjects to rebellion.[77] These were but a few of the varying interpretations utilized by Du Moulin and d'Argentré in evaluating customary law, but they illustrate the Parisian's use of certain concepts, largely extra-legal, in the unification of custom, and likewise d'Argentré's defense of the rights of his province through preserving the strict detail of local usage. The approach and emphasis of Du Moulin were to triumph and were of definite influence in reducing the customary law to subordinance under the royal authority, but the attitude of d'Argentré was closer to the spirit of the period in which those customs had had their origin.

If the movement for unification of customary law in the works of the legists witnessed the application of certain ideas

---

interdum graues et sordidas seruitutes, quae homines ad fraudes sollicitent. Hic quidem Molinaeus aut impingit in rectam rationem, aut non video, qui ex omnibus vsquam contractibus maiori in pretio esse debeat feudi datione, cum continuam et successiuam habeat beneficentiae causam, et in quo exuberare bona fides magis debeat, aut commercii fides enixius obseruari, aut maiori favore dignus sit. . . ." Bertrand d'Argentré, *Commentarii in patrias Britonum leges, seu consuetudines generales antiquissimi ducatus Britanniae* (Paris, 1621), Tit. II, "Des droicts du prince," Art. LXXVI, nota 2, no. 2.

[76] *Commentarii*, Tit. I, § 33, glo. I, no. 125.

[77] "Neque enim Consuetudo minorem auctoritatem tribuit conuentis, et prouisione hominis inductis, quam a se ipsa, cum legitimis conuentionibus inductae sunt in concessionibus feudalibus, et negatio talium iniuriam, et ingratitudinem arguat eius, qui a lege beneficium accepit, cui hoc modo Molinaeus fauet, et fauere docet recusantibus." *Op. cit.*, Tit. XIII, "Des executions," Art. CCXXX, glo. I, no. 3.

tending to subordinate that law to the ruler, the actual process of redaction resulted in a similar tendency. Custom may have had its origin and final authority in the people's legal right, but redaction was an act of administration and could be carried out only under royal authorization. In the sessions of the local estates, there was close cooperation between deputies and the royal commissioners. The latter prepared a preliminary draft of the local regulations, directed the discussion of individual items in the sessions of the estates, and completed the redaction, while decision concerning points of law rested with the assembled deputies, or, in case of disagreement, with a higher court. The resulting body of written custom was published in the local Parlement and was recognized as the law of the province. The mere outline of the procedure utilized suggests a large and often predominating influence of the legal practitioners over the opinions of the popular representatives, and such was increasingly the case as the century progressed. The case of the successive redactions of the *coutume de Paris* is enlightening: the redaction of 1507–1510 was carried out strictly in accordance with the right of the people to establish the customary law regulating their legal position and rights.[78] But the redaction of 1580 was carried out by the practitioners from the Parlement of Paris almost heedless of the wishes of the deputies, the reformation of the law being effected largely in the light of principles established through judicial decision and the writings of certain theorists, particularly Du Moulin.[79] In this fashion, codified custom tended more and more to become practitioners' law rather than the law established by the people. As such, it came effectively under the control of the royal officers. This factor, together with the royal authorization necessary to legalize the process of redaction, had definite influence in placing customary law below the royal prerogative.

Intimately allied with these several factors tending to sub-

---

[78] Olivier-Martin, *Histoire de la coutume de la prévôté et vicomté de Paris* (Paris, 1922), I, 108–109.

[79] Olivier-Martin, *Histoire*, I, 113.

ordinate custom to the ruler was the important and increasing
inclination of the jurists to find the source of all constitutional
law in original acts of the king. Each school of political thought
examined thus far had variously set forth this interpretation.
Its influence in regard to customary law resulted in a general
tendency among the jurists to assert that codified and written
custom did not draw its authority from popular consent but
from the act of the king permitting the redaction. Specifically,
these ideas caused writers to identify codified custom with
royal ordinance, stating that each rested similarly upon royal
authorization. This idea was very difficult to establish, not
only because of the differing origins of custom and ordinance
but also because of the opposite spheres of legal practice to
which each normally applied. Yet it was seized upon as providing a valuable point to support the growing idea of the king
as legislator, and it appears frequently in contemporary treatises. Early in the century, Chasseneuz had written that custom, as such, was undoubtedly the work of the people and that
the process of redaction, while necessarily authorized by the
prince, did not involve the making of new law but was simply
in order to preserve extant usage.[80] Nevertheless, he insisted
that the royal approval of written customs caused them to
become laws and constitutions of the prince because he had
imparted his authority to them.[81] His contemporary, Rebuffi,
wrote that customs approved by the prince had the force of
leges.[82] Certain later constitutionalists presented the same idea.
Simon Marion did not hesitate to state that custom which had
been promulgated by authority of the king had the character
of royal law,[83] while Fontanon wrote that since customs were

---

[80] *Consuetudines*, pp. 1a, 6b, 11b, 381a.

[81] "Et aduerte, quia ex quo princeps approbauit has consuetudines, sunt leges
et constitutiones ipsius principis, cum omnia nostra facimus, quibus a nobis
autoritas impartitur." *Consuetudines*, p. 381a.

[82] "Et antequam a principe sint approbatae, priuatae dici possunt consuetudines, postea notoriae, et ab omnibus tanquam leges obseruandae. . . ." Rebuffi,
Tractatus de consuetudine, usu, et stylo, p. 586, in *Commentarii in constitutiones
seu ordinationes regias*, III.

[83] His text was that used by Chasseneuz: "Ioint, qu'estant homologuée par

codified in virtue of the royal authority, they were held to partake of the same legal qualities as the ordinances.[84] These statements from widely scattered sources are sufficient to indicate that ideas permitting the identification of written custom and royal ordinance were present and gaining strength.

If the legists held, in any sense, that the king enjoyed the continual authority to make law, they identified it with his issuing of the royal ordinances. All writers included the prerogative to make law and ordinances (*faire loi et ordonnances*); consequently an exact definition of that authority is necessary in evaluating the relative positions of the king and the law, and in understanding the nature of the prerogative. Certain of the ablest modern authorities on French constitutional history have developed the interpretation that the true sphere of royal edicts and ordinances was in matters pertaining strictly to government and administration, that is, public affairs as such. Royal ordinances, being a manifestation of the prerogative, normally pertained to questions of justice and administration alone; they did not trespass upon the domain of customary law and private rights. If there was any element of legislation in the ordinances, it dealt strictly with public affairs, not popular rights, for the latter were the domain of customary law.[85] The writings of the sixteenth-century jurists did not present this interpretation in such sharp focus, and it was particularly obscured by those

---

authorité du Roy et de la Cour, *ex eo potest dici lex Regia: Quia omnia nostra facimus quibus auctoritatem nostram impertimur.*" *Plaidoyez*, p. 261.

[84] "*Consuetudo a consensu tacito populi, qui olim habuit potestatem legis condendae: estque ideo ius ciuile, et quae in iis constituta sunt vim plenissimam iuris habent. . . .* Toutesfois *ex eo* que les coustumes sont redigees par autorité du Roy, *censentur eodem iure* que les ordonnances." Antoine Fontanon, *Les Edicts et ordonnances des roys de France* (Paris, 1580), I, 499. Cited by Lebrun, *op. cit.*, p. 93. For a general treatment of this question, see Lebrun, pp. 79–82, 92–94.

[85] Paul Viollet, *Histoire des institutions politiques et administratives de la France* (Paris, 1898), II, pp. 201–202. More recently, Professor Olivier-Martin has given this interpretation a more precise and comprehensive character: ". . . le domaine normal de l'ordonnance est le droit public, comme le domaine normal de la coutume est le droit privé." *Précis d'histoire du droit français* (Paris, 1934), p. 215. This idea has been adopted and developed in able fashion by Olivier-Martin's pupil, René Filhol. *Op. cit.*, pp. 64, 71–77.

aspects of legal thought causing theorists increasingly to find something resembling a general legislative authority in the ruler. However, much in their doctrine points to an acceptance of the major implications of the principle. The legists held that the prerogatives of jurisdiction and administration summed up the major elements in the crown, and they frequently defined royal ordinances as simply the means utilized in exercising those authorities. Charondas wrote that edicts and ordinances were made for the administration of justice and the affairs of the realm.[86] Du Haillan, as we have noted, regarded the prerogative of the king to make laws and ordinances as little more than that regulatory authority which the Bartolists had attributed to each duke and baron within his sphere of jurisdiction.[87] And Du Moulin wrote that the common law of the realm was to be found in custom rather than in the royal constitutions, for the latter dealt mainly with individual persons and cases and were often merely temporary regulations.[88] It may be accepted that at least a representative body of writers regarded the normal sphere of the ordinances as the regulation and direction of the central administration alone.

Admittedly, there were unusual instances in which the king, through edict or ordinance, regulated the details of customary law, but in this connection the attitude of the courts is enlightening. The practitioners in the Parlement of Paris held that the king might quash a custom if necessary through royal act and that the courts should, as a general rule, apply such edicts and ordinances as portions of the law of the land.[89] But in actual practice, the courts exhibited an extreme freedom in

[86] *Pandectes*, pp. 6–7. See chapter IV of this work, "Des loix et ordonnances."

[87] See above, n. 46.

[88] *Commentarii*, Tit. I, *proemium*, no. 106.

[89] "Et à la verité nos Roys ne sont astraincts aux Coustumes et Loix Municipales que les subiects font par leur permission, si estroitement qu'ils ne les puissent reformer et faire vne Loy contraire vniuerselle en tout le Royaume, et telles loix generales sont de plus grand effect que les Coustumes qui sont particulieres, et selon les meurs des Prouinces." Barnabé Levest, *CCXXXVII arrêts celebres et mémorables du Parlement de Paris* (Paris, 1612), p. 683. This is a small portion of a remarkable discussion of that question contained in an *arrêt* of the Parlement of Paris.

dealing with royal acts concerning customary law. The edict of 1581 making the *retrait lignager* effective in the *pays de droit écrit* remained a dead letter.[90] The *Edit des mères*, of 1567, which was framed specifically for the *pays de droit écrit*, was refused application in Guyenne by the Parlement of Bordeaux in an *arrêt* of August 18, 1597, because that court had not enregistered the edict. And when the case was appealed to the *grand conseil*, the earlier decision was upheld.[91] On the other hand, when the jurists approved of a royal edict regulating the customary law, they would extend its application to cases quite beyond its letter. The *Edit des secondes noces* of 1560, forbidding a widow at remarriage to prejudice the heritage of her children by her first husband through donations to the second, suffered this extension. The judges interpreted it to apply not only to widows but to widowers, to gifts to children by the second marriage, to acquisitions by the partner recently deceased, and to all such contingencies in which property rights were concerned.[92] This extreme freedom of the judges in their treatment of royal acts regulating the customary law reveals great independence of the judiciary in accepting the efforts of the central administration to decree concerning the rights of the subjects.

In the light of these devious currents tending to reduce customary law to subordinance under the royal authority, it is important to examine the relevant statements made by the legists of the more traditional stamp. Those taking a broader and more theoretical approach, less grounded in the practical details of law and further from the routine of the profession, illustrate

[90] Isambert, *Anciennes lois françaises*, XIV, 505. Cf. Filhol, *op. cit.*, p. 75.

[91] By *arrêt* of September 30, 1600. The account of these proceedings is to be found in Choppin, *Coûtume d'Anjou*, pp. 33–34, 363. Choppin said that the *grand conseil* should have applied the edict regardless of the lack of its registration in the local Parlement because it was made expressly for that region. He would limit the prerogative of registration in favor of the royal right to regulate custom. For this edict, see Isambert, *Anciennes lois francaises*, XIV, pp. 221–224.

[92] Georges Louet, *Recueil d'aucuns notables arrests donnez en la cour de Parlement de Paris* (Paris, 1612), pp. 652–654; *Dictionnaire des arrêts*, III, pp. 47–49; Bacquet, *op. cit.*, pp. 464–471.

most clearly the influence of those currents making for increased royal control over custom,[93] but they were visible in the works of the strict constitutionalists as well. One of the most revealing statements was made by François de Gravelle who wrote late in the century and was not abreast of intellectual developments, representing rather the attitude of the provincial nobility. Written custom, he said, was more sure than royal ordinance and ought not to be abolished by the king without the consent of the local estates. Although the legists habitually placed the king over custom, he would do best to submit to it and live according to its dictates.[94] This passage from Gravelle is strong evidence of the maintenance, at least in the provinces, of the traditional, dual spheres of right, recognizing customary law as the basis of the legal authorities of the people and the logical impossibility of encroachment upon it by the prince. Gravelle's complaint that the legists placed the prince above custom was highly justified, but in answer he could but assert that the king ought to live according to, and under, the law of the land. His was one of the clearest statements of the older attitude, and the fact that it appeared in the provinces in 1596, partially as a protest against theories current among the professional jurists, reveals much concerning the flow of ideas concerning the nature of the constitution.

The ideas feared by Gravelle had long been gaining strength

---

[93] The thought of those men will be examined in the following chapter.

[94] ". . . estimons les coustumes auiourd'huy reduites par escrit, plus fortes qu'aucunes loix, voire plus asseurees que les ordonnances des Princes, lesquelles peuuent estre par eux abrogees, mais non pas les coustumes, sans le consentement des estats du pays, assemblez à ceste fin. . . . Il est encores moins licite au Roy de corrompre les loix naturelles, comme de permettre meurtre sans cause. . . . Encores moins sera-il licite au Roy d'enfreindre et corrompre les loix diuines, lesquelles tous hommes sont tenus d'obseruer. . . . Mais quant aux loix ciuiles positiues, et qui ne sont point interpretatiues du droit diuin ou naturel, ny fondamentales de l'estat, le Prince en est estimé absouls par les legistes. . . . Toutesfoys il fera plus louablement, si en tout et par tout suiuant la resolution de l'Empereur Alexandre et de Theodose, il se sousmet aux loix du pays et vit selon icelles, affin qu'il puisse sainement iurer apres le bon Empereur Trajan, de n'auoir iamais rien faict contre les loix." François de Gravelle, *Politiques royales* (Lyon, 1596), pp. 144–147. Gravelle was *sieur de Fourneaux et d'Arpentigny*.

among the legists of the capital. Du Tillet was among the most judicious of that group and set forth one of the most circumspect statements concerning the royal authority over custom, and yet he wrote that it was an undoubted prerogative of the ruler to abolish custom according to public necessity.[95] Although Du Tillet made the reservation that the ruler should be guided by the dictates of justice in all things, the examples which he gave leave no doubt concerning his idea of the royal prerogative to dispense with custom. However, he introduced a distinction: the king in quashing a custom might not break a man's legal right. A member of the royal administration, Du Tillet accepted the inferences to be drawn from the multitudinous currents making for the supremacy of the king over customary law, but he refused to draw the conclusion that the king might abolish a man's right, even as a measure necessary in government. The distinction between the authority of the king over customary law but not over the rights of the people had appeared earlier in the century and represented a stage of transition from a theory of complete separation of the spheres of legal right to one permitting the dominance of the king over custom and popular rights alike. Du Tillet's refusal to accept the latter conclusion, and the careful framing of his statements concerning the royal rights over custom, reveal at once the pres-

[95] "Encores sont lesdits Rois pardessus leurs ordonnances et coustumes du Royaume, pour la souueraineté qu'ils ont: qui est à dire qu'ils en peuuent dispenser, changer, reuoquer lesdites ordonnances: mais ce qu'ils sont ministres et lieutenans de Dieu, responsibles à luy et iusticiables de luy . . . quelque plenitude de puissance qu'ils ayent, elle doit estre par eux exercee auec equité et iustice. . . . Les rois abolissent les coustumes s'ils veulent quant à leurs contracts, non quant à ceux de leurs subjets, pour tollir leur droit. Car les coustumes sont accordees par lesdits subiets, non ordonnees par lesdits Roys. . . . Le Roy Philippes de Valoys en ses deux testamens faicts mil trois cens quarante sept, et trois cens cinquante, pour la validité d'iceux, derogea à tout droict escrit, disant n'y estre suiet quant à la temporalité, et aux coustumes de son Royaume, comme estant pour son regard par dessus icelles. Luy mesme par la donation qu'il feit à la Roine sa femme le vingt et vniesme Nouembre, mil trois cens trente, de tous ses ioyaux, bagues et meubles de son hostel, ou vsage qu'elle auroit lors de son decez, s'il mouroit le premier, osta pour la validité toutes coustumes, loix et vsages contraires. Qui suffira pour exemple de bien vser du pouuoir que les rois ont par dessus les loix et coustumes." *Recueil des roys,* pp. 251–252.

sure of certain doctrines making for a new interpretation and the hesitance of the legists to accept its ultimate implications. This reticence likewise characterized the thought of Simon Marion, who, as we have seen, did not hesitate to assert on occasion that written custom received its authority from the king.[96] The rising theory of kingship may have placed custom, as such, under the royal discretion, but the legists refused to accept the logical corollary that the king held authority over any man's legal right.

The theory of Pasquier was more precise. Custom, he said, was made by the people; law (*loi* or *lex*) was the work of the prince. Codified customs were published under the royal authority, but such did not attribute to them the character of ordinances; redaction was effected merely in order to render them more readily available.[97] But if Pasquier was thus quite traditional in his ideas concerning the exact nature of custom, he was equally definite in attributing to the prince an authority over the same. Partially on the basis of precepts drawn from Roman law, he stated as a general principle that the king had the undoubted right to abolish custom.[98] Although customary law formed a vital part of the constitution, it might be over-ridden by royal ordinance, moral or natural precepts, religion, or public necessity.[99] In these statements appears important evidence in regard to the rising theory of king and constitution.

---

[96] "S'ensuiuent ces propres mots: *De nos certaine science, plaine puissance, et authorité Royale, par nostre Arrest et jugement diffinitif, Auons fait, dit, et ordonné: disons et ordonnons, etc.* Ce qui ne fut jamais veu, et ne peut aussi estre par raison en Arrest quelconque, concernant le droict et l'interest des particuliers decisiuement; parce qu'en cela les Roys n'vsent jamais de puissance absolue, mais de distribution ordinaire, selon les regles communes de la Iustice." *Plaidoyés*, p. 200.

[97] *Plaidoyé*, p. 1092.

[98] ". . . c'a toujours esté une régle géneralle que la loy du prince derogeoit à la Coustume: à Rome, par la loy 3, § Diuus Adrianus, *De sepulcro violato.*" *Interprétation des Institutes*, p. 34. Also: "Et neantmoins c'est une regle tres-certaine, que non seulement dedans Rome, ains dedans ce Royaume, voire par les Loix mesmes du Roy Louys le Debonnaire, la Loy generale du Prince efface par un seul trait de plume, toutes les Coustumes particulieres de chasque Province." *Lettres*, Liv. XIX, no. 15, p. 577.

[99] *Interprétation des Institutes*, p. 34.

Pasquier may have maintained older ideas concerning the essence of customary law, but when he attributed to the prince the authority to quash custom, he took a major step toward a theory of absolutism. Instead of regarding the constitution as a rigid framework composed of two independent and mutually exclusive spheres of right and law, he recognized the supremacy of the crown over that portion of law reflecting popular rights, thereby obscuring the primary meaning of the dual spheres of legal authority. Pasquier did not exaggerate the implications of his statements, and it must be remembered that Parisian legists almost without exception accepted to a similar extent this subordination of custom to the royal prerogative. Although this interpretation remained quite innocuous in the thought of such men as Pasquier, it opened the way for political doctrines which would have met with his complete disapproval.

Choppin held theories quite similar to those of Pasquier, but their emphasis reveals a further step in the direction of increased royal authority. Like his predecessor, Choppin maintained the double interpretation that the people were the source of custom, which, however, was subordinate to the royal prerogative.[100] His royalist leanings were indicated in his heavy emphasis upon the requirement that the king authorize all codification of local customs: the procès verbal he called the soul of the resulting *coutumier*, insisting that in it resided the strength and the authority of the reformed customs.[101] Thus, for Choppin, there was little difference between codified custom and royal ordinance, as concerned their bases of authority; each rested upon the royal prerogative. And in explanation of this interpretation, he set forth the very important idea that the king alone held the authority to give laws to his subjects, that is, only he might permit them to establish their customary law.[102] Here appeared the union of the royal prerogatives to

---

[100] *Coûtume d'Anjou*, pp. 3–4, 39–40, 43.

[101] *Coûtume d'Anjou*, p. 43. His phrase is "l'ame de la coustume."

[102] ". . . car le Roy seul donne des loix à son Peuple, ou est seul Auteur à ses subiects de se former et établir des Coustumes . . ." *Coûtume d'Anjou*, p. 48.

authorize redaction of custom and to give law to the people. The latter item had undergone immense changes during the period just previous to Choppin's writing, and he was doubtless influenced by the newer ideas. But the identification of the royal authority to give law to the people with that permitting redaction of custom — heretofore merely the authorizing of an administrative matter — was of great importance in bringing customary law under the royal prerogative, because it all but clinched the identification of custom and ordinance. Each was held to rest upon royal authorization, and in consequence all law of the constitution, save the two fundamental laws, was brought under the royal discretion. Choppin's emphasis reveals certain highly adverse effects which the newly formulated theory of legislative sovereignty was to exercise upon the traditionally independent legal rights of the subjects as expressed in customary law. Seyssel's check of *la police* was fast disappearing.

In conclusion, we may merely reiterate the interpretations illustrated by the authors cited above. The concept of the state based upon law may have been subject to changing emphases and diverse intellectual currents, but in the works of the constitutionalists it remained largely intact. It rested upon the fundamental assumption that the state was a commonwealth composed of individual but mutually dependent units, each with its rights and prerogatives which found their expression and guarantee in the law of the land. Those rights and laws were divided into two distinct categories consonant with the two major divisions of the state: the social structure composed of the myriad units in hierarchical arrangement, and the royal authority as the right of government. Fundamental law regulated the reception and exercise of the prerogative, while the customary law maintained the rights of the subjects. The latter was the work of the people and rested upon the authority which they gave it. In regard to the fundamental law, there were wide variations in theory concerning its origin and exact nature, but all parties were agreed concerning its importance in contributing the legal basis and limitations of the royal authority. The currents of thought relative to the customary law were more complex and of much greater significance in the evolution of constitutional thought.¹ Principles of Roman law, the increasing emphasis upon divine right and the consequent change in the idea of the king as judge, the growing use of abstract criteria in evaluating custom, the continual expressions of royal approval necessary in the redaction of that law, the attempted assimilation of the *coutumiers* with the ordinances, and finally the effects of the new theory of legislative sovereignty all tended increasingly to make the king the master of customary law. The consequent evolution in the idea of the state is manifest. The constitutionalists maintained intact the conception of the state based upon law and the primary duty of the king, as judge and administrator, to preserve and enforce that law, but the respective positions of the two spheres of legal right were distinctly altered. From a theory of state based upon the mutually exclusive spheres of public and private right, they tended inevitably toward an imposition of the public over the private and consequently a new definition of the latter.

The dominance of a legal theory of the state is best illustrated by the jurists' constant reiteration that any change in the law necessarily involved a breakdown of the social organism. This was no mere apology for the *status quo* but was an integral part of their thought necessitated by their approach through strict legality. The Estates General of Blois in 1576 witnessed great stress upon this idea, doubtless in reaction to the chaotic condition of French society at that period. Bauffremont, the orator for the nobility, said on one occasion that his estate asked nothing more from the king than that he permit them to live under the ancient laws, customs, and ordinances of France.[103] Pierre d'Epinac, the speaker for the clergy, elaborated upon that idea when he said that since the established laws had sufficiently provided those things necessary for the preserva-

---

[103] ". . . les Gentilshommes François . . . ne vous demandent que ce qu'ils demanderent au Roy Charlemagne, par un Gentilhomme, qui porta la parole pour la noblesse: c'est que vous nous laissiez vivre et vieillir és anciennes loix, coustumes et ordonnances de la France." Claude de Bauffremont, *Proposition pour toute la noblesse . . . en l'assemblee generale des estats de ce royaume en la ville de Bloys l'an 1577* (Paris, 1577), p. 13.

tion of the state, the observation of those laws, which provided the standard for all things, seemed to be much more profitable than the creation of new ones. And since reformation consisted simply of a return to the ancient form, his estate merely recalled in its *cahier* the observation of the old laws rather than seeking the erection of new ones.[104] Here appeared in striking form the ideas that the state rested upon a permanent legal foundation essentially unchanging, that innovation was necessarily bad, and that reformation of the law meant merely a return to the original form of the constitution. This concept was held generally by the constitutionalists; their theory of state admitted no fundamental changes nor even an evolution along given lines. The state was an approximation of a fixed ideal; that ideal was partially embodied in the law, and while the law might be reformed in terms of that ideal, both were in themselves essentially static. Any process of reformation necessarily took the form simply of restoration of the ancient constitution. It was admitted on occasion that there might be necessity for new measures, but there was no integration of an idea of real change into the bases of constitutional thought. Apart from his elimination of obvious abuses, the primary duty of the king was to preserve the law of the land unaltered. Not as yet had the legists become aware of the insufficiency of the ancient constitution to meet the demands of a new situation.[105] They were conservative in the true sense of the word.

[104] "Or puisque auec vne si belle maniere nous trouuons que les ordonnances et loix de France, ont suffisamment pourueu à toutes les choses necessaires à la conseruation d'vn estat, l'obseruation de ces anciennes loix, à laquelle nous ramennons toutes choses, semble estre beaucoup plus profitable et vtile, que d'en chercher ou composer de nouuelles. Car nous sommes enseignez qu'il n'y a rien de plus pernicieux à vne Republique, qu'vne trop grand multitude de loix. . . . Et puis que la reformation n'est autre chose, que leuant les choses en leur premiere et ancienne forme: auec bon droit et iuste occasion nous auons par nos remonstrances plustost rappellé l'vsage et obseruation des vieilles loix, que n'auons esté curieux d'en chercher de nouuelles." *Harengue prononcée deuant le roy*, pp. 37–38.

[105] Two quatrains of Pibrac may be regarded as representative of the legists' attitude:

> La loy sous qui l'Estat sa force a prise,
> Garde-la bien pour grosse qu'elle soit:

B. The Institutions of Government

Simon Marion said in 1572 that sovereignty was the true mark of royalty and must reside perpetually in the prince who was unable to separate it from himself or communicate any portion of it to another individual.[1] Although the circumstances in which this statement was made necessitated insistence upon the indivisibility of the royal authority, the idea was in complete accord with concepts held by the overwhelming majority of legists throughout the century. Their theory of the state was based upon the fundamental idea of two spheres of law and right, and they lent that concept a rigidity of interpretation which made impossible the sharing of the crown — one division of legal authority — between the king and other men, even the members of the royal administration. We have seen how the legists of the Renaissance developed a concept of the king's complete and unshared title to the prerogative. In that approach, all governmental officers were regarded simply as constituted agents, or, in the case of the permanent courts, as part of the royal person.[2] The undeniable fact that thousands of men from the various social estates were carrying out innumerable tasks of administration had caused Seyssel to assert that the political organization of the realm combined elements of monarchy, aristocracy, and democracy; but it is clear that he meant this to reflect the facts of administrative organization, and not to indicate a division of governmental authority.[3] Later in the century, Du Haillan repeated Seyssel's statement,[4]

> Le bon-heur vient d'où l'on ne s'apperçoit,
> Et bien souvent de ce que l'on méprise.
>
> Changer à coup de loy et d'ordonnance,
> En fait d'Estat, est vn poinct dangereux:
> Et si Lucurge en ce poinct fut hereux,
> Il ne faut pas en faire consequence.

Guy du Faur de Pibrac, *Les Quatrains* (Paris, 1640), nos. LXXXIX, XCII.

[1] See above, ch. III, pt. A, n. 10.
[2] See above, pp. 52–55.
[3] See above, p. 40.
[4] "Car bien que ce ne soit vne Monarchie, si est ce que par l'institution

and like Seyssel, he encountered severe criticism because of it. In a later edition of his *Estat et succez*, he found it necessary to reply to his critics by inserting a passage wherein he denied that he had implied a sharing of the prerogative between the king and his administrators. Such merely seemed to be the case, he said, because the work of administration was being effected by men drawn from each of the three estates.[5]

One of the best statements of sixteenth-century theory concerning the authority of royal administrators is to be found in the works of Du Moulin. Writing during the period of absolutism, his ideas concerning many details of constitutional thought closely resembled those of the Romanists discussed above, but in regard to this question there was essential agreement between the absolutists and later constitutional writers. Concerning the concession of authority to royal officers, he wrote that even though this were done *omni iure*, it did not include delegation of regalian rights. The prince might transfer *dominium utile* to the recipient, but all authorities which he held as *rex* he retained completely, because all regalian rights were inseparable from the crown.[6] Thus, he said, magistrates

---

d'vne infinité de belles choses politiques qui la rendent florissante, il semble qu'elle soit composee des trois façons de gouuernement, c'est à sçauoir de la Monarchie qui est d'vn, de l'Aristocratie qui est le gouuernement des personnages graues et sages, choisis et receus au maniement des affaires, et de la Democratie (c'est à dire du gouuernement populaire). Premierement il a le Roy, qui est Monarque, aimé, reueré, craint, et obey. . . ." *Estat et succez*, pp. 78b–79a.

[5] "Il y a quelques escriuans bien hardis et qui donnent à tort ou à trauers leur iugement sur toutes choses, qui ont escrit que c'est crime de leze Majesté de dire que l'Estat de la France fut composé de trois choses publiques. . . . Nous ne disons point que la France soit vn Estat composé de trois façons de gouuernement, ny diuisé en trois en puissance absolue et esgalle, chascune ayant la sienne: mais nous disons seullement qu'il semble qu'il le soit, veu les authoritez des trois Estats, tous toutesfois soubzmis à la puissance du Souuerain qui est le Roy, de laquelle ils tirent la leur, comme nous tirons du Soleil la clarté que nous voyons; et y a bien grande difference entre semble ou estre. Car il n'y a nulle doubte qu'il ne soit absolument Royal, Monarchique, et Souuerain, accompagné de toutes les marques d'absolue puissance et de souueraineté, qu'on peult desirer ou former en vn Monarque." *Estat et succez* (Paris, 1580), pp. 154a–154b.

[6] "Declaro tertio vt in concessione castri, vel ducatus, aut comitatus, facta per supremum principem cum omni imperio, etiam cum hac clausula, *omni iure*

have no right in jurisdiction, for all title to it remains strictly in the possession of the prince; officers have merely the exercise of that authority.[7] For this reason, Du Moulin advocated that all acts creating royal officers contain the limitation *quandiu nobis placebit*.[8] Jurisdiction, he said, is commonly spoken of as though it might be sold, divided, or dealt with like anything with the qualities of property. But considered in itself, it is not a patrimony and cannot be sold or treated as such; it is as far from property as sacred things are from profane, public from private. Thus it is absurd and pernicious to allow it to be sold; it belongs of right only to the king.[9] Although the logic of Du Moulin's theorizing had caused him to fly in the face of several aspects of prevailing legal usage — in particular the consequences of venality of office — the great majority of sixteenth-century jurists accepted without question his dictum that all right in governmental authority was held by the king alone, and that all royal officers merely exercised a portion of the prerogative which remained unbroken.

In the broad outlines of sixteenth-century political thought, the Huguenot writers were the only major group who seriously challenged the doctrine that the king held all authority of rulership. The best example of this Huguenot variation is to be found in a work which Théodore de Beza devoted to the problem.[10] Beza's celebrated theory of the minor magistrates

---

quod habet nullo reseruato, non veniant nec transeant regalia, et alia reseruata regiae majestati in signum supremae potestatis: sed solum ea quae possunt conuenire illi, cui sit concessio, seu cuilibet inferiori, et domino particulari castri. nam duplex ius habet rex in castro, vel re concessa, vnum tanquam dominus specialis et vtilis ipsius castri, quod forte emerat, et illud censetur transferre. aliud tanquam rex, quia habet dominium directum et ius regium vniuersaliter in toto regno, et de isto iure regio, nihil transfertur. . . . Ratio est duplex, prima, quia huiusmodi regalia sunt de iuribus coronae, et illi annexa, et inseparabilia: nec sunt in commercio." *Commentarii*, Tit. I, § I, glo. V, no. 53.

[7] "Vera igitur ratio est, vt dixi, quod habens huiusmodi officium, nullum habet ius in iurisditione, nullam possessionem, sed nudum exercitium et administrationem nomine domini." *Commentarii*, Tit. I, § I, glo. V, no. 59.

[8] *Commentarii*, Tit. I, § I, glo. V, no. 59.

[9] *Commentarii*, Tit. I, § I, glo. V, nos. 63, 64.

[10] Théodore de Beza, *Du droit des magistrats sur leurs sujets*. This work was originally written in Latin but was first published in French, in 1574. Our

represented those men as sharing the prerogative with the king in such manner that the ruler and his officers held varying degrees of authority and together formed a corporate entity which as a unit filled the crown.[11] The minor magistrates, he said, formed an intermediate element between sovereign and people, and, in terms of their authority, were officers of the crown or the realm, rather than of the king.[12] They might be subordinate to their sovereign who commanded and invested them, but they did not hold their authority from him but from the general body of sovereignty.[13] Likewise the king, he said, before receiving his sovereign authority, swore fidelity to the crown according to the conditions imposed by his oath, after which he administered the oath to the said officers.[14] Continuing his assignment of separate spheres of authority within the crown to the king and the magistrates respectively, Beza gave that doctrine additional coherence by describing the ruler and

---

references are to the edition in the *Mémoires de l'estat de France sous Charles IX* (Meidelbourg, 1578), II.

[11] Beza's work contains many indications that he assigned final authority in political matters to the people and placed them above king and magistrates alike, even in matters of government. Mesnard (*op. cit.*, p. 325) and others have made this the basis for statements that Beza's theory was democratic, in the exact sense of the term. However, the relevant passages appear to present little more than that theory examined above, namely, the original priority of the people over the government which they had instituted and over which they retained a final and extraordinary authority. At any rate, there is little doubt that Beza believed the realm to be governed normally in virtue of a body of authority — the crown — which was shared by king and magistrates.

[12] "Je vien maintenant aux Magistrats inferieurs, et qui sont comme en degré subalterne, entre le souuerain et le peuple, entendant par ce nom, non pas les officiers de la maison d'vn Roy, et plustost affectez à vn Roy qu'à vn Royaume; mais ceux-là qui ont les charges publiques, et de l'estat, soit touchant l'administration de Iustice, soit du fait de la guerre, appelez pour ceste cause en vne monarchie, Officiers de la couronne, et plustost du Royaume que du Roy, estant ces deux choses bien differentes." *Du droit*, p. 492b.

[13] "Or faut-il entendre que tous ceux-ci, encores qu'ils soient au dessous de leur souuerain (duquel aussi ils reçoiuent commandement, et lequel les installe, et approuue) toutesfois ne dependent proprement du souuerain, mais de la souueraineté." *Du droit*, p. 493a.

[14] ". . . le souuerain mesmes, deuant qu'estre mis en vraye possession de son administration souueraine, iure fidelité à la souueraineté sous les conditions apposees à son serment, comme puis apres il baille le serment ausdits officiers. . . ." *Du droit*, p. 493a.

officers as a corporate unit filling the crown. From the fore-
going, he said, it appears that there is a mutual obligation
between the king and the officers of the realm. All authority
of government is not placed within the hands of the king, but
only the highest degree of that authority, while the officers
each have their portion according to their preeminence, all alike
being subject to certain conditions binding all members.[15] In
developing this concept, Beza utilized very skilfully several
generally accepted tenets of legal usage, in particular the current theory of office. However, when he set forth his idea that
the crown was divided among the magistrates and the king,
with the latter as simply the highest among many officers who
shared authority of government, he definitely broke with the
current theory of royal sovereignty. The fact that his treatment constituted a variation from accepted doctrines may be
established by examining the arguments put forward by others
in answer to the various works supporting Beza's position. The
publicists who wrote in defense of the predominant ideas concerning this question were invariably inferior to Beza in ability,
but it is noteworthy that they found it sufficient to meet his
arguments simply by repeating the contrary interpretations
generally accepted by the legists of the century. It was in this
vein that Arnault Sorbin, one of the least able among the royal
historiographers, composed his *Vray Reveille-matin*,[16] in answer to the pamphlet probably by Hotman. The distinction
between officers of the king and those of the realm, he said, was
simply a subterfuge used to justify rebellion. Is not the prince
alone the head of the social organism? [17] True, the ruler ought

---

[15] "Par cela il appert qu'il y a vne mutuelle obligation entre vn Roy et les
officiers d'vn Royaume: duquel Royaume tout le gouuernement n'est pas mis
entre les mains du Roy, ains seulement le souuerain degré de ce gouuernement,
comme aussi les officiers y ont chascun leur part selon leur degré, et le tout à
certaines conditions d'vne part et d'autre." *Du droit*, p. 493b.

[16] Arnault Sorbin, *Le Vray Reveille-matin des calvinistes, et publicains françois: où est amplement discouru de l'auctorité des princes, et du deuoir des
suiets enuers iceux* (Paris, 1576).

[17] "Ceux cy veulent, que les Officiers soient distinguez en Officiers du Roy,
et Officiers du Royaume. . . . A quoy on peult respondre, que telles diuisions

not to order all things according to his fancy and should respect the *counsel* of his officers, but the entire authority for carrying out the various acts of government rests entirely with him.[18] Several years later, François de Clary, an equally strong royalist, writing against the machinations of the League, upheld a theory of magistrates in the same vein.[19] These clear assertions of the dominant theory regarding the authority of the king and his officers were set forth in order to combat doctrines upheld by the two major parties which broke from the traditional constitutional thought — first the Huguenots and later the Leaguers. The concepts set forth by writers on both sides of the controversy reveal that the claims made by the opponents of the government were essentially different from the ideas held by the great body of legists. In developing their arguments, the latter considered it sufficient to reassert theories which had been accepted by writers before the outbreak of religious strife. Thus, the Gallican *politique* jurists appear as the center party throughout the Wars of Religion, maintaining

---

ne sont que de vrayes allumettes de partialitez, pour nourrir les mauuaises affections de ceux, qui sont bien aises d'auoir dequoy couurir les vilainies de leurs rebellions, ligues et factions. Car si vne Monarchie, ou Estat d'icelle, n'est qu'vn vray corps, duquel le Prince est le chef, qui sera celuy qui dira, que les autres parties du corps ne soient autant membres de la teste, que du corps?" *Op. cit.*, pp. 36b–37a.

[18] "Or quant à ceux, qui sont vrais Catholiques, comme ils ne veulent pas dire, qu'il soit loisible aux Princes d'ordonner de toutes choses à leur fantasie, et sans conseil ny demy; estant certain que les Constitutions de Theodose et Valentinian, par lesquelles est ordonné, que les Empereurs approuueroient les arrests de leur conseil, sont tresque iustes: Mais aussi ne peult on nier, qu'il n'y ait des choses, qui dependent de la pure volonté du Souuerain. . . ." *Op. cit.*, p. 44a. He goes on to list the various marks of sovereignty.

[19] "Car ce sont les Roys qui ont departy et donné les charges aux Magistrats, qui leur ont inspiré ces esprits de grandeur qui leur ont communiqué l'honneur mesme de leur dignité Royale, pour la tenir sous leur authorité et adueu, et pour leur seruice. . . . Car pour les grandes habitudes, respectes, et raports qui doiuent assembler et vnir les Magistrats et Officiers auec le Roy: ils ne constituent, ny ne forment point de membre separé de la Royauté, et ne font point de corps à part en la conuocation des Estats generaux du Royaume, comme tous les autres ordres. Ils sont censez du corps mesme du Roy, tenus et reputez pour dependences, et suittes necessaires de sa dignité, comme instruments et ressorts de sa couronne, comme parties essentielles meslees, et confuses auec la Royauté." François de Clary, *Philippiques contre les bulles, et autres pratiques de la faction d'Espagne* (Tours, 1592), pp. 86b–87b.

the traditional interpretation against the attacks of the Huguenots and later against the challenge of the League.

Although the great majority of jurists assigned all public authority to the king, they nevertheless insisted that he should govern *par très grand conseil*, to use Beaumanoir's phrase. It was through counsel and legal limitation, rather than by a division of authority, that they hoped to temper the royal policy. In spite of widespread ideas concerning the necessary excellence of kings and the enlightenment of their minds by agents beyond the capacity of ordinary mortals, the legists continued to assert heavily that no monarch could carry out wise and adequate government without the counsel of the constituted bodies in the central administration.[20] Often it was asserted that only through counsel could the king know the true state of the land.[21] Furthermore, the idea was widespread that enlightened policy might be achieved only through the exercise of reason; even justice and truth might be found through that process, and consequently the best policy might be established only through free deliberation. Although the king made the final decisions, his mind had been enlightened by the free play of reason in the preceding discussions.[22]

The various bodies in the central administration capable of counselling the ruler may be classed as belonging to one of two groups: first, those whose counsel was simply advice, without binding qualities, and secondly, those whose decisions limited the king because they embodied legal elements serving as constitutional limitations upon his discretion.[23] To the first category may be assigned the "born" counsellors and the royal councils, in the narrow sense. Du Haillan described the *conseil secret* and the *conseil privé* as key instruments in the central

[20] In this connection, the legists frequently cited as precedent the fact that even Moses had required counsel for efficient government! E. g., L'Alouette, *op. cit.*, pp. 128–130.

[21] Charondas, *Pandectes*, p. 134.

[22] Charondas, *Questions diverses*, pp. 90–96.

[23] Although the undifferentiated competence of many administrative bodies caused a corresponding lack of precision in contemporary thought concerning the same, each falls readily into one of these categories.

administration. It was in the former where the king and his small, select group of advisers formulated decisions of greatest weight, while in the latter, the highest officers of the several branches of administration assembled and expedited important matters, particularly those of justice and finance.[24] Although the advice and activity of those bodies had great immediate influence upon the tenor of royal policy, Du Haillan regarded neither as specifically controlling the king's acts. It was the *fact* of their activity, rather than the binding qualities of their decisions, which enabled those bodies to alter on occasion the course of royal policy.

In the royal councils, the born counsellors often exercised important influence, and the prevailing theory of their position paralleled closely that concerning those bodies as complete units. The remnants of the medieval duty of counsel — become a privilege by the sixteenth century — were ascribed to these born counsellors, and their membership was strictly limited to include the peers of the realm and the princes of the blood. Regarding the counsel given by the princes of the blood, Du Tillet wrote that they enjoyed the especial right of deliberation in the Parlement. They swore no oath to that court and enjoyed their special judicial competence solely because of the nature of their dignity.[25] Pasquier regarded the peers as the aristocratic element in the constitution and maintained that their counsel should have great weight in shaping royal policies.[26] Yet if writers insisted upon the necessary influence of the born counsellors, they assigned to them neither a portion of governmental authority nor any prerogative to prescribe bonds of law upon the ruler, but only an external influence upon the formulation of royal policy.

Of very different import was the activity of those governmental organs whose competence enabled them to make pronouncements based upon accepted law, and thus to limit the

---

[24] *Estat et succez,* pp. 83a–84a.
[25] *Recueil des roys,* pp. 314–316.
[26] *Pourparler du prince,* p. 1040.

king's freedom of action. In this group may be placed the Chancellor, the *chambre des comptes*, the Parlement, and, according to certain thinkers, the Estates General, although predominant concepts denied this attribute to the latter institution. The great majority of royal officers may have been regarded as little more than royal agents, but the Chancellor held the seals of state and was thus enabled to pronounce concerning the justice and legality of all documents which came under his supervision. Du Haillan wrote that the Chancellor might quash royal letters contrary to accepted usage and act as controller of the king's ordinances, edicts, orders, commands, and gifts.[27] Similarly, it was invariably stressed by the constitutionalists that the *chambre des comptes* might limit the king's extravagance by refusing to permit the execution of those donations and favors which were contrary to the good of the state and legal usage.[28] In these capacities, the Chancellor and the *chambre des comptes* may be said to have represented the position of the Parlement in miniature.

The Parlement of Paris was the most important among the constituted bodies within the central administration, and any evaluation of its position must take into consideration not only the relative authorities of the king and his courts but also the function of the latter in making judicial decisions binding upon all men, including the prince. Although essentially a court for the administration of highest justice over a great portion of the realm, the functions and attributes of the Parlement were sufficiently unspecialized to permit it to claim the authority to evaluate royal edicts and ordinances and to supervise a host of lesser matters, such as economic measures and municipal administration. It was, however, the capacity of the Parlement

[27] "Ce mot de Chancelier vient de *Cancellare*, qui signifie rompre, c'est à dire, que c'est à luy à rompre les lettres qui ne sont ciuiles. . . . Il est comme seuere contrerooleur des ordonnances, Edicts, volontez, commandemens, et dons du Roy." *Estat et succez*, p. 136b.

[28] E. g., Du Haillan, *Estat et succez*, p. 84b; Louis Le Roy, *Les Politiques d'Aristote* (Paris, 1568), pp. 376–377; Pasquier, *Lettres*, Liv. XIV, no. 11, pp. 427–428.

as the highest judicial body in the realm which represented its true nature and from which its many functions were derived. Concerning the source and nature of the Parlement's authority, the jurists invariably set forth ideas in strict accord with their fundamental concept which attributed all public authority to the king and represented the administrators simply as exercising a portion of the prerogative. In this sense, Pasquier asserted that although the king was the fountain of justice, it flowed from him to his subjects through the medium of the sovereign courts; the Parlement necessarily drew its authority from him. In its sessions, the king was always assumed to be present, and its decisions were carried out as representing his word.[29] Even more conclusive concerning this interpretation was a statement made by the court itself in 1556: God had given to the prince the entire body of power and jurisdiction. The essence of sovereignty was justice, and that the king had committed to his judges, superior and inferior. The sovereign courts might give supreme justice, but they always spoke for the king, never for themselves.[30] At no time during the century did the Parlement or the jurists claim for that body any independent authority in addition to that which it held from the king. As an administrative body, it was created and endowed with authority by the king, and if it claimed to check or limit him, that was simply in virtue of its position as guardian of the law. It was part of the royal administration, but its function was the dispensing of justice, right, and law which even the king was bound to respect. Thus, the independence of the Parlement rested upon its function rather than upon any

---

[29] *Plaidoyé*, p. 1075.

[30] "Dieu a ordonné le roi comme monarque en son royaume en unité de pouvoir et de jurisdiction; et la souveraineté est si étroitement conjointe avec la justice que séparée elle perdrait son nom et serait un corps sans âme. Le roi, pour la multitude du peuple et grandeur de son Etat, ne pouvant exercer personnellement la justice, a dû la commettre à des hommes de confiance: première à des juges subalternes, baillis, prévôts, etc. . . . qui jugent par obeissance de ressort; puis aux Cours souueraines établies en divers pays, pour le soulagement des sujets, qui jugent en souveraineté et pour cela ne parlent en leurs arrests, mais font parler le roy." Quoted by Edouard Maugis, *Histoire du Parlement de Paris* (Paris, 1913), I, viii.

independent source of authority. Such was the basis of its claim to regulate the acts of all men in the realm, including the sovereign.

The greater portion of the Parlement's work as highest court represented merely the application of substantive law to disputes between subject and subject, but it entertained as well much litigation between the people and the ruler. The jurists may have regarded the king as above the law, in the sense that he might judge according to equity and even dispense with specific details of local usage, but they continued to maintain that he could err in terms of the law of the land and therefore was subject to correction by the courts of justice. Such was the essence of Seyssel's check of *la justice*, and the doctrine appears with such frequency throughout the century — in the works of constitutionalists and absolutists alike — that it may be regarded as representing the dominant opinion among contemporary legal writers. During the reign of Francis I, Du Moulin wrote that there was such genuine justice in the realm of France that if a poor man had a case against the king and lacked the means of prosecuting it, the king would furnish him with legal counsel in order that the truth of the matter might be revealed.[31] At a somewhat later date, Pasquier recalled that the king frequently lost his case, plead in the Parlement by his Procureur General in order to avoid intimidation of the opposite party. Such judicial recourse against the ruler was necessitated by the requirements of justice and truth.[32] Louis Le Roy repeated without change many of Seyssel's statements

---

[31] ". . . tam sinceram iustitiam esse in regno Franciae, quod si aliquis pauper habet litem cum rege, et non habet vnde litis impensas faciat, quod rex ei subministrat aduocatum vt veritas causae eruatur. . . ." *Commentarii*, Tit. I, § XLI, glo. I, no. 1.

[32] "Et quant à nous, nous ne trouvons nullement estrange que le Roy perde la sienne; et de fait, pour ne nous intimider point sous le nom de Sa Majesté, nous ne plaidons point contre luy; mais contre son Procureur General que l'on tire du Collège des Advocats, afin que nous ne nous estonnions en telles Causes: en quoy nos Roys nous ont montré qu'ils estoient perpetuellement debonnaires, et que combien qu'ils eussent en grande recommandation ce que l'on disoit estre de leur Domaine, si ont-ils tousjours eu en plus grand'estime ce qu'ils voyoient estre de la justice et la verité. . . ." *Plaidoyé*, p. 1083.

concerning the judicial check upon the monarch,[33] while Jean
de Montluc, in speaking before the Polish Diet in 1573, listed
as one of the glories of France the system of jurisdiction
whereby the subjects might defend their rights by calling their
ruler to trial before the Parlements.[34] The same opinion was
upheld by writers of a more absolutistic bent. In commenting
upon the *legibus solutus* clause, Bugnyon, a very strong Ro-
manist, wrote that the king was not free from the law, since
he submitted to judicial decisions and authorized their execution.[35] And finally, William Barclay, one of the most important
exponents of the rising doctrine of absolutism at the close of
the century, retained intact this judicial check upon the monarch. Although he stressed the fact that the royal monopoly of
all judicial authority rendered impossible any subjection of the
ruler to the court, he represented the king as freely submitting
to its decisions and allowing the trial of cases between himself
and his subjects.[36] The inescapable conclusion is that Seyssel's

[33] *Politiques d'Aristote*, pp. 376–377.

[34] "La Gaule a tousiours esté fort estimee et prisee par les nations estrangeres
de sçauoir bien administrer la Iustice, et rendre droict à vn chascun . . . on a
institué les Parlemens qui semblent auoir esté diuinement concedez à noz ancestres, afin que iusques au plus bas et plus petit du peuple, mais principalement
aux Nobles et aux Gentilshommes, il fust loisible d'agir, et de poursuiure leurs
droicts en Iustice à l'encontre des Roys mesmes. Car l'institution des Parlemens
est telle que nostre Roy peut estre appellé en Iustice deuant eux, par tous ses
subiects, qui pensent que l'on leur face tort: et voit on bien souuent qu'en
choses de tresgrands poix, le Roy deschet de sa cause, et pert son procez." Jean
de Montluc, *Harangue faicte et prononcee . . . en l'assemblée tenue à Warssauie,
pour l'election du nouueau Roy*. (Paris, 1573), pp. 11b–12a.

[35] "Nonobstant donc les droits precedens, Les Roys de France se soubmettent
volontairement aux Arrests et jugemens de leurs Cours de Parlemens, de leurs
Bailliages et Seneschaucées, esquels Arrests et jugemens ils acquiescent et obeissent, comme font leurs subjects, mesme veulent que les Commissions ottroyées
soubs leurs noms soyent executées selon leur forme et teneur." Philibert Bugnyon, *Legum abrogatarum et inusitarum in omnibus curiis, terris, jurisdictionibus
et dominiis regni Franciae tractatus* (Brussels, 1666), p. 336. Bugnyon likewise
criticized Budé for using the authority of Aristotle to place the king above the
law: "Mais l'opinion d'Aristote ne convient ny s'accorde point à la raison: et
semble qu'elle soit pleine de sycophantie et flaterie, pour peut estre gratifier et
complaire à Alexandre futur successeur de Philippe de Macedone." *Ibid*., p. 337.
The passage which he criticized is that given above, ch. II, n. 52.

[36] "Rex vult sibi ius dici ab omnibus Curiis regni sui et quotidie inter eum
et priuatos controuersiae per eius procuratorem in iudiciis agitantur: an Rex
idcirco Curiis subiicitur? nugae. Quicquid potestatis habet Curia, id totum a

check of *la justice* retained great significance in the eyes of legal writers throughout the century. Although this specific limitation upon the royal discretion was suffering constant attacks from many directions, it remained dominant throughout the period here under consideration.

When the sixteenth-century jurists represented the Parlement as an administrative body drawing its authority from the king and yet pronouncing judgments superior to him, they set forth a dual relationship between king and court sufficiently complex to permit great divergence of interpretation regarding the exact position of the court, according to the royal or constitutional bias of the individual author. A crucial question was the irremovability of the magistrates constituting the court. Apart from the consequences of venality of office, the majority of writers upheld permanent tenure of judges in one form or another. Seyssel had insisted that judges ought to be irremovable except for offenses established by the court. The necessity of free administration of justice, especially in cases involving the king, and the idea of office as property, gave weight to this very important constitutional doctrine. Charondas, in considering the question from the point of view of efficient judicial administration, emphasized the need of freedom and security for the members of the judiciary. He concluded that the magistrates in the sovereign courts were permanent officers and could hardly be otherwise without opening the way for the subversion of the entire legal ordering of the state.[37] The attitude of the constitutionalists was well summarized by La Roche-Flavin early in the following century when he wrote that the officers of the Parlements were perpetual and might not be dismissed except through adjudged forfeiture.[38]

Rege habet." William Barclay, *De regno et regali potestate adversus Buchananum, Brutum, Boucherium, et reliquos monarchomachos, libri sex* (Paris, 1600), p. 302.   [37] *Questions diverses*, pp. 51b–60b.

[38] "Les officiers des parlemens estre perpetuels, et ne pouuoir estre destituez, que par forfaicture jugée." Bernard de La Roche-Flavin, *Treze Livres des Parlemens de France* (Bordeaux, 1617), pp. 601–602. Although this work appeared early in the following century, it may be regarded as synthesizing the earlier, constitutional position in regard to the Parlement.

Although the strict constitutionalists maintained that the officers in the Parlement should and did enjoy inviolable tenure of office, there was a contrary current of thought visible in the works of the legists and of increasing importance as the century progressed. It was constantly maintained at the royal court and by writers under its influence, even the more circumspect, that since the Parlement had been instituted by the king and held its authority from him, he might abolish it at will. The court not only held its authority from the prince but existed at his discretion. This interpretation rested upon the theory, accepted by all, maintaining the royal monopoly of governmental authority, and it denied any independence to the judiciary in virtue of its function. There are traces, although slight, of this royalist attitude in the works of Du Tillet. While admitting that judges ought to be irremovable for the good administration of justice,[39] he drew from the idea of indivisible rulership a double conclusion which went far toward denying the independence of the courts. First, he regarded the Parlement of Paris as similar to the council (*conseil privé*) in representing merely a mouthpiece of the king.[40] And secondly, he stated that since the king was the source of the Parlement's authority, he might withdraw its power of jurisdiction and grant the same to others at will.[41] The idea that the king held title to all right of adjudication was denied by no member of the court, but to assert that the king might authorize the dispensing of justice by any person in the realm, regardless of office or status, went far toward denying the independence of the judiciary.

The expressions of opinion by the central government in-

---

[39] *Recueil des roys*, p. 423.

[40] ". . . ils n'ont superieur apres Dieu que le Roy, qui parle absent, és Arrests dudit Parlement, comme en ceux dudit Conseil." *Recueil des roys*, p. 425.

[41] ". . . le Roy, qui n'a qu'vne iustice souueraine par luy commise à ses Parlemens, lesquels ne sont qu'vn en diuers ressorts: peut sa maiesté la commettre à d'autres, et l'oster ausdits Parlemens." *Recueil des roys*, p. 425. This passage contains the parallel idea that the king might remove any case from one court and give it to another. Contrast Pasquier's attitude toward such evocations: above, ch. III, pt. A, n. 62.

variably upheld the royal authority to create and abolish the sovereign courts at will. Two examples of such statements will suffice to indicate their tenor. After the Day of the Barricades, May 12, 1588, the Parlement sent a deputation to Henry III at Chartres in an attempt to make amends for the acts of the Parisian populace. In his answer, Henry expressed a desire for reconciliation with his rebellious subjects but did not hesitate to threaten retaliation upon the capital by abolishing the Parlement, the *chambre des comptes*, the *cour des aides* and other bodies.[42] In the following year, when circumstances forced Henry to decree the transfer of the Parlement from Paris to Tours, his edict recalled the fact that all courts had been suppressed earlier, as a preliminary measure.[43] Although it was constantly asserted in official pronouncements that the courts should enjoy freedom of action in administering justice, the government always maintained its prerogative to deal with its courts as it saw fit. It may be noted that the royalist doctrine concerning their position was simpler than that of the constitutionalists because the former rested squarely upon the accepted concept of royal sovereignty which denied independent authority to the judiciary. Those writers who supported the freedom of the courts and the inviolable tenure of judges were forced to base their claims upon the prevailing theory of office and the courts' function of making judicial pronouncements binding the ruler. These latter factors, while of great significance in contemporary constitutional thought, were regarded by the royalists as confusing the question, which they interpreted strictly according to spheres of authority. And with the rise of monarchy less and less reverent for bonds of

[42] ". . . je puis, comme vous savez, revoquer ma Cour de Parlement, Chambre des Comptes, des Aydes et autres Cours et Université, qui leur retourneroit à grande ruine." *Mémoires de la ligue* (Amsterdam, 1758), II, 364.

[43] "Nous aions par notre Edit du présent mois, pour les raisons amplement déduites en icelui, révoqué nôtre Cour de Parlement, Chambre des Comptes, Généraux des Aydes, Chancellerie, Bureaux de nos Finances, Chambre de Monnoies, Sieges Présidiaux, Bailliages, Sénéchaussées, Prévôtés, Elections et autres Corps et Compagnies, tant de Judicature que de Finance. . . ." *Mémoires de la ligue*, III, 224–225.

law and the dignity of that body which pronounced them, the inviolability of the court's position consequently declined. The only basis of irremovability which the monarchy of the seventeenth century was unable to challenge was venality of office, but that was decried by both parties: by the constitutionalists because of its disastrous effects upon the administration of justice, and by the royalists because it limited the king's freedom to appoint officers and raised up a new aristocracy on a basis less vulnerable than that of the feudal lords over whom the rulers had triumphed but recently.

The activity of the Parlement in enregistering royal edicts and ordinances and in sending up relevant remonstrances to the king was the most important manifestation of its authority to determine the legality of royal policy. Like the court's pronouncement of judicial decisions against the ruler, this function of enregistering and remonstrance constituted an important judicial check upon the royal discretion. After the submission of an edict or ordinance to the Parlement, there was, in theory, free discussion of the act, following which it was inscribed upon the register of the court and became law in that court's circumscription. Similar procedure was necessary in the provincial Parlements in order to render the act binding in their territories. If for any reason the court disapproved of the act in question, the magistrates customarily sent up remonstrances to the ruler, and negotiations would continue until one party triumphed or a compromise was agreed upon. In case of enforced registration following *lettres de jussion*, the court usually appended the phrase *de mandato regis*. Such did not prejudice the character of the act as binding upon the people, but it indicated the definite disapproval of the judges who frequently allowed the act to fall into disuse. The necessity of registration in order to validate all royal edicts and ordinances was denied by very few writers during the century; but the character and significance of that procedure were sufficiently nebulous to permit great latitude of interpretation to contemporary writers concerning the same, both in regard to the meaning of the court's action and the weight of its decisions in determining the policy of the central administration.

One interpretation of enregistering and remonstrance, surprisingly widespread, represented the court as wielding that authority over royal acts because it was the permanent representative of the Estates General. The prevailing ideas concerning the historical origins of those two institutions lent this concept a coherence which it otherwise would have lacked. Contemporary writers invariably pictured the Estates and the Parlement alike as stemming from the ancient assemblies held by the Merovingian and Carolingian kings. The Estates General was the larger unit, assembled but intermittently, while the Parlement was the permanent, sedentary portion of the original body.[44] The resulting idea, that the Parlement stood as permanent representative of the larger assembly, contained highly explosive implications when made the basis of the court's activity in judging royal edicts and ordinances. A minor current of interpretation during this period attributed to the Estates General a final, extraordinary prerogative over important matters of public policy because of the original priority of the people over the state.[45] Simon Marion regarded this preservative function as exercised only at rare intervals by the Estates General, but he took the very important step of identifying this power of the Estates with that exercised by the Parlement in enregistering and remonstrance.[46] Such an inter-

---

[44] This idea concerning the origins of the Parlement and the Estates General was held generally by sixteenth-century writers. E. g., Pasquier, *Recherches*, Liv. II, ch. 2; Du Haillan, *Estat et succez*, pp. 84b, 89a; Charondas, *Questions diverses*, p. 3; Budé, *Annotationes*, pp. 96–98; François Ragueau, *Indice des droicts royaux et seigneuriaux* (Paris, 1583), s. v. "Parlemens."

[45] See above, pp. 86–88, and below, 156–159.

[46] "En quoy noz Peres ont esté si sages, que se sousmettans au Roy par eux choisy, et à ses successeurs selon le droict du sang, ils ont retenu pour marque insigne de proprieté la conuocation des Estats generaux. Mais parce qu'il estoit impossible d'assembler à toutes occurrences vn corps composé de tant de membres espars ça et là; non par les quartiers d'vne grande Cité, mais dedans les bornes amples et diffuses des fleuues . . . ceste authorité vrayement supreme a esté reseruee pour vn dernier remede, aux accidens nouueaux qui peuuent suruenir: et la puissance ordinaire du Prince prudemment temperee par l'institution de ce Parlement, qu'on peut appeller vn abregé des Estats de France:

pretation of the court's authority over royal enactments would
have altered the entire course of the Parlement's history, had
it won general acceptance, because it attributed to that body
an authority drawn from popular rights rather than from the
crown. Instead of existing merely as a unit in the central
administration, exercising a portion of the royal prerogative, it
would have stood outside the royal government in the narrow
sense, wielding a power of judicial control from a position
beyond the confines of the governmental organization, and
thereby immeasurably strengthened in its effective defense of
popular rights. The idea that the court was the permanent
representative of the Estates General, or of the three social
classes at large, was not confined to a few theorists but appeared in the pronouncements of those two institutions themselves.[47] And if the Parlement had habitually acted in virtue
of an independent source of authority in popular rights, the
prevailing lack of differentiation in its activities [48] might have

---

parce qu'il est egalement ouvert à chacun des trois Ordres, et que ses functions
correspondent à la dignité de ce qu'il represente. . . . Les Loix, les Edicts, les
Traittez de Paix et de guerre, les Priuileges, les Contracts publics, et autres tels
actes touchans à l'estat, sont faicts par le Roy: mais il sont verifiez en ce
Parlement, qui les peut refuser, restraindre, ou modifier." *Plaidoyez*, pp. 267-
269.

[47] In 1593, the Parlement declared itself to be an "abrégé des Trois Etats,
image et raccourci de tous les Ordres du royaume." Maugis, *op. cit.*, I, xiv.
The Estates of Blois, 1576-77, made the very inclusive statement: "Et si bien
la puissance du Roy est tres-grande comme d'vn tres-puissant monarque, si
est ce que les Roys de France par leur debonaireté n'ont iamais pensé leurs
puissance et auctorité estre limitee, ou diminuee, se submettans de ne pouuoir
faire ny ordonner pour le reiglement du royaume qu'entant qu'il seroit selon
la raison et les loix d'icelle: d'ou vient quil fault que tous edicts soyent verifiez
et comme conterollez és cours de parlement, quant qu'ilz obligent à y obeir:
lesquelles combien qu'elles ne soyent qu'vne forme des trois estats racourcis au
petit pied, ont pouoir de refuser, suspendre, modifier, lesdits edicts." *Instruction*, no pagination. The same assembly of the Estates allowed the Parlement
to consent to taxes in its circumscription during the intervals between meetings
of the deputies. Robert Villers, *L'Organisation du Parlement de Paris et des
conseils supérieurs d'après la réforme de Maupeau* (Paris, 1937), p. 12.

[48] The lack of differentiation between the activities of the Parlement and the
Estates General, in the minds of certain writers, is illustrated by the following
passage from Du Haillan: "Et pour reuenir à ce mot de Parlement, d'autant
que les plaintes et doleances publiques se faisoient en ces Parlemens premiers,
et que par l'institution du Parlement de Paris, faicte par le Roy Philippes le

produced in that body a concentration of powers which would have changed immeasurably its activity throughout its centuries of existence. However, the Parlement never seriously pressed its claim to act for the general body of the populace. Such was hindered by the friction between the court and the Estates General, caused by the desire of each to preserve the identity of its membership and to prevent the other's appropriating its functions.[49] Furthermore, the idea ran counter to the rapidly crystallizing doctrine of royal sovereignty and the indivisibility of public authority. In practical affairs, the theory that the Parlement represented the Estates General was utilized merely to attribute an additional, though badly defined, authority to the court in evaluating royal edicts. The Estates General itself finally gave up its claim to independent power in matters of government; consequently the Parlement could hardly find a basis for such authority in its capacity as representing the former.

The great majority among sixteenth-century jurists regarded enregistering and remonstrance by the Parlement as simply that procedure necessary for the evaluation of edicts and ordinances according to law and justice. In that fashion, the Parlement, as highest court, was held to declare concerning the consonance of royal acts with accepted criteria of right and equity, and it was generally believed that such enactments could not be truly just unless they were verified by unconstrained decision of the court. However, the great breadth and undifferentiated nature of contemporary criteria of legal justice

---

Bel, il n'auoit cognoissance que des causes ciuilles et criminelles en dernier ressort sans appel, lesdictes doleances, plaintes, et remonstrances publiques furent remises à vne assemblee qui fut lors erigee, baptisee d'vn nouueau nom, et appellee les trois Estats, et le nom de Parlement demeura à l'assemblee des Cours souueraines et des audiences publiques, qui sont tenues par certain nombre de Presidens et Conseiliers establis . . ." *Estat et succez*, p. 89a.

[49] The Estates wished to dispense with the Parlement's verification of royal ordinances based upon the *cahiers* of the deputies, while the court insisted on carrying out that procedure. Also, the Parlement emphatically denied that it was represented in the sessions of the Estates and that the will of the deputies automatically expressed the court's desires. Maugis, *op. cit.*, I, Liv. III, ch. V; Georges Picot, *Histoire des états généraux* (Paris, 1872), IV, 210.

and truth permitted widely varying interpretations regarding
the exact nature of the values thus employed by the Parlement.
Many jurists seem to have regarded the court's approval of a
given act as signifying its consonance with general and highly
abstract principles of justice and equity, without necessarily
including conformity with the law of the land. It was in this
sense that L'Alouette attributed to the court the prerogative to
determine whether a given act was just and reasonable.[50] This
phrase (*juste et raisonnable*) appears constantly in the treatises
of the period as that criterion according to which the Parlement judged royal enactments. Its meaning was as nebulous
as its place was important in contemporary theories of the
court's activity. In the mind of L'Alouette, a member of the
Parlement, the concept seems to have included only intellectual
values, and such was the major emphasis of Charondas in his
very important statement concerning this function of the
court.[51] In this interpretation, the magistrates were held to act
in the light of those universal principles which sixteenth-century

[50] ". . . n'ont pas voulu que leurs edits et ordonnances eussent pouuoir et
autorité dessus leur peuple, qu'ils n'eussent passé par la censure de leur Cour
de Parlement ou de leur Chambre des comtes, encore que tout son conseil d'Etat
et priué les eût aprouués: et apres tant de sortes d'examens et deliberations,
elles sont publiées et enregistrées, s'il ne se trouue rien de deraisonnable et sont
mises à l'impression et publiquement distribuées à vn chacun par les rues. . . .
Les lois etans ainsi faites, elles seront tenues pour iustes et raisonnables." *Des
affaires d'état*, pp. 7–8. Cf. Jean de La Madeleine, *op. cit.*, pp. 35a–35b.

[51] "La premiere et principale puissance desdicts Parlemens, c'est de verifier
les Ordonnances et Edits du Roy: et telle est la loy du Royaume, que nuls
Edicts, nulles Ordonnances n'ont effect, et on n'obeyt à iceux: ou plustost on
ne les tient pour Edits et Ordonnances, s'ils ne sont verifiez aux Cours souueraines . . . et par la libre deliberation d'icelles: qui est vn vray moyen pour
asseurer l'estat de la Monarchie, quand le peuple cognoist que le Prince ne veut
rien ordonner et establir, que par l'aduis et auctorité de ses Cours souueraines:
d'autant que par telle maniere le Roy se rend plus aimable au peuple. . . .
Car . . . deuant que publier une loy, il en faut sagement et meurement deliberer,
et premierement considerer si elle est iuste, en apres si elle est utile: parce que
si elle est du tout inique, il la faut reietter, quelque profit qui en puisse
aduenir. . . . Et apres en auoir deliberé, quelquefois est ordonné que la publication s'en fera, que quelquefois sont faicte remonstrances à sa maiesté." *Pandectes*, p. 142. The character of Charondas' criteria is illustrated more precisely
by the following passage: ". . . il ne conuient à sa Maiesté de faire Edicts,
Ordonnances, mandemens ne lettres quelsconques, contraires à la loy, qui est la
droicte raison, et vraye regle de iustice et equité." *Ibid.*, p. 100.

theorists without exception believed to be binding upon all men, including the prince. As such, the procedure constituted, in the eyes of these writers, an undoubted judicial check upon the ruler's freedom of action. However, the nature of this argument caused it to be limited to those treatises of a more speculative bent, and such were written largely by those who tended toward an expansion of the royal prerogative and a corresponding lessening of this limitation. Often the expedient was represented as setting forth little more than equitable procedure. The abstract character of the criteria applied did not in itself vitiate this check upon the ruler, and it was preserved largely intact in the works of Charondas. Nevertheless, a superabundant emphasis upon the purely speculative quality of the legal bonds within which the king was free to act played into the hands of the later absolutists who would remove all effective limitations upon the royal discretion.

The school of thinkers that insisted most heavily upon the bonds of law hedging the ruler represented the Parlement as judging royal edicts and ordinances not only according to their consonance with general principles of right but also in the light of their conformity with the law of the land. The complete fusion of legal precedent and concepts of justice and truth, in sixteenth-century constitutional thought, caused many jurists to regard the court as applying the entire scale of legal values when judging royal acts. In this sense, the Parlement was held to evaluate the king's enactments according to the legal principles embodied in the constitution, and the primary purpose of that procedure was the preservation of established law. Seyssel had said that royal letters should be judged in the courts according to their *civilité*; such was an important portion of his check of *la justice*. Much more definite concerning the relations of the king and his Parlement, however, was the idea which Pasquier seems literally to have projected into the constitutional writing of the century. Although he attributed absolute authority to the king, he insisted that the ruler should submit his orders to the censure of the Parlement, thereby reducing his will to the *civilité de la loy*.[52] This phrase appears constantly throughout Pasquier's works as the criterion according to which the court should judge royal acts, and the exact content which he ascribed to it is synonymous with his idea concerning the meaning of enregistering and remonstrance. That he believed the court to judge royal orders according to general tenets of justice and equity is manifest from one of his very important statements regarding that procedure,[53] yet for him the *civilité de la loy* included a strong admixture of constitutional precedent as well. Not only is this indicated by his wording of the phrase, but it is also borne out by his detailed statements. It will be recalled that Pasquier accepted the widespread idea that the law of the constitution had originated through acts of the king,[54] but in addition he stressed that such law gained additional sanction through long acceptance and usage.[55] For him, the law at the basis of the state consisted of

[52] "Grande chose veritable, et digne de la Majesté d'un Prince, que nos Roys, ausquels Dieu a donné toute puissance absolue, ayant d'ancienne institution voulu reduire leurs volontés sous la civilité de la loy: et en ce faisant que leurs Edicts et Decrets passassent par l'alambic de cet ordre public." *Recherches*, Liv. II, ch. 4, p. 66.

[53] "O aveugle opinion de tout le monde, de penser que les Roys mesmes, se pensent par dessus la loy! . . . ou la Loy est raison, ou contrevenante à icelle: si contrevenante à icelle, quoy que sous honneste pretexte les Roys pretendent en abuser, si ne merite-t-elle nom de Loy: mais si elle se rende conforme à une equité naturelle, d'estimer que les Roys soient encore dessus la raison . . . ceux qui sous cette puissance leur voulurent ainsi applaudir, au lieu de leur gratifier, dirent en un obscur langage, que les Roys n'estoient point hommes, ains Lyons. . . . Et au contraire, nos Roys . . . despouillans toute passion se voulurent soubmettre à la Loy, et ne faire par ce moyen chose qui ne fust juste et raisonnable: de maniere que leurs patentes sont sujectes à la verification des Cours de Parlement, non seulement sur les obreptions, comme à Rome, ains sur la Justice ou injustice d'icelles. Et posé le cas que parfois elles soient de leur mouvement, toutesfois fort aisément passent-elles en force de chose arrestée, ains se sont tousjours reservées les Cours, la liberté d'user de remonstrance au Roy, pour luy faire entendre que ses mouvemens doivent s'accorder à raison: autrement, sous l'ombre d'une clause derobée, plusieurs favoris feroient d'une passion une Loy." *Pourparler du prince*, pp. 1041–1042.

[54] See above, pp. 84–85.

[55] ". . . les loix, qui sont quelque-fois brusquement proposées au peuple, reçoivent avec le temps polissure, à mesure qu'elles sont mises en œuvre. Et c'est pourquoy l'on a dict, que le vray truchement de la loy c'estoit l'usage." *Lettres*, Liv. VI, no. 2, p. 156. Also: "Davantage que les veilles loix s'estans tournées en coustume, elles se tournoient tout d'une suitte en nature, joint que

royally instituted regulations which had achieved effective import largely through long observance. The king he regarded as preserving this authority to add points of law to the constitution, but he insisted that in so doing, the ruler must submit his enactments to the censure of the court; otherwise they were not binding.[56] The limits within which the king might make new regulations were fixed in the main by the compass of constitutional laws established by his predecessors, and it was the duty of the court to prevent his serious infringement upon existing usage. Such was the meaning of Pasquier's assertions that the purpose of judicial verification of edicts and ordinances was to reduce the king's authority to the royally ordained constitution, or to the *civilité des loix royales de la France*.[57] Such statements leave no doubt that Pasquier believed the Parlement to evaluate royal enactments according to their consonance with constitutional law. His conception was not dissimilar to that of Charondas, since both regarded the court as applying the entire, undifferentiated body of legal values as its basic criterion. The variation of the two writers lay rather in their differing emphases, Charondas stressing the highest elements in the scale of values, while Pasquier gave

---

ce qui estoit d'une longue main empraint dedans nous, estoit beaucoup plus aise à digerer, ores que moins bon: et les ordonnances, quelque fruict qu'elles nous promissent, coustoient infiniment à un peuple, avant que de pouvoir tomber en usage." *Recherches*, Liv. VIII, ch. XII, p. 784.

[56] "Il est certain que le fondement de toute Republique est la Loy, ou pour mieux dire, c'en est l'Ame, sans laquelle nulle Republique ne peut avoir vie. Et combien que les Loix prennent, en cette France, leur premiere source du Roy; toutesfois si n'ont-elles vogue, qu'apres qu'elles ont esté bien et deuement verifiées par ces trois Ordres [Parlement, *chambre des comptes, cour des aides*], en ce qui les concerne. C'est une Loy fondamentale de nostre Estat." *Lettres*, Liv. XII, no. 8, p. 345. Cf. Liv. VI, no. 1, p. 146; Liv. XII, no. 2, p. 327; Liv. XIX, no. 15, pp. 576–577.

[57] "Ce sont les façons que nous apportons en ceste France, en la publication d'un Edit, lequel estant verifié . . . adoncques nos Roys, par une bienveuillance naturelle qu'ils portent à leurs subjects, reduisants leur puissance absolue sous la civilité de la Loy, obeissent à leur Ordonnance." *Lettres*, Liv. XIX, no. 15, p. 577. Also: "Il ne faut rien esperer de bon, si le Roy par sa bonté ne reduit sa puissance absolue, sous la civilité des Loix Royales de la France, comme ont fait ses Predecesseurs: en ce faisant, il aura la paix avec Dieu, il l'aura dans son Royaume, il l'aura avec ses Subjects. . . ." *Ibid.*, Liv. XII, no. 8, p. 346.

greater weight to the substantive law of the constitution. The final implications of these varying approaches to the same general pattern led ultimately to the extremes of constitutional and absolutist thought, as they appeared in the sixteenth century, yet Pasquier and Charondas were essentially agreed concerning the general nature of this judicial check. Both writers, moreover, were at one in regard to its form as an administrative expedient; it did not serve as an active control upon the ruler's actions but simply permitted remonstrances setting forth legal principles which it was his duty to obey.[58] The king was under the law, and the function of the court was to maintain the accepted legal limitations binding the ruler, but it could do so only through declaration and counsel.

Pasquier's concept of enregistering and remonstrance enjoyed wide acceptance among the jurists of the century. His statements were repeated verbatim by Du Haillan who made them his major treatment of the question.[59] An examination of the latter's interpretation reveals that he followed Pasquier in all, save possibly in an even greater stress upon the monarch's subjection to constitutional law.[60] And Choppin very definitely set forth a theory similar to that of Pasquier when he wrote that the Parlement, having sworn to preserve the royal edicts, could modify or refuse to receive new enactments contrary to preceding ordinances or equity.[61] The idea that the court accepted or rejected royal acts according to their consonance with established law seems to have provided the basis of the constitutionalists' position regarding this question.

---

[58] Pasquier wrote that the Parlement had been established ". . . non pour servir de controlle à nos Roys, ains par les humbles remonstrances duquel se passoient les confirmations des affaires generales." *Lettres,* Liv. VI, no. 1, p. 146.

[59] Du Haillan repeated several statements from Pasquier concerning this matter, including that given above, n. 52. *Estat et succez,* pp. 87a–87b.

[60] This impression results largely from Du Haillan's constant repetition of Seyssel concerning the legal limitations upon the king.

[61] "Car Messieurs du Parlement ayans fait serment de garder les Edicts Royaux, si aucuns leur sont presentez qui ayent esté par faveur ou surprise extortuez du Prince, qui soient contraires aux precedentes Ordonnances ou à l'equité, ils ont coustume de les modifier, et de iuger s'ils doivent estre receus par tout le Royaume, suiuant les traces et coutume de leurs predecesseurs." *Eloge de l'auctorité qu'a la cour de Parlement,* p. 409, in *Œuvres,* III.

A very important aspect of this problem concerned the authority of the Parlement as guardian of the fundamental laws of the realm. It was generally accepted among sixteenth-century jurists that any and all infringements upon fundamental law could be valid only if approved by that court whose duty it was to prevent violation of such law. Parallel with statements presented above, Simon Marion wrote that all alienations of the royal domain should be approved by the Parlement because it represented the Estates General, that body which had originally endorsed all such acts.[62] The majority of contemporary legists believed the Parlement to hold jurisdiction over infringements upon fundamental law simply in virtue of its capacity as highest court. This was the emphasis of Du Vair in 1593, when he exhorted the magistrates to declare illegal the plans of the League to depose Henry IV and to erect their candidate as king, thereby breaking the Salic Law.[63] Certain statements of the jurists concerning the alienation of royal prerogatives, however, reveal more explicitly the manner in which contemporaries regarded enregistering and remonstrance as a vital expedient for preserving fundamental law. The royal domain was defined so as to include not only the crown's landed properties and their fruits but also such royal prerogatives as the right to levy tolls and customs, the *droit d'aubain, droit de bâtardise, droit de déshérence,* and others.[64] Thus, the fundamental law prescribing the inalienability of the domain rendered illegal any transfer of those prerogatives to other persons, and it was the duty of the court either to prevent such alienations or to approve them through registration if it

[62] "Mais quand il s'agit de l'alienation de ce domaine ou de la donation de ces droits de souueraineté, les rois seuls ne se sont iamais attribué la puissance ny l'autorité d'en cognoistre; mais l'ont faict iuger par les Estats. Et parce que cest assemblée d'Estats est pénible et laborieuse, il fut trouvé plus commode d'establir et constituer le Parlement, qui tient le lieu d'Estats." Quoted in Cougny, *op. cit.,* p. 13.

[63] ". . . un seul arrest le fera, quand vous declarerez que c'est chose contraire aux loix du Royaume, que ceux qui sont assemblez n'ont point de pouvoir d'en disposer, et que vous condamnerez ceux qui feront le contraire et les jugerez coulpables, comme ils sont, d'avoir violé les loix fondamentales de l'Estat." Quoted in Radouant, *op. cit.,* p. 126.

[64] Choppin, *Traité du domaine,* pp. 11–12; Bacquet, *op. cit., passim.*

saw fit to do so. In this vein, Bacquet wrote that letters of naturalization did not require verification, but if the king desired to alienate his *droit d'aubain* over a given province, that transfer should be enregistered because it involved alienation of a domanial right.[65] Bacquet made similar statements regarding the *droit d'annoblissement* and the *droit d'amortissement*.[66] Thus it is clear that he was at one with his contemporaries concerning the exact sphere of action assigned to the king. The issuance of letters of naturalization was an undoubted royal prerogative, and as long as the king contented himself with the exercise of that right, he violated no law and could not be limited. But if he attempted to alienate a portion of that authority in virtue of which he issued such letters, he trespassed upon the fundamental law regulating his tenure of the crown. Hence, his acts in that direction might be valid only if approved by the Parlement through registration. Early in the following century, Charles Loyseau penned similar statements in connection with the king's authority to create peers. In analyzing the dignity of a peer, Loyseau concluded that it contained such great rights and prerogatives [67] that the erection of a peerage automatically involved the alienation of certain

[65] "Et combien que le droict d'Aubein soit domanial, toutesfois il n'est pas besoin, que les lettres de naturalité obtenues par vn particulier soyent verifiees en la Cour de Parlement, comme il seroit requis, si le droict d'Aubein estoit remis et quitté par le Roi en quelque prouince. Car en ce cas la verification de tel don seroit requise en la Cour de Parlement, comme contenant alienation de droict domanial. . . ." *Œuvres*, I, 114–115.

[66] *Op. cit.*, II, 107, 191.

[67] Loyseau wrote that among the great officers of the realm, only the king and the peers enjoyed dignities which combined the qualities of office, fief, and seigneury. *Cinq Livres du droit des offices* (Cologne, 1613), Liv. II, ch. II, nos. 21, 43. He listed the following as special prerogatives of the peers. They held their offices as dignities from the crown rather than from the king. They held the authority to deliberate in sessions of the Parlement and to have all cases touching their persons and dignities tried in that court. And they not only held the wide judicial authority inherent in their dignities but also a superior justice to which appeal might be made from their regular justice. This was a true *droit de ressort*, in virtue of which a peer might send annual or semi-annual commissions or *grands jours* through his territories, similar to those sent out from the Parlement under royal commission. *Traité des seigneuries* (Paris, 1608), ch. VI, nos. 7, 49, 50, 54, 55, 57, 58.

royal authorities over the lands assigned to the peer. This was the foundation of his reasoning when he wrote that it was not necessary to enregister the erection of lesser offices, but only of peerages which were offices of the crown and a portion of the Parlement. In contradistinction, the erection of other seigneuries did not involve alienation of domain nor a privilege against the laws; hence there was nothing to limit the king's making such erections in perpetuity.[68] The parallelism between Loyseau's statements and those of Bacquet is manifest: both required judicial verification of all acts involving alienation of royal prerogatives contrary to fundamental law, while both would permit all strictly legal acts of the king to pass unchallenged. These statements, appearing in the works of two major authorities on constitutional problems, indicate that many jurists believed enregistering and remonstrance by the Parlement to provide a major defense against infraction of fundamental law.

Early in the seventeenth century, La Roche-Flavin summed up the constitutional theory of enregistering and remonstrance. His method of composition was to quote verbatim from the major writers of the previous century, and he set forth his ideas concerning this question merely by repeating the earlier statements of Pasquier and Charondas.[69] This is evidence that the apparent divergence of those writers was one of emphasis alone rather than any inherent disagreement. The *civilité de la loy* was a broad conception, but the constitutionalists were clear that it included precedent as well as more abstract values

---

[68] "En quoy ne seruiroit rien de rapporter l'erection d'vne Chastellenie faicte par vn Baron, ny d'vne Baronnie faicte par vn Comte. Car c'est chose toute certaine qu'autre que le Roy ne peut faire telles érections, encor moins, que des simples iustices. Voire mesme on ne se contente pas à present d'en auoir les lettres patentes du Roy, ains encor on les fait verifier et enregistrer au Parlement: ce que pourtant ie n'estime pas estre absolument necessaire, fors és érections de Pairie, qui sont offices de la Couronne, et du corps de Parlement: mais quant à l'érection des autres seigneuries, ce n'est point vne alienation de domaine, ny priuilege contre les loix: bref rien n'empesche, à mon aduis, que le Roy seul ne puisse faire ces érections à perpetuité." *Seigneuries*, ch. IV, no. 74.

[69] *Op. cit.*, pp. 701–702. The passages which La Roche-Flavin quoted are those given above in notes 51 and 52.

when utilized by the court as its criterion in accepting or reject-
ing royal acts. The pronouncements made by the Parlement
itself were in that vein. The remonstrances which Christofle
de Thou, the First President, presented to Henry III on Janu-
ary 29, 1580, contained one of the most complete statements
made by the court regarding the import which it ascribed to its
verification of royal acts. In that document, the court insisted
that although royal enactments, the registration of which had
been forced by express command of the king, might bind the
subjects, such acts had weight simply as personal orders or
mandates from the prince. They might be revoked by him
through a simple letter or verbal order, and being his work
alone, they expired with him. Likewise, the earlier kings had
not found it strange that the magistrates, instructed in the
truth by law and reason, had refused verification of such
letters.[70] Thus the court readily admitted that all royal orders
bound the people as acts of authority, but it refused to admit
to them any additional weight through their consonance with
the law unless they conformed with established usage and the
principles of right. Royal enactments contrary to such values
existed merely as personal mandates resulting from the king's
immediate exercise of the prerogative and died with him, while
those in accord with law were binding perpetually. The refusal
of the court to verify certain acts constituted a denial of their

---

[70] "Et quant, nonobstant toutes remonstrances, le roi a voulu qu'il fût passé
outre, la Cour ayant fait ce qui était en elle, a mis sur les registres que telles
lettres étaient lues, publiées et registrées du commandement très-exprès du roi
par plusieurs fois réitéré; laquelle clause a servi pour montrer que, *Non patrum
vollontate, sed mandato et jussu regis*, elles avoient passé. Et cela signifiat que
*toutes et quantes fois qu'il plaira au roy que telles lettres ainsi publiées fussent
révoquées, cela se pouvait par une simple lettre missive, mesmes par une seule
jussion et ordonnance verballe.* Mesmes on a voulu tenir *que les lettres publiées
de mandato expresso expiraient et n'avaient lieu après le décès du roy*, par le
commandement très-exprès duquel telles publications avaient été faites, d'autant
que *morte mandantis expirat mandatum.* . . . Et n'ont les rois trouvé mauvais
ne estrange que ceux du Parlement, qui jugent et doivent juger en leurs con-
sciences, *bien informés de la vérité par la loy et par la raison*, respondissent,
en la vérification des lettres dont ils étaient poursuivis, qu'ils ne pouvaient
procéder à la vérification desdites lettres, usant de ces mots: *Non possumus,
neque debemus*." Quoted in Maugis, *op. cit.*, I, 630. Italics in the original.

consonance with accepted legal values; such was the meaning of the great body of jurists who wrote that edicts and ordinances had no weight as law unless they had been enregistered in the Parlement. As such, that procedure served as a very severe limitation upon the king's freedom of action. In its essence, this constitutional expedient took the form simply of the declaration of law by the court, and its ultimate success depended upon the monarch's respect for law. Nevertheless, contemporaries regarded it as an important and effective check of *la justice*.

The fact that enregistering and remonstrance constituted a limitation of very serious consequences in the work of government is revealed by the constant efforts of the royal administration to abolish that procedure altogether. The aim of those wishing to achieve that end was to limit the court strictly to the judging of cases between subjects and to reduce its remonstrances to mere counsel. The speech which Chancellor L'Hospital delivered before the court in 1561 contained sharp statements in this vein.[71] L'Hospital may have been justly indignant concerning the obstructions which the Parlement opposed to all conciliatory measures which might have lessened the religious strife of the period, but if his ideas had been put into practice by the central government, the court would have been deprived of a major prerogative to check royal policy. This was the aim of L'Hospital's Ordinance of Moulins, 1566, which declared royal acts to be legally valid notwithstanding remonstrances by the court and even if not published by that body. Remonstrances were to be allowed when edicts were contrary to public utility or required interpretation, but such

---

[71] "L'estat du parlement est de juger les différends des subjectz et leur administrer la justice. . . . Aultre prudence est nécessaire à faire les loyx, que à juger les differentz. . . . Les remonstrances ont tousjours esté bien reçeues par les roys et leur conseil; mais quelquefois on passe l'office de juges; et ce parlement, qui est le premier, et le plus excellent de tous les aultres, y peult mieulx regarder. . . . Quand les remonstrances d'ycelles sont bonnes, le roy et son conseil les suyvent, et changent les edictz, dont la court se deust contenter, et, en cest endroict, cognoistre son estat envers ses supérieurs." *Œuvres complètes de Michel de L'Hospital* (Paris, 1824), Duféy, ed., II, pp. 12–14.

did not diminish their legal validity. Publication was to take place immediately after reception of the ordinances, and no repeated remonstrances were to be permitted.[72] The reaction of contemporaries to this limitation, if not abolition, of the court's authority over edicts and ordinances indicates the degree to which the ordinance departed from accepted usage. The Parlement presented a vigorous resistance which lasted through long negotiations and forced the administration to agree to certain modifications of the act.[73] In his commentary upon the ordinance, Bugnyon, who was not among the strongest constitutionalists of the century, apologized for the measure on the basis of headstrong opposition of the court to royal policies;[74] but in his conclusion he returned to accepted ideas requiring the enregistering of all royal acts, with remonstrances if necessary, and cited Pasquier as his authority.[75] These expressions of opinion represented fairly the reaction of the legal profession to the effort of the government to limit the court's right of enregistering and remonstrance. Actually, the ordinance had little effect upon the use of that procedure.

The last resort of the king wishing to force the enregistering of an edict was the *lit de justice.* During this ceremony, the king appeared in the court in person and simply ordered the registration of one or more edicts. The Parlement had no grounds for resisting such procedure, in terms of its authority, because it claimed no independent source of jurisdiction and admitted that it held its authority strictly from the prince. Thus the jurists were entirely logical in maintaining, as they did without exception, that in the presence of the king, all power held by the court reverted to him, depriving the magistrates of their jurisdiction. There was no theory that the *lit de justice* constituted an invasion of the rights and prerogatives

---

[72] Isambert, *Anciennes lois françaises,* XIV, pp. 190–191.

[73] Maugis, *op. cit.,* I, pp. 615–618.

[74] Philibert Bugnyon, *Commentaire sur les ordonnances faictes par le roy Charles neufiesme en la ville de Moulins au mois de feurier, l'an mil cinq cens soixante six* (Lyon, 1567), pp. 15–17.

[75] *Commentaire,* pp. 18–19.

of the court, as was asserted by a few constitutionalists during the following century, because there was no theory that the court held an authority independent of that of the king. The most that the judges might claim under such circumstances was the right to discuss freely and to give counsel. Furthermore, the jurists were loath to recognize the king's misuse of the *lit de justice*. Throughout the century, that phrase was used merely to denote the king in his court giving justice. The presence of the monarch in his highest court continued, it would seem, to be regarded as representing the traditional function of the king as judge, and his appearances there were valued as of real benefit to his subjects.[76] In spite of the actual evolution of the *lit de justice* from an expedient for the dispensing of justice to a means of forcing the court to enregister royal edicts, the great majority of legists retained the older idea that the ceremony constituted nothing more than the king in his court giving justice according to his traditional duty.

[76] Choppin wrote: "Et pleust à Dieu que son successeur à la Couronne Henry IV eust quelque relasche des guerres qu'il a contre l'Espagnol, afin qu'il peust quelquefois venir et seoir en son lict de Iustice, en sa Cour de Parlement, pour monstrer en public à ses subjets combien il est grand amateur de la droicture et équité, et auec quelle ferueur il l'a tousiours embrassée." *Coutume de Paris*, pp. 73–74. Cf. Pasquier, *Plaidoyé*, p. 1082. Ragueau defined the *lit de justice* as "Quand le Roy est seant en son Parlement." *Indice, s. v.* "Lict de Iustice." There were countless expressions of this opinion during the century. However, there is evidence that at the close of the century the members of the Parlement were beginning to fear the *lit de justice* as a weapon for encroachment upon the sphere of the court. The old as well as the new attitudes were well expressed in a letter of Achilles de Harlay, the First President, concerning the *lit de justice* of May 21, 1597: "Ce jour le Roy est venu en sa court faire publier des édicts en sa presence: c'est la premiere entree en son parlement depuys son heureux advenement à la couronne; laquelle ie lay souvent supplié de faire et venir en son lict de justice, ce que ses predecesseurs avoient faict et voulontiers: l'asseurant que lapplaudissement de ses subiects seroit si grand quil en recevroit contantement. . . . Je n'y ay peu assister pour mon Indisposition, aiant porté daultant plus impatiemment mon absence que S. M., aiant declaré avoir grand mescontentement de la Compagnie et monsieur le Chancelier declamé contre le parlement, M. le pr. qui a porté la parolle ny les gens du roy n'ont rien relevé ny proposé les justes defences que nous avions, et se sont estendus à louer Sad. Maiesté et le remercier d'estre venu en son parlement: ce que ie n'eusse pas faict, comme il ne mest poinct advenu en semblables occurrences envers le feu Roy que dieu absolve." Quoted in Albert Chamberland, *Le Conflit de 1597 entre Henri IV et le Parlement de Paris* (Paris, 1904), pp. 50–54.

However, the increasing use of the *lit de justice* to force the enregistering of royal acts constituted a definite threat to the court's function of enregistering and remonstrance. Henry III was especially offensive in his frequent use of this procedure, which, if it was not regarded as an invasion of an independent sphere of authority, was certainly believed to violate customary usage which required judicial verification of all royal enactments. It was a major grievance against Henry's rule and was severely criticized in several anonymous pamphlets of the period as a denial of justice.[77] Likewise, both the king and the court regarded the *lit de justice*, when used in this fashion, as a very extraordinary measure, if not a flagrant abuse.[78] The

[77] "Mais quoy? nostre mal est là, que la porte est fermee à toutes remonstrances, vos Officiers des compagnies n'ont plus d'audience: ou il est question d'argent et de vostre proffit, practiquant le sordide prouerbe, *Pallet oratio auro loquente.* Cependant vous forcez les Cours et compaignies de verifier voz edits par menaces: Ou bien vous allez en personne en vostre Parlement: Et là vostre Chancelier et vos Procureurs et Aduocats, vous applaudissent trompans vous et vostre peuple, et puis vous verifiez vous mesmes vos Edicts, et non pas vostre parlement: et par apres vous dictes, et voulez qu'on dise qu'ils sont verifiez en Parlement, et qu'ils soient tenus pour tels. Voyez, ie vous prie, et iugez quelle iustice c'est là, et s'il y a pas raison de s'esbahir comment on ause vous donner ce conseil trompeur et inique, et comment vous l'approuuez et executez, pour vn profit souuent tres-esloigné de ce qu'on a imaginé. Si chacun n'auoit veu ces choses, ie ne sçay si on les voudroit croire l'oyant raconter." *Remonstrances treshumbles au roy de France et de Pologne Henry troisiesme de ce nom, par un sien fidele officier et subiect, sur les desordres et miseres de ce royaume, causes d'icelles, et moyens d'y pouruoir à la gloire de dieu et repos vniuersel de cet estat* (1588). No place of publication, pp. 76–77. This work has been attributed to Nicolas Rolland and was certainly written by a member of the royal administration. It is one of the most severe criticisms of Henry III's weakly tyrannical rule and decries vehemently his habitual violation of the constitutional rights of persons and institutions. It is a very important document in revealing the temper of many men during the period.

[78] The opening sentences of Henry III's speech in his *lit de justice* of June 16, 1586, express this attitude: "Messieurs, l'acte que je fays aujourdhuy en ce lieu m'apporte autant de deplaisir que le dernier que j'ay faict m'apporta de contentement." Quoted in Radouant, *op. cit.*, p. 208. The reaction of the legal profession to this *lit de justice* is indicated by the following memoir: "Le Roy vint en son Parlement ou il feit publier vingt et sept edicts qui tendoient tous à recouvrer deniers pour ayder à faire la guerre. Chacun fut esbahy de ce grand nombre d'edictz publiez tout à coup et par ce que plusieurs y avoyent interest, l'on n'oyoit parler d'aultre chose par toute la ville, et le lendemain, qui fut le mardy, l'on n'alla point au pallais par ce que c'estoit le jour destiné pour le lendit de messieurs, et le lendemain, qui fut le mercredi, les procureurs

jurists and members of the court did not question the right of
the king to come into his Parlement; they did not question the
reversion of their authority to him when he was present. But
they did claim that such procedure constituted a denial of the
court's function of evaluating the acts of all persons, including
the ordinances of the king, in terms of law and justice. Their
specific objection to forced registration invariably centered
upon the king's denying their freedom to discuss his acts.[79]
The restriction of royal enactments within the *civilité de la loy*
was the essence of the Parlement's sphere, and in order to do
so, freedom of discussion was indispensable. This was the
substance of the remonstrance made by Achilles de Harlay, the
First President, before Henry III during the *lit de justice* of
March 7, 1583.[80] And in his more famous speech which he

du parlement, que l'on vouloit contraindre d'achepter leurs offices par l'ung
des precedens edictz, prirent leur resolution de plus ne venir au palais, et de
faict ils cesserent d'y venir et par ce moyen toutes les plaidoyeries ont cessé et
toutes autres affaires qui despendoient desdits procureurs." Guillaume Aubert,
Mémorial juridique et historique. Extract from the *Mémoires de la société de
l'histoire de Paris et de l'Ile de France.* Paris, 1909. XXXVI, 28.

[79] Pasquier wrote: "Et nos Roys prenoient ordinairement leurs humbles remonstrances, en payment: pour cela en estoient-ils moins obeis par leurs subjets?
Au contraire, par ceste correspondance et entrelas de la puissance du Roy
avecques les trés-humbles remonstrances de ces trois Compagnies [Parlement,
chambre des comptes, cour des aides], chacun demeuroit content, nos Roys en
bien commandant, le peuple en bien obeissant. Maintenant qu'on les contrainct,
tantost par commandemens absolus, tantost par la presence du Roy, ou des
Princes de son sang, sans recueillir les voix et opinions des Juges, tout aussi-tost
se sont les affaires de nostre France desliées, et la desobéissance logée au coeur
des sujets." *Lettres,* Liv. XII, no. 2, p. 327.

[80] "*Sire*, vos predecesseurs ont fait cet honneur à vos Parlemens de regler la
balance de la Iustice par leur conseil et aduis: Et combien qu'ils peussent vser
de puissance absolue comme vous, toutesfois ils ont tousiours eu cette maxime
engrauée en leur esprit de reduire leur puissance à la ciuilité des Loix. . . . Ne
changez point les formes accoustumées, soit en la distribution de la Iustice, soit
en la publication des Edicts, lesquels bien qu'ils n'ayent force que sous vostre
authorité, toutesfois vous auez tousiours voulu qu'ils ayent esté deliberez et
resolus en vostre Parlement, que de là ils prissent leur origine, comme de l'ocean
les eaues prennent leur source, et aprés fussent publiez, non de *puissance absolue*,
que vous auez depouillé pour ce regard, mais *requerant vostre Procureur General.*
Ces deliberations, *Sire*, sont tres-necessaires pour le bien de vostre seruice, et le
soulagement de vostre peuple, parce que souuent les Edicts qui vous sont
proposez semblent de prime face fort specieux, mais ayans esté examinez, se
trouuent esloignez de vostre intention sans apparence de Iustice, et trop dom-

delivered during the *lit de justice* of June 16, 1586, de Harlay went to the length of assimilating the court's freedom of discussion with fundamental law of the land.[81] Such remained his major objection to the *lit de justice* throughout his long career.[82] From the statements contained in his speeches may be drawn the essence of the constitutionalists' theory regarding this function of the Parlement. It was an administrative body created by the king and with no authority independent of the crown, and royal edicts and ordinances drew their coercive force solely from the royal prerogative. However, only the Parlement was able to determine their consonance with justice and law. For that purpose, it necessarily enjoyed the right to evaluate royal acts free from outside interference. Edicts and ordinances became law not only on the basis of the king's

mageables à vos suiets. Et puis qu'il vous plaist tant honorer cette Compagnie que d'y venir, faites nous aussi cet honneur, et donnez ce contentement à vostre peuple de prendre conseil sur ce que voulez estre executé. . . . Ainsi ont fait vos predecesseurs venans aux Parlemens. . . . Et quand vous direz *Ie suis Roy*, ie ne repliqueray point, parce que ie sçay que sous ce mot ie me dois humilier: Mais bien m'enhardieray-ie de vous remonstrer en toute humilité, que la Verification en seroit plus fauorable, et de plus facile execution, si elle auoit esté faite par les formes ordinaires, et accoustumées en vostre Parlement, parce que l'obseruation des formes fait vne partie de la Iustice." Quoted in Théodore Godefroy, *Le Cérémonial de France* (Paris, 1619), II, pp. 598–599. It is extremely unfortunate that de Harlay, a great leader of the Parlement in a crucial period of its history, did not leave in writing his theories concerning the court's authority. In the absence of such, his speeches must suffice. This one, given in full by Godefroy, is one of the most valuable. Italics in the original.

[81] "Nous avons (Sire) de deux sortes de loix; les unes sont les loix et ordonnances des Roys, les autres sont les Ordonnances du Royaume, qui sont immuables et inviolables, par lesquelles vous estes monté au throsne Royal et à ceste couronne, qui a esté conservée par vos predecesseurs jusques à vous. . . . Mais ceste loy publique n'est pas seulle; il y en a d'autres aussi, dependantes de ceste là, qui concernent le bien public et le repos du peuple à l'endroit de son Roy et souverain Seigneur. Celle la entre autres est l'une des plus sainctes et laquelle vos predecesseurs ont le plus religieusement gardée, de ne publier loy ny ordonnance qui ne fut deliberée et consultée en ceste compagnie. Ils ont tousjours estimé que violer ceste loy estoit aussi violer celle par laquelle ils sont faicts Roys et donner occasion à leur peuple de mescroire de leur bonté." Quoted in Radouant, *op. cit.*, pp. 216–217. De Harlay meant this not in the sense that verification of edicts was in itself a portion of fundamental law but that it was an all-important means of preserving the legal bases of the state. Cf. Pasquier, above, n. 56.

[82] For other instances, see a second speech quoted in Radouant, *op. cit.*, pp. 221–228, and Maugis, *op. cit.*, I, 522, and II, 272.

puissance absolue but also through their conformity with justice and law. The king should not force registration or deny free discussion but should merely request, through his Procureur General, the acceptance of his acts by the court. The forms of administering justice were essential to justice itself, and the king could no more deny that primary function of the Parlement than he could deny his own submission to the dictates of justice and the law of the land.

Such was the greatest extent to which the constitutionalists upheld an authority of the Parlement in public affairs. The theory represented a logical elaboration of that conception of the state wherein the king and the people formed two distinct entities with legally constituted rights, and wherein the court, although existing as an agent of administration created by the king, exercised a judicial check proportionate with its function of preserving the legal bases of the whole. Enregistering and remonstrance were fundamental to its preventing the encroachment of one legal entity upon the rights of the other. If those values used as criteria by the court were held to include not only customary usage but also a higher and more abstract justice, the court nevertheless utilized the procedure for the preservation of the law of the constitution. The theory maintained the strictly traditional approach; its essential principles were those embodied in Seyssel's check of *la justice*. But in the face of increasingly autocratic government, the concept was ultimately to prove insufficient as a check upon kingship. The constitutionalists of the Fronde were forced to claim for the Parlement a sphere of authority independent of that of the king;[83] and while the spirit of their approach was closer to that of the earlier legists than was found among the royalists, it constituted nevertheless a complete break with the older conception concerning the relations of the king and his Parlement.

Concerning no other institution in the realm did constitutional theories vary as greatly as they did in regard to the

[83] E.g., Claude Joly.

Estates General. The infrequent appearances of that body and its lack of well defined authority over the matters with which it dealt rendered theories concerning its exact sphere and competence variable in the extreme. The major writers during the first half of the century — Seyssel as well as the absolutists — seem to have held that affairs of government could be carried out entirely without the Estates. Later in the century, the institution was revived, and with it appeared considerable speculation concerning its true place in the life of the state. But its lack of permanence and the prevalence of theories similar to those of Seyssel caused great divergence in the resulting theoretical treatments. This variation was in no manner proportionate with a given legist's desire to place legal limitations upon the king: witness the attitude of Pasquier who, although a major constitutionalist, regarded the assemblies of the Estates as practically worthless.[84]

It was in connection with the Estates General that the theory of the priority and ultimate supreme authority of the people in political affairs found its most readily adaptable field. The indications given above in connection with fundamental law and the Parlement indicate that that conception, while not dominant in either consideration, was far from inconsiderable. It is readily apparent that such a theory of the Estates offered a very advantageous position to the opponents of the government, and it was upheld in varying fashions by the two major factions resisting the central administration, first the Huguenots and later the League. It is not entirely accurate to accuse the apologists of the League of appropriating theories propounded earlier by the Huguenots; a more likely explanation is that the prevalence of this theory made it the logical recourse of any strong party wishing to oppose the royal government. Proof of its widespread acceptance is to be found not only in

---

[84] Pasquier wrote concerning the Estates: "C'est une vielle follie qui court en l'esprit des plus sages François, qu'il n'y a rien qui puisse tant soulager le peuple, que telles assemblees: au contraire, il n'y a rien qui luy procure plus de tort, pour une infinité de raisons." *Lettres*, Liv. IV, no. 9, p. 84.

its being upheld by writers of those two parties but also by its appearance in the works of the constitutionalists and in the sessions of the Estates themselves. Yet in the final analysis, such an approach to the position of the Estates necessitated a division of governmental authority and proved incompatible with the dominant theory of state which predicated undivided royal sovereignty.

The *Francogallia* of Francis Hotman may be regarded as the best presentation of this theory of the Estates as developed in the Huguenot pamphlet literature. The ancient constitution of France was, in Hotman's eyes, the work of the *francsgaulois* who, being enamoured of liberty and enlightened in the ways of tyrants, had instituted their king in such manner as to subject his rule not only to limitations of law but also to the will of the people expressed in the Estates General.[85] Although the Estates had originally given authority to the king, they had not divested themselves of final right over the monarch, a fact which was revealed by their election of successive rulers and deposition of offending ones. Under the first and second races of kings, these rights were regularly exercised.[86] Furthermore, the Estates were habitually consulted in regard to all great matters under all three races of rulers and well into recent times.[87] The implication — inevitable in the eyes of contemporaries for whom historical precedent was synonymous with rightful procedure — was that the Estates retained these powers over king and crown, and that non-observance of them constituted little less than the abandonment of time-honored principles.

[85] "Satis igitur demonstratum esse arbitramur, Regibus Francogaliae non immensam atque infinitam potestatem a suis ciuibus permissam fuisse: vt legibus omnibus soluti dici possint: sed eos certis legibus et pactionibus obligatos esse: quarum primam esse summam hanc fuisse ostendimus. Vt publici concilii auctoritatem sanctam inuiolatamque seruarent: eumque conuentum, quoties vtilitas Reip. postularet, sua praesentia concelebrarent. Ac leges quidem quibus Reges astrictos esse constat, permultae sunt. . . . Prima igitur haec esto: Vt ne quid quod ad statum Reip. in vniuersum pertineat, Regi sine publici Concilii auctoritate statuere liceat. . . ." Hotman, *op. cit.*, pp. 188–189.

[86] *Op. cit.*, chs. 6, 7.

[87] *Op. cit.*, ch. 21.

Although Hotman did not discuss the question in abstract terms, his insistence upon consultation of the Estates General concerning all weighty matters of government was revolutionary when coupled with his inference that final authority lay with the Estates and not with the king.[88] It is evident that his interpretation denied the absolute authority of the king in matters of government. And Hotman's statements were not far removed from later assertions of the Leaguers who sought to establish the supremacy of the people, represented in the Estates General, in order to depose a heretic king and preserve the unity of the faith. The version of this theory adopted by the League was well presented in the anonymous pamphlet *De la puissance des roys*,[89] one of the ablest and more moderate of its type. More clearly than Hotman, the author of this work recognized that the supremacy of the Estates necessitated a division of governmental authority. Although the prerogative might reside *souverainement* in the king, he held only a portion of the whole. The Estates General retained the other division, and they might reassume the entire body of public authority if the king, their creature, were false to his trust.[90] The patent

[88] In their response to the *Francogallia*, Anton Matharel and Papire Masson stressed especially the idea that the Estates held no authority whatsoever in public matters and merely gave counsel to the ruler. The great majority of writers upheld this concept, save in its application to royal taxation. Anton Matharel, *Ad Franc. Hotomani Franco-Galliam Antonii Matharelli, reginae matris a rebus procurandis primarii, responsio* (Paris, 1575), *passim*. Ronzy has shown that this work was written by Masson as well as by Matharel. Pierre Ronzy, *Un humaniste italianisant: Papire Masson* (Paris, 1924), pp. 171–175.

[89] See above, ch. III, pt. A, n. 34.

[90] "Ie dy que le Roy est le chef des Estats, les deputez sont ses conseilers, qui sont les membres desdicts Estats. Tout se doit publier au nom du Roy comme chef, et non au nom des Estats, qui ne sont que les membres. Le chef n'ordonnera toutesfois rien contre l'aduis d'iceux, puis que la teste ne doit discorder d'auec les membres. Et par ainsi la puissance estant au Roy comme chef, il reste que ce ne sera pas vne pure Aristocratie de plusieurs seigneurs en puissance egale, comme quelque Politique [*] a escrit, mais vne mesme puissance que celle du Prince et des Estats, qui reside souuerainement au Prince. Les Estats ont eu premierement ceste puissance de Dieu, puis l'ont transferré au Prince, afin d'en vser legitimement pour leur defense et protection. Tant qu'il en vsera ainsi, les membres ne se separeront point de leur teste, mais lors qu'elle ne sera plus saine, ains infectée et pourrie, en danger euident de corrompre le

departure of this author from the more generally accepted theory is strikingly illustrated by his disagreement with Bodin concerning the indivisibility of the royal prerogative, an aspect of the latter's thought in which he was at one with the great majority of legists.

The theory of the Estates General accepted by the legal profession as a whole was little concerned with the original holder of public authority. Writers frequently asserted that the right to govern had originally been given to the king by the people, but they insisted that the transfer was complete and that the Estates retained no independent authority of their own.[91] In effect, such ideas varied but slightly from those upheld by the proponents of direct divine authorization of kingship, for it mattered little in practical affairs whether the people acted as the transmitting agent or were omitted altogether in the divine grant to the king. Either interpretation divested the people of all active control over public matters. Regarding the specific functions of the Estates General, the statement of Pierre Matthieu may be accepted as representative. First, the assembly was called to make decisions concerning a disputed succession to the crown or a regency, and secondly in order to

reste du corps, le corps s'en separera: car ce n'est pas vne teste née naturellement, mais volontairement imposée. Voila comment en celle question agitée entre les Politiques, si le Roy est pardessus les Estats, ou au contraire les Estats par dessus le Roy, nous deuons dire, que lors que le Prince vse bien de sa puissance souueraine, sans commettre generale iniustice, les Estats ne sont pas par dessus luy, puis qu'ils luy ont transferé leur puissance pour en vser ainsi: seulement aux cas reseruez à la cognoissance des Estats, il prendra leur conseil et le suiura, car il ne peut ny doit rien faire sans conseil: et se sont ses vrays conseillers, et ses conseillers en tels affaires: mais lors qu'il en vse autrement, c'est sans doubte que les Estats luy sont superieurs, parce qu'ils ne luy ont donné ceste puissance pour en vser ainsi." *De la puissance des roys*, pp. 32–34. At the point indicated (*) he cites Bodin's *Republic*, Bk. I, ch. 8.

[91] "Doncques par necessité, la communauté en soymesme a puissance de la nature, de faire tout ce qu'est necessaire, ou profitable en vne assemblee bien ordonnee, a puissance de la cedder à son Roy, et en somme, ou qu'elle soit au peuple, ou au Roy, telle puissance pour sa conservation et bon gouvernement est en soy absolue, et à tout pouvoir. . . . et alors ordinairement les Estats n'ont puissaunce aucune, l'ayant auec l'election transferee au Roy." Mathieu Zampini, *Des estats de France, et de leur puissance* (Paris, 1588), pp. 21b–22a. Zampini was a third-rate writer but representative of a large body of opinion.

"reform the realm," correct abuses of officials, and to restore things to their original state. This was the fashion in which Matthieu summed up the presentation of the *cahiers*. Third, the Estates were called in order to consent to taxes.[92] All were regarded as extraordinary measures, and none required a claim by the assembly to independent authority in matters of government.

One of the most widely accepted definitions of the Estates General was that given by Chancellor L'Hospital in the opening session of the Estates of Orleans, 1560.[93] In that celebrated address, he elaborated carefully not only upon the nature of the Estates but also their purpose and functions.[94] From his statements may be constructed a complete theory of the institution. The representatives of the people were called together in order

[92] "La premiere, quand la succession et le droit de la Couronne estoit douteux et controuersé, ou qu'il estoit necessaire de pouruoir à la Regence et gouuernement du Royaume, durant la captiuité ou minorité des Rois, ou quand ils estoient troublez et perclus de l'vsage de leur entendement. La seconde quand il est question de reformer le Royaume, corriger les abus des Officiers et Magistrats par les troubles et seditions, et ramener les choses à leur entiere et premiere institution et integrité. La troisiesme pour les necessitez du Roy et du Royaume, en ces assemblees des deputez de toutes les parts du Royaume on representoit au peuple en quel estat estoient les affaires du Roy, et on l'exhortoit gracieusement aux subsides, subuentions, aydes, et ottrois: car les Rois autresfois se contentant de leur domaine pour maintenir la splendeur de la dignité Royale ils n'auoient accoustumé d'imposer et faire leuer à leur plaisir sans le consentement d'iceluy, et ne disoient pas comme disoit Loys onziesme que la France estoit vn Pré qui se tondoit trois fois l'annee." *Histoire des derniers troubles* (Lyon, 1594), Liv. III, pp. 273–275.

[93] "Il est certain que les anciens roys avoient coustume de tenir souvent les estats, qui estoient l'assemblée de tous leurs subjects, ou des députez par eulx. Et n'est aultre chose tenir les estats, que communiquer par le roy avec ses subjects, de ses plus grands affaires, prendre leur adviz et conseil, ouyr aussi leurs plaintes et doléances, et leur pourvoir, ainsi que de raison." L'Hospital, *Œuvres*, I, p. 378.

[94] "Les estats estoient assemblez pour diverses causes, et selon les occurrences et les occasions qui se présentoient, ou pour demander secours de genz et deniers, ou pour donner ordre à la justice et aux genz de guerre, ou pour les apanaiges des enfans de France . . . ou pour pourvoir au gouvernement du royaume, ou autres causes. . . .

"Il est sans doubte que le peuple reçoit grand bien desdicts estats; car il a cet heur d'approcher de la personne de son roy, de luy faire ses plaintes, luy présenter ses requestes, et obtenir les remèdes et provisions nécessaires. Aulcuns ont doubté s'il estoit utile et profitable aux Roys de tenir les estats, disant que

to communicate with their sovereign regarding certain matters of vital interest to the state. The part of the deputies in that procedure took the form of counsel enlightening the ruler concerning the condition of the land and their petition for redress. The king, as a true paternal ruler, weighed the counsel, and, by exercising that authority which he alone possessed, answered the petitions according to the dictates of his conscience. He was not bound to redress grievances but should follow counsel in all things if he were to be true to his office. Thus, the institution had little purpose but that of advising the ruler. It was he who retained all authority to make final decisions concerning those matters discussed by the assembled deputies. It is to be noted that there was a complete absence of differentiation between judicial and administrative measures in this definition of the Estates' activities. As the kingship continued to be defined in terms of adjudication, likewise matters of administration could not be dissociated from the redress of wrongs.[95]

With such an approach, the legists were entirely able to accept the statement of Henry III in opening the Estates of Blois, 1588, that the purpose of that assembly was to reform the realm through *les bons conseils des subiets, et la saincte*

le roy diminue aulcunement sa puissance, de prendre l'adviz et conseil de ses subjects, n'y estant obligé ne teneu. Et aussi, qu'il se rend trop familier à eulx; ce qui engendre mespris, et abaisse la dignité et majesté royale.

"Telle opinion me semble avoir peu de raison. Premierement, je dis qu'il n'y a acte tant digne d'ung roy, et tant propre à luy, que tenir les estats, que donner audience générale à ses subjects, et faire justice à chascung. Les roys ont été esleus, premièrement pour faire justice, et n'est acte tant royal faire la guerre, que faire justice." *Œuvres*, I, 379–380. These statements were repeated very frequently by others later in the century: Louis Le Roy quoted the passage given in note 93. *Politiques d'Aristote*, pp. 517–518. Du Haillan made L'Hospital's treatment the basis of his ideas concerning the Estates General. *Estat et succez*, pp. 89a–90a.

[95] This union of the judicial function of king and Estates with the reformation of the ills of the land appeared in another important statement concerning the place of that institution: the speech of Charles de Marillac, Archbishop of Vienne, at the Assembly of Fontainebleau early in 1560 when he urged the assembling of the Estates. The speech is preserved in Regnier de La Planche, *Histoire de l'estat de France, tant de la république que de la religion, sous le règne de François II*, pp. 352–360, included in Jean Alexandre Buchon (ed.), *Choix de chroniques et mémoires sur l'histoire de France* (Paris, 1836), XIII.

resolution du Prince.[96] Yet it was only gradually established that the *cahiers de doléances* presented by the deputies had no force other than that of counsel and petition. The Estates of 1576–77 witnessed the crucial struggle in regard to this question, for at one time or another during that assembly, the clergy, nobility, and third estate were alike determined to insure that the unanimous resolutions of the three estates should have force of law. It was proposed that each order appoint twelve members to a council of thirty-six which would oversee the translation of the *cahiers* into ordinances. It is manifest that this movement was based upon the doctrine which maintained the original and ultimate authority of the people in matters of government and recognized a division of the prerogative between king and Estates, for if the deputies held the right to transform their *doléances* into law, they must have held an authority independent of the king and sufficiently great to contravene his desires during the assemblies. This was clearly recognized during the crucial debates on the question in the third estate.[97] Had it not been for the fear of the third that the other two orders would force decisions binding all, the movement might have succeeded; but it met defeat not only through friction between the estates but also because many deputies definitely held that they had no authority in public administration. Such was the tenor of Bodin's report to the clergy regarding the decision of the third estate.[98] The fact

---

[96] *Sommaire de toutes les harangues*, p. 802.

[97] ". . . alléguant plusieurs qu'il n'etoit raisonnable que le roi l'accordât, d'autant qu'il prejudicioit à son droit de souveraineté, qui ne permit que le roi s'assujetisse à la volonté de ses sujets; d'autre part, qu'il auroit excuse de dire qu'il ne savoit pas ce qu'on lui vouloit proposer. — Les autres opinoient au contraire, et disoient que le roi ne faisoit point de tort, d'autant que ses Etats et sujets ne lui vouloient demander que choses concernant l'honneur de Dieu, le repos du royaume et le bien du service du roi; remontroient que la monarchie en étoit toujours plus élevée, quand, par le consentement commun des trois Etats, elle établissoit une ou plusieurs loix sur les trois choses susdites . . . et ici on alléguoit les exemples de la convocation et puissance des Etats du temps passé." Quoted in Picot, *op. cit.*, II, pp. 382–383.

[98] ". . . apres avoir longuement débattu, enfin avoient resolu de ne faire aucune élection des députés de leur corps, et supplier le roi de ne prendre personne pour assister au jugement ni à la conférence desdits cahiers; d'autant que

that Bodin's theory of state was of a type to preclude such action by the deputies, together with his great influence over the sessions of the third, speaks much concerning the reasons for the final failure of the proposition; it was he who persuaded the clergy and nobility to permit the royal government to answer the *cahiers* in the traditional fashion.[99] Yet the undoubted intentions of the clergy and nobility to attribute legal force to decisions of the three estates, discarded only because of the refusal of the third to cooperate, reveals widespread acceptance of a theory recognizing independent authority in the assembly.

However, the legal writers of the period were overwhelmingly emphatic in denying independent authority to the Estates in the framing of the ordinances. They regarded the *cahiers* as counsel and petition, to be considered by the king but in no manner binding. It might be advisable for the ruler to follow counsel, for the exercise of reasoned judgment by many minds brought the best decisions; but the authority to make the final choice rested with him.[100] In spite of the contrary current in the Estates of 1576–77, the assertions made in the great majority of assemblies throughout the century were in this vein. Even in that of 1576, there appeared many statements of theory resembling that of Bodin.[101] Likewise, the *cahiers* of the deputies invariably embodied this approach to the problem of the Estates. It must be concluded that the predominating theory attributed governmental authority solely and entirely to the king. Those who found a separate, extraordinary prerogative in the Estates, while receiving widespread support in certain quarters and basing their ideas upon a deep-rooted tradition, moved nevertheless against the dominant current of

les états n'avoient pas cette puissance. . . ." Jean Bodin, *Relation journalière de tout ce qui s'est negotié en l'assemblée générale des états*, in Mayer, *Des états généraux et autres assemblées nationales* (Paris, 1788), XIII, 278.

[99] Picot, *op. cit.*, II, 356–358.

[100] This was the opinion of L'Hospital and Marillac, as shown in the works cited above, and it was upheld by the great majority of jurists, many of whom followed the ideas of these two authorities.

[101] E.g., the speech of Bauffremont for the nobility.

political thought. The movement in the Estates of 1576–77 to establish the deputies' control over the framing of the ordinances was the last of its kind, and it was defeated in part by the activity of the legists themselves.

A word must be included to clarify the attitude of the jurists toward the process involved in the removal of abuses by the Estates General. If the purpose of those assemblies was to reform the realm by redressing wrongs and solving problems of general import, that procedure would have had wide implications if either party had been allowed real freedom of action. But writers held a very definite idea of reforming the realm, namely, the restoration of affairs to their original form.[102] Theorists were all but unanimous that the law ought never to be changed, and this was well illustrated in their idea of the removal of abuses by the Estates. It was a characteristic idea of the period of the Renaissance and the Reformation that the original form was the best, that the ideal was unchanging, and that, as Pierre d'Epinac said in 1577, reformation was nothing more than the removing of recent introductions and abuses and the restoring of things to their ancient and original form.[103] And if the deputies regarded their role as the reviving of ancient customs and the elimination of recent, extraneous innovations, popular opinion hoped for a revival of the state through exactly that method.[104] Contemporaries considered the action of the Estates to be reformation in the exact sense of restoration, a perfection in terms of a constant ideal. The law of the land and the values which it contained were regarded as permanent, and the reforms effected by king and deputies in concert were regarded largely as rectification along the lines of a previously conceived and unchanging plan. In spite of the great

---

[102] Cf. Matthieu, above, n. 92.

[103] See above, ch. III, pt. A, n. 104.

[104] E.g., *Remonstrance d'vn bon catholique françois, aux trois estats de France, qui s'assembleront à Blois* (1576). No place of publication. The entire work is a presentation of the traditional customs, some of which were as "recent" as five or six centuries (a fact for which he apologizes), urging the Estates to put them into effect in their pristine purity as the best means of reviving the life of the state.

changes occurring in contemporary society, men continued to regard the traditional fundamentals of the state as entirely sufficient.

The third occasion for summoning the Estates General, according to Matthieu, was to inform the people concerning the finances of the central government and to ask for taxes sufficient to care for necessary expenses, for in earlier times the king had contented himself with his domain and had not levied taxes at pleasure from the populace.[105] The implication of this statement was double: that the king ought to secure the consent of the deputies before levying extraordinary taxes, but that recent rulers had dispensed with that procedure. That this change in royal policy was deplored by many constitutionalists who felt the pinch of personal government may easily be gathered from a survey of contemporary writings, yet concerning no detail of equal importance was there greater hesitation and disagreement than in regard to consent to taxation. If, in a theory recognizing the unity of governmental authority in the sovereign, there was any sphere for independent action on the part of the Estates General, it was in consent to taxes; for taxation touched private property which formed the essence of those legal rights enjoyed by the people, in contrast to the prerogative rights of the prince. In this sense, there was an independent authority in the Estates arising from its representation of the legal rights and immunities of the populace. Constitutional thought of long standing distinguished between ordinary and extraordinary levies, the first accruing from the royal domain and customary dues, while the second included all non-customary taxes assessed upon private lands and persons according to the needs of the central government. It was the second group which might be taken only with popular consent. In spite of the fact that the royal administration had long ignored the theoretical necessity of consent to all non-

---

[105] See above, n. 92. This discussion of consent to taxation is necessarily incomplete because we have reserved two major defenders of consent, Bodin and Coquille, for treatment in later chapters.

customary taxation, many constitutionalists maintained firmly that the ordering of the state into two spheres of legal right implicitly necessitated that all such levies take the form of grants by the Estates General.[106] The best men in the royal administration accepted the fundamentals of this theory as a working approach: witness a statement of L'Hospital in his speech before the Estates of Orleans, 1560.[107] Although there was great difference of opinion concerning the exact point where the authority of the prince over private property, for meeting expenses of government, might cease and the independent right of the immediate holder might begin, the constitutionalists were all but unanimous that the king did not hold as a prerogative right the authority to collect taxes at will. It was not a part of the crown.[108] During the second half of the century, royal taxation became a burning issue. The extravagant and aimless government of Henry III aroused bitter and widespread animosity which found reaction in the promises of the Huguenots and the Leaguers to reduce levies and brought many bitter, anonymous criticisms of his rule.[109] That the Es-

---

[106] The widespread acceptance of this idea is reflected by its appearance in the works of Masuer and Ragueau, which were intended to be used as practitioners' manuals. "Item, Rex vel Princeps pro vrgenti necessitate potest subditis talliam imponere . . . hoc forte de consensu trium statuum, scilicet nobilium virorum, ecclesiasticorum, et habitantium ciuitatem et villas regni, seu patriae, quia ita est fieri consuetum." Jean Masuer, *Practica forensis* (Lyon, 1577), p. 354. "Et seroit expedient qu'aucune taille, aide, subside ou imposition nouuelle ne fust leuee sur le peuple sans l'aduis, deliberation et consentement des Estats de ce Roiaume, comme il fut arresté aux Estats tenus du temps du Roy Louis Hutin, et du Roy Philippes de Vallois, et de ce les Rois Charles 9. et Henry 3. ont esté requis aux Estats d'Orleans et de Blois: d'autant que les tailles ne sont point deuës de deuoir ordinaire, ains ont esté accordees durant la nécessité des affaires seulement." Ragueau, *Indice, s. v.* "Tailles."

[107] "Je vouldrois aussi que les roys se contentassent de leur reveneu, chargeassent le peuple le moins qu'ils pourroient, estimassent que les biens de leursdicts subjects leur appartiennent, *imperio, non dominio et proprietate.*" *Œuvres,* I, 392.

[108] Choppin, *Traité du domaine,* p. 5.

[109] "C'est chose prodigieuse de voir ce mauuais menage et qu'il faille que vous ne viuiez, et ne faciez voz affaires sinon par impositions et daces nouuelles: et que aussi promptement qu'elles sont ordonnées, aussi tost elles soient vendues et alienées, et tous les deniers du principal incontinent despendus et dissipez, tellement qu'il faut aussi soudain repenser à nouuelles daces et impositions." [Rolland], *Remonstrances,* pp. 81-82.

tates General was fully conscious of its role as defender of the property rights of the subjects appears from the fact that in every assembly during the century, the right of consent to taxation was upheld by the assembled deputies.[110] Bodin's heroic resistance to the demands of Henry III at Blois, in 1576–77, was but one phase in the struggle to establish and make effective this right of the Estates. And among theorists closely associated with the Estates, its authority over taxation was upheld until the institution ceased to exist.[111]

As the framing of royal ordinances and the redress of grievances were effected through the absolute prerogative of the ruler, likewise the assembled deputies held the right of giving or withholding their consent to extraordinary levies. Certain constitutionalists, Pasquier in particular, evinced keen perception in maintaining that it was in consent to taxation that the Estates found their surest foundation of authority and influence, and that if that function of the institution were denied, it would lose its reason for existence. Pasquier's criticism of the assemblies was not that they had no juridical basis but that they had been warped by the central administration to the point of becoming mere tools in the hands of the ruler. Instead of effecting a transaction between two independent parties, each acting in virtue of a designated sphere of authority, the institution was used simply as a means of placating the turbulent populace and of giving an appearance of legality to the arbitrary acts of the central government. In regard to the deputies' right of consent to taxes, Pasquier recalled that it was for that purpose that the institution had been created by Philip IV, as a measure to quiet a rebellion resulting from the collection of several non-customary levies.[112] In similar vein, he described the provincial estates as giving their consent to local, extraordinary taxes.[113] Such was the original and rightful order of

---

[110] Picot, *op. cit.*, IV, p. 201.

[111] E.g., Jean Savaron, *Chronologie des estats generaux* (Paris, 1615), written in connection with the Estates of 1614.

[112] *Recherches*, Liv. II, ch. 7, pp. 87–88.

[113] *Plaidoyé*, p. 1071.

things, for the early kings conducted their affairs with such prudence that the income from the royal domain sufficed to meet all ordinary expenses of government.[114] The earliest non-customary levies were accorded only for necessities of war and were limited to one year; but — and here he struck a note so frequent among legal writers — those temporary levies based upon consent were gradually transformed into permanent taxes for which consent was not needed.[115] And in addition to making permanent the tailles and aids, the central administration had undermined the deputies' power of consent by subtracting all meaning from the transaction between the assembly and the king. For reasons only too well founded, Pasquier knew that it was vain to expect significant results from the ordinances based on the *cahiers*. In the eyes of the central government, he held, the purpose of calling the deputies together was merely to effect a formal justification of new taxes; the ordinances obtained in return were invariably ineffective. The bargain was not a bargain but only a one-sided affair in which the government secured formal approval of levies and gave nothing in return.[116] Thus the Estates' vote of taxes, far from representing a free gift by persons holding independent proprietary rights and according levies in return for definite concessions by the ruler, was but a convenient means whereby the administration secured justification of its acts through an appearance of legality. For these reasons, Pasquier concluded that the assemblies of the Estates were quite worthless, either as a means of defending popular legal rights or as an agent in reordering the realm. Only the sovereign courts, by insuring the king's submission to the law, he believed capable of effecting a reformation of the state.[117] Convinced by the facts of experi-

---

[114] *Pourparler du prince*, p. 1038.

[115] *Recherches*, Liv. II, ch. 7, p. 88.

[116] The following was Pasquier's caustic comment: "En ce lieu quelques bonnes Ordonnances que l'on face pour la reformation generale, ce sont belles tapisseries, qui servent seulement de parade à une posterité. Cependant l'impost que l'on accorde au Roy, est fort bien mis à effect. . . . Invention grandement sage et politique." *Recherches*, Liv. II, ch. 7, pp. 86–87.

[117] ". . . la Couronne de France s'estoit maintenue, par l'authorité de ces

ence rather than by legal doctrine, Pasquier thus denied any value to the Estates General.

The majority of constitutionalists were unwilling to emulate Pasquier's severe condemnation of that institution. Their insistence upon the theoretical necessity of popular consent to taxation — supported by Pasquier without question — caused them to attribute a proportionate value to the assemblies. However, only a limited number of jurists published straightforward statements requiring the consent of the Estates to all non-customary levies. The fact that the king was taking taxes largely without the consent of his subjects was recognized by all, and although deplored by many, was hardly an aspect of royal policy which they felt capable of condemning outright. Although the fundamentals of their thought logically required consent to taxation, as political theorists and particularly as jurists, they found it very difficult to construct constitutional systems which flew in the face of commonly accepted practice and at the same time purported to reflect current legal usage. Many constitutionalists who wished to preserve consent to taxation solved their difficulty, however unsatisfactorily, simply by recounting the historical origins and development of relevant royal policy and leaving the conclusion to the reader. This type of treatment is to be found in the works of Choppin and Belleforest, not the best of their school but representative of a large body of opinion. In reference to the royal domain, Choppin showed that the king formerly lived of his own; but when such became insufficient, new taxes were added, consent

---

trois Ordres [Parlement, *chambre des comptes, cour des aides*] ; diminuant leur authorité, vous diminuerez d'autant la Majesté de nos Rois: que le Roy donc maintienne ces trois Cours Souveraines en leurs anciennes prerogatives; il ne faut point d'Assemblée des trois Estats, pour restablir nos affaires; elles se restabliront d'elles-mêmes. Jamais on ne fit plus d'Assemblées que l'on a fait, sous ce regne, pour la reformation de l'Estat; et jamais Estat ne fut tant difformé, que le nostre. La convocation generale des Estats tenus à Blois, l'an 1576. la particuliere, faite à S. Germain en Laye en l'an 1581. les Deputez envoyez par les Provinces, pour donner ordre aux desordres: à quoy est revenu tout cela, sinon à rien? Un trait de plume l'a effacé tout d'un coup." *Lettres,* Liv. XII, no. 8, p. 346.

being given by the Estates General.[118] But successive rulers, relying upon the argument of manifest necessity, gradually transformed those granted levies into permanent taxes, until "the common people of France are greatly oppressed with tailles, under the pretext of war, a procedure which has been followed for more than two centuries." [119] Argument from historical precedent had immense weight with men of the sixteenth century, and the implication of these statements was that the true procedure according to law required that the king secure consent to all new taxes, following the original practice. Yet in a great number of contemporary writings, that conclusion was present only through implication. This hesitance on the part of a large number of writers reveals at once the difficulties of their position and the fact that this detail of constitutional thought might be maintained only in the face of strong pressure, theoretical and practical.

The influence which factual considerations might exert upon a given theorist's political doctrine is well illustrated in the statements of Du Haillan regarding royal taxation. His treatment of that question dealt principally with the historical development of royal finances: first the domain, and later those extraordinary levies which were originally granted by the Estates General only to become permanent taxes.[120] Like the others of his school, he decried the great increase in royal levies, but he did not insist that the king revert to the original practice of securing popular consent. On the contrary, he seems to have believed that the mere fact of royal policy rendered legitimate the levies taken. Through continuous administrative procedure, those levies which had originated through popular grant had become the proprietary right of the kings.[121] Far from consti-

---

[118] *Traité du domaine*, p. 305.

[119] *Traité du domaine*, p. 306. Cf. François de Belleforest, *Les Chroniques et annalles de France des Pharamond, jusqu'au roy Charles neuvieme* (Paris, 1573), p. 183.

[120] *Estat et succez* (Paris, 1580), pp. 223b–229a. The first édition contains only a very short treatment of extraordinary taxation, merely decrying the increasing of such levies (pp. 116b–117a).

[121] "Mais la coustume est venue que ce qui estoit accordé par grace, est depuis

tuting an invasion of the legal rights and immunities of the subjects, the permanent taille and others of its type were owed to the king simply on the basis of long usage. In this fashion, Du Haillan not only incorporated the practices of the central government into his political system but gave taxation which was originally arbitrary and illegal the sanction of prescription. Such clear assertion of the final legality of force, when combined with a completely constitutional system, seems to be unique in the century, yet the fact that it was an integral part of his thought is shown by his similar interpretation in regard to fundamental law.[122] Du Haillan's utilization of force as an ultimate criterion may have been caused in part by his keen sense of political realities, but its presence in his works serves as an indication of those currents which were ultimately to undermine the older system and to substitute a theory of absolutism.

If the doctrine of prescription, when utilized after the manner of Du Haillan, was essentially foreign to the constitutional thought of the century, there were other, less drastic means whereby writers might incorporate the facts of royal policy into their juridical systems and thus eliminate the necessity of consent to taxes. The reader will recall that beginning in 1523, Francis I initiated a series of financial reforms which abolished forever the ancient system of administration based upon the division of royal income according to ordinary and extraordinary sources of revenue. In its stead, all permanent levies of either type — domain, tailles, aids, and such — were concentrated in the *trésor de l'épargne*, while uncertain or intermittent revenues were assigned to the *bureau des parties casuelles*.[123]

---

venu patrimonial et hereditaire aux Roys, et ordinaire, sans faire distinction de guerre ny de paix: et ne se sont contentez desdictes Tailles, mais peu à peu ont mis sur le dos du pauure peuple, les impositions susdictes, desquelles ayant esté abusé par les ministres des Roys, plusieurs grosses seditions s'en sont esmeües, et depuis on a mis Taille sur Taille, et Imposition sur Imposition." *Estat et succez* (Paris, 1580), p. 227a.

[122] See above, pp. 85–86.

[123] G. Jacqueton, "Le Trésor de l'épargne sous François I," *Revue historique*, LV (1894), 1–43; LVI, 1–38. E. Meynial, "Etudes sur l'histoire financière du

The effect of this reshuffling of governmental income was to render meaningless the traditional distinction between ordinary and extraordinary revenues, as far as the central administration was concerned, since both were regarded as permanent by the officials who administered them. Legal doctrines requiring popular consent to the tailles and similar levies became little more than polite fiction. Following this altered state of affairs, Charondas Le Caron discarded as useless the traditional division of royal income into ordinary and extraordinary, and classed all levies simply as certain or uncertain.[124] And the certain taxes could but be those which were regularly collected in virtue of the royal authority.[125] Such statements eliminated entirely the need for popular consent and seemed entirely logical to many writers who followed Charondas in arguing from the facts of royal policy.

Those jurists who thus attributed to the ruler the authority to collect taxes at will frequently brought strong arguments to the support of their case. It was widely accepted that the people had originally transferred to the ruler all governmental authority, and for many it seemed a logical consequence that the royal prerogative should include competence over all things necessary to public administration, including the collection of taxes.[126] From the generally accepted position recognizing undivided royal authority, it was but a step to attribute to the ruler the right to take taxes at will, simply as acts of government. The writers who upheld this interpretation attributed to the Estates General no more than the right to give advice to the king regarding his financial policy. Like the *cahiers*, the representations of the deputies concerning royal taxation had

---

XVIᵉ siècle," *Nouvelle Revue historique de droit français et étranger*, XLIV (1920), 451–515; XLV (1921), 459–583.

[124] *Pandectes*, p. 122.

[125] ". . . la certaine est celle de laquelle se faict estat certain et ordinaire, comme sont les tailles, taillons, aydes, subsides, decimes, gabelles, daces et autres impositions, qui se leuent ordinairement par l'auctorité du Roy, comme secours perpetuel de son estat et affaires du Royaume, à cause de sa puissance Royale sur ses subiects et leurs biens. . . ." *Pandectes*, p. 133. See below, p. 255.

[126] E.g., Matharel, *op. cit.*, cap. X.

weight only as counsel and petition.[127] Such a definition of the Estates' function reduced that institution to the position of a mere advisory body, incapable of decisive action in any sphere.

The chief aspect of constitutional thought tending to disrupt the traditional consent to taxation appeared in the distortion of the equally traditional doctrine concerning the mutual obligations of king and people. Crystallizing in the Middle Ages in a body of reasonably well defined rights and duties determining the position of each party, that concept had long been impregnated with a peculiar mystic value which had gathered impetus through the fifteenth century and which eventually provided the focal point of the growing national consciousness. It was around these quasi-spiritual aspects of kingship that centered the patriotism which had arisen at the close of the Hundred Years' War to crystallize about the Renaissance monarchs. The position of the king as feudal lord might be subject to tolerably exact definition through feudal custom, but the intangible qualities of kingship constituted values extremely difficult for the legists to handle and yet of definite influence upon their thought. A large number of jurists regarded the king as inherently superior to the mass of his subjects, and the thought of the most practical constitutionalist was infused with an ideal of strong paternal rule. In such as intellectual atmosphere, the idea of mutual obligations of king and people tended to lose the sharpness lent by its strictly legal details and to be dissolved into a concept in which the old, reciprocal relationships tended to take the form of obligations on the part of the people and prerogative rights on the part of the prince. With the increasing emphasis upon enlightened paternal rule, both as an ideal and as offering the only effective means of saving the state from collapse, such was the inevitable result. It is only through an appreciation of the role played by these extra-legal factors that the attitude of sixteenth-century jurists

---

[127] Matharel, *op. cit.*, cap. X; Marillac, in La Planche, *op. cit.*, p. 357, col. 2; L'Alouette, *Traité des nobles et des vertus dont ils sont formés* (Paris, 1577), p. 265b.

toward taxation and consent may be understood; legal principles alone will not suffice. The prince, as L'Hospital said, might be owner of all wealth in the state *imperio, non dominio et proprietate*, but if entire confidence were placed in a ruler animated by mystical, super-human qualities, the inevitable tendency was to blur the line of definition between the rights enjoyed by the ruler and subjects respectively and to alter the balance in favor of the king. The rights of the crown tended to overshadow and to subjugate the rights in private property. The results of such intellectual currents are clearly visible in the words of Renaud de Beaune, Archbishop of Bourges, at the Estates of 1588.[128] Similar statements appeared in the works of François de Gravelle [129] and Jean de La Madeleine [130] whose ideas reflected widespread opinion. The remarkable similarity of the fundamentals and argument in these three passages re-

---

[128] "Toute Monarchie, tout Royaume, Empire, Republique et Estat, ne se peut maintenir sans Finances et argent, c'est le ciment et liaison du bastiment, ce sont les nerfs du corps: ainsi les appele Ulpian Iurisconsulte, nerfs de la Republique, dont l'intendence et administration comme de toutes autres choses, apartient au Prince souuerain. Il y a vn commerce et correspondance mutuel entre le Prince et son peuple. Le peuple doit à son Prince l'honneur, l'obeyssance et le tribut. Et c'est ce que dict l'Apostre à qui l'honneur, l'honneur, à qui tribut, le tribut. Et reciproquement le Roy doibt vser de ses tributs et argent qu'il leue sur ses subiects comme vn bon pere de famille de son bien et substance: Il doibt estimer que s'il a l'amour et dilection de ses subiects, laquelle il peut acquerir les traictant doucement, que tout ce qui est à eux est à lui, pour s'en ayder en toutes necessitez occurentes." *Declaration ou harangue faicte aux estats tenus à Bloys* (Blois, 1589), p. 46.

[129] "Quant à ce que dit Isocrate traictant de ce propos, que les biens du peuple sont au prince, cela s'entend de l'vsage et à cause de la communion qui est entre le Roy et les subiects, lesquels comme ils sont estimez faire vn corps politic, aussi sont ils commis en biens, et comme ceux du Roy sont reputez public, ainsi ceux des particuliers Royaux, le Prince representant le public, et pouuant vser d'iceux comme vn bon pere de famille. . . . Vray est que le Prince est le dispensateur des biens publics, et peut en prendre de ceux des particuliers autant que la necessité le requiert." *Op. cit.*, pp. 202–203.

[130] "Nous ne penserions point auoir deuement traicté du debuoir et office d'vn bon Roy enuers ses subiects, si nous n'auions faict quelque particuliere despute des tailles, tribuz et subsides que les Roys preignent et leuent ordinairement sur leurs peuples, tant pour le maintien et entretenement de leur estat que pour subuenir à la necessité de leurs affaires . . . lesquels tribuz et subsides le Roy peult quand il luy plaist prendre et leuer sur son peuple: Car il est seigneur et maistre des personnes et des biens. Et ses subiects luy doibuent seruice et du bien et de la vie par tout droict diuin et humain." *Op. cit.*, p. 70a.

veals the importance of such intellectual factors in making for the elimination of consent to taxation. It is evident that an approach through exaggerated paternalism thus had the result of altering the traditional relations of ruler and people, thereby making taxation an undoubted royal right. Emphasis upon one aspect of political thought had proceeded to the point of invalidating a major tenet of the system. And when applied to the political situation obtaining in the newly formed national state, this altered concept of the mutual relationships between king and people was to have disastrous effects upon the inviolability of private property rights. It was a major factor causing the metamorphosis of the populace from vassals to subjects.

It was to be expected that the government at Paris would exploit to the full these theories making for the cessation of consent to taxes, thereby eliminating the Estates General as an institution with which it had to contend. The most important presentation of the "official" theory concerning taxation was in the book of Jean Combes.[131] In stating his position, Combes invariably utilized contemporary administrative procedure as his point of departure, yet his work makes full use of the various ideas which others had utilized to eliminate the necessity of consent. Admitting that popular assemblies frequently considered the question of royal taxation, he interpreted such procedure simply as deliberation concerning the advisability of new levies.[132] Although he thus defined the action of the Estates as counsel and not consent, he was entirely aware of the legal questions involved. There are writers, he said, who maintain that the ruler may not acquire the right to levy taxes from the people even through long usage, that prescription does not validate taxation instituted contrary to common and natural law, the guarantee of popular immunities. This position, how-

[131] Jean Combes, *Traicté des tailles, et aultres charges, et subsides, tant ordinaires que extraordinaires, qui se leuent en France* (Paris, 1576).
[132] ". . . la cause de telle conuocation est, à mon iugement, à fin d'entendre par le Roy, la commodité ou incommodité de ses subiects, sçauoir s'ils ne seront pas surchargez de payer ce qui leur sera demandé, et les ouir en leurs plaintes." *Traicté*, p. 7a.

ever, he neutralized with arguments of manifest necessity, the super-human qualities of the monarch, the ideal of strong paternal rule, and the natural obligations of the people toward their king.[133] Popular consent to taxes had no place in the established order of things, for the will of the king was law and it was the duty of the people simply to place their trust in the inherent justice and equity of his rule.[134] The interpretation was complete. The legal basis of consent to taxation had been met and defeated, in the eyes of Combes, by the ideal of quasi-divine paternal monarchy and the resulting concepts of the

[133] "Il y en a qui soustiennent, que les Roys ou Monarques ne peuuent arroger n'attribuer auoir acquis ce droit de leuer si grands deniers sur leurs subiets, nonobstant la continuation de iouissance et perception, de si longues annees qu'elle peut auoir duré: voire quand ce seroit de quatre ou cinq cens ans. Et taschent de le prouuer par raisons escrites, adioustans qu'vne telle perception et iouissance immemoriale, a esté plus tost prinse et exigee par vn Roy sur ses subiets, ou par force ou par crainte, que non pas autrement. Tellement qu'elle ne peut subsister sans tiltre et droit constitué. . . . Concluans par ce moyen qu'vn Roy ne peut onques vsurper ny prescrire contre ses subiets, ce qui est institué contre le droit commun et naturel: qu'est la franchise et immunité de tous subsides et contributions. Mais telles ou semblables allegations n'ont point de lieu en ce Royaume de France, auquel les Roys ont esté forcez par la malice du temps . . . de continuer la leuee des tailles, emprunts et autres subsides: auec certaine resolution neantmoins, qu'aussi tost que Dieu (par sa grace) aura donné quelquefois relasche à leurs guerres et autres affaires, de moderer lesdites tailles et imposts. . . . En quoy nostre souuerain Prince . . . se declare estre pere pitoiable du pais, vigilant pasteur de son peuple . . . vray ministre ou plustost la vray image de Dieu, vnique protecteur de iustice, voire la loy viuant mesmes, et finalement fidele gardien et defenseur de la Republique qui n'est autre chose qu'vn corps mystique, dont le Prince est le chef, auquel se voyant ces deux beaux sens, l'ouye et la veue, pour ensemble l'intelligence regir tout le corps, laquelle aussi en recompense, est redeuable à sondit prince selon tout droit diuin et humain, d'honneur et obeissance, tributs et subsides." *Traicté*, pp. 18a–19b.

[134] "Mais les Roys de France qui ont esté pressez et plongez en telle necessité, que de recourir à ce remede extraordinaire, y ont procedé d'vne mesuree puissance, et autorité qui appartenoit à leur dignité. Et dont le peuple François se peut à bonne cause glorifier, sur tous les autres peuples du monde, qui dependent de la volonté d'vn seul Roy. Il est certain, que le Royaume de France est absolu: tellement que là où la volonté du Roy est, c'est loy: sa parolle, arrest: et sa vie, discipline exemplaire de bien ou mal faire . . . nostre Roy est si prudent, et son Conseil si sage et aduisé, qu'ils ne permettroient que lesdits deniers fussent leuez sans necessité grande, et apres bien dispensez et administrez, pour les occurrentes affaires et necessitez du Royaume, dont certes nous deuions estre contents, et nous reposer sur la prouidence de sa Magesté." *Traicté*, pp. 12b–13a, 16b.

natural subjection of the people and their obligations to the ruler. The majority of his ideas, minus the conclusion concerning taxation, had appeared in the works of the constitutionalists themselves; thus their theory contained the seeds of its own destruction. It may be observed that had the constitutionalists stated their theory of consent and the legal bases upon which it rested as clearly as Combes presented the divergent ideas making for its disruption, the conception of the former might have had better opportunity of survival.

Such was the theory of the French constitution, in its elements and variations, as it was understood by that remarkable body of jurists who wrote from approximately 1540 to 1600. The state has been found to consist, in their eyes, of two primary portions: the social structure and the governmental authority. Each found its basis and limitations in the law of the land. The constitutionalists retained these legal fundamentals largely intact; in relation to the public authority they were as conscious of the checks of *la police* and *la justice* as was Seyssel. However, even in its strictly legal aspects there were signs of a coming breakdown of their system. The king was, through devious means, becoming master of both the customary law and the property rights of his subjects. The Parlement as a check remained essentially unchallenged; yet the basis of its influence lay in the respect of the monarch for law, and that was definitely diminishing. As for the Estates General, its most certain reason for existence, consent to taxation, was subjected to constant pressure from the government in Paris which hoped to end that limitation upon the prerogative and to abolish the institution altogether.[135] The delicate balance of rights and relations set forth by Seyssel was suffering from pressure brought by one of its component parts. And as the sovereign courts were powerless to exercise a definite control over the

---

[135] Zampini, a hanger-on at the royal court, concluded his work with the statement that since the authority to govern had been given completely to the king by the original act of the people, the Estates General was now purposeless. *Op. cit.*, pp. 139b–140a.

monarch and could act as a stabilizing force only by declaring the law to which the ruler ought to submit, adequate checks were lacking to counteract effectively the rising irreverence for the legal bases of the system. Because of these qualities, the traditional constitutionalism bade fair to succumb to an aggressive personal government and to ideas of theorists who justified its policies in advance.

CHAPTER IV

THE KING AND THE SUBJECTS

PERHAPS the most far-reaching alteration of constitutional thought in the sixteenth century was the transition from the medieval conception of the social organism as composed of a great complex of individuals of varying rights, status, and consequent position in the hierarchical structure, to a theory wherein the people, if continuing to possess unequal rights and privileges as individuals, were reduced substantially to a great body of subjects alike in their subordination to the monarch. This was the most important result of the many and devious currents of thought which caused the jurists to break from the older constitutionalism, as outlined in the previous chapter, and to substitute in its stead a theory of absolutism. The strong monarchs controlling the newly crystallized national states demanded more from their subjects than the conditioned obedience enjoyed by the earlier feudal rulers; yet the traditional relations of king and people were extremely resistant to change and could be altered by the legists in favor of the monarch only through the most guarded and painstaking effort. The facts and theories involved in this general development were extremely complex and obscure. They were very imperfectly recorded in the formal treatises written during the period and may be analyzed only by piecing together a variety of sources each quite incomplete. The ultimate effects of this change were not manifest until long after 1600, but the essential break from medieval theory and practice occurred during the century here under discussion. In this chapter we propose to treat three major portions of sixteenth-century political thought which stand forth as landmarks in the decline of the older constitutionalism and the rise of absolutism.

A. Du Moulin and the Devitalizing of the Feudal System

An important advance in this process of undermining the legal system stemming from feudal society and of substituting a national and rigidly monarchical economy is to be found in the works of Charles Du Moulin. One of the most eminent jurisconsults of the mid-sixteenth century, his influence upon the development of French law, in theory and practice, was as great, if not greater, than that of any other writer in the century. The outburst of praise which greeted the publication of his *Commentarii in consuetudines Parisienses*, in 1539, the first and one of his most important works, bears witness to the widespread acceptance of his ideas and their value relative to the current standards of jurisprudence. Recently, it has been established that the *Coutume de Paris* passed through three distinct periods of development during the sixteenth century: the redaction of 1510, the commentaries of Du Moulin, and the redaction of 1580.[1] Thus, it was of crucial importance in the history of French legal thought that Du Moulin was a major proponent of an increased royal authority and the subordination of all portions of the social organism which might interfere with strong personal government by the monarch. In the long line of Parisian legists who aided in fashioning the strong monarchy of the *ancien régime*, Du Moulin stands as one of the most important. However, his contributions, like those of so many of his colleagues, often took the form of subtle distinctions and recombination of accepted ideas, rather than that of specific innovation. A partial index to his originality may be had by comparing his most important interpretations with the parallel statements of Chasseneuz who wrote somewhat earlier in the century, and who likewise favored strong royal government.

Although of vital importance in the decline of the feudal

---

[1] Olivier-Martin, *Histoire de la coutume de la prévôté et vicomté de Paris*, I, 57–60, 110.

hierarchy as the basis of the state, the theories of Du Moulin represent but one stage in that development, for if he was inspired by ideas of omnipotent royal authority, he could not, as a responsible legist, make arbitrary changes in the law of the land. His approach to the feudal structure of society maintained its framework and yet went far toward devitalizing the entire system because his fundamental concepts were such as to increase the royal authority at the expense of the barons and to lessen the inequalities among men. His willingness to preserve the hierarchical legal structure, as such, is apparent from his treatment of property rights, the cornerstone of feudal society. In his discussion of the terms *proprietas* and *dominium*, he stated clearly the differences between the concepts of ownership in the Roman and the medieval systems,[2] and he specifically discarded the Roman in favor of the later theory recognizing a series of varying rights in the same piece of land.[3] This feudal theory of property he made the basis, in strictly traditional fashion, of his discussion of the proposition "the vassal of my vassal is not my vassal." [4] There is, he said, a complete scale of rights in property giving rise to certain legal relationships between lord, vassal, and subvassal. After subinfeudation, the lord does not retain rights in the portion of the subvassal, but rather the relations incidental to tenure are entirely between the vassal and the subvassal.[5] Thus the lord may not seize the fief of the subvassal for failure to give dues or services; such may be carried out

[2] Du Moulin perceived the difference between the absolute ownership in the Roman system and the series of rights in the same piece of land which characterized the feudal system; he showed how Baldus, in attempting to fit Roman terminology to the later system had been forced to label *dominium directum* as *proprietatem superiorem*, and *dominium utile* as *proprietatem inferiorem*. Du Moulin concluded: "Imo passim in iure [Romano], proprietas simpliciter et absolute, supponit pro dominio simpliciter et absolute sumpto." *Commentarii*, Tit. II, § LXXVIII, glo. IV, no. 12.

[3] "Sed bene quod plura iura, et plures possessiones subordinatae possunt concurrere: nec est inconueniens, quum hoc diuersis iuribus, et diuersis respectibus fiat." *Commentarii*, Tit. I, § I, glo. VI, no. 8.

[4] The subject of Tit. I, § I, glo. VI, in *Commentarii*.

[5] *Commentarii*, Tit. I, § I, glo. VI, no. 1.

only by him from whom the subvassal received his holding.[6] However, such does not deny the proprietary right of the overlord or of any other member of the feudal scale, however many there may be between the subvassal and the final overlord; each enjoys his rights according to his tenurial relations with the persons above and below him.[7] Thus, it may be said that Du Moulin retained the medieval theory of property without significant alteration. In this he was entirely in agreement with Chasseneuz and the great majority of his contemporaries. It is noteworthy that the feudist d'Argentré at a later date found no aspects of Du Moulin's treatment of this question with which to take issue and cited him as an authority on this department of customary law.[8]

Du Moulin's approach to the land law, in its relation to the royal authority, was one of strict definition and restriction. The king, in his capacity as *dominus*, was the ultimate source of all infeudated properties in the realm; all fiefs were, in the final analysis, held from him.[9] This did not mean that the king was the owner of all real property in the realm. In accordance with the fundamental concept of dual spheres of proprietary right, Du Moulin stated explicitly that the king was not the proprietor of· the realm but merely its supreme overlord and administrator.[10] As he was the original grantor of all lands, holdings forfeited by their tenants reverted eventually to him, the title moving automatically up the feudal scale; in this fashion many lands had been changed from

---

[6] *Commentarii*, Tit. I, § I, glo. VI, nos. 1, 11.

[7] *Commentarii*, Tit. I, § I, glo. VI, no. 10.

[8] D'Argentré cited this gloss of Du Moulin at least twice as authoritative on the proposition "the vassal of my vassal is not my vassal." *Op. cit.*, Tit. XVI, "Des fiefs," Art. CCCXXXI, no. 3; Tit. XV, "Des Promesses," Art. CCCIII, no. 1.

[9] ". . . in hoc felici regno Franciae omnia fere feuda emanant et dependent a supremo rege nostro tanquam ab vno crebriore principio, et fonte ad quem redeunt et terminantur per recognitiones, tam immediatas quam mediatas." *Commentarii*, Tit. I, § III, glo. IV, no. 8.

[10] ". . . non censetur dominus seu proprietarius regni sui, sed administrator." *Commentarii*, Tit. I, § III, glo. IV, no. 17. "Imo etiam supremus princeps non est fundatus in dominio rerum particularium, nec dicitur vniuersalis dominus nisi quoad iurisdictionem et protectionem." *Ibid.*, Tit. I, § LXVIII, glo. I, no. 5.

feudal holdings to alodial.[11] If Du Moulin thus adhered to the legal details of hierarchical relations of rights in land, his critical attitude toward such provisions appeared in his treatment of alodial holdings. In that type he saw his ideal of land owing no services, owned absolutely, and hence true *proprietas* [12] of a type which, if widespread, would bring all men directly under the king. In answering the crucial question concerning the assumption to be made in case of doubt concerning a piece of land claimed to be alodial, he outlined theories quite contrary to those of the feudists. As a general approach, he urged that a piece of land ought usually to be assumed to be alodial. Feudal tenure involved servitudes, a condition which ought not to be assumed unless proven.[13] True, such could not be followed as a general rule of law. Du Moulin introduced the distinction that if the disputed land lay within a feudal unit with badly defined boundaries, it was assumed to be alodial, but if it lay within one with well established limits, it should be regarded as feudal.[14] But the emphasis of his approach is indicated in his statements regarding the means of proving alodial tenure. It was not necessary that the holder show the original grant or specific title; the freedom of a piece of land might be established by simple declaration in regard to alodial holding resting upon long usage.[15] Thus, although as a legist he felt incapable of urging the unqualified assumption of the free character of land, his interpretation was as close to such as was possible in com-

[11] *Commentarii*, Tit. I, § III, glo. IV, nos. 13–15.

[12] *Commentarii*, Tit. I, § LXVIII, glo. I, no. 1.

[13] ". . . videtur iudicandum pro possessore seu pro domino particulari aut proprietario fundi, quia in dubio quaelibet res praesumitur libera. . . . Sed feudalis et censuraria conditio est quaedam seruitus. . . . Vnde nulla res praesumitur esse feudalis nisi probetur." *Commentarii*, Tit. I, § LXVIII, glo. I, no. 5. His fundamental attitude was expressed in the clause: ". . . in dubio res praesumitur alaudialis." *Ibid.*, Tit. I, § LXVIII, glo. I, no. 11. These passages were not conclusions but points in argument. However, his final conclusion was but slightly modified.

[14] *Commentarii*, Tit. I, § LXVIII, glo. I, nos. 6, 7.

[15] "Secundo autem modo accipiendo titulum dico, quod etiam simplex titulus declaratorius, vel literae verificationis nullo modo requiruntur. . . ." *Commentarii*, Tit. I, § LXVIII, glo. I, no. 13.

bination with his preserving the fundamentals of the feudal system of ownership.[16]

Du Moulin's favoring of alodial holdings was but a minor point in his interpretations tending to equalize the status of all men by reducing the nobility and raising the lower classes; it did not attack the fundamentals of the hierarchy in property rights. Much more important was his definition of the exact content of a fief. The major significance of the medieval law of property as a basis of social organization, the reader will recall, was that it not only distributed landed properties, the major form of wealth, among persons in the realm but that it also fixed the positions of the holders of those lands in the hierarchical structure. A man's tenure of land not only provided his wealth but also gave rise to his personal relationships with those above and below him in the scale and placed upon him consequent dignities or servitudes according to the nature of his holdings. The pyramidization of lands and persons together formed the primary elements of the feudal hierarchy, and in the case of a given individual, his tenure and status were largely synonymous. It was this complete fusion of personal position and proprietary right which had long caused the jurisconsults to regard a fief as combining both elements; the definition of a fief most widely quoted in the early sixteenth century, that of Raynaudus, laid especial stress upon these twin aspects.[17] Often the jurists went to the lengths of giving greater weight to the personal element than to the proprietary; such had characterized the ideas of the Bartolists, and it is found repeated in the thought of

[16] Chasseneuz, like Du Moulin, preserved the feudal hierarchy of lands but favored alodial holdings because of the unnatural character of feudal servitudes: "Ratio rationis est, quia seruitus regulariter non habet causam naturalem, sed impositam aut praescriptam . . . feudum est quaedam seruitus . . . ergo in dubio praesumitur res allodialis: et sic libera, non autem feudalis." *Consuetudines*, p. 110a.

[17] "Feudum est beneuola, libera et perpetua concessio rei immobilis vel aequipollentis, cum translatione vtilis dominii proprietate retenta, sub fidelitate et exhibitione seruitiorum." This definition, apparently originated by Raynaudus, was repeated by almost every legist early in the century.

Chasseneuz. After repeating Raynaudus' definition,[18] Chasseneuz wrote that personal servitude was owed because of the very nature of a fief.[19] Real servitudes, on the contrary, did not characterize true fiefs, and in support of this statement he quoted the dictum of Baldus that a fief adhered rather to the person than to the patrimony because the cause of the fief was rooted in the person, that is, in personal servitude.[20] It is readily apparent that Chasseneuz maintained to the fullest extent those legal interpretations which preserved the hierarchy of persons in the feudal system. Because of this fundamental emphasis, his thought set forth in full rigor a multitude of concepts stemming from the Middle Ages: the natural quality of the reverence and service owed by the vassal to his lord, parallel ideas of homage and fealty, the necessity and inherent justice of feudal dues and services, and, most important, the absence of direct personal contact between the king and the great mass of his subvassals.

It was in Du Moulin's treatment of the fief that appeared one of his most apparent deviations from his near-contemporaries and likewise one of his most important contributions. Like Chasseneuz, he approached the problem by repeating the definition given by Raynaudus,[21] but he immediately gave it a novel signification by adding that a fief might exist without the obligation of servitudes.[22] The lord, he explained, has no right in the person of the vassal but only in that thing which the vassal holds from him as a fief.[23] *Dominium utile* is not a

[18] *Consuetudines*, p. 98b.
[19] ". . . ex natura feudi debetur seruitium personale." *Consuetudines*, p. 98b.
[20] ". . . non est proprie feudum si praestetur seruitium reale. . . . Nam tale seruitium reale alterat eius naturam . . . vnde et dicit Bal. in aut. si quas ruinas, in antepe. col. C. de sacrosan. eccle. quod feudum magis cohaeret personae quam patrimonio, quia causa feudi est radicata in persona, id est in seruitio personali." *Consuetudines*, p. 99a.
[21] *Commentarii, proemium*, Tit. I, no. 114.
[22] ". . . potest subsistere feudum absque obligatione seruitiorum." *Commentarii, proemium*, Tit. I, no. 114.
[23] ". . . dominus nullum ius reale, nullam seruitutem habet in vasallum, sed tantum in rem quae ab eo tenetur in feudum." *Commentarii*, Tit. I, § I, glo. V, no. 1.

condition of servitude but simply a lesser proprietary right;[24] if any servitudes are involved in the tenure of land, they are real and not personal because the vassal is a free person.[25] It is evident that Du Moulin made a careful and far-reaching distinction between the personal and the proprietary elements in feudal tenure and defined a fief strictly in terms of the latter. Thus it happened that he expressly reversed the statement of Baldus, referred to above, and asserted in its stead that a fief adhered rather to the patrimony than to the person; its cause was rooted in the thing conferred as a fief.[26] The dictum of Baldus was true, he explained, only when applied to lands held immediately from the ruler; only in the tenure of liege fiefs was there personal subjection to the overlord, the king.[27] The attack of Du Moulin upon the feudal organization of society thus becomes evident at once: he would preserve its details complete as concerned the law of property and the tenurial rights of lords and vassals, but would remove its significance in regard to the personal status of the individuals concerned. The laws of property might necessitate a hierarchy of rights and relations, but for Du Moulin, only lands were pyramided; status and tenure were distinct and to be treated separately. Thus his legal theory of property became largely devoid of significance as a basis of social organization; to interpret the laws of feudal tenure as involving only proprietary right was to deny the hierarchy of persons

[24] ". . . dominium vtile non est seruitus, sed quaedam inferior proprietas." *Commentarii*, Tit. I, § I, glo. VI, no. 7.

[25] "Tamen huiusmodi seruitus est realis, ratione scilicet vtilis dominii rei seruientis directo: non autem personalis, quia vasallus apud nos est mere libera persona. . . ." *Commentarii*, Tit. I, § I, glo. V, no. 2.

[26] "Sed habet locum totum oppositum, quod feudum magis cohaeret patrimonio, quam personae: et eius causa est radicata in re concessa in feudum." *Commentarii*, Tit. I, § I, glo. V, no. 4.

[27] "Secus in feudis ligiis, quae a solo supremo principe recognoscuntur in feuda ligia: quia in istis proprie procedit illud dictum Bal. quod cohaereat magis personae quam patrimonio." *Commentarii*, Tit. I, § I, glo. V, no. 5. ". . . vasallus non ligius non obliget personam nisi ratione feudi, et in consequentiam rei: tamen vasallus ligius principaliter et absolute obligat et subiicit personam domino, et in consequentiam personae omnia bona." *Ibid.*, Tit. I, § I, glo. V, no. 8.

according to their holdings of land and to devitalize the entire feudal system. Du Moulin's distinction, by removing the tangible basis of personal status, weakened the relations of a given individual with those above and below him in the scale. And when to this was added his double interpretation — that all men were assumed to be free and that there was personal subjection only to the king — an effective contact had been established between the ruler and all others below him. The metamorphosis of the latter from vassals to subjects is quite apparent in Du Moulin's treatment; his interpretations were of vital influence in undermining the hierarchical structure of society and establishing a theory of state based upon the primary concepts of king and subjects. Yet if the significance of his contribution was extreme, it was not seriously challenged by the great majority of later theorists.

Having separated personal status from tenure of land, Du Moulin proceeded to interpret the position of the individual with great freedom. In this connection, his hostility to feudal services and dues becomes very significant. The ease with which he evaluated those obligations according to abstract principles of right and justice was permitted in part by the long tradition of the equitable content of the customary law, but it was facilitated by his separation of status and tenure and given its guiding criterion by his assumption of the freedom of all persons and things. We have witnessed his well-nigh complete condemnation of all feudal services and dues as *sordidae servitutes* contrary to liberty, and likewise the defense of them by d'Argentré who found them to be just and equitable because based upon customary law.[28] In treating the obligations of the lower classes to their feudal lords, Du Moulin went to the lengths of advocating the reduction of all reliefs to a single lump payment,[29] which would have

[28] See above, ch. III, pt. A, n. 74. Chasseneuz, like d'Argentré, upheld the necessity and justice of feudal dues. See *Consuetudines, passim*, but especially p. 108b, where he shows that many dues, even in addition to those specified by custom, were owed by the vassals because of their duty to support their lords.

[29] *Commentarii*, Tit. I, § XXXIII, glo. II, no. 3.

had the effect of making them purely nominal. His ideal was
the entire removal of servitudes of all kinds and the placing
of all men directly under the rule of the king, for, as he said,
"to live under a single and supreme king is greatest liberty." [30]

Du Moulin's definition of a fief, through its restricted
nature, favored the immediate rule of the king over all his
subjects through another interpretation, although this was by
no means contrary to current legal thought. In the sixteenth
century, the doctrine *fief et justice n'ont rien de commun*
had been accepted by the legists all but universally as a consequence of the indivisible royal authority of jurisdiction. In
dealing with the prerogative, Du Moulin purposely laid heavy
stress upon the supreme jurisdiction of the king as an important means of establishing direct contact between ruler
and subjects. Like his colleagues in the capital, he insisted
that the entire judicial authority in the realm was owned by
the king; no other person however high his rank or office had
a right to such authority and might not exercise the same
unless in virtue of specific concession by the ruler.[31] A fief,
by its nature, had nothing to do with jurisdiction; if the
latter were held by the tenant of the fief, it was simply an
additional right added to his holding.[32] Furthermore, as the
king held jurisdiction over the whole of the realm and all its
parts, he should rightfully have authority of immediate justice over all persons, and not merely the right of highest
judicial decision.[33] Thus all acts of jurisdiction, even those
effected by the barons, were but manifestations of the royal
prerogative. In this fashion, Du Moulin fused the authority

[30] *Commentarii*, Tit. I, § I, glo. V, no. 64.

[31] *Commentarii*, Tit. I, § III, glo. III, no. 10. This general problem has been
discussed above, ch. III, pt. B. This was likewise the interpretation given by
Chasseneuz. See above, ch. II.

[32] "Imo posset territorium esse sine iurisditione, et iurisditio sine territorio
. . . et sic licet sit addita feudo, tamen dicitur augmentum extrinsecum: imo
omnino alterius naturae et qualitatis." *Commentarii*, Tit. I, § I, glo. V, no. 44.

[33] ". . . ex quo liquet delirare eos qui putant regem solum esse fundatum in
vltimo gradu appellationis, siue (vt eorum verbo vtar) *in vltimo ressorto*:
quia imo in omni gradu et specie iurisdictionis est fundatus in toto regno et in
qualibet eius parte." *Commentarii*, Tit. I, § III, glo. III, no. 10.

of the ruler into the entire feudal scale and placed the sovereign authority directly over all men, high or low.

The constituted agents exercising jurisdiction throughout the realm included the officers in the royal administration and the feudal lords. Du Moulin did not differentiate between these two types in terms of their authority and simply regarded each as exercising a portion of the royal prerogative. However, his hostility toward baronial jurisdiction appears in innumerable statements; the elimination of the nobles' activity in such matters was among his principal objectives. Strictly, he said, only the royal justices have authority according to common law and in the name of the king. The barons hold their jurisdiction only through special law, and if they misuse it, it reverts at once to that fountain from which it was drawn.[34] The same emphasis is revealed in his statements concerning judicial procedure. Specifically, Du Moulin allowed royal justices to entertain cases between vassals of a feudal lord who held judicial rights, the only limitation upon the competence of the justices to do so being an immediate complaint by the lord or the fact that he had already begun to hear the case. The parties to the case might not refuse to have it tried before the royal officers, for the latter represented the highest authority in the land. If the case were in process of being tried, it might be taken up to the royal justices through appeal; but the transfer did not rest solely with the litigants. If for any reason it seemed that the feudal lord or his procureur were denying justice, the king's officers might evoke the case to themselves and give final judgment.[35] Du Moulin's treatment always returns to the fundamental idea that the royal justices necessarily ex-

---

[34] "Igitur solus iudex regius, est vere ordinarius et fundatus de iure communi nomine regio in omni iurisditione totius sui territorii, vt praefectus vrbis, seu praeses prouinciae Parisiensis in tota vrbe, comitatu et prouincia. Inferiores autem domini, habentes iurisditionem nomine proprio, in terris et dominiis suis, quae possident infra eandem prouinciam, sunt fundati solum de iure speciali: et sic de iure ex sola eorum neglentia iurisdictio eorum deberet reuerti ad ordinariam et regiam a qua emanauit." *Commentarii*, Tit. I, § III, glo. III, no. 11.

[35] *Commentarii*, Tit. I, § III, glo. III, no. 12.

celled by far all others.[36] For the best administration of justice, he concluded, it would be highly advantageous to reduce all feudal jurisdictions, lay and ecclesiastical, to a single type, thus removing the innumerable gradations of authority and the gross inefficiency of administration.[37] Only in that fashion might equitable justice be dispensed, as was necessary, under the supervision of the king. As he would reduce all feudal dues to a single payment, likewise he would regiment all baronial jurisdictions under the authority of the monarch.

Although Du Moulin retained the medieval law of property which gave basis to the principle "the vassal of my vassal is not my vassal," he insisted that the great exception to that rule was the king, for the monarch was immediate lord over all men.[38] Du Moulin's separation of status and tenure, we have observed, largely eliminated the feudal hierarchy of persons and opened the way for direct contact between the king and all other men in the realm, no matter how far they might be removed from him in the feudal scale. Thus Du Moulin could readily assert that throughout the entire realm not only the immediate vassals of the king but also all sub-

---

[36] ". . . iudices regios longe maiori praerogatiua caeteros antecellere." *Commentarii*, Tit. I, § III, glo. III, no. 13.

[37] "Quis enim non viderit vtile futurum reip. si barones, castellani, et reliqui temporales domini, siue seculares, siue ecclesiastici, qui ex munificentia et concessione regia habent iurisditionem omnimodam in terris et dominiis suis, vnum tantum iurisditionis gradum haberent, eumque longe melius et diligentius administrandum, quam duos aut plures, oppositum notorie cedere in nimiam dilationem, ne dicam priuationem iustitiae, cuius summus ipse rex est debitor, et in damnum et depauperationem subditorum, atque adeo collatorum regis?" *Commentarii*, Tit. I, § III, glo. III, no. 10. Chasseneuz had said the same thing earlier: "Vnde quaeri posset, an Rex Franciae qui est imperator et monarcha in regno suo, posset tollere omnes iurisdictiones inferiorum quae sunt in regno suo, et reducere ad iuris. regales: et pro certo credo quod esset maioris vtilitatis quo ad iustitiam administrandam: et populus non esset cruciatus, prout est, a multis dominis temporalibus habentibus iuris. subalternas. Et quod possit, etiam sine causa . . . quia in concernentibus iurisdictionem superioris potest princeps sine causa reuocare, et de nouo aliud facere." *Consuetudines*, p. 21a.

[38] "Et fallit illa regula vulgata quod vasallus vasalli mei, vel homo hominis mei, non est vasallus, nec homo meus, quia omnes subditi magis sunt clientes et homines Regis, quam cuiusuis alterius, etiam proprii domini." *Commentarii*, Tit. I, § I, glo. VI, no. 12.

vassals and their lords without exception were his clients and
subjects, not only in the first instance and as a superior, but
also, if necessary, to the exclusion of any lord whatsoever.[39]
In support of this all-embracing conception, Du Moulin did
not hesitate to vary the connotation carried by many details
of legal usage. His definitions of homage and fealty are valuable commentaries upon his ideas of the necessary freedom
of all men and their immediate relationship with the king.
Any oath of fealty, he said, should include the phrase *sicut
debet iurari* which was sufficient to indicate that the oath
excepted that fealty due to the king from every man. It was
not necessary to name the king, for he was understood to be
excepted in all such oaths.[40] The ceremonies necessary in
taking the oath, he held, clouded the issue by seeming to
involve personal subjection of the vassal to the lord as well
as to the king. On the contrary, the vassal was under no
personal servitude before his lord; no man should kneel in
the presence of another except when swearing before the
prince.[41] In the phrase *devoir la bouche et les mains, la bouche*
signified merely the taking of the oath in the mouth of the
vassal rather than in that of his agent, while *les mains* meant
simply that the agreement should be made with the joined
hands of the two parties.[42] His interpretation invariably

[39] "Istud illatum limito in vniuersali et supremo domino, qualis est serenis-
simus noster Francorum Rex, quia in toto regno suo, nedum sui vasalli im-
mediati sed subuasalli omnes, et eorum domini (nullo excepto) sunt clientes, et
subditi sui, nedum primario et praelatiue, sed etiam (si opus sit) exclusiue, ad
quemcunque alium dominum. . . ." *Commentarii*, Tit. I, § I, glo. VI, no. 12.
The distance which Du Moulin had travelled from the older, feudal concepts is
illustrated by comparing his statement with the following passage from Chasseneuz. ". . . homo enim hominis mei non est homo meus . . . vassallus vassalli non est primi vassallus . . . licet barones et alii comites et duces in regno
Franciae sint immediate vassalli siue homines ligii regis Franciae, tamen homines
ipsorum baronum non sunt homines ipsius regis . . . bene tamen omnes homines
baroniae qui sunt in regno, sunt sub potestate et principatu regis Franciae."
Consuetudines, pp. 38a–38b. Cf. pp. 106b, 107a.

[40] *Commentarii*, Tit. I, § III, glo. IV, no. 2.

[41] *Commentarii*, Tit. I, § III, glo. III, no. 15.

[42] *Commentarii*, Tit. I, § III, glo. III, no. 16. Chasseneuz, on the other hand,
believed that homage and fealty necessitated true personal subjection of the
vassal to his lord. *Consuetudines*, pp. 106b, 108a.

denied personal subjection, except to the monarch. Du Moulin's insistence upon the general obligation of liege homage and fealty to the king marked no essential break from doctrines long accepted, but the emphasis of his statements proclaims a desire to utilize these older forms in any fashion that might strengthen the direct contact between the king and all his subjects. His commentaries upon such ceremonies reveal in striking manner his determination to evolve from the traditional, mutual obligations animating feudal society a theory of state effecting the personal freedom of all men, with the single, all-important exception of their subjection to the king.

The final detail in Du Moulin's forging of the links between the king and all other persons in the realm was his assertion that all should serve first the king against any man according to the best interests of the state. Vassals were not bound, he said, to serve in the private wars of their lords but only in public wars undertaken for the service of the king and the common good of the realm.[43] As a general conception, he maintained that all men, whether vassals or subvassals, were required to give aid to the extent of their holdings against all others, even their immediate lords, if such were required for the defense of the realm and the needs of the state.[44] Thus Du Moulin sought to achieve that end long desired by the Parisian legists, namely, the elimination of baronial revolts and the illegality of all military activity except that undertaken by the king. In these passages there is little that lacked precedent in established law, but it will be noted that in each the emphasis is not only upon the service due to the king before all others, thus effectively eliminating the parallel and conflicting relationship between lord and vassal; the

---

[43] ". . . vasalli inferiorum suorum, non tenentur seruire patronis immediatis in bellis priuatis, sed solum in bello publico pro seruitio regis et communi bono totius reipub. Franciae." *Commentarii*, Tit. I, § III, glo. IV, no. 8. Cf. Tit. I, § I, glo. VI, nos. 13, 14.

[44] "Et tenentur Regi, tam vasalli quam subuasalli sui, secundum conditionem feudi, auxilium praestare contra omnes, etiam contra eorum dominium immediatum, si illum infidelem aut perduellionem esse contingat, pro defensione regni, vtilitate, et necessitate reip." *Commentarii*, Tit. I, § I, glo. VI, no. 12.

underlying principle and the reason advanced is the interest of the state. Throughout Du Moulin's works there is visible a conscious effort to recast the great body of accepted law in such form that it might fill the needs of the expanding national economy. It was for this reason that he sought to eliminate the remnants of feudalism and to aid in establishing that rigidly monarchical regime which alone seemed to him capable of supplying the necessary foundation of the national unit.

And finally, Du Moulin's approach to political problems was such that he could but focus the life of the nation in the king; his strongly monarchical bent caused him practically to identify the will of the ruler with the good of the state. As reasons for the general obligation of all men to serve in public wars, he placed side by side the service due to the king and the common good of the realm.[45] Likewise he stated that all subjects (*subditi*) must obey the orders of the prince, regardless of their desires; he who disobeys commits a serious offense and should be punished accordingly. If a royal order is found to be impossible of execution, the subject may petition the prince and beg for exoneration, whereupon he should receive due justice from the ruler who is *iustitiae vigor, ipsa iustitia, et lex animata*.[46] The aim and end of the interpretation were thus achieved. The direct ties between the king and his subjects had resulted in the absorption of all personal relationships into the obligation of all men to serve the king. This was combined with the concept of the king as the embodiment of justice, the major tenet of contemporary theory of enlightened monarchy. And the whole was focused so as to identify the policy and profit of the king with the good of the state. In this fashion, Du Moulin developed a complete social theory in which all men were subjects of a wise and paternal king and could but submit to his rule, not only because it resulted from his supreme and unshared authority

[45] See above, n. 43.
[46] *Commentarii*, Tit. I, § IX, glo. VI, no. 9.

over all but also because it was synonymous with the best interests of the state and represented justice itself.

Such were, in barest outline, the main aspects of the thought of Charles Du Moulin through which he attempted to evolve from the established constitution a legal theory of state based upon the concepts of king and subjects. Commensurate with its incompleteness, this treatment necessarily represents a distortion of his thought, yet the details listed are sufficient to indicate that Du Moulin elaborated a theory of great significance in the evolution of political ideas reflecting the newly formed national unit. The majority of royalists during the period contented themselves with little more than a multiplication of points of law making for the exaltation of kingship; Du Moulin was one of the few who interpreted the great mass of substantive law in that direction. The limitations imposed upon his approach through the law of the land are revealed by his maintaining the more resistant portion of it untouched, in particular the theory of property. But likewise, it was Du Moulin's manner of legal interpretation, both in method and emphasis, which was to have vital consequences upon the rights of the individual against the state. The practical consequences of those changes which he sought may have seemed, in his eyes, to bring greater liberty to the subject, and such was undoubtedly their effect in his day. But the ultimate effect of the direct subjection of all men to the monarch was to deny many rights which the populace had enjoyed under the earlier system.

B. JEAN BODIN AND HIS CONTEMPORARIES

Before we consider the constitutional thought of the greatest French legist of the century, certain features of the previous evolution of political concepts must be recapitulated. This course is necessary in order to establish the position achieved by that body of doctrine during the 1570's and to place Bodin's contribution in the setting provided by the prevailing modes of thought, thereby supplying a partial index to his originality. As an approach to the generally accepted tenets of legal doctrine, we may do no better than to outline the concepts of Charondas Le Caron who summed up and presented in completed form the major portion of traditional constitutional thought. Although at one with the great majority of his profession, Charondas' philosophical approach to legal problems caused him to draw conclusions of a more advanced character than those held by many of his colleagues. His system, while thus marking no radical break from those of his predecessors, provides an excellent panorama of those concepts which led to, and made possible, the contribution of Bodin.[1]

In his ideas concerning the sovereign authority, Charondas was entirely agreed with the majority of his contemporaries in regarding the king as the supreme magistrate who governed in conformance with law and the best interests of the state. His chief duty was the preservation of the social organism and the laws at its foundation; hence he remained for the jurists essentially a judge. Charondas merely reiterated the ideas of his predecessors when he said that the principal mark of sovereignty was the equitable and supreme administration of justice, either distributive or commutative.[2] Appended to that judicial authority and in close association with it, Charondas listed many additional marks of sovereignty: the making of laws and ordinances, the *regale,* power of life and death over subjects through justice, authority to give graces, remissions, and pardons, the assembling and dissolution of the courts and the Estates General, liege homage and fealty, the creation and abolition of offices and dignities, military affairs, letters of naturalization, legitimation, and many others.[3] It is clear that the royal authority continued to be

---

[1] Charondas wrote before and after Bodin but was apparently quite uninfluenced by the latter's works. In one passage, he referred to Bodin as "homme de singuliere et meslee doctrine." *Pandectes,* p. 94.

[2] "La principale marque de souueraineté est la droicte et souueraine administration de la Iustice, soit distributiue ou commutatiue." *Pandectes,* p. 2.

[3] *Pandectes,* pp. 63–77.

thought of as a mosaic of various rights summed up in the dispensing of justice and the authorizing of administrative activities, as far as there was any dominating interpretation.

This all-important prerogative of dispensing justice according to law Charondas defined in a broader and more inclusive manner than did many of the legal practitioners. The basis of the state was its law, and he regarded that law as including not only the customs of the land and ordinances of the prince, but also those higher tenets of equity and justice which were over all things and upon which all earthly forms of law ultimately rested. He preserved quite intact the traditional scale of legal values extending from eternal law to earthly custom; the conception permeates his treatment of all portions of the constitution and appears particularly in his statements regarding the exact manner in which human law reflected divine justice.[4] The law of the constitution, he held, was a reflection and partial embodiment of that justice which could be defined only in terms of final principles resting ultimately in the Divinity. Hence his insistence that all laws rested upon natural and divine law; thus also his statement that religion was the foundation of all laws.[5] In these interpretations, Charondas merely lent increased weight to concepts held by the great majority of contemporary legists. However, his superabundant emphasis upon the equitable content of established law created in him a disdain and even a distrust of such lowly but important types as the custom of the land,[6] thereby coloring his entire treatment of constitutional problems. Furthermore, Charondas insisted as heavily as any

---

[4] "Elle [la justice] est la vraye et droicte reigle des Lois, lesquelles ne sont establies que pour la Iustice, sçauoir pour remonstrer et publier aux hommes, ce que la Iustice diuine leur a naturellement commandé et comme seellé et engraué en leurs ames." *Pandectes*, p. 3.

[5] These interpretations appear throughout Charondas' works. *Pandectes*, pp. 1-2, 9, 11-12; *La Claire, ou de la prudence de droit* (Paris, 1554), pp. 20-21. Many of his statements represented merely a development of his idea: "La loy est reputée un don de Dieu, et qui veut qu'elle commande veut aussi . . . que Dieu regne et commande." *Questions diverses*, p. 11.

[6] See below, pp. 198-199.

other Gallican, *politique* jurist upon the miraculous, super-human qualities of kingship. The king, through his direct institution by God, he believed to be inspired by agents beyond the capacity of ordinary men. His judgments partially reflected divine truth; thus he was peculiarly fitted to set the standard for society and to guide it toward its ultimate ends.[7] Again, Charondas' ideas were subscribed to by the great majority of his contemporaries, but in his thought they received greater emphasis. Consequently, while his system marked no essential break from that upheld by others of his school, he stressed to an increased degree two major aspects of prevailing thought which tended to disrupt the traditional constitutionalism, namely, the superior value and immediate applicability of highest legal values, in preference to established custom, and the quasi-divine qualities of kingship.

These fundamental conceptions provided the basis for Charondas' placing the king over the law of the constitution. Like all jurists of his day, he placed the king below natural and divine law and the few certain fundamental laws. More difficult, he said, was the problem of the great body of civil law.[8] In examining this question, he fell back upon the nature of monarchy itself, arguing that the prince should serve as the model of conduct for all persons in the realm and should set the standard by obeying the laws over all others. Furthermore, the laws of the land were rightly consonant with natural and divine law; thus the prince should observe the lower type because he was subordinate to the higher.[9] However, Charondas did not seriously press the latter idea. His ideal of a quasi-divine monarch who served as a living law and a dispenser of justice according to highest equity, when complemented with the legal concepts listed below, caused him inevi-

[7] These ideas appeared with greatest emphasis in the various "panegyrics" which Charondas addressed to Charles IX, but they were entirely in accord with those set forth in his more formal treatises.

[8] His phrase is: "les loix establies pour l'estat public, honnestes et politiques." *Pandectes*, p. 17.

[9] *Pandectes*, pp. 17–18.

tably to regard the ruler as master of all mundane codes of law. He reviewed the various categories of such law — custom, edict, ordinance, and Roman law — and placed all under the authority of the prince to make or break.[10] Thus the several currents tending to attribute to the ruler unquestioned mastery over the legal guarantees of popular rights had triumphed completely in Charondas' system. With the exception of natural, divine, and fundamental law, the king was above all portions of the constitution.

The jurists who reasoned in this fashion concerning the royal authority invariably proceeded to the conclusion that the king stood as an active source of law. Since he was master of all civil law, it seemed to follow that such law existed upon his suffrance and necessarily drew its authority from him. And from that position, it was but a step to assert that since the royal prerogative provided the foundation of all civil law, the king held authority to add individual legal regulations at will, according to the needs of the state. This dual interpretation, recognizing at once the king's supremacy over civil law and his authority to give new laws to the populace, appeared in those statements which Charondas set forth in support of his dictum placing the ruler over such law. Like so many of his colleagues, he regarded the king as the originator of the constitution, a capacity which permitted him to add new points of law as needed.[11] When the people first instituted their ruler over themselves, had they not conferred upon him all authority of government, including the control of legal regulations within the state?[12] Even more important were Charondas' statements in regard to customary law. Custom, he said, is regarded as having legal weight because it is ac-

---

[10] ". . . tout le droict François depend de la souueraine aucthorité du Roy, qui peut casser, abroger et reuoquer tous les statuts coustumes et loix de son Royaume, concernans seulement le gouuernement humain." *Pandectes*, p. 101.

[11] See his *Livre au roy nostre souverain prince et seigneur*, in *Sommaire de toutes les harangues*, livre 12.

[12] Charondas gave the usual statements on this question and cited as precedent the Roman *lex regia. Pandectes*, p. 11.

cepted by the people at large, but strictly it is not law because it was not introduced by the sovereign authority.[13] The redaction of customary law should be carried out under the authority of the king, not only because he alone holds the right to assemble the local estates but also because it is his prerogative to give law to the people.[14] Continuing, Charondas differentiated sharply between the qualities of law and custom. Law was the work of the prince and necessarily equitable; it was founded upon justice and reason. Custom, on the other hand, was but fortuitous usage, often unjust and arbitrary, and thus lacked those two elements vital to true law, namely, consonance with justice and a basis in the authority of the ruler.[15] It is evident that Charondas believed the king to be the sole active source of civil law and that he approached very close to a theory of legislative sovereignty.

However, in the thought of Charondas and all of his stamp, the king remained primarily a judge. Through elaboration of certain generally accepted concepts, Charondas had reached the point of attributing to the ruler the twin prerogatives of

[13] "La coustume, encores qu'elle ait force de loy, parce qu'elle est gardée comme loy par ceux qui en vsent, et longuement en ont vsé, n'est toutesfois proprement loy: mais à cause du long consentement que le peuple a donné aux choses introduites par coustume, elles sont obseruees, comme si elles auoient esté ordonnees et publiees par le commandement du souuerain, soit Monarque, le peuple ou un corps de seigneurs. . . ." *Pandectes*, p. 167.

[14] "Dauantage la redaction des coustumes se doit faire par l'auctorité du Roy suiuant ses lettres patentes, et par Commissaires deputez et choysis des Cours souueraines. Car il n'appartient aux estats d'vn pays d'assembler sans la permission du souuerain: et en France le Roy seul a puissance de donner loix à ses suiects, ou leur octroyer d'en faire accorder entre eux." *Pandectes*, p. 169. This idea was expressed even more emphatically in an earlier work, *La Claire*, pp. 139–145.

[15] ". . . la loy est vne ordonnance generalle, laquelle à la descrire proprement, si elle n'est iuste, et produite de la droicte raison, ne peut estre telle reputee: mais la coustume est vne commune observance, qui s'est coullee doucement par vn taisible consentement de ceux qui en ont vsé, et quelquefois plustost pour le profit ou commodité des plus puissans, que par iuste et droite raison: et souuent n'est generale, ains particuliere du pays, où elle a pris force et authorité: tellement que contre l'opinion de Dion, je compare la loy au Roy, et la coustume au tyran . . . le Roy gouverne de pleine puissance, non par force, ains par les loix. La coustume n'a souvent pour raison que l'vsage: mais la loy est fondee en raison naturelle ou civile. . . ." *Pandectes*, p. 167.

giving law and of judging according to it; but for him the royal authority of legislation continued subordinate to that of adjudication. As we have noted, Charondas believed that the king dispensed justice according to the highest ideals of right and equity, the judicial function thereby serving as a very important means of establishing those values in human society. The making of laws was for him but another procedure for accomplishing the same end. The giving of justice, he repeated, is the first mark of sovereignty, and from it arises the authority of the king to establish laws.[16] Thus the laws of the prince necessarily embody and make manifest to the people that higher justice which is over all men.[17] Charondas might define a civil law simply as a command of the sovereign power,[18] but he insisted that the law thus created must take its place in the unbroken scale of values which included higher concepts. In very medieval fashion, he defined human law as an interpretation of, or an addition to, divine and natural law; human law in contradiction to those higher types was impossible.[19] Thus it is clear that Charondas regarded the making of law by the king largely as an aspect of his ideal jurisdiction according to highest equity. Legislation and

[16] ". . . la Iustice est la premiere marque de souueraineté: car d'icelle depend la puissance de faire Loix et les casser pour le bien et salut de la Republique, qui contient la conseruation de l'estat du souuerain, et la tranquilité des subjects. . . ." *Pandectes*, p. 3.

[17] ". . . ce Royaume (par la grace de Dieu) est le premier et mieux doué de toutes choses que nuls autres: aussi a il communement esté de tout temps mieux regi et gouuerné, que nulle autre Monarchie, en iustice: laquelle y a esté iustement et esgallement administrée à tous sans acception de personne, mesmes en tant qu'il a peu toucher les desirs, vouloirs, et affections des Roys nos predecesseurs, lesquels en eux voulant acquitter enuers Dieu et leurs subiects ont fait et estably plusieurs bonnes, sainctes, iustes et tres-vtiles constitutions et ordonnances, pour à l'honneur de Dieu faire rendre et administrer deue et vraye Iustice au peuple et subiects qu'il leur a commis." *Pandectes*, p. 9. This interpretation is borne out by the general treatment given in ch. IV, "Des Loix et ordonnances." Likewise: ". . . la loy est l'œuvre de la Iustice, et par les loix sainctement ordonnées Iustice se fait cognoistre." *Panegyrique ou oraison de louange, au roy Charles VIIII. nostre souuerain seigneur* (Paris, 1566), no pagination.

[18] ". . . vne ordonnance faite par celuy ou ceux qui ont puissance souueraine en la Republique." *Pandectes*, p. 11.

[19] *Pandectes*, pp. 23–26.

adjudication were simply different means of applying certain fixed values, and the preservative nature of that dual function rendered it inevitable that those theorists who interpreted the royal authority in such fashion should regard the king as primarily a judge. This was the type of legislation, if we may use the word, which was upheld by those legists who were content to develop concepts of long standing. Together, the Romanists and the constitutionalists of Charondas' stamp pushed the prevailing idea of kingship to those limits consonant with the essentials at its basis. They made long strides toward the creation of a theory of legislative sovereignty, but the fundamental nature of their thought was such that they were unwilling to break from the older conception of the king as judge. In spite of much significant evolution of legal doctrine, there was still needed a different approach to permit the formulation of a theory of sovereignty in which the king was primarily a maker of law.

It is readily apparent that the traditional theory in which the king was essentially a judge rested fundamentally upon a concept of the state as a permanent, unchanging entity. The duty of the king as judge was primarily that of preserving the extant legal system and the ideals which it embodied. In his dispensing of justice, he maintained and applied the law of the constitution which was regarded as permanent. If the king was placed over that law by many theorists, they nevertheless insisted that the law was the basis of the state and that the king should preserve it as such. Furthermore, the ideal which the law embodied, however imperfectly, remained fixed, and in relation to this aspect of the theory, the greatest freedom that could be permitted to the king in changing the law was reformation in terms of that ideal. Thus, the state and the law upon which it rested were regarded as necessarily permanent, and the institution of kingship was primarily for the purpose of maintaining the constitution as it stood. Such was the attitude of all schools of legal thought examined thus far. We have observed the heavy and unani-

mous insistence that the law of the land should be preserved
at all costs, the slightest innovation being rooted out because
it was dangerous to the continued existence of the legal system.[20] It was widely accepted that the primary function of
the institutions of government was the better ordering of the
state in terms of fixed laws. The Estates General was called
in order to reform the realm in accordance with the original
law of the land which the king was often requested to enforce
in its pristine purity.[21] Quite similar was the work of the
Parlement. As a court, it was interested primarily in the
preservation of accepted law; it even followed that criterion
in judging royal acts. The lengthy speeches made at the
opening sessions of the court invariably interpreted its function as the preservation of the law of the land, both in terms
of its specific content and the more general concepts of justice and equity.[22] And it is certain that many contemporaries regarded the work of the court as a major bulwark
against innovations which seemed to threaten the life of the
state.[23]

Perhaps the aspect of sixteenth-century thought which revealed most clearly the dominant concept of the state as
essentially unchanging was the contemporary idea concerning
the value of historical study. During the period there appeared
in France for the first time historians worthy of the name,
and it was invariably insisted by those writers that the teachings of history were to be explored not only because of their
cultural value but also because they provided ready solutions
for present problems. Since the constitution was regarded as
remaining the same throughout the centuries, those remedies
which had proved their value in meeting past difficulties were

---

[20] See above, pp. 41–42, 72–73, 119–120.

[21] See above, pp. 164–165.

[22] E.g., *Premier recueil des publicques actions de l'éloquence françoise contenant trente une remonstrances faictes aux ouvertures des parlements et autres
cours de ce royaume* (Lyon, 1604); *Harangues et actions publiques des plus
rares esprits de nostre temps* (Paris, 1609).

[23] E.g., *Remonstrance aus parlemens de France, touchant l'observation de la
paix* (1581). No place of publication.

held to retain their efficacy undiminished. Such was the approach of the entire body of writers who investigated the past history of the state; often they wrote for the specific purpose of instructing their prince concerning the best manner of government.[24] This intellectual characteristic of the period accounts for the frequent literary treatment of contemporary constitutional problems in terms of past regulations; consent to taxation was often upheld, as we have seen, by showing long historical usage rather than through the more direct course of logical reasoning from extant law. Historical precedent had immense weight in the eyes of men holding this attitude, for since the law was regarded as unchanging, to establish with certainty a given usage enjoying long acceptance in the past meant to give it validity in the present system. This explains the great influence of such a book as Hotman's *Francogallia* and caused writers of such different stamp as Budé and Du Haillan to seek elaboration of, and justification for, their conceptions in the past history of the state. True, there appeared during the century many new factors making for a more closely articulated historical sense. The humanistic school of Roman law, best represented by Cujas and his followers, placed that body of law strictly in its historical setting and thus tended to dissociate it from contemporary legal practice. The innumerable discoveries and broadened intellectual outlook of the age undoubtedly caused men to become increasingly conscious of historical and geographical variation. But these and other factors, which were eventually to give rise to a concept of state very different from the static idea inherited from the Middle Ages, were slow in influencing the ideas of historians concerning the practical value of their labors. The most important book on historical method produced at the close of the century, that of

[24] From a host of possible examples illustrating this approach, we may cite: Seyssel, *Appian Alexandrin*, dedicatory epistle; Budé, "De l'institution du prince," 15ʳ, 114ᵛ; Du Tillet, *Recueil des roys*, dedicatory epistle; Le Roy, *Politiques d'Aristote*, p. 368; Jean de Serres, *Inventaire general de l'histoire de France* (Paris, 1597), Introduction.

La Popeliniere,[25] upheld the idea that history, as an accurate representation of previous human life and experience, provided teachings which were to be regarded as social truths. Certain passages in his work show the marks of increasing doubt concerning the validity of this interpretation,[26] but he concluded with the orthodox statement that the principal aim of the historian was to provide lessons of practical value in serving the needs of the state.[27] Although the historians of the period had made great advances in the study of the past through written documents, they lacked almost entirely any sense of historical relativity such as was developed by their followers in subsequent centuries. That was because their idea of the value of historical study was but one portion of an all-embracing attitude in which the state and the law at its basis were necessarily unchanging.

[25] La Popeliniere, Lancelot Voisin, sieur de, *L'Histoire des histoires* (Paris, 1599).

[26] La Popeliniere's fundamental attitude, together with his doubts concerning its validity, appear in the following passage: "Veu donc que l'estat, gardien de nos biens, vies et honneurs est la plus louable et necessaire institution, qui fut oncques introduite, pour l'entretien de cette societé humaine: Et que l'histoire est la vraye et seule representation d'iceluy: Si quelqu'vn s'esmerueille, qu'vn seul peuple ne s'en est moyenné vne digne de ses actions: à fin que si precieux Thresor, et tant digne conserue de la memoire du passé, luy fut pour reigle asseuree à tout le present et aduenir: doit considerer, que tous les autheurs Grecs et Latins, ont attribué les principales occasions, non seulement de ce, mais de toutes les fautes que les hommes font à conceuoir et manier les choses humaines: tant à la difficulté des choses, qu'à la foiblesse des hommes. Qui sont, à bien dire, vrayes: encor qu'on en peut adiouster d'autres. Mais pour la difficulté, elle se peut iuger en la multitude, grandeur, varieté, et incertitude des choses humaines. Les Philosophes, les politics, et autres, qui comme plus pratics, ont les mieux remarqué le nuageux et si fort embrouillé cours de la Nature: peuvent magistralement enseigner combien il est mal-aisé de conceuoir, descouurir, et apprendre à autruy, les forces et qualitez des choses humaines." La Popeliniere, *L'Idee de l'histoire accomplie*, p. 193, printed with *L'Histoire des histoires*.

[27] "Les bons Historiens sont aussi remarquez: si rassemblans en vn tous les auantages qu'ils peuuent recueillir de l'Histoire ils rapportent tous les propos, actions et Conseils des hommes à la forme et conduite d'vn estat bien policé. . . . Car outre ce que le principal but de l'Histoire, qui est vne action publique, est de tendre à bien former et entretenir l'Estat sous lequel elle est dressee. La fin seconde de l'Historien, doit buter au bien des particuliers sur lesquels comme vne douce pluie descendent les graces qu'il iette sur le public." *L'Idee de l'histoire accomplie*, p. 324.

However, as the century progressed and the diverse currents — economic, social, and religious — causing rapid and increasingly apparent evolution of the social structure became more and more pressing upon the minds of the political theorists, they began vaguely to realize that the traditional law of the constitution was impossible to maintain and that willynilly something else was taking its place. This conviction appeared primarily, as might be expected, in the minds of men who were forced to deal with these new problems through their work in the royal administration; and of their number, Chancellor L'Hospital was by far the greatest of the period. Faced with the growing dissention between social factions and with the all-important break in the religious unity of the state, he was one of the first to express in precise form ideas permitting definite change in the law to account for the new situation. While continuing to hold that the king was essentially a judge and that the law of the land provided at once the basis and the ideal of political and social life, he insisted that it was occasionally necessary to make adjustments in that law to accord with actual conditions, in the same manner as a mariner changes the set of the sails according to the variations of the wind.[28] A major aspect of his program of governmental reform included the reevaluation of much accepted law, both in terms of ultimate principles and the changed condition of the state.[29] Even more precise was his

[28] "Quand ilz considéreront que les édictz sont faictz sur choses incertaines, journellement ils ne trouveront estrange que l'on les change selon le temps, à l'exemple du gouverneur d'un navire, lequel calle la voile et la tourne çà et là, selon que le vent est: aussy les loyx humaines et politiques ne peulvent tousjours demeurer en ung estat; mais les fault changer quelquefois, selon que le peuple est." *Harangue au parlement de la part du roy . . . touchant les edicts faicts par le roy sur le faict de la religion,* [June 18, 1561], in *Œuvres,* I, 424.

[29] ". . . aussy semble il nécessaire d'examiner aujourd'huy les loyx et ordonnances de ce royaulme, qui est nostre droict françois, soubs la reigle duquel nous vivons, rejetter les superfleues, retrancher ce qui se trouvera inutile et hors d'usaige, restablir et faire revivre celles qui, par nostre nonchalance ou par nos dissolutions et maulvaises moeurs, ne sont plus en practique, bien qu'elles soient pleines d'esquité et de justice; abroger vertueusement celles que la corruption du siècle a introduictes; conserver les bonnes, utiles et esquitables. . . ." *Traité de la réformation de la justice,* in *Œuvres,* V, 101.

statement made before the Estates General at Saint-Germain-
en-Laye in 1561 when he said that it was not only necessary
to consider whether the law was just but also whether it was
propitious for the time and the men for whom it was made.[30]
His approach marked a definite break from that of the majority of legists who continued to assert that it was sufficient
to maintain intact the law of the constitution, with the possible
exception of slight reformation in terms of a fixed ideal;
L'Hospital definitely advocated changing the law as far as
necessary in order to take account of the new situation. His
attitude arose from a conviction that the seriousness of contemporary social upheavals precluded any return to the traditional order of things. The religious question was without
doubt the greatest with which he was forced to treat; his
desired solution of that problem through toleration is well
known. And as his acceptance of two religions grew from a
willingness to regard as irreparable the break in the traditional religious unity of the state, thus also his equanimity
before the necessary sacrificing of portions of accepted law
arose from the same attitude in secular affairs. Religious
unity and the traditional law of the constitution were part and
parcel of the same thing; and when the *politiques* accepted
the loss of the former, it was but logical for them to permit
correlative changes in the latter. Their attitude had great
importance not only regarding theories of the religious nature
of the state but also concerning the increasingly apparent
evolution of the secular constitution.

As the best means of achieving the necessary rectification
of the law, L'Hospital could but advocate an extension of the
royal prerogative permitting the king to bring about needed
changes through acts of authority. Contemporary political
concepts which attributed to the sovereign all right in matters

---

[30] "Il ne faut considerer seulement si la loy est juste en soy, mais si elle est
convenable au temps et aux hommes pour lesquelz elle est faicte." *Harangue à
l'assemblée des états-généraux, à Saint-Germain-en-Laye,* [August 26, 1561], in
Œuvres, I, 450–451.

of government left him no alternative. It was for this reason that L'Hospital laid especial stress upon the authority of the king to give law to his subjects; his statements show that this function was intimately allied, in his thought, with the preservation of order in the state.[31] Yet it should be noted that L'Hospital did not outline any theory of legislative sovereignty; in his thought the king remained primarily a judge, and legislation was subordinate to adjudication.[32] His insistence upon the authority of the king to give law to his subjects was simply an effort to find in the royal prerogative an authority sufficient to stem the tide which was rapidly assuming fearful proportions. Thus his thought reveals with extraordinary clarity the manner in which the social upheavals and progressive changes in accepted law were forcing thinkers to alter their older modes of thought and to feel their way toward the later theory of legislative sovereignty.

If L'Hospital was painfully conscious of the rapid changes going on about him and was forced to alter his political ideas accordingly, such was increasingly the case among the professional jurists. Even the more traditionally minded among that group were becoming increasingly sensible of the unmistakable changes in accepted law, but their approach to political problems through the established and theoretically static constitution created in them such a conservative frame of mind that they frequently confined themselves to recording and deploring the specific breaks from former usage. This position is well illustrated by the thought of Du Haillan; the changes which he perceived to be taking place in the law of the land may easily be established by comparing the successive editions

[31] "Rien n'est plus honorable et magnifique à ung Roy que de donner la loy à ses subjects sans diminution de ses debvoirs; rien n'est plus louable à ung saige prince qui cognoist que les fureurs et dissensions civiles sont la mort des grands estats, d'y appliquer, par sa prudence, le remède convenable, et si dextrement manier les esprits qu'il guérisse leurs playes, et saulve de ruyne, par ce moyen, ses subjects et sa seigneurie." *Mémoire addressé à Charles IX et à Catherine de Medicis*, in *Œuvres*, II, 202.

[32] This appears throughout his works. For a detailed statement, see his *Traité de la réformation de la justice*, in *Œuvres*, IV, p. 38.

of his *Estat et succez*.[33] When, during the late 1560's, he
wrote that portion of the book outlining the French constitution,[34] he did not hesitate to borrow the majority of his doctrines from Claude de Seyssel. Although he admitted that
much in Seyssel's system, the traditional system, had been
corrupted and lost permanently during the intervening half-
century,[35] such did not prevent his quoting at length from
Seyssel's works and modeling the structure of his treatment
after that of his predecessor.[36] However, the turbulence of
the times soon forced Du Haillan to recognize further and
rapidly mounting changes in constitutional organization and
practice. The additions which he felt obliged to insert into the
edition of his book which appeared in 1580 reveal his perception of several specific breaks from older usage,[37] while in
that of 1595, he did not hesitate to admit that great portions
of the traditional constitution had fallen into discard.[38] Yet

[33] The editions which we have used are those of Paris, 1571 (identical with
the first edition of 1570), Paris, 1580, and Paris, 1595.

[34] Book II in the first edition; book III in subsequent editions.

[35] "Qui sont les mesmes mots de Claude de Seissel en son liure de la Monarchie
de France, lesquels (bien qu'ils sentent l'antiquité) nous n'auons voulu changer:
toutesfois on voit bien que ce bel ordre institué en nostre Monarchie, est corrompu, et que nous ne retenons que l'ombre de ces belles premieres constitutions." *Estat et succez*, p. 82a.

[36] Du Haillan appropriated the section on constitutional matters in Seyssel's
introduction to his translation of Appianus and made it the working outline of
his book on the French constitution, simply using Seyssel's statements as topic
sentences and expanding each category with relevant material.

[37] After stating that justice was available to all who sought it, he added:
"La licence de ce siecle est si grande que cest article se trouue auiourd'huy sans
effect en plusieurs endroicts de la France." (p. 156a) After showing that the
sovereign courts checked the alienation of the royal domain, he added:
". . . mais auiourd'huy ceste craincte est ostee, car chascun se fourre à acheter
le Domaine, et à se faire nommer le Conte, ou le Baron de la terre du Domaine
par luy achetee. Ce qui attend vne tresnecessaire reformation." (p. 158b) After
outlining the system of the royal councils, he added: "Mais la façon des conseils
change souuent, comme on l'a veu souuent changer depuis vingt cinq ou trente
ans, ayans esté augmentez de Secretaires de finances, et de Greffiers dudict
Conseil, et changez en façon et en cognoissance des affaires." (p. 161a)

[38] After discussing the grandeur and preeminence of the nobility, he added:
"Cela estoit jadis, mais depuis nostre Noblesse s'est merueilleusement licenciee.
Le temps a apporté ceste licence, vn autre temps la luy ostera, et la fera reuenir
à ce qu'elle estoit." (p. 173b) After showing that the king governed with the
counsel of his officers, he added: "Nous parlons de la forme de viure et de

throughout his writings, he offered no solution save to return to the older forms.

In contrast with Du Haillan's uncompromising conservatism, there appeared during the mid-sixteenth century several legists, usually of a more speculative bent, who not only perceived contemporary changes in political life but also attempted to frame a corresponding theory of state. Among those endeavoring to deal with the legal aspects of the changing situation, Charondas stands as one of the most important. He was entirely orthodox in regarding the law as the basis of the state, and like his contemporaries he insisted that for the preservation of the social organism the law ought to be maintained intact.[39] But even in his early works the newer current made itself felt. In very definite terms he stated that changed circumstances necessitated corresponding changes in the law.[40] As L'Hospital in his work of administration had realized that it was impossible to maintain the law without change, likewise Charondas among theorists had come to the same conclusion. In the thought of both, this conviction was a vital factor in causing them to attribute to the king the power to make law. We have observed the manner in which the various intellectual currents causing theorists to regard the king as a giver of law were brought together in Charondas' thought.[41] His idea of the law-giving function of the monarch

---

regner de nos anciens Roys. Elle a esté bien changée. Leurs successeurs ont voulu faire beaucoup de choses sans conseil, et pour auoir voulu trop faire les Roys, ils se sont trouuez en tel Estat qu'ils ne l'estoyent plus." (p. 176b) After his statement that the king willingly submitted his edicts and ordinances to the approval of the Parlement (the passage which he borrowed from Pasquier), he added: "Nous parlons du temps passé, car cela est changé." (pp. 182b–183a) After discussing the Estates General and their benefit to the people, he added: "Ouy iadis, mais ces derniers Estats ont esté la ruine de la France." (p. 186a) And as a commentary upon the central judicial system, he did not hesitate to add: "Tout cela a changé de forme, comme toutes autres bonnes constitutions de la France." (p. 188a)   [39] *Pandectes*, p. 16.

[40] ". . . la dissemblance et diuersité des actions humaines et inconstance des choses ne peut porter vne seule constitution et tousiours semblable ains desire que selon les diuerses circonstances la loi pareillement soit changée." Charondas, *Les Dialogues* (Paris, 1556), p. 22. Cf. *Pandectes*, p. 7.

[41] See above, pp. 198–199.

allowed little more than the promulgation of new regulations strictly in conformity with natural and divine law, but Charondas believed that such procedure allowed the ruler sufficient latitude of discretion to cope with changes in contemporary society. He even made it the basis of a theory of continuous change and corresponding alteration of the law by the king.[42] That he did not regard the law of the constitution as entirely temporary and precarious is illustrated by his increased caution in his more formal treatises,[43] but his moderation did not lessen the strength of his conviction that the ruler should alter the law according to manifest necessity. In his thought, this interpretation was carried very largely to the possible limits within the framework of his approach. His heavy insistence upon divine and natural law in the working of the political system gave rise to a double emphasis in his thought: first, the ability of the legislator to deal very freely with the law of the constitution because it was admittedly but an approximation of an ideal. Since the circumstances of earthly society were visibly changing, that approximation must needs change accordingly. But secondly, Charondas retained the older idea of rulership as essentially adjudication, that is, rule in terms of a fixed criterion. He had developed his concepts to the point of allowing the prince to give out new law according to circumstances, but in the final analysis the king did not find his major rule of procedure in society around him, either in legal facts or in the changing situation, but rather

---

[42] "Le Legislateur ne peut de telle prudence constituter les lois, que par le diuers cours des ans et changement des choses, ses successeurs ne trouuent souuent à redire. Car c'estoit asses à lui de publier les plus exquisement qu'il pouuoit de qui lui sembloit vtile à la Republique. Afin donc que ce qui a esté premierement introduit à l'vtilité des hommes, ne soit conuerti en leur dommage, et la tranquilité politique n'empire: le bon Roi ne sera tant superstitieux, qu'il doute de changer, abolir et entierement renuerser les lois anciennes, si elles lui semblent contraires ou à la raison, ou à la societé humaine." *Les Dialogues*, p. 20.

[43] "Toutesfois ie ne doute qu'il ne soit quelquefois necessaire de changer les Loix et ordonnances anciennes, ou desroger et retrancher d'icelles: mais il y fault vser de grand' prudence, et le faire petit à petit, et auec le iugement du temps et de la necessité." *Pandectes*, p. 17.

in the eternal principles over and above society. For that reason, the monarch remained for him essentially a judge, and legislation was but a subordinate portion of the royal right of adjudication.

The attitude of Louis Le Roy toward changing the law of the constitution was similar to that of Charondas, although resting upon somewhat different fundamentals and thus less favorable toward unrestrained innovation because of immediate necessity. Ideally, he said, the law should be preserved intact.[44] However, such was recognizedly impossible because of the instability and constant fluctuation of human affairs.[45] Thus, Le Roy recognized clearly the dilemma of the constitutionalists of his day. Torn between their desire to maintain accepted law and their growing consciousness that rapid social evolution was making the older positions increasingly untenable, they could but seek a solution by permitting to the king, in varying degrees, the actual creation of law. Less conscious than Charondas of the possibility of changing the law according to circumstances and yet maintaining its partial consonance with final ideals, Le Roy concluded that in spite of urgent necessity, it was sufficient to limit the abolition of laws to those unquestionably barbarous and without value, preserving even those with manifest imperfections because of the risk involved in any process of change within the social structure.[46] If this was a solution, it was but partial. The evolu-

[44] "Combien que la nouuelleté soit aggreable aux curieux: toutefois elle est dangereuse à introduire. . . . Ie dis que la mutation en toutes choses, fors es mauuaises, est tresdangereuse en toutes saisons, en la diete des corps et meurs des ames, et absolument en tous cas. . . ." *Politiques d'Aristote*, p. 203.

[45] "Il seroit tresbeau, tresutile, et trescommode user tousiours de mesmes loix. Mais puis que les meurs, opinions, coustumes, affections, sont uariables comme toutes choses humaines: lon est par necessité constrainct faire ça et la incessamment loix nouuelles, abroger les anciennes, corriger les mauuaises, moderer par dispensations les trop rigoureuses ou seueres. Il ne fut iamais autrement, ny sera tant que le genre humain durera." *Politiques d'Aristote*, p. 213.

[46] "S'il est utile ou non muer les loix anciennes et receues d'un estat, resoluant celles loix estre à changer, qui sont evidemment barbares et inutiles: mais que sans manifeste utilité lon ne se doyue mettre à y rien changer ou innouer: à fin de ne perdre l'auctorité et obeissance de la loy, qui ne s'acquiert que par longueur de temps: de maniere qu'il est plus expedient tolerer quelques imper-

tion of older constitutional doctrine had proceeded sufficiently to account for definite changes in the law of the land and the making of law by the monarch, and yet the legists could but be dissatisfied with a body of thought which, while maintaining the traditional insistence upon complete preservation of the law, nevertheless advanced ideas permitting the violation of that principle. The hesitance of theorists concerning this important change in interpretation reveals at once an unwillingness to part with the older conceptions and a groping for a new and more adequate theory of state.

It was in this tangled intellectual situation that appeared the *Republic* of Jean Bodin.[47] Contemporaries recognized the value of the book at once, and henceforth Bodin was cited as a foremost authority on problems of law and constitutional theory. The double purpose of the work was quite in line with those forces making for the development of political concepts: not only did Bodin wish his book to take its place among the theoretical treatises in the field, but he also desired it to be of value in aiding contemporary monarchs to solve practical problems of government.[48] As such, it reflects not only very wide study of contemporary and earlier political doctrines but also a close acquaintance with the administrative machinery of the French state. And since Bodin was very well grounded in the theory and practice of contemporary jurisprudence, his work was necessarily in close conformance with much that had been set forth by earlier writers. With the exception of his greatest contribution, his theory of sovereignty, the major portion of his thought reflected closely that of Charondas and Le Roy.[49] But it was Bodin's superior

---

fections des loix et fautes des magistrats, si elles ne sont trop preiudiciables, qu'en les cuidant corriger, renuerser un estat." *Politiques d'Aristote*, p. 205. Cf. *De l'excellence du gouvernement royal* (Paris, 1575), pp. 22b–23a.

[47] Jean Bodin, *Les Six Livres de la république* (Paris, 1576). Our references are to this edition and to the Latin translation printed at Frankfort, 1622.

[48] This is explained in the preface.

[49] In innumerable instances, Bodin's concepts appear as a hybrid product which combined current legal theories, of the type upheld by Charondas, with the Renaissance version of Aristotelian philosophy, similar to that embodied in

insight and precision of thought which enabled him to arrive at conclusions lacking heretofore. His new conception of kingship may have been founded upon widely accepted political doctrines, but he defined it in such fashion that it was better able to meet the necessities of the moment than that of any earlier writer. These qualities enabled Bodin's contribution, in spite of its complexity, to be adopted by a host of followers. In this manner, his constructive effort served to deflect the evolution of legal concepts into very definite channels and was of immense moment in the growth of political thought.

There is no doubt concerning Bodin's pressing consciousness of the changes occurring in French society and the need for solution of the concomitant problems. The evidence of his historical studies as well as the social upheavals going on about him caused him to perceive that the secular state was anything but the static affair so important in the outlook of his predecessors. In an earlier work, his *Methodus,* he had listed as causes of the mutation of states the abolition of slavery, the rise of new religions, and the decline of the feudal system.[50] And it was because of his search for the causes and nature of those changes that he was moved to treat political problems in abstract terms. He was the first to make full use of certain scattered threads of interpretation presented in writings before his time and to set forth something resembling a complete and well integrated system permitting the evolution of the social organism.

Bodin believed certain occult and inscrutable forces to be the primary causes of the mutation of states. He was far from alone in this; previous to the *Republic,* Le Roy had set forth essentially the same theory in considerable detail.[51]

the works of Le Roy. Because of the limitations of this study, we have placed greater stress upon Bodin's intellectual relationships with Charondas, merely indicating his similarities with Le Roy through citations in the footnotes.

[50] Jean Bodin, *Methodus ad facilem historiarum cognitionem* (Paris, 1572), p. 341. This work was first published in 1566; our references are to the edition of 1572.

[51] "Il est certain que comme toutes autres choses commencees finissent, et augmentees diminuent, et veillissent: les unes tost, les autres tard, selon la

Even more elaborately than in the several works of Le Roy, Bodin treated at length the celestial causes of the rise and fall of earthly societies. While admitting that human action and the policies of rulers were of definite effect, he insisted that the principal causes of such changes lay in natural forces beyond the control of man.[52] Bodin found in astrology one of the few means, however imperfect and unsatisfactory, of observing and calculating the natural forces over human destinies. Hence his detailed treatment of that science and his efforts to correct the errors of his predecessors in order to arrive at more accurate conclusions. Certain numbers in the chronology of a state's existence he believed to exercise definite influence over its progress and decline, and he strove to find a clew to the fate of realms in the implications of the perfect numbers 6, 28, 496, and 8128.[53] Admittedly, he concluded, it was extremely difficult to calculate the rise and fall of states in this fashion, but such a study dealt with the forces determining human destinies and had value as such. Details apart, the implications of his approach reveal that he believed certain natural forces to preside over the lives of men and states, and that they were partially within the capabilities of the human mind.

---

disposition de la matiere dont elles sont composees, et par l'influence des corps celestes, desquelz procede ceste uicissitude continuelle de generation et de corruption: Ainsi sont les estatz publics constituez, accreus, maintenus, abbaissez, changez, destruict, conuertis et remis les uns des autres par l'ordre de nature: ayans les mieulx fondez en religion et iustice leur puissance plus asseuree et plus durable, sans toutefois qu'il en soit perpetuelz, quelque bonne police qu'on y mette: ains voyons tous se corrompre par succession de temps, et finablement perir par leurs vices propres, et naturelz, qui les suyuent et accompaignent." *Politiques d'Aristote*, p. 540. See pp. 799–807 of the same work; *De la vicissitude ou variété des choses en l'univers* (Paris, 1575), *passim; De l'excellence du gouvernement royal*, pp. 25b–27a; *Exhortation aux françois pour vivre en concorde et jouir du bien de la paix* (Paris, 1570), pp. 26–28.

[52] "Quand ie di causes naturelles, ie n'entends pas les causes prochaines, qui de soy produisent la ruine ou le changement d'vn estat: comme de voir les meschancetez sans peine, et les vertus sans loyer en vne Republique . . . mais i'entends les causes celestes, et plus esloignees. . . . Or il n'y a personne de sain iugement, qui ne confesse les merueilleux effects des corps celestes en toute la nature: où la puissance de Dieu se monstre admirable. . . ." *République*, pp. 429–430.   [53] *République*, pp. 431–438.

The record of the rise and fall of states Bodin found in that great and amorphous body of historical knowledge which had been amassed by writers before the mid-sixteenth century. In the study of history, he found not only a guide to the past existence of states but also a key to those factors determining their rise and fall and thus an indication of the best means of coping with the resulting social difficulties. In this latter emphasis, he was at one with other writers of his time; like them he advocated the solution of present problems through the application of lessons to be gathered from the past experiences of men.[54] But his fundamental interpretation of that question differed from the treatment found in the majority of sixteenth-century writings. The greater number of men advocated that procedure simply because of their conscious and natural identification of contemporary problems with those which had confronted men in the past. Since the state was rightly unchanging, all political troubles were but variations of the same thing and might be remedied by those measures which had previously proved their efficacy. Bodin, on the other hand, believed the uncritical use of such procedure to be quite inadequate because of the multitudinous variations among peoples arising from differences in location, climate, chronological development and other factors which influenced the natural evolution of any social organism. And yet he preserved the older idea concerning the practical value of the lessons derived from history. This was permitted to him by his manner of using historical data. Far from advocating an indiscriminate borrowing from earlier practices, he sought to utilize the materials of history as a guide to the true nature of states.[55] Through historical investigation, he felt that the universals in human life might partially be discovered and could be used as a basis for solving present difficulties. This approach he believed to be especially valuable in the study of

---

[54] *Methodus, proemium.*

[55] On this question, see Jean Moreau-Reibel, *Jean Bodin et le droit public comparé, dans ses rapports avec la philosophie d'histoire* (Paris, 1933), pp. 52–70.

political and legal phenomena. In the sixth chapter of his *Methodus*, the *De statu rerumpublicarum*, he urged the comparative analysis of the laws and customs of various present and historical states as a valuable means of establishing the best type of constitution.[56] And it is quite evident from Bodin's writings that such was his own method. His lengthy examination of innumerable constitutions and his evaluation of them in terms of his main contribution, his theory of sovereignty, illustrate the fact that he regarded his theory of the royal authority as drawn from, and applicable to, all present and historic constitutions and thus partially consonant with the truths of social and political existence.

In addition to the celestial forces determining man's course, Bodin insisted heavily upon the influence of such environmental factors as geographical location and climate. This approach, which he first set forth in his *Methodus* and later gave greater place in his *Republic*, provides additional evidence concerning those natural forces which he believed to surround men.[57] In developing this interpretation, generally called his theory of climate, he dwelt at length upon the variations of peoples in character, aptitudes, laws, and institutions according to climate and ·geographical location. More important than the details of his theory, however, was his correlation of it with his science of government. These exterior and natural factors he believed to act as determinants upon the life of a given state, and it was the duty of the ruler both to take cognizance of them and to order the constitution in accordance with them.[58] Far from finding a single, universal justice to be applied to all peoples without distinction, he

---

[56] ". . . si viri prudentes omnibus omnium Rerumpublicarum moribus ad legibus collectis, eas inter se comparent, et ex his optimum Reipublicae genus constarent." *Methodus*, p. 230.

[57] Bodin's development of this theory occurs in chapter five of the *Methodus*, and in book five, chapter one of the *Republic*. It was also set forth by Louis Le Roy in his *Politiques d'Aristote* (p. 123) and in his *Excellence du gouvernement royal* (pp. 37a–37b).

[58] ". . . accommoder la forme de la chose publique à la nature des lieux, et les ordonnances humaines aux loix naturelles." *République*, p. 516.

insisted that their natures were sufficiently diversified by natural law itself to necessitate variation in institutions and the ordering of states.[59] But he did not conclude from the manifest differences in human institutions and from the varying criteria of justice among states that there was no single universal animating all. The fundamental aim of his approach was the discovery of those values which he held to be present in all manifestations, however varied, of human life.

It is apparent from these statements that Bodin's approach to political problems was largely rational and empirical, and as such it was certain to cause him to draw conclusions at variance with those reached by the majority of contemporary thinkers. One of his most important deviations from his predecessors was in his lessened emphasis upon religious considerations. He held that religion was of definite value in the life of any state and that the prince should preserve it for that reason; he might even refer to it as the basis of the state. But he had no conception of a single religion as the true one as contrasted with all others; in his approach to all problems it was reason which dominated his analysis. Throughout the vagaries of his religious thought and experience, he held largely to a "natural religion" resting upon broad, unspecialized beliefs and a cultivated rationalism.[60] Such an attitude tended to eliminate religion as the dominant consideration in human affairs, and in its stead, Bodin found

[59] "Il faut donc que le sage gouuerneur d'vn peuple sçache bien l'humeur d'iceluy, et son naturel, au parauant que d'atenter choses quelconque au changement de l'estat, ou des loix. Car l'vn des plus grans, et peut estre le principal fondement des Republiques, est d'accommoder l'estat au naturel des citoyens, et les edits et ordonnances à la nature des lieu, des personnes, et du temps. Car quoy que die Balde que la raison, et l'équité naturelle n'est point bornee ny attachee aux lieux, cela reçoit distinction, c'est à sçauoir, quand la raison est vniuerselle, et non pas où la raison particuliere des lieux et des personnes, reçoit vne consideration particuliere. Qui fait aussi qu'on doit diuersifier l'estat de la Republique, à la diuersité des lieux: à l'exemple du bon architecte, qui accomode son bastiment à la matiere qu'on trouue sur les lieux." *République*, p. 518.

[60] Bodin's religion has provided the subject for several studies. *See* Roger Chauviré, *Jean Bodin, auteur de la république* (Paris, 1914), pp. 142–172, and the same author's article, "La Pensée religieuse de Jean Bodin (d'après des documents nouveaux)," *La Province d'Anjou* (1929), pp. 433–451.

the immediate aim and end of man's existence in the secular state. Partially after the manner of Aristotle, he defined the highest good of man as the contemplation of things natural, human, and divine, that is, the exercise of the intellect concerning the universals at the basis of human existence. And the facilitation of this, even the thing itself, was to be found through living in the state. The greatest good and most perfect life of the individual were entirely consonant with the aim and end of the state; it was through harmonious existence in the social organism that man could best achieve that highest aim in life.[61] This was strictly in accord with the classical erudition of the age, yet in the sixteenth century such an interpretation of human existence was little short of revolutionary. Not only did it deny the traditional emphasis, if not all the implications, given the religious fundamentals of the state, but it assimilated the aim and end of man's existence with those things which were available in secular society. The state was thus made the all-inclusive framework into which the individual fitted completely. It is clear that such was hardly a fitting frame of reference in which to maintain independent rights of the subject against the government.

Bodin's insistence upon the natural forces and universal values active in human existence was sufficient to establish them as dominant in his thinking, yet there has been considerable difference of opinion concerning the seriousness and exact import of these considerations in his political thought. It is true that he minimized the place of religion in the state. It is also true that he gave great weight to force in political affairs; the origins of states he accounted for in that fashion,[62]

---

[61] "Or si la vraye felicité d'vne Republique, et d'vn homme seul est tout vn, et que le souuerain bien de la Republique en general, aussi bien que d'vn chacun en particulier, gist és vertus intellectuelles, et contemplatiues, comme les mieux entendus ont resolu: il faut aussi accorder que ce peuple là iouist du souuerain bien quand il a ce but deuant les yeux, de s'exercer en la contemplation des choses naturelles, humaines, et diuines, en rapportant la louange du tout au grand prince de nature. Si donc nous confessons que cela est le but principal de la vie heureuse d'vn chacun en particulier, nous concluons aussi que c'est la fin et felicité d'vne Republique." *République*, pp. 3–4. [62] *République*, p. 50.

and he even asserted that force frequently determined the holder of governmental authority.[63] His ideas of paternal authority and royal sovereignty included heavy insistence upon the value and necessity of coercion. Furthermore, when considering practical necessities of social life, he gave great weight to mere utility as a criterion of judgment and often sacrificed apparently higher considerations for stability almost as an end in itself. His conception of justice often appears as the actualities of the moment in combination with those norms to be discovered through the use of reason; the wise man he defined as the measure of justice and truth.[64] These aspects of his thought have caused certain writers to represent Bodin as separating practical government from higher ideals; if he preserved a place for the latter in his system, they were dissociated from immediate affairs sufficiently to give them little weight other than purely speculative and to break down the traditional unity of higher principles and human conduct.[65] And yet Bodin's statement that the rational man is the measure of justice, in combination with his thought as a whole, provides the key to his system. Although his approach occasioned a distinct laicization of political ideas, both his method and his major conceptions indicate that he believed certain fundamental universals to be ever-present in human society.

We have included this brief excursion into the broader aspects of Bodin's intellectual system because they provided the framework within which he developed his political thought. Specifically, they indicate the paramount importance which he ascribed to natural law. Since Bodin believed that such law formed the universal basis of all things, he could but make it the foundation of his theories concerning the French

[63] *République*, p. 428.
[64] *République*, p. 4.
[65] This is the interpretation given by Chauviré. *Op. cit.*, pp. 276–299. Garosci, a recent author, is even more extreme and presents Bodin as little more than a utilitarian. A. Garosci, *Jean Bodin, Politica e dritto nel Rinascimento francese* (Milan, 1934).

constitution.[66] His definitions of the major portions of the state — the family and the sovereign authority — were in terms of their natural position and functions in the social structure. Parallel, his ideas of the necessary authority in each of those divisions — that of the father over the family and of the sovereign over the state — rested upon fundamental conceptions of natural law and justice. His definition of the crucial phrase *droit gouvernement* is enlightening in regard to this matter. Public authority (*publica potestas*) he believed to form a natural and necessary element in every true state, but it must be based upon law and justice and have a sanction other than mere force. True authority did not exist among a band of robbers because such a society lacked natural law and that element of justice which was necessary at once to a true state and to legitimate authority.[67] Mere rule of force was not only insufficient to give rightful authority; it was the antithesis of legitimate government. Similarly, in regard to the authority of the husband over the wife, Bodin held that marriage conferred upon the husband the element of right over his wife which was necessary in order to render his command legitimate. Coercion of male over female under any other circumstances, such as that of a youth over his fiancée or in the case of concubinage, lacked

[66] The majority of writers who have considered Bodin's constitutional thought have stressed this dominating element of natural law and justice. From among many possible examples, we may cite Allen, *op. cit.*, p. 423, where he makes the statement that Bodin's greatest contribution was his idea that the state and the sovereign authority were facts of nature. This has been accepted by Carl Joachim Friedrich, *Politice methodice digesta of Johannes Althusius* (Harvard University Press, 1932), lx. *See* Esmein, *Eléments de droit constitutionel français et comparé* (Paris, 1921), I, 540; Otto von Gierke, *Natural Law and the Theory of Society* (Cambridge University Press, 1934), I, 37; and the same author's *Das Deutsche Genossenschaftsrecht* (Berlin, 1913), IV, 286 ff. Moreau-Reibel, *op. cit.*, pp. 151–152; Lemaire, *op. cit.*, pp. 111–128. Max Adams Shepard, "Sovereignty at the Crossroads: A Study of Bodin," *Political Science Quarterly* (1930), pp. 580–603.

[67] ". . . cela ne doibt estre appellé société, ny amitié, ny partage en termes de droit: ains coniurations, voleries, et pillages: car le principal poinct auquel gist la vraye marque d'amitié leur defaut, c'est à sçauoir le droit gouuernement selon les loix de nature." *République*, p. 3. See below, p. 231.

justice and right and was consequently mere force.[68] The same idea appeared in Bodin's statements concerning the acts of governmental institutions. Although he denied to the Parlement any control over matters of public policy, he did urge the necessity of enregistering and remonstrance on the basis that the court should judge royal enactments in the light of justice and equity and thus act as a strong deterrent against the monarch's violation of those principles which were necessary to his authority and just rule.[69] These examples should suffice to indicate that Bodin placed the major portion of his political thought upon a basis of natural law.

In the light of Bodin's clear perception of those factors underlying the impermanence of human society — celestial influences over men and states, variation according to geographical and climatic factors, and progressive historical development — it is interesting to examine his attitude toward change within the French constitution. His first reaction to this proposition was not unlike that of his contemporaries: that any change was necessarily dangerous to the life of the state because it touched its legal foundations and therefore threatened ruin.[70] However, he clearly realized that the ideal of complete preservation was impossible to maintain in the face of the many factors making for certain change. He had incorporated the latter into his intellectual system and could hardly insist upon maintaining the law intact in spite of them. Reluctantly, it seems, he admitted that the nature of men and things was subject to change to the extent that new regulations were constantly necessary to meet new situations, although that remedial procedure should be carried out with caution and in accordance with manifest necessity.[71] But to these orthodox statements, he added interpretations drawn from the fundamentals of his system. The evolution of states was caused by natural forces, and it was necessary to approach the problem through such media. It was the duty of the

---

[68] *République*, p. 15.
[69] *République*, p. 340.
[70] *République*, p. 452.
[71] *République*, p. 453.

governor to make regulations not only in view of visible changes but also according to those forces at their basis. This could be done only through the exercise of reason. Bodin argued that although the natural laws causing the evolution of states might be beyond the power of man to check, they were not entirely beyond his comprehension. The wise man was not subject to celestial influences to the same degree as the beast; he might understand and evaluate them, at least in part. Hence, it was the duty of the ruler to perceive the nature of the disruptive forces at work, to introduce measures accordingly, and thus check, although not arrest, their influence upon the life of his realm.[72] And finally, it was largely for the purpose of meeting the perilous situation of contemporary society that Bodin developed his theory of sovereignty. In the king he willingly placed sufficient authority and legitimate discretion to permit him to act effectively against those forces making for social disruption. In his ideal ruler, Bodin pictured an enlightened monarch with great rational capabilities, exercising a very wide authority not only because such was necessitated by the chaotic condition of the realm but also because of the necessity of such authority in a well ordered state. It may be said that Bodin's theory of sovereignty was his answer not only to those political factions opposing and seeking to weaken the government, but also to those forces, natural and social, which he perceived to be causing increased disorder in the social organism. In this fashion, Bodin both took account of those factors causing the progressive evolution of the state and proposed a con-

[72] ". . . par la sagesse, et prudence que Dieu a donné aux hommes, on peut maintenir les Republiques bien ordonnees en leur estat, et preuenir les ruines d'icelles. Car tous les Astrologues mesmes demeurent d'accord, que les sages ne sont point sugets aux astres: mais bien que ceux-là qui lachent la bride aux appetits déreiglez, et cupiditez bestiales, ne peuuent eschaper les effects des corps celestes. . . . Si doncques on a decouuert que la force des astres, qu'on pensoit ineuitable, se peut affoiblir, et que les sages Medecins, ont trouué des moyens pour changer les maladies, et alterer les fieubures, contre leur cours naturel, afin de les guerir plus aisément: pourquoy le sage Politique, preuoyant les changemens qui aduiennent naturellement aux Republiques, ne preuiendra par conseil, et remedes conuenables la ruine d'icelles?" *République*, pp. 449–450.

crete solution in terms of governmental policy and authority. He may be regarded as the first political theorist to substitute for the traditional, static conception a dynamic theory of state.

Turning now to the details of Bodin's constitutional thought, it should be stressed that he regarded the family as the primary natural element in the social structure. The republic itself was but a legitimate association of families under a sovereign authority;[73] consequently the origin and principal substance of the state were to be found in the domestic unit.[74] Bodin emphasized the natural character of the family as a social entity. Its existence was a fact of nature, and hence it not only provided the material basis of civil society but was consonant with natural law governing human life. Thus all things pertaining to it should be treated in terms of their natural basis and necessity. One of the most important attributes of the family, quite necessary to its existence, Bodin found in the authority of the father over all other persons within the group.[75] The element of command was needful and natural in any social body; it was inherent in any ruler who enjoyed rightful authority over a group of individuals, whether they constituted a family or a state.[76] Bodin defined natural liberty as the complete freedom of the individual, save for subjection to God and to reason which was consonant with God,[77] but he insisted that in any organized society such liberty must be brought under the authority of the one who

[73] "Republique est vn droit gouuernement de plusieurs mesnages, et de ce qui leur est commun, auec puissance souueraine." *République*, p. 1.

[74] ". . . la vraye source et origine de toute Republique, et membre principal d'icelle." *République*, p. 8. This idea had appeared earlier in the works of Le Roy. *Politiques d'Aristote*, pp. 8, 31; *Excellence du gouvernement royal*, p. 7.

[75] "Mesnage est vn droit gouuernement de plusieurs sugets, soubs l'obeissance d'vn chef de famille, et de ce qui luy est propre." *République*, p. 8.

[76] "Le mot de puissance [potestas], est propre à tous ceux qui ont pouuoir de commander autruy. Ainsi le Prince, dit Seneque, commande aux sugets, le magistrat aux citoyens, le pere aux enfans." *République*, p. 21.

[77] "Nous appellons liberté naturelle de n'estre suget, apres Dieu, à homme viuant, et ne soufrir autre commandement que de soymesme: c'est à dire, de la raison, qui est tousiours conforme à la volonté de Dieu." *République*, p. 14.

commands.[78]   Although the authority held by one member might take the form of outright coercion, it was bestowed upon the father and the sovereign by natural law, the element which differentiated it from mere force. It was because of Bodin's approach to the question of political power through conceptions of natural law and necessity that he was thus enabled to represent the authorities of the father and the king as but different manifestations of the same thing.[79] And since he regarded the family as the state in miniature, it is very revealing concerning his theory of sovereignty to examine his statements regarding the rights enjoyed by the head of the family. He maintained the contemporary ideas of the natural and legal superiority of the husband over the wife in all their rigor, insisting heavily upon the inherent imperfection of the female, and elaborating that concept in terms of the legal systems of various nations past and present.[80] Even more uncompromising was his idea concerning the rights of the father over his children. The power of life and death, he said, was assigned to the father by natural and divine law.[81] Such had been the order among the Romans during their greatest period, and the lessening of its rigor had proved a vital factor in the decline of their state. Bodin admired the more Spartan aspects of the Roman social system, pointing out that domestic authority and discipline had enabled them to preserve not only the family but also those virtues which had made them great.[82] He concluded that contemporary rulers could do no

---

[78] "Toute Republique, tout corps et college, et tout mesnage se gouuerne par commandement, et obeissance: quand la liberté naturelle, qu'vn chacun a de viure à son plaisir, est rangee soubs la puissance d'autruy. . . ." *République*, p. 14.

[79] Tout ainsi donc que la famille bien conduitte, est la vraye image de la Republique, et la puissance domestique semblable à la puissance souueraine: aussi est le droit gouuernement de la maison, le vray modelle du gouuernement de la Republique." *République*, p. 8.

[80] *République*, Bk. I, ch. III.

[81] *République*, p. 24.

[82] "Car ils tenoient que la iustice domestique, et puissance paternelle, estoit vn tresseur fondement des loix, de l'honneur, de la vertu, et de toute pieté." *République*, p. 24.

better than to revive the ancient laws of paternal authority, if only in order to insure greater stability in the social system.[83] Nothing could emphasize more strikingly Bodin's insistence upon the large measure of legitimate discretion necessary and natural to governmental authority than his ideas concerning the rights enjoyed by the father of the family. Although in the same vein as many other writings of the period, the emphasis of his statements was definitely more rigorous.[84]

As the family was the natural social entity, so those things necessary to its existence rested, in the eyes of Bodin, upon an inviolable basis of natural law. Property was by far the most important of these; it summed up those things which Bodin took care to include in his definition of the family as *ce qui luy est propre*. His interpretation of such property rights was of crucial importance in his political thought, for private property represented the general body of popular immunities, that sphere of legal right traditionally independent of the royal authority. Bodin definitely included in his concept the specific and varying property rights held by the populace according to the established legal organization of the state. On this basis, he criticized Plato's communism as contrary to the institution of the family and thus not only inimical to the organization of the state but inadmissible in natural law.[85] The important fact to be noted is that although Bodin included the multitudinous proprietary rights recognized by contemporary legal usage, he placed them upon a basis of natural law.[86] Instead of representing popular rights

---

[83] *République*, pp. 28–29.

[84] The majority of writers, even the Romanists, usually confined their remarks to stating that the Roman laws concerning the *patria potestas* had no force in France. E.g., Bugnyon, *Legum abrogatarum*, pp. 18–20, 48, 265–266, 351–352. It is to be noted that Bodin came to adopt this attitude toward parental authority only after developing his theory of sovereignty. In his *Methodus* (p. 313), he had found the likeness of the *pater familias* in the seigneurial monarch ruling without bonds of law, rather than in the legitimate or royal monarch.

[85] *République*, p. 11.

[86] This is illustrated by a passage in which he criticized the egalitarian tend-

as resting simply upon customary law made by the people, he found the ultimate basis of their inviolability in their concordance with the law of nature. As such, property rested, in Bodin's system, upon a basis beyond the capacity of the prince to violate, but his natural-law interpretation of that issue marked a changed conception of the two spheres of legal right reflected in the constitution.

It was in his theories concerning the sovereign authority that Bodin made his greatest contribution. The right of government he believed to be inherent in every true state,[87] as natural and necessary in every organized society as the power of the father over the family. Approaching the problem of political power through its foundations in natural law, Bodin was led to emphasize the concept of legitimate power in his theory of sovereignty. He consequently set forth an interpretation novel to the age, although sufficiently close to older ideas to be adopted by a majority of writers after 1576. For heretofore, the sovereign authority had been defined as a mosaic of legally defined rights, a series of marks of sovereignty, the sum-total of which constituted the crown. But Bodin was not greatly concerned with the specific content of that authority; his emphasis was upon the abstract concept of power and the element of command. Instead of showing the royal prerogative to consist of certain specific rights, he represented it simply as a body of power which was absolute, undivided, perpetual, and responsible only to God.[88] Although

encies of democracy, as contrasted with the more just proportion maintained by monarchy: "Mais le plus grand inconuenient est, qu'en ostant ces mots tien et mien, on ruine les fondemens de toutes Republiques, qui sont principalement establies pour rendre à chacun ce que luy appartient, et defendre le larcin, comme il est porté par la loy de Dieu, qui a disertement voulu, que la proprieté des biens fust gardée à chacun. et ne faut dire que la nature a fait toutes choses communes. . . ." *République*, p. 682.

[87] ". . . la souveraineté [maiestas] est la puissance absolue et perpetuelle d'une Republique." *République*, p. 125.

[88] Bodin treats his concept of sovereignty in Bk. I, ch. IX in the first edition of the *Republic*, and in ch. VIII in all later editions. On this question, see especially the following: Hermann Rehm, *Allgemeine Staatslehre* (Freiburg, 1899), pp. 40-70, and his *Geschichte der Staatsrechtswissenschaft* (Freiburg, 1896),

he likewise insisted that there were certain inviolable rights which the king could not touch, his theory of sovereignty permitted, and even required, wide exercise of the royal discretion. The emphasis was no longer upon the exact legal rights enjoyed by king and people respectively; it was upon a concept of natural and legitimate power inherent in every true state. It is readily apparent that such a concept of sovereignty, being based upon fundamentals varying from the older approach, would give rise to a distinctly new interpretation of the innumerable rights and duties of the monarch, and of his relations with his subjects.

Nothing illustrates more clearly the vital place of sovereignty in the social organism, in Bodin's system, than his classification of states and his idea of revolution. As the state was composed of a group of families under a sovereign authority, so the exact body exercising that authority determined the character of the state. Bodin was not greatly concerned with the origin of governmental authority. He might assert that it had been given to the king by the people, insisting that the transfer had been complete and perpetual,[89] but his major conception was that sovereignty was a fact of nature. He insisted that in every true state, large or small, sovereignty was to be found in one person or group of persons. The exact place of that authority provided the basis of his classification of states, and he passed in review a great number of constitutions, past and present, applying his doctrine and finding in each a single unit which exercised absolute sovereignty. He concluded that the historic classification of states

---

pp. 218–231; E. Hancke, *Bodin, Eine Studie über den Begriff der Souverainetät* (Breslau, 1894); Max Landmann, *Der Souveränetätsbegriff bei den Franzosischen Theoretikern, von Jean Bodin bis auf Jean Jacques Rousseau* (Leipzig, 1896), pp. 40–91; Adolf Dock, *Der Souveränetätsbegriff von Bodin bis zu Friedrich dem Grosse* (Strassburg, 1897); Georg Jellinek, *Allgemeine Staatslehre* (Berlin, 1900), pp. 394–445; Otto von Gierke, *Das Deutsche Genossenschaftsrecht* (Berlin, 1913), IV; Marcel De la Bigne de Villeneuve, *Traité général de l'état* (Paris, 1929), I; Charles H. McIlwain, *Constitutionalism and the Changing World* (Cambridge University Press, 1939).
[89] *République*, pp. 128–129.

into monarchies, aristocracies, and democracies included the only possible types, since any mixed constitution was contrary to the nature of the sovereign authority.[90] Thus, any transfer of governmental power from one person or body to another constituted a complete revolution.[91] The place of the prerogative determined the character of the state; the sovereign authority *was* the state, not in the sense that it represented the entire realm and summed up the life of the social organism, but in the sense that it included that entire body of authority necessary to bring existence to the state, to determine its exact form, and to render it a legitimate association according to natural law.[92]

Although Bodin regarded the sovereign authority as an undifferentiated body of rightful power, he felt obliged to elaborate upon its content in the traditional fashion of listing certain marks of sovereignty. The first and most vital mark of rulership, important to the point of including all others, he found in the authority of the prince to make law.[93] His break from the older conception is apparent at once. Instead of regarding the king as primarily a judge, Bodin emphasized the monarch's authority over the law and his ability to give it to all his subjects. True, judicial authority was a necessary royal prerogative. Bodin listed it as fourth among the marks of sovereignty,[94] but such only emphasized its subordinance to the right to make law. Furthermore, he advocated that the king allow his supreme right of jurisdiction to be exercised by the sovereign courts, implying that the ruler, while retaining the authority of highest jurisdiction, wielded it but rarely.[95] Among other subordinate marks of sovereignty,

---

[90] *République*, Bk. II, ch. I.   [91] *République*, p. 402.

[92] The idea that the place of sovereignty in the state determined its form and nature was also upheld by Le Roy. *Politiques d'Aristote*, pp. 308, 325, 419. Both borrowed the idea from Aristotle.

[93] ". . . la premiere marque du Prince souuerain c'est la puissance de donner loy à tous en general, et à chacun en particulier." *République*, p. 197.

[94] *République*, pp. 204–207.

[95] *République*, pp. 485–486. This is the emphasis of Bk. IV, ch. VI, "S'il est expedient que le prince iuge les sugets, et qu'il se communique souuent à eux."

Bodin listed the right to make war and peace, to appoint magistrates, to give graces, receive liege homage and fealty, to coin money, and to collect taxes.[96] But he always returned to the royal authority to make law as the most important mark, summing up all others.[97] This was because Bodin's idea of the law-making power represented simply his concept of the natural authority of the monarch to command translated into terms of practical government.

It was in this fashion that Bodin was moved to define the royal authority in terms of legislative sovereignty. For him, sovereignty and the power to make law were all but synonymous, and he rightly claimed to be the first to define the royal prerogative in this manner.[98] In regard to the specific qualities which Bodin assigned to the legislation of the prince, it has been stressed above that his approach to that problem through concepts of natural law caused him to attribute to the prerogative in question a large element of command. But Bodin was primarily a jurist and could understand the making of law only in terms of accepted legal concepts. He distinguished carefully between *lex* and *jus*, the former being the law made by the sovereign, while the latter included broad principles of justice and equity, consonant with natural law. Although the distinction was clear, it did not involve separation. The laws and commands of the prince, far from being devoid of justice, should always be in accord with higher ideals.[99] As

---

[96] *République*, Bk. I, ch. XI in the first edition; ch. X in others.

[97] "Soubs ceste mesme puissance de donner, et casser la loy, sont compris tous les autres droits, et marques de souueraineté: de sorte qu'à parler proprement on peut dire qu'il n'y a que ceste seule marque de souueraineté, attendu que tous les autres droits sont compris en cestui-là. . . ." *République*, p. 199.

[98] *République*, p. 125. It is to be noted that Bodin reached this conclusion only after long study and observation. In his *Methodus* (p. 261), he defined the authority of rulership after the older manner of listing marks of sovereignty, such as the appointment of magistrates, the making and abrogating of laws, war and peace, supreme jurisdiction, etc.

[99] ". . . le mot de Loy [lex] sans dire autre chose, signifie le droict commandement de celuy ou ceux qui ont toute puissance par dessus les autres sans exception de personne. . . ." *République*, p. 193. The emphasis is sharper in his Latin translation: ". . . leges propria sui acceptione definiemus, recta sum-

emphatically as his predecessors did Bodin insist that human laws contrary to those of God and nature were not law but iniquity.[100] Thus the prince, when making law, should cause his enactments to conform with higher principles to the point of embodying them; in making *leges*, he incidentally promulgated *jus*. But the element of command was of great weight in his interpretation. Immediately following the definition cited above, Bodin added the statement that law was merely the general command of the sovereign.[101] Furthermore, it was not the equitable content of the laws of the prince which rendered them binding upon his subjects but the fact that they issued from him as rightful ruler. It was necessary that such laws conform to principles of right and justice, but in relation to the people, they were simply acts of authority.[102] It was in this fashion that Bodin's theory of royal legislation combined traditional ideas of law with that large measure of authority which he would attribute to the prince.

When compared with earlier theories of the royal prerogative, it is evident that Bodin's concept of legislative sovereignty gave rise to a marked expansion of the legitimate royal discretion. One very important reason for Bodin's willingness to attribute greater authority to the prince was his fear that the more limited rights held by earlier rulers allowed insufficient freedom of action in dealing with entirely new problems. His consciousness of change and sense of historical relativity exercised definite influence upon his theory of sovereignty. It was in order to enable his ideal ruler to cope with the innumerable difficulties arising from rapidly changing circumstances that Bodin would attribute to him authority to make laws *selon l'exigence des cas, des temps, et des per-*

---

mae potestatis iussa, siue vnius, siue omnium, siue paucorum sit potestas." Edition cited, p. 235.

[100] *République*, p. 147.

[101] ". . . loy est le commandement du souuerain touchant tous les subiects en general, ou de choses generales. . . ." *République*, p. 193.

[102] ". . . les loix du Prince souuerain, ores qu'elles fussent fondees en bonnes et viues raisons, neantmoins qu'elles ne dependent que de sa pure et franche volonté." *République*, p. 133.

sonnes.[103] New laws might be required to conform with general principles of right and justice, but the criterion of the prince in making them was, for all practical purposes, the situation in society at any given moment. No longer did he seek to remedy social ills simply by restoring the ancient constitution. That was gone forever, and thinkers had no choice but to attribute wider authority to the prince in the hope that it would enable him to check those forces which threatened the life of the state.

Although Bodin's theory of sovereignty was characterized by a material expansion of the king's discretionary power, he nevertheless incorporated into his system certain specific limitations upon the ruler's freedom of action. First in importance were those limits inherent in his conception of authority itself. Being based upon natural right, the royal prerogative could but be exercised according to those values imposed by justice and natural law. Bodin insisted that the laws made by the prince should conform with such principles. A true republic was by definition one which was governed by a policy of *droit gouvernement*,[104] and the specific content which he assigned to that concept was strictly in accord with his basic approach to political questions through theories of natural law. Bodin distinguished sharply between royal and seigneurial monarchy. The former, being the only legitimate type, he defined as that in which the king abided by the laws of nature and preserved the natural liberty and property of his subjects unmolested. On the other hand, seigneurial monarchy was characterized by the ruler's unqualified mastery over the persons and property of his subjects, ruling them like slaves.[105] Bodin's entire political doctrine, from his funda-

---

[103] *République*, p. 142.   [104] See above, p. 220.

[105] "Donc la Monarchie royale, ou legitime, est celle où les sugets obeissent aux loix du Monarque, et le Monarque aux loix de nature, demeurant la liberté naturelle, et proprieté des biens aux sugets. La Monarchie seigneuriale, est celle où le Prince est faict Seigneur des biens, et des personnes, par le droit des armes, et de bonne guerre, gouuernant ses sugets comme le pere de famille ses esclaues." *République*, p. 234. Cf. p. 238. Also, Le Roy, *Politiques d'Aristote*, pp. 6, 45-46, 465.

mental approach to his most refined details of interpretation, may be regarded as an elaborate statement of his concept of royal monarchy, that type in which the ruler exercised an authority at once based upon, and limited by, values of natural law. Although he would increase the scope of the royal power, he was throughout a theorist of right, not might. As such, he was poles apart from Hobbes.

It was in this fashion that Bodin retained the traditional concept of the royal authority as absolute within its sphere but suffering very definite limitations. However, his approach to that problem through natural law rather than established constitutional usage varied from that followed by the majority of his contemporaries and caused him to draw divergent conclusions in regard to specific details of law. As Gierke has observed, Bodin may have retained the three classical divisions of law, *jus naturale*, *jus gentium*, and *jus civile*, but his emphasis upon natural law caused him to interpret almost all legal matters either in terms of *jus naturale* or *jus positivum* and to render *jus gentium* binding upon the prince only when it conformed with *jus naturale*.[106] The legal elements in political thought he interpreted largely in terms of positive or natural law; these were his fundamental categories. The vital importance of this tendency in Bodin's thought was that he retained the supremacy of natural law over the prince but made him, with few exceptions, the master of all portions of the constitution which rested upon *jus positivum*.

---

[106] Gierke, *Natural Law*, I, p. 38 and note 27. This tendency of Bodin to make *jus gentium* binding over the prince only if it was in accordance with *jus naturale* apparently grew in importance in his thought, as is revealed by the following text from the first edition of the *Republic* and its later Latin translation: "Vray est, que ces docteurs ne disent point que c'est de puissance absolue, car si nous disons que celuy a puissance absolue, qui n'est point suget aux loix, il ne se trouuera Prince au monde souuerain, veu que tous les Princes de la terre sont sugets aux loix de Dieu, et de nature, et à plusieurs loix humaines communes à tous peuples." *République*, p. 131. "Quid autem sit absoluta, vel potius soluta lege potestas, nemo definit. Nam si legibus omnibus solutam definiamus, nullus omnino princeps iura maiestatis habere comperiatur, cum omnes teneat lex diuina, lex item naturae; tum etiam lex omnium gentium communis, quae a naturae legibus ac diuinis diuisas habet rationes." Edition cited, p. 132.

The most apparent exception to this rule appeared in Bodin's treatment of fundamental law. He maintained that the Salic Law determined succession to the crown and thus might not be broken by the holder of the prerogative.[107] Likewise, he upheld in traditional fashion the inalienability of the domain as a limitation upon the royal discretion.[108] However, he reduced the significance of these laws to limitation only; he discarded the concept of the royal authority as based upon such law and interpreted it rather in terms of natural necessity. The traditional fundamental laws were reduced to regulations upon the royal discretion in the administration of the royal domain and in provision for the succession to the crown. As such, they constituted definite but small limits upon the king.

The two fundamental laws represented a seemingly extraneous quantity in Bodin's system of legal values. All other portions of the constitution he placed in one of two categories: natural or positive law. Those details of legal usage falling in the former division were beyond the authority of the prince to touch, while those of the latter type were distinctly subject to his discretion. This all-important feature of Bodin's legal system is borne out by an examination of his statements in regard to three very important constitutional matters: contracts, private property, and customary law. Bodin considered the question whether a king's contracts with his subjects were binding and beyond his authority to break through unilateral action. In answer, he maintained that if the contract were unjust or contained fraud, that is, if it were contrary to natural law, it might be broken; but if it were just and reasonable, it should be maintained.[109] He stated clearly his reasons: a contract was a bilateral action in which the parties stood on an equal footing; thus the breaking of the contract by one party injured the other unjustly and was therefore contrary to natural right and law.

---

[107] *République*, p. 136.
[108] *République*, pp. 618–619.   [109] *République*, p. 133.

The prince, being subject to that type of law, was bound by his contracts.[110]

Private property formed the most important limitation which Bodin placed upon kingship and was of crucial significance in his theory of the constitution. It will be recalled that he believed the family to form the basic natural entity in the state, and that he insisted in consequence that those things necessary for its maintenance were based upon natural right and law. Such was the foundation of his argument in favor of the inviolability of private property rights. The prince, he said, is bound by the laws of God and nature and thus may not take a man's property without just and reasonable cause. He defined just cause as an emergency in which it was necessary to act quickly for the preservation of the state. In such a case, the good of the realm was the good of the individual, but even in that instance, the subject ought to be reimbursed. As a general proposition, Bodin insisted that the king might not take a man's property without his consent,[111] and he quoted approvingly from Seneca: "to kings belongs authority over all; to private persons, property." [112] If Bodin listed the taking of tailles among the marks of sovereignty, he did so merely in order to emphasize that such authority could never be held by a feudal lord, even on the basis of prescription.[113] In answer to certain critics who accused him of lessening the bonds of law upon the king, he recalled his emphasis upon the monarch's subordination to divine and natural law, contracts, and the legal requirement

---

[110] *République*, pp. 146–149.

[111] "Si donc le Prince souuerain n'a pas puissance, de franchir les bornes des loix de nature, que Dieu, duquel il est l'image, a posees, il ne pourra aussi prendre le bien d'autruy, sans cause qui soit iuste et raisonnable . . . mais la raison naturelle veut que le public soit preferé au particulier, et que les sugets relaschent non seulement leurs iniures, et vengences, ains aussi leurs biens, pour le salut de la Republique. . . . Et toutesfois on doibt chercher touts les moyens de recompenser la perte des vns, auec le profit des autres. . . . Cessant donc les causes que i'ay dit, le prince ne peut prendre, ny donner le bien d'autruy, sans le consentement du seigneur." *République*, pp. 150–151. Cf. p. 138.

[112] *République*, p. 151.

[113] *République*, pp. 213–216.

of consent to taxation.[114] It is clear from his explicit statements and from the framework of his thought that he regarded taxation as legitimate only if carried out with the consent of the people. Otherwise, it violated fundamental principles of natural right and law. In the system of Bodin, such a doctrine was entirely sufficient to preserve the traditional inviolability of private property, but he made the vital change of finding its basis not in the customary law of the land but rather in the more abstract concept of natural law. When adopted by later writers, the ultimate effects of that deviation were immense.

Bodin's treatment of customary law reveals in striking fashion the effect of his theory of sovereignty upon traditional constitutional thought. It likewise provides an excellent index to the manner in which his new conception of kingship necessitated an expansion of the royal discretion at the expense of the older legal limitations. Bodin's insistence upon those limits which were provided by natural and divine law, contracts, and consent to taxation, indicates his real willingness to preserve bonds of law upon the ruler. Actually, his original position was much more constitutional and included additional limitations of customary law. In his *Methodus*, he had stated that in every legitimate monarchy not only the people and the magistrates were bound by law but also the king. At his coronation, he swore to preserve the laws of the realm, and these Bodin explicitly defined to include private as well as fundamental laws. Likewise, he denied that the ruler might alter established custom without the consent of the three estates.[115]

---

[114] This occurs in the prefatory epistle which first appeared in that edition of the *Republic* printed in Paris, 1578.

[115] "Alterum est eorum, qui non modo magistratus ac priuatos, verumetiam seipsos legibus constringunt, vt Principes Christiani, paucis exceptis, ac Poeni: qui cum sacris initiantur, magno iureiurando verbis conceptis a Pontificibus et regni proceribus sese obligant, ex legibus imperii et aequo bono Rempublicam gesturos. formula quidem initiationis regum nostrorum, non modo verborum et antiquitatis eximia specie, sed etiam pondere et grauitate sententiarum pulcherrima visa mihi est: in eo maxime, quod Princeps ante Pontifices per Deum

However, in developing his theory of sovereignty, Bodin was forced to discard these limits of customary law upon the ruler. Since he defined the sovereign authority in terms of law-making power, it seemed logically necessary that he attribute to the ruler an authority superior to all positive law, a position in which it was impossible to retain those limitations arising from custom. This accounts for Bodin's effort to place all remaining checks upon a basis of natural law. Likewise, the dynamic element in Bodin's theory required that the king stand above custom, if only to enable him to alter it according to changing circumstances.[116] Thus it happened that Bodin expressly reversed himself in regard to the limitations which custom placed upon the king. The coronation oath, he said, did not bind the monarch to preserve the laws and customs of the land.[117] The changing of customary law was ordinarily done according to the advice of the local or general estates, but the opinions of the deputies had no weight other than that of counsel and could not bind the ruler who held all authority to make law.[118] Custom, he con-

---

immortalem iurat, se omnibus ordinibus debitam legem ac iustitiam redditurum: et quanta poterit integritate ac religione iudicaturum. neque vero iuratus fidem violare facile potest, aut si possit, nolit tamen. ius enim illi dicitur vt priuato cuique, et iisdem legibus tenetur. leges autem totius imperii proprias conuellere non potest, nec de moribus ciuitatum et antiqua consuetudine quicquam immutare, sine trium ordinum consensu." *Methodus*, pp. 313–314.

[116] "Car il faut que le Prince souuerain ait les loix en sa puissance pour les changer, et corriger, selon l'occurence des cas . . . tout ainsi que le maistre pilote doit auoir en sa main le gouuernail, pour le tourner à sa discretion: autrement le nauire seroit plustost peri, qu'on auroit bien l'aduis de ceux qu'il porte." *République*, p. 140.

[117] "Aussi le serment de nos Roys, qui est le plus beau, et le plus bref qui se peut faire, ne porte rien de garder les loix et coustumes du pays ny des predecesseurs." *République*, p. 135.

[118] "Mais quant aux coustumes generales, et particuliers, qui ne concernent point l'establissement du royaume, on n'a pas accoustumé d'y rien changer, sinon apres auoir bien et deuement assemblé les trois estats de France en general, ou de chacun bailliage en particulier: non pas qu'il soit necessaire de s'arrester à leur aduis, ou que le Roy ne puisse faire le contraire de ce qu'on demandera, si la raison naturelle, et la iustice de son vouloir luy assiste. Et en cela se cognoist la grandeur, et maiesté d'vn vray Prince souuerain, quand les estats de tout le peuple sont assemblez presentans requestes, et supplications à leur Prince en toute humilité, sans auoir aucune puissance de rien commander, ny discerner, ny

cluded, drew its weight from the prince alone and had force
only as long as it pleased him;[119] he might quash it through
simple royal act if he so desired.[120] In this fashion, Bodin
was forced by the logic of his own position to discard certain
older limitations upon kingship. His statements marked the
completion of a dual current noted above in earlier writings,
namely, the subordination of customary law to the ruler, and
the separation of that law from the inviolable legal rights of
the subjects. In Bodin's system, the people retained their
rights in property, but the immunity of the same rested upon
their basis in natural law. Customary law, on the contrary,
was reduced to subordinance under the authority of the legislator. The multitude of legal guarantees contained in that
body of law, and representing the heritage of centuries, was
subjected to the will of the prince. With the exception of the
two fundamental laws, the only legal provisions remaining to
bind the king were those based upon the abstract concepts of
the laws of God and nature.

Bodin's ideas concerning the various institutions of government were in strict accord with his theory of sovereignty.
Public authority, he held, was situated entirely in the king.
There could be no division of it between the ruler and any
other individual in the state, no matter how high that person
might stand in office or dignity. Sovereignty was by its nature
perpetual and complete; if it were granted to the ruler with
limitations either in time or content, he held no true sovereignty because final control rested with that power which had
made the grant.[121] For this reason, a regent, lieutenant, or
other officer with a delegation of full authority did not hold

---

voix deliberatiue: ains ce qu'il plaist au Roy consentir, ou dissentir, commander,
ou defendre, est tenu pour loy, pour edit, pour ordonnance." *République*,
pp. 136–137.

[119] ". . . la coustume n'a force que par souffrance, et tant qu'il plaist au
prince souuerain. . . . Et par ainsi toute la force des loix et coustumes, gist au
pouuoir du prince souuerain." *République*, p. 198.

[120] *République*, pp. 137–140, 147. He cited as an example the *Edit des mères*
(p. 140).

[121] *République*, pp. 127–129.

true sovereignty; he held his right merely by *commission précaire*. Between the holder of sovereignty and all other men, even the members of the government, there was a great and fixed distinction, that of ruler and subjects.[122] Consequently, Bodin regarded the Estates General as holding no authority in matters of government or legislation. The *cahiers* of the deputies were for him simply counsel and petition, incapable of binding the ruler.[123] It was only in the granting of taxes that the Estates exercised authority distinct from that of the king, and that was because taxation touched the natural right of the subjects to property.

In similar vein were Bodin's conclusions concerning the authority of the Parlement and the general body of magistrates in the central government. The Parlement he regarded as a key unit in the royal administration, since it represented the ancient body of counsellors and continued to advise the king in regard to weighty matters.[124] Likewise, he retained the doctrine that royal edicts and ordinances should be enregistered by the court. If the magistrates found that an enactment was not just and reasonable, he said, they should send up appropriate remonstrances to the ruler.[125] Bodin believed that remonstrances might well embody precepts of natural law and justice which bound the ruler; such was the meaning which he ascribed to the court's objections to edicts which were not just and reasonable.[126] Thus he reiterated the traditional concept that the court might limit the king by declaring the law which bound him. In spite of Bodin's desire to expand the royal authority, he retained the essentials of the judicial check, making it clear, however, that in verifying royal enactments the court exercised no authority to make

[122] ". . . l'vn est prince, l'autre est suget: l'vn est seigneur, l'autre est seruiteur: l'vn est proprietaire, et saisi de la souueraineté: l'autre n'est ny proprietaire, ny possesseur d'icelle, et ne tient rien qu'en depost." *République*, p. 127.

[123] See above, pp. 162–163.

[124] *République*, p. 293.

[125] *République*, p. 340.

[126] *République*, p. 340.

law.[127] Remonstrances were merely counsel and statement of the law; the court exercised no further control over the sovereign.[128] And finally, he insisted heavily upon the generally accepted idea that when the king was present in his Parlement, that body lost all right of judgment because its entire authority reverted to the king who was its source.[129] These portions of Bodin's system merely duplicated accepted ideas concerning the institutions of government, and reveal the manner in which he caused his theory of sovereignty to fit into the framework of accepted legal theory.

In conclusion, it is necessary to evaluate the implications of Bodin's political thought concerning the reciprocal relations of king and subjects. His system marked a definite advance over every earlier one in the elimination of the feudal, hierarchical structure of the state and the substitution of a theory based strictly upon the entities of ruler and ruled. His fundamental concept, representing the social organism as composed of innumerable families under a single sovereign, provided the basis of that interpretation. As a legist, he could not eliminate at a stroke the multitudinous details of law continuing the older system, yet the larger aspects of his thought predetermined his treatment of the relevant legal problems and caused him to minimize the pyramidal arrangement of the social structure, much after the manner of Du Moulin. The most resistant portion of the legal system inherited from the Middle Ages — that perpetuating the pyramidization of lands — Bodin regarded as an extraneous feature introduced into the Roman system after the barbarian invasions, reflecting the remnants of the seigneurial monarchies of the East and thus inherently unjust. Like his predecessor, he favored alodial holdings and the Roman system of ownership.[130] Con-

---

[127] *République*, p. 145.

[128] *République*, p. 301.

[129] *République*, p. 227. It is to be noted, however, that in the same passage he allowed free discussion in the presence of the king for the purpose of counsel. Thus his attitude was closer to that of de Harlay than to that of Henry III.

[130] These points occur in his discussion of seigneurial monarchy. "Et si on dit

cerning the immediate relationships and mutual obligations of ruler and subjects, Bodin repeated that the king owed protection and security, while the subjects should give faith, submission, obedience, and aid.[131] The bond between king and people was the most vital in the state and transcended all degrees of the feudal scale, bringing all men directly under the monarch. It was the duty of the subjects to consecrate their lives and goods to the service of the monarch; in this Bodin found the true mark of subjection, owed by the people not as vassals and subvassals but as natural subjects.[132] But it must be noted that Bodin did not follow the widespread tendency of distorting those relationships stemming from the feudal system. When applying the idea of reciprocal duties to the national state, many writers altered that concept to the point of regarding taxes as owed through natural obligation, thus completely eliminating popular consent. Bodin avoided this pitfall through his insistence upon the natural basis of property rights.

When untrammeled by the remnants of the feudal system,

qu'il n'y a Monarque en Europe, qui ne pretende la seigneurie directe de tous les biens des sugets, et qu'il n'y a personne qui ne confesse tenir ses biens du Prince souuerain: Ie di que cela ne suffist, pour dire que le Monarque soit seigneurial: attendu que le suget est auoué du Prince vray proprietaire, qui peut disposer de ses biens: et que le prince n'a que la droicte seigneurie. encores y a-il plusieurs terres allodiales, où il n'a, ny proprieté, ny droite seigneurie, non plus que les Romains, qui n'ont iamais cognu ceste droite seigneurie: et ne se trouueront point en tout le droit Romain, ny mesmes au Code, ny aux authentiques ces mots, *Dominium directum, et dominium vtile*: mais ils sont venus, apres l'inuasion des Hongres, nation Tartaresque, et leur entree en Europe, qui monstrerent l'exemple aux Alemans, Lombards, et François, de la Monarchie seigneuriale, soy disans seigneurs de tous les biens. . . . mais depuis que les Alemans, Lombards, Francons, Saxons, Bourguignons, Gots, Ostrogots, Anglois, et autres peuples d'Almaigne eurent gousté la coustume des Hongres Asiatiques, ils commencerent à se porter seigneurs, non des personnes, ains de toutes les terres des vaincus, et peu à peu, se contenterent de la droitte seigneurie, foy, et hommage, et de quelques droits, qui pour ceste cause sont appellez seigneuriaux, pour monstrer que l'ombre des Monarchies seigneuriales est demeuree, et toutesfois beaucoup diminuee." *République*, pp. 235–236.

[131] *République*, p. 72.

[132] ". . . la vraye marque de sugetion, que le vassal, et arriere-vassal doibuent seulement au prince souuerain, non pas en qualité de vassaux, ains en qualité de sugets naturels. . . ." *République*, p. 74.

Bodin elaborated in considerable detail the relations of king and subjects. This aspect of his thought represented a distinct crystallization of several intellectual currents which reflected the appearance of strongly knit national states. Bodin defined the citizen as the free subject living under the sovereignty of another.[133] His approach through the concept of the citizen reveals in itself his preoccupation with the national unit. The most representative citizen he found in the father of the family; all other persons in that group, such as wife, children, or slaves, were under additional servitudes.[134] The liberty enjoyed by the true citizen was greater than that of inferior members of society, but it was necessarily under the rule of the sovereign. None the less, the capacity of citizenship included the basic rights of liberty and property. In addition, Bodin listed certain legal immunities enjoyed by the citizen, largely reflecting the disabilities of foreigners in the state. However, the latter type was quite different from those resting upon natural law, for they not only varied from state to state and city to city but were based upon positive law and therefore subject to the will of the prince. Although Bodin recognized the value of the legal rights of the citizen, he did not regard them as the true test of citizenship. Rather, such was found in the exact relationships existing between ruler and ruled.[135] And in accordance with the implications of these categories, the mass of the people could but take their place as subjects directly under the rule of the sovereign.

Such was the final emphasis of Bodin's conception of legitimate government. Throughout his treatment, he preserved the traditional dualism of legal spheres within the social organism: the authority of the prince and the rights of the subjects. Yet his work brought a definite alteration of the older ideas, largely because of his precision of thought and

---

[133] ". . . le franc suget tenant de la souveraineté d'autruy." *République*, p. 49.

[134] *République*, pp. 50–51.

[135] ". . . il faut bien dire que les priuileges ne font pas le citoyen, mais l'obligation mutuelle du souuerain au suget, auquel, pour la foy, et obeissance qu'il reçoit, il doit iustice, conseil, confort, aide, et protection. . . ." *République*, p. 61.

his emphasis upon natural law. Instead of regarding the prerogative as a mosaic of legal rights authorizing specific capacities, he gave it a natural basis and ascribed to it the all-inclusive authority to command and to make law, an emphasis which necessitated a definite expansion of the legitimate royal discretion. Of equal importance was his treatment of the social position and rights of the subjects. By elaborating his approach to the state through the natural units of sovereign and families, he grouped all men as substantially equal under the prince. This interpretation was motivated by the all-important rise of strongly ruled national states and was of increasing importance in sixteenth-century political thought. But the fact that Bodin's theory was far in advance of that held by the more traditional constitutionalists is revealed by comparing his ideas with those of Du Haillan who maintained the hierarchical structure of society largely intact and applied the term "subject" merely to the lower population on the land.[136] In regard to the specific rights enjoyed by the populace, Bodin maintained the long tradition of the inviolability of property, yet he believed such to be beyond the capacity of the prince to touch only because it rested upon a basis of natural law. All rights guaranteed by customary law were distinctly subject to his discretion. Bodin's ideal citizen, while continuing to enjoy many legal rights, held all subject to the will of the prince, save those resting in abstract concepts. The absolute authority of the ruler remained limited, but those limitations were essentially upon a theoretical basis. Bodin's constitutional system presented a complete, logical, and well-rounded whole and as such it must be admired; but its ultimate influence, in part through its distortion by his followers, proved disastrous to the older constitutionalism.

[136] "Il y a difference entre vassaux et subiects. Les vassaux sont ceux qui tiennent les Fiefs: les subiects sont les Paisans qui doiuent la censiue, la poulle, le chappon de rente, et la couruee: travaille, et iournee de leur corps: toutesfois plusieurs confondent le nom des Vassaux et subiects ensemble, et prennent souuent les uns pour les autres. Car souuent vous verez que monsieur le Gentilhomme parlant de ses terres et de ses hommes, dit mes subiects." *Estat et succez* (Paris, 1580), p. 221a.

C. The Divine Right of Kings

The appearance of Bodin's *Republic* marked, in a sense, the beginning of a new era in French political thought, for the majority of theorists who wrote after 1576 were directly influenced by his contribution. The important mutation in political concepts which resulted from Bodin's ideas was brought about chiefly by the general adoption of his theory of legislative sovereignty. Not only was his definition of the royal authority as a body of power found to provide a theoretical concept superior to the former approach through various marks of sovereignty, but the wider discretion which Bodin attributed to the ruler was adjudged by contemporaries to provide the prince with that enlarged measure of authority which was necessary to enable him to cope with an increasingly difficult social situation. And in the realm of ideas alone, Bodin's statements were regarded as filling a vital need. Theorists had long been feeling their way toward a political conception representing the king as primarily a legislator, and more recently many had become keenly aware of the need for a dynamic conception of the state. Thus, for the jurists of the period, Bodin's system not only drew together and marshalled in logical order many ideas which had heretofore lacked a well defined place in political thinking, but also presented conclusions found to be of value both in the theory and practice of contemporary political life. Because of these qualities of Bodin's doctrine, his conception of the royal authority became the basis of relevant political speculation within a remarkably short period of time.[1]

[1] As indices to the widespread adoption of Bodin's theory of sovereignty, we may list, in addition to the treatises examined below, two works intended to serve as reference manuals in very different fields. Ragueau defined sovereignty as the ". . . pouvoir de donner loy à tous en general et à chacun en particulier de decerner la guerre ou traicter la paix: d'instituer les principaux Officiers et premiers Magistrats: et au dernier ressort. . . ." *Indice, s. v.* "Droicts de souueraineté." Secondly, the *Academie françoise* of Pierre de La Primaudaye. This was first published in Paris, 1577, before the author had read Bodin's *Republic*. The revisions of the second edition, appearing in 1579, were made

As is seemingly inevitable in the subsequent influence of great intellectual systems, it was not Bodin's thought as a whole which was adopted by his followers but rather certain salient features which were appropriated because of their immediate value or appeal to contemporary writers. And in the process of adoption by others, those portions of Bodin's system undergoing such treatment could but be distorted because of their removal from their original context. Certain important concepts were seized upon, torn from their immediate milieu, and, through association with other ideas, were attributed meanings entirely lacking to Bodin. Such was the fate of his most important contribution, his theory of sovereignty. It will be recalled that in the great majority of constitutional systems examined above, the element of divine right was present and of increasing influence. Such an interpretation was lacking from Bodin's fundamental approach; he may have included the usual statements concerning the divine authorization of the political power and the responsibility of the king solely to God, but the basis of the sovereign authority he found in its necessity in every legitimate state as a fact of nature. However, the approach through divine right was a favorite with the great majority of the *politiques*,

---

largely on the basis of Bodin's interpretation. La Primaudaye's method of revision consisted merely of incorporating passages from Bodin verbatim into his treatment and altering his own statements by inserting significant words and phrases drawn from Bodin; consequently, a comparison of the two editions gives a very sharp picture of Bodin's influence upon contemporary political thought. Two short examples of this interpolation follow, the additions being indicated by italics. "Pour la conclusion de nostre present propos, apprenons *que les Loix et ordonnances ciuiles dependent seulement du Souuerain, et qu'il les peult changer selon l'occurrence et bien des affairs de l'Estat*. Que toute Loy se doit rapporter à la reigle infallible de la Iustice et volonté diuine, et à l'vtilité commune de la ciuile societé. . . ." *Academie*, p. 151b, ed. of 1577; p. 182a, ed. of 1579. "Quant à nostre Monarchie Françoyse, on la peult bien dire aussi participer des trois [monarchy, aristocracy, democracy], *en ce qui touche son gouuernement: combien qu'à la verité, l'Estat d'icelle est simple, et pure Monarchie*. Car le Roy y est Monarque, aimé, et reueré ensemble: lequel iaçoit qu'il ayt toute puissance et authorité *souueraine* de commander et faire ce qu'il veult. . . ." *Ibid.*, p. 157a, ed. of 1577; p. 189a, ed. of 1579. The latter statement originated with Seyssel and was repeated by Du Haillan, from whom La Primaudaye doubtless appropriated it, modifying it according to Bodin's ideas.

and when they adopted Bodin's theory of sovereignty, they inevitably placed it in a theoretical framework in which the royal authority rested upon direct divine authorization. It was this all-important union of legislative sovereignty and the divine right of kings which caused the major distortion of Bodin's idea of rulership and foreshadowed the major developments in political theory during the remainder of the century. It would not be great exaggeration to attribute the origins of seventeenth-century absolutism to this union of concepts. But the appearance of that new theory of state was not delayed until the strong rule of the Bourbon kings; it was set forth in its essentials very soon after the publication of the *Republic* because of the immediate adoption of Bodin's contribution by the royalist writers who turned it to account in maintaining the cause of the legitimate monarch, whether Henry III or Henry IV.

Among the legists who wrote during the decade after 1576, this eclectic manner of thought appears best in the works of Jean Duret, François Grimaudet, Pierre Grégoire, and the Gallicized Scot Adam Blackwood. Of these, Duret was by far the least able, and his statements often represent little more than a clumsy attempt to superpose Bodin's ideas upon the older modes of thought without making the necessary adaptation of either. But Grimaudet, Grégoire, and Blackwood were all highly capable thinkers. Each constructed a logical and well-rounded political system and incorporated into it the essentials of Bodin's theory of legislative sovereignty.[2] Although these three writers, and particularly Blackwood, drew conclusions invariably more absolutistic than had Bodin, throughout they were mindful of the niceties of statement and

---

[2] François Grimaudet, *Opuscules politiques, passim*, esp. pp. 3b, 19a, 34b. This work was first published in 1580; our references are to the *Œuvres* of Paris, 1670. Pierre Grégoire, *De republica libri sex et viginti, passim*, esp. Lib. I, V, VI, VII, IX. First published in 1578; our references are to the edition of Lyon, 1609. Adam Blackwood, *Adversus Georgii Buchanani diologum, de iure regni apud Scotos, pro regibus apologia, passim*, esp. pp. 34, 35, 37, 49, 51, 56, 67, 86, 135. First published in 1581; our references are to the *Opera* of Paris, 1644.

interpretation necessary to formal treatises, and they frequently hesitated to push their ideas to their logical conclusions. But such was not the case with a later group of writers of lesser abilities but of equal importance in the evolution of political concepts. These were the militant pamphleteers who wrote in defense of legitimate monarchy during the chaotic period between 1588 and 1593, when the League was at its height and the royal authority had sunk to its lowest ebb. Among these publicists were such men as Louis Servin, Pierre de Belloy, François Le Jay, and Jacques Hurault, and all were close to the royal administration. In developing their position, they invariably followed the example of earlier followers of Bodin by combining his theory of sovereignty with divine right, but unlike their predecessors, they did not hesitate to utilize to the full the potentialities of their arguments. Their pamphlets present but one portion of contemporary controversy, but it was their party which ultimately triumphed, and their doctrines, although brought forth in the heat of battle, were of definite influence upon subsequent theories of state and kingship. The major elements of later absolutism were present in those informal but very purposeful works written in defense of legitimate monarchy when it met its greatest challenge. Thus, it may be said that the theory of absolutism was developed indirectly from Bodin during the chaotic period following his writing, as a distortion of his ideas brought about by the necessities of the moment.

The theory of the divine authorization of kingship was a vital force in the political thought of the sixteenth century. The conception was believed to provide the most satisfactory basis upon which to establish the legitimate character of the political power, and as such it influenced strongly even those legists whose immediate concern was constitutional law. A theorist such as Charondas may have been exceptionally conscious of the philosophical implications of his legal system, yet his ideas that the king was instituted by God, was the image of God, and was responsible to God were accepted by the great majority of his colleagues who were Gallicans and *politiques* almost without exception. Among major writers of the century, there were very few who would have denied that monarchy was a divinely ordained institution, that the king was authorized by God as His agent in temporal government, and that the king was in a strict sense God's vicar. That Bodin's approach to kingship through its natural and human basis, rather than its divine, varied from that of his contemporaries is revealed by the criticisms which Duret levelled at him because of his unorthodox statements on that point.[3] Likewise, Grimaudet and Blackwood, while accepting Bodin's theory of the sovereign power, insisted heavily upon its basis in divine institution.[4]

Among the immediate followers of Bodin, Pierre Grégoire outlined the most complete theory of divine right. His *De republica* is permeated with that conception, and he utilized it as an initial approach to countless political problems. As his point of departure, he stated that the pope and the king stood as God's appointed agents in spiritual and temporal governments respectively.[5] Thus the government of the prince was under the constant influence of God's will and necessarily embodied His dictates.[6] And since the king was no less than the actively inspired agent of the Deity, the people had no choice but to give reverence to their ruler as to the divine

---

[3] Jean Duret, *Commentaires aux coustumes du duché de Bourbonnois* (Lyon, 1584), p. 53.

[4] "Le moyen de rendre les subjetz obeyssans à la loy est . . . si le Prince croit qu'il est un Dieu, s'il le craint, s'il gouverne ses subjets suivant les commandemens de Dieu." Grimaudet, *op. cit.*, p. 476. ". . . la premiere que Dieu en sa perfection administre tout par justice: la seconde est, que les Roys et Princes . . . sont par la distribution de iustice . . . faits à la semblance de l'image de Dieu, qui regit et gouverne, n'ayant besoing ny de Phidias, qui la taille, ny de Polycletus, ny de Miron, ains eux mesmes se forment au moulle, et patron de Dieu, conformans leurs gouvernemens à sa volonté. . . ." *Ibid.*, p. 517. Blackwood wrote: "Quid enim aliud est mortalis ista monarchia, nisi caelestis illius simulachrum et imago?" *Op. cit.*, p. 49. "Nostri reges nihil acceptum populo ferre tenentur, sed Deo, a quo potestas omnis et imperium, eique soli rationem sui reddere muneris et officii." *Ibid.*, p. 65.

[5] *Op. cit.*, Lib. VI, cap. I, no. 6, and cap. II, nos. 6, 13; Lib. VII, cap. I, no. 8.

[6] *Op. cit.*, Lib. VI, cap. I, no. 6, and cap. II, nos. 3, 8, 13.

majesty itself.[7] Thus the prince represented God on earth and should be obeyed as such;[8] to resist him was to revolt against the will and commands of the Deity.[9] This uncompromising logic often carried writers of this school to the point of asserting that the prince himself represented a fusion of the human and the divine. Grégoire hesitated before that idea, preferring to regard the king as a strictly human individual upon whom a divine capacity and authority had been bestowed.[10] But Blackwood carried the glorification of divinely authorized monarchy to its conclusion, stating that the person of the king, no less than his authority, was divine and that he was a god on earth in a literal sense.[11]

In this fashion, the writers of the 1580's presented a complete theory of the divine authorization of the political power. Although certain among their number placed heavy emphasis upon the majesty and quasi-divine qualities of the king, their major conception was concerned with the royal authority rather than the person of the king. Strictly, the theory was one of the divine right of kingship rather than of kings. Although Grégoire placed very heavy stress upon the exalted qualities of royal government, he preserved the distinction between the person of the king and his office, making it clear that the divine character and consequent glory of regality adhered strictly to the latter.[12] Thus, although his statements

---

[7] *Op. cit.*, Lib. VI, cap V, *passim.* "Imago vero Dei, in potestate et authoritate, est princeps." Lib. VIII, cap. X, no. 9.

[8] "Deum tradit imperium constituisse de coelo. Deus in terris dicitur princeps, vt Deus in coelis. . . ." *Op. cit.*, Lib. VI, cap. V, no. 4.

[9] *Op. cit.*, Lib. V, cap. III, no. 6, and cap. IV, no. 12; Lib. VIII, cap. IV, no. 1.

[10] "Neque in principibus, tam inspicimus vel considerare debemus quid ipsi per se et tanquam homines sunt: sed quantum illis concessum aut permissum a Deo sit. Neque in principibus tam personam singularem reueremur, quantum maiestatem Dei et imaginem potestatemque consideramus ex parte illius cuius delegati sunt et vicarias in terra partes gerunt. . . ." *Op. cit.*, Lib. VI, cap. II, no. 9. Cf. Lib. VI, cap. III, no. 1.

[11] See below, n. 21.

[12] "Querat ergo princeps quis ipse sit: inueniet se hominem similem aliis natura, et pares in ea sibi esse subditos. . . . Proinde si quando princeps coronam, diadema, purpuram, ornamentaque regia admirari, et in his sibi complacere coeperit: statim quoque reminisci debet, quod caput et corpus, cui haec

developed to the fullest extent the time-honored concept of the divine right of the governing power, he did not break with older ideas to the point of attributing a divinely sanctioned claim to the individual holding the crown. The novelty of his treatment was merely one of exaggerated emphasis.

The logical content of many current political concepts and the desire of writers to enhance to the fullest extent the majesty of secular government were forcing thinkers increasingly toward a theory recognizing the personal divine right of the monarch. This conception, which was to win acceptance in England at a date not far distant, attributed to the king a personal right to the crown similar to private legal inheritance according to customary law. The ruler was regarded as that divinely chosen individual who enjoyed a proprietary right in the entire body of public authority. Thus, the divine authorization was shifted from the crown to its holder, and the theory became one of the divine right of kings in the strictest sense. However, the appearance of this theory was long delayed in France because of the very strong tradition of fundamental law. It had long been a primary tenet of the constitutionalists that the Kings of France acceded to the throne according to the order of succession fixed by fundamental law, and that far from holding a proprietary right to the royal authority, the reigning prince merely held the prerogative as a trust committed to him for the duration of his reign. The ruler was chosen by law, and the authority which he wielded was accorded to him and limited by law; if there was any element of divine right involved, it adhered to that dignity which the king was called upon to exercise rather than to the king himself. The strength of this tradition was occasioned in part by the unusual character of the Salic Law among the legal systems of the various European states,[13]

exterius accedunt, mortalia, humana, morbis, lapsibus, et ludibrio fortunae obnoxia sunt: quod illa extranea non propria, sed accidentalia sunt: et ne iniuriam sibi faciat, si se extraneo inferiorem profiteatur." *Op. cit.*, Lib. VI, cap. III, no. 7.

[13] French writers were highly conscious of the unusual nature and superiority

but whatever were the reasons for the vigor of the conception, there is no doubt concerning its continued strength throughout the sixteenth century. Although Bodin's successors enhanced to the fullest extent the miraculous and quasi-divine qualities of kingship, occasionally representing the king as a super-human individual, they did not break with this all-important conception of legal succession to the crown. Grégoire outlined very sharply the differences between royal succession according to private, patrimonial right and according to fundamental law, making it clear that the Kings of France acceded strictly in virtue of the latter type.[14] Likewise Blackwood, the most absolutistic of the group, stated explicitly that royal succession was according to fundamental law rather than private right.[15] Thus the tradition representing the crown as a dignity conferred by law upon its holder remained unbroken in the writings of Bodin's immediate successors. Their major importance was in their amalgamation of his theory of sovereignty with the prevailing concepts of the divine basis of the prerogative, a development of very great importance. But they did not proceed to the further conclusion that the monarch himself enjoyed divine right.

When Bodin's followers gave his theory of sovereignty a

---

of the Salic Law. The following statement is representative: "Nullum enim est in toto orbe, fuit, aut erit, diuturnius Regnum, et Imperium, quam Francorum: istis scilicet duobus fundamentis: primo, quod filii Regnum a patre accipiunt, non electione, sed successione: secundo, quod mulieres a Regno arcentur." Matharel, *op. cit.*, p. 54.

[14] "Quamobrem aliud est in regno succedere in locum demortui, iure haeredi-tario, aliud iure legis et proximitatis seu primogeniturae in regno antiquo generis. Nam quando regnum defertur iure haereditatis et nouum siue quaesitum est, quod fuerit in libera morientis dispositione, ne electionis alia lege obstrictum, ex voluntate defuncti succeditur vel expressa per testamentum, vel tacita ab in-testato. . . . At quando principatus antiqui per legem regni deferuntur proxi-miori et antiquiori, vel alio modo, licet retinere principatum ei qui in gradu vel qualitate requisita idoneus inuenitur, reiecta haereditate, et reiecto imposito grauamine, nisi ipse ei se obligauerit, et debetur principatus filio aut proximiori etiam non haeredi." *Op. cit.*, Lib. VII, cap. XII, no. 1. Cf. Lib. VII, cap. XVI, no. 9.

[15] "Neque enim iam haereditas est, proprium adeuntis patrimonium, cuius ei pleno dominium acquiritur, non a patre, non a populo, sed a lege." *Op. cit.*, p. 46.

basis in divine authorization, they took a major step toward the later theory of absolutism. This was not because of any resulting change in ideas concerning the rights of the king to the crown, but rather because that development altered the conception of the royal authority itself. This appears particularly in the tendency to attribute more comprehensive qualities to royal legislation and in the further expansion of the monarch's dominion over the traditional rights of the people, especially those in private property. In regard to royal legislation, it was a very real danger that such an altered conception of sovereignty would give the unrestricted will of the prince the force of law. His commands of all types would be legally binding, for whatever he did would be *ipso facto* just. Bodin's conception of sovereignty had attributed to the ruler the combined authorities to make new law and to enforce its execution. And when royal authority of that type was given a basis in divine authorization, the resulting idealization of the monarch's rule caused thinkers increasingly to regard the law made by the king as the earthly manifestation of God's will, or at least to believe that it was inspired by agents beyond the capacity of ordinary mortals.[16] Thus the king was a living law in the most complete sense. Likewise, he could do no wrong, for he himself might establish the standard according to which his acts were evaluated. However, the majority of contemporary jurists refused to go to such lengths in regarding the king's laws and commands as *ipso facto* just. They were unwilling to break with the time-honored tradition that the king could err in terms of well established criteria of justice and that he could even be condemned in court for the same. Grimaudet considered this

[16] "Cette puissance [souveraine] est par dessus les loix, car elle peut les abolir, en faire de nouuelles, les interpreter, et modifier, le tout par Iustice à laquelle elle mesure toutes actions, et sa volonté: c'est à dire ses ordonnances tenues pour loix. Le Prince au gouuernement qu'il faict par ceste puissance, est l'image de Dieu." Grimaudet, *op. cit.*, p. 478. "Est igitur legis iustitia finis, lex munus principis, princeps cuncta moderantis, recteque et ordine constituentis simulacrum Dei." Blackwood, *op. cit.*, p. 188.

general issue in relation to the question whether an officer was bound to carry out iniquitous orders of the prince. Certain writers, he said, argue that since the ruler has authority superior to the law and may make law, any orders must be carried out even if contrary to accepted law; the will of the prince necessarily has the force of law because his authority is superior to legal limitation. This reasoning Grimaudet held to be specious. True, he said, the king as king cannot err because a legitimate ruler measures all his acts according to justice. But it is entirely possible that commands of the ruler may go against right and justice, in which case he no longer remains a just and legitimate ruler but degenerates into a tyrant.[17] And he cited Bodin's distinction that officers were bound to carry out orders of the prince contrary to the law of the land but not those contrary to natural and divine law.[18] Thus, although Grimaudet attributed a very wide discretion to the prince and recognized his freedom from the major portions of constitutional law, he did not exaggerate his doctrine to the point of attributing legal weight to the indiscriminate will of the prince. That pitfall he avoided by maintaining a large body of precepts, however intangible, which the king was bound to follow and which served as criteria in distinguishing between legitimate rule and tyranny. He held that the king as king could do no wrong, but such did not preclude the possibility of injustice in certain acts of the ruler. The

[17] "Sur ce est fait question. Si le Prince commande à ses officiers, ou à l'vn de ses subjets faire quelque chose d'injustice, s'ils doiuent obeyr? Il semble que non par les raisons cy-dessus alleguees: car le commandement du Prince ne peut estre dit injuste, sinon en tant qu'il commande faire chose contre la loy. Or il a toute puissance sur la loy, peut icelle abolir, à icelle deroger, et lever la deffence portée par icelle. Partant lors que le Prince aura commandé faire quelque chose, Tel commandement n'est plus d'injustice, puis qu'il contient la volonté du Prince, qui est la loy, et oste la deffence qui estoit auparauant. Par ceste raison Innocent est d'auis que le subjet doibt executer le commandement du Prince, encores qu'il soit inique: ce qui est flaterie trop impudente et faulse; car il est impossible que le Roy (comme Roy) commande chose iniuste, parce qu'il rapporte toutes ses actions à Justice, qui ne peut estre au Prince, qui fait injustice, lequel où il commetra les deportemens de Caligula, Nero, Domitian. . . ." *Op. cit.*, pp. 479–480.

[18] *Op. cit.*, p. 480.

will of the prince had force of law, but it was by definition
his just will; unjust commands emanating from him were not
legally binding because they were contrary to natural and
divine law and thus ran counter to the inherent qualities of
kingship.[19]

Although Grimaudet thus refused to regard the orders of
the prince as just unless they conformed with that justice
which characterized true kingship, the criteria according to
which he would establish the legitimacy of such acts were
largely abstract and hence could impose very indefinite and
uncertain limits upon the king's discretion. With the subjection of all constitutional law, save the fundamental laws, to
the prince, those thinkers who preserved the older concept of
justice as a body of precepts above and apart from the ruler
were forced to find their standards of right and equity in
natural and divine law. These conceptions were of vital importance in the intellectual systems of such thinkers as Bodin
and Grimaudet. But the fact that such criteria of justice
offered ineffective barriers to the rising tide of opinion favoring royal absolutism is illustrated by the willingness of Blackwood, the most absolutistic of the group, to regard the will
of the prince as just almost without qualification. Following
the example of Budé, Blackwood not only attributed to the
prince a blanket authority over all civil law but insisted that
the voluntary submission required by the *digna vox* might be
understood only as applying to the final principles of natural
law governing all men equally.[20] And like Budé, he called
upon the authority of Aristotle to demonstrate that the king,
far from standing on the same plane as his subjects, was a

---

[19] "Parquoy ce qui est dit, et tant de fois repeté, que ce qui plait au Prince,
doit estre tenu pour loy, sera entendu pource qu'est juste et raisonnable."
Op. cit., p. 478. "Aussi qu'il est escrit, ce qu'il plaist au Prince, a force de loy,
non ce qu'il plaist à Cesar: esquelz motz y a grande force, pour entendre quand
l'ordonnance du Roy doit estre tenue pour bonne, car l'Empereur (comme
Cesar) peut faillir, et faire des oppressions, mais comme Prince il ne peut:
d'autant que par ce mot de Prince, est entendu un homme juste et de valeur, qui
pour ses vertus est le chef du peuple. . . ." *Ibid.*, p. 524.

[20] *Op. cit.*, pp. 188–190.

god among men and a law unto himself.[21] The ruler stood as a living law not only because he embodied in himself the ideals of human aspiration [22] but also because he necessarily modeled his enactments after the highest principles of justice and truth.[23] Blackwood may have preserved natural and divine law as higher values above the prince, but his emphasis upon the superhuman qualities of the ruler and the automatic concordance of his laws with highest justice all but equated his enactments with justice itself. For all purposes of practical government, the will of the prince was *ipso facto* just.

The second important alteration of constitutional thought which resulted in part from the fusion of Bodinian sovereignty and divine authorization was the elimination of consent to taxation. Bodin had placed property rights upon an inviolable basis of natural law, and he retained in consequence the requirement of popular consent to all non-customary levies. Although his interpretation shifted the basis of property rights from customary law and usage to one of natural law, the latter was entirely valid and sufficed in his system to guarantee the inviolability of private property. However, in the evolution of political concepts, Bodin's changed conception of proprietary rights marked an important step toward the elimination of consent to taxation, because the inviolability ascribed to property by natural law alone was not sufficiently rigid to withstand the impact of those absolutistic conceptions

[21] "Princeps enim animata lex est in terris, cuius potestas atque iurisdictio non alia lege quam ipsius voluntate in angustum cogi potest. Aristoteles regem quasi Deum inter homines censendum ait. . . . Necessarium est, inquit, legislationem inter eos esse qui sunt et genere, et ciuili facultate pares. In illos autem huiuscemodi nulla prorsus est legislatio, quippe qui ipsi lex sunt." *Op. cit.*, p. 59. See above, ch. II, n. 52.

[22] "Reliquorum ciuium vt quisque vel opibus, vel virtute, vel maiorum meritis, vel antiquitate generis, vel apud principem gratia maxime pollet, ita longissime distat ab ignobilis vulgi faece, principis ideam quandam ac imaginem referens, non aliter ac princeps Dei." *Op. cit.*, p. 60.

[23] "Nunc vero quemadmodum, vt Cyprianus ait, ad diuinum imperium de terris mutuamur exemplum: sic caelestis imperii similitudine terrena metiamur. Principes enim cuncta moderantis simulachra sunt Dei: terrena politia caelestis est imago." *Op. cit.*, p. 181. See above, n. 16.

which were taking shape in the late sixteenth century. In the midst of widespread reaction against the older conception of kingship and the substitution of divine-right sovereignty, there was certain to result a metamorphosis of the traditional relationships between king and people. In such an intellectual atmosphere, it was very easy to define natural law as the legal basis for the obligation of taxes to the ruler, rather than as the basis of the inviolability of property. The consequent elimination of consent to taxation was made doubly certain, for many thinkers, by the element of divine right: from a position attributing to the king a divinely bestowed authority over all matters of government, it was but a step to attribute to him a right over all matters *necessary* to government, such as taxation. The interpretation did not deny the two traditional spheres of legal right, but it effectively eliminated popular consent to taxation.

The fact that Bodin's political doctrines were in themselves a step toward the elimination of consent to taxation is indicated by the flat denial of that constitutional expedient by the great majority of contemporary writers who followed a similar approach to the problem. Such was the case not only with Bodin's immediate followers but also with his intellectual predecessors, such as Charondas and Le Roy. Charondas had stated that circumstances occasionally constrained the ruler to levy new taxes from the people, and he made it clear that the taking of such levies was effected simply in virtue of the king's authority over his subjects and their property.[24] However, Charondas did not intend to imply that the ruler was owner of all property in the realm; he preserved the concept of popular proprietary rights as constituting a sphere of legal immunity apart from the royal prerogative. The true prince, he said, would recognize the rights of the people and refrain

[24] ". . . il est quelquefois contrainct d'imposer et leuer sur le peuple nouvelles tailles, aides et subsides, ou augmenter les anciennes: qui est un droit de souueraineté. Car telle imposition procede de la puissance, qu'a le souuerain sur ses suiects, qu'il ne doit communiquer à autre seigneur." *Pandectes*, p. 87. See above, ch. III, pt. B, n. 125.

from claiming them as his own, but he likewise maintained that such constitutional provisions were entirely compatible with the monarch's supreme authority over private property.[25] In this fashion, Charondas maintained the traditional distribution of proprietary rights in the realm and at the same time attributed to the monarch the prerogative to take all levies necessary for the support of the government, thus eliminating consent to taxation.

The theory of Louis Le Roy concerning royal taxation was more precise, and the close parallel between many of his ideas and those of Bodin renders his interpretation doubly valuable in evaluating the potentialities of their approach. In discussing the organization of the state and the respective duties of the various social classes toward its maintenance, Le Roy placed upon the third estate the unqualified obligation to give those taxes which were necessary to meet public expenses.[26] Equally explicit were the legal aspects of his system. Taxes, he said, were owed to the king according to all law, human and divine. The only limitation upon the authority of the ruler to collect such levies was his own sense of moderation. Le Roy advised the king to avoid excessive taxation and extortion arising purely from passing whims, but he placed no definite limits of law and he did not mention consent.[27] The

---

[25] "Si quelqu'vn corrompu de la poison de Cour pour mettre en desordre l'Estat du Royaume, propose que le Roy n'a grand interest d'aliener, et engager son domaine, parce qu'il est seigneur de tous les biens de ses subiects, esquels consiste le fonds de ses finances, d'autant qu'il peut, quand il veut, et par diuers moyens tirer et espuyser de leurs bourses tout ce qu'il commande: ie respondray qu'vn bon Prince (comme tousiours ont esté nos Rois), reiectera telle proposition comme tyrannique: ains s'estimant tuteur, defenseur et pere de la patrie dressera tout son soin et ses pensees au salut et profit de ses subiects, tant en general qu'en particulier: et combien qu'il ait puissance sur leurs biens, toutesfois il recognoistra qu'ils sont à eux en domaine, et dira auec Tertullian, si tous les biens sont au Prince, si tout est permis au Prince, que sera-il à Dieu?" *Pandectes*, p. 122.

[26] *Politiques d'Aristote*, p. 340. His statements regarding this question are very similar to those made by Seyssel in his *Grande Monarchie*.

[27] "Car les subsides sont deuz aux Princes par droit diuin et humain, pour soustenir les grandes despenses de leurs estats, et entretenir la dignité de leur maison, Pourueu cependant qu'ils n'oublient qu'ils sont constituez en ce lieu

definitions of royal and seigneurial monarchy given by Le Roy and Bodin were highly similar, varying only in regard to the inviolability of private property and the necessity of consent to taxation.[28] Le Roy's legal interpretation of that question may be summed up in the statement that the third estate owed taxes to the prince according to human and divine law. The ease with which he interpreted natural law as constraining the people to give all necessary taxes reveals in striking fashion the insufficiency of Bodin's conception, likewise founded upon natural law, to preserve the inviolability of property rights and to require popular consent to extraordinary levies.

Although Bodin's immediate followers appropriated great portions of his thought, they invariably refused to follow his dicta in regard to royal taxation. Grimaudet was the most hesitant concerning this matter. He maintained uncompromisingly the distinction between public and private property and denied that the king might confiscate at will, but he did not equate this with consent to taxation.[29] In his writings in connection with the Estates General, he mentioned the question of the tailles but did not include the right of the assembly to assent to such levies.[30] He seems to have avoided that delicate issue entirely. But Grégoire attributed to the king the unqualified prerogative to levy all taxes necessary to government. For him, public necessity was synonymous with just cause for taxation, since, he argued, the good of the state is higher than the property rights of any individual.[31] In

---

eminent, pour estre peres du pais, pasteurs du peuple, gardiens de paix, protecteurs de iustice, et pour bien mesnager ce qu'ils leuent de la propre et necessaire substance de leurs subiects: à fin qu'ils n'en abusent par prodigalité, et qu'ils les despendent en saine conscience deuant Dieu." *Excellence du gouuernement royal*, p. 40. "Que les tributs et imposts sont duez aux Princes par droit diuin et humain, pour soustenir les grandes despenses de leurs estats, et entretenir la dignité de leur maison." *Les Monarchiques* (Paris, 1570), p. 101b.

[28] *Politiques d'Aristote*, pp. 6, 46, 116, 465.

[29] *Op. cit.*, opuscule VII.

[30] *Remonstrance aux estatz d'Anjou* (Lyon, 1561).

[31] *Op. cit.*, Lib. III, cap. IV, no. 2; Lib. VII, cap. XX, no. 41.

similar vein, he insisted heavily that if the monarch went beyond the needs of the royal administration and appropriated subjects' wealth simply for personal gain, he degenerated into a tyrant.[32] However, Grégoire established no legal limitation upon the ruler's right to appropriate wealth, save the extent of public expenses. As a general proposition, he insisted that the king held by divine grant an absolute authority over the persons and property of his subjects.[33] The Estates General, he said, might discuss the expediency of new levies, but that body had no determinative voice concerning the same. He concluded that it would be preferable to dispense with the Estates altogether and to consult instead the members of the Parlement who were better acquainted with administrative problems.[34]

Even more explicit were the statements of Duret. While recognizing that the tailles were of recent origin and had grown from an extraordinary levy,[35] he emphatically stated that the monarch might appropriate a man's property accord-

---

[32] *Op. cit.*, Lib. III, cap. IX, no. 14.

[33] "Atque in his omnibus desideramus iustas causas et modos iustos acquirendi, vel imponendi, conseruandi seu augendi, et expendendi pecunias vel bona reipublicae. Praecipue hic prudentia principis, et affectio in causam communem, potius quam in priuatum commodum primas partes habebit. . . . Sic necessarium fuisse harum pecuniarum exactionem pro ratione necessitatis referri ad principem, tanquam ad cerebrum et gubernaculum totius corporis ciuilis: vt nulli alii liceat quam principi, aut illis qui gerunt in republica supremum imperium, de his se immiscere sine eorum iussu et authoritate. Et quanquam fuerit disputatum a quibusdam, de iure et potestate regum, num quae praescripta sunt per legem regiam, prolatam iussu Dei per Samuelem in creatione regis Saulis, pertinerent ad tyrannum vel ad regem legitimum. Placuit tamen saniori iudicio, ad vtrosque pertinere posse: ad tyrannum quidem, si sine cerebro, ratione, et necessitate publica, exigat ibi concessa; vt ad bonum principem, si vtilitas publica requirat et suadeat illis iuribus vti: vt etiam possit iuxta praedictam legem, agros et vineta subditorum addecimare, imo et bona illis tollere et dare seruis suis, nempe si suadeat publica vtilitas, et debeant illi esse subditi tanquam serui. Postquam enim commissa est potestas a Deo principi in subditos absoluta, non est dubitandum quin et bona eorum et personae sint illi subiectae, et ex potestate principis, possessionum diuisionem et proprietatem pendere. . . ." *Op. cit.*, Lib. III, cap. II, no. 10. Cf. Lib. IX, cap. I, nos. 11–13, 30. Also, Grégoire's *Syntagma iuris universi* (Lyon, 1587), Lib. III, cap. II to X.

[34] *De republica*, Lib. XXIV, cap. V, nos. 3, 4.

[35] *Op. cit.*, p. 185, col. 2.

ing to the necessities of government, since all acts of the king were assumed to be just and reasonable; taxation was simply a matter of his pleasure.[36] The authority of the king to levy taxes was a regalian right; to question it was to disavow the rule of the sovereign who alone had the right to determine policy and to cause his subjects to contribute to the public chest.[37] And Blackwood likewise asserted that the king might take all necessary taxes simply in virtue of his undoubted right over such matters.[38] In explanation of this statement, he set forth a theory of property and ownership with extremely absolutistic implications. All lands, he said, were originally held by the king and were granted by him to others; thus when a fief was forfeited to the ruler, it merely reassumed its original nature as a royal possession.[39] And the granting of fiefs by the king was but a partial transfer; all lands owed tribute to him and remained subject to his authority. Likewise he retained *dominium directum* over all.[40] Whereupon

---

[36] ". . . le Monarque auec cognoissance de cause et pour le bien public, qui doit estre preferé au particulier, peut despouiller le subiect de ce qui luy appartient, payant la iuste valeur: et ensaisiner vn autre qui n'y auoit rien. Il peut defendre au priué de faire poursuitte de ses dommages et interests, et les remettre s'ils sont adiugez. Qui plus est, s'il n'appert de la cause pourquoy il le veut ainsi, elle sera tousiours entendue estre iuste et raisonnable. D'ailleurs si vous considerez la plenitude de sa puissance, il n'y faut autre chose que son bon plaisir. . . ." *Op. cit.*, p. 61, col. 2.

[37] ". . . resolvons sans distinction, que qui est subiect doit obeir à la volonté de son Seigneur souuerain. . . . Car veu qu'imposer est vn droict accompagnant la royauté, qui est le subiect qui puisse dire le plaisir du Prince estre desbordé? Ne seroit ce pas retourner au commencement et mal à propos receuoir l'effect de l'inferieur contre son souuerain? C'est au seul Roy d'imposer et la quottite est remise à son bon plaisir. C'est à luy d'aduiser les necessitez du royaume, et pour y subuenir contribuer les subiects, faire emprunts sur les aisez, et autrement s'en ayder, ainsi qu'il preuoira estre meilleur. [*] C'est à luy et non à autre, de donner permission et auctoriser toutes collectes." *Op. cit.*, p. 199, col. 2. At the point indicated (*), he cites Grassaille. See also Duret's *Harmonie et conference des magistrats romains auec les officiers françois* (Lyon, 1574), pp. 36–37.

[38] "Verum vbi res ita tulerit, vbi maiores sumptus publica necessitas exegerit, quam quos fiscus, quos regium patrimonium suppeditare queat, iure suo, ac regni lege priuatorum facultatibus vtetur vt suis." *Op. cit.*, p. 142.

[39] *Op. cit.*, pp. 166–167.

[40] "Nec ab his institutis abhorruere nostrates, quibus nihil possessionum, nihil agrorum est, quod censui, quod tributo non sit obnoxium, quod regiae ditionis

Blackwood, by a singular extension of these ideas of the king's original lordship over all lands, the subjects' incomplete title to their holdings, and the ruler's capacity as a fleshly god on earth, drew the conclusion that the king alone held true property rights, and that all other persons in the realm held mere temporary possession which entitled them to the use and the fruits of their holdings but to nothing else.[41] Such a statement eliminated at a stroke the fundamental conception of dual spheres of legal right because it attributed title to all private property — the essence of popular legal rights — to the prince. In making such a sweeping and revolutionary statement, Blackwood stood almost alone in the century, but its appearance in his works illustrates the lengths to which the proponents of divine-right sovereignty were willing to extend their doctrine.

It was during the period of the Wars of Religion dominated by the League that the theory of the divine right of kings received its greatest impetus and extension. Roughly between 1585 and 1593, the royal authority faced its most severe challenge during centuries of existence, and that was because the heir to the throne was a heretic incapable of fulfilling the capacities of the Most Christian King. The opposition rested its claims squarely upon the religious issue; such was the rallying cry and the *raison d'être* of the League. The pamphlet literature of the period reflects well the fact that the main lines of the struggle, at least as concerned the royal authority,

---

sit immune." *Op. cit.*, p. 167. "Quae certissimo sunt argumento praediorum omnium dominium directum ad reges pertinere." *Ibid.*, p. 167.

[41] "Omnes enim clientelae, omnia praediorum beneficia regno inhaerent a quo profecta sunt. Rex patronorum omnium supremus est patronus: eoque clientis regii cliens regius etiam cliens est: vt non iniuria post Vegetium Baldus doctissimus Romani iuris interpres, regem in suo regno corporalem Deum appellarit, quod eius nutu moueantur omnia, eius nutu quiescant: quod eius omnia sint mancipio, singulorum vsu: quod eius omnium sit proprietas, singulorum fructus." *Op. cit.*, p. 167. "Regum enim omnia sunt dominio, singulorum vsu. Regum sunt omnia proprietate, singulorum possessione." *Ibid.*, p. 141. As authority for the latter statement, Blackwood cited Seneca's *De beneficiis*; but the manner in which he utilized this passage is a definite and very revealing departure from Seneca.

were drawn in terms of the relative importance of fixed succession, symbolized by the Salic Law, and the religious attributes of kingship. The Salic Law was regarded by the legitimists as the necessary legal basis of the succession, important not only in itself but as a symbol of the entire legal structure of the state which would be threatened with collapse if that most fundamental law were violated. Their emphasis was upon social stability, legal right, and legitimate rule. The religious element, while not as well established in terms of law, was regarded as a vital quality of kingship essential in a state whose ultimate ends were defined in terms of religious values. The vital place and all-absorbing quality of the religious life of the state were made manifest by the immense strength of the League, and as long as the great body of the population held Catholicism to be vital to kingship, the League could hardly be challenged on its own grounds. The compromise solution through the acceptance of the legitimate heir, recently converted, is well known. But before Henry IV was able to make good his claim to the throne, the realm had passed through a series of violent struggles which had been waged with the pen as well as the sword and which were to exercise permanent influence upon French political thought.

It was in order to meet the Leaguers with something resembling their own arguments that the royalist party of the period placed very heavy emphasis upon the divine right of kings. In adopting this position, the purpose of the royalists was not to deny the religious life of the state but rather to establish the indefeasible claim of the legitimate heir to the throne and to checkmate the doctrines of the Leaguers permitting papal domination over purely French affairs. This they sought to achieve by reiterating in exaggerated form the long-standing tenets of Gallicanism. The leaders of the League, insisting that the religious attributes of kingship were of highest importance, upheld the authority of the pope to pronounce concerning the fitness of the successor to the throne of France because of papal superiority over all secular rulers,

a superiority which included in their eyes not only supremacy
in spiritual matters but also the power of direct intervention
in affairs of state. In 1585, Sixtus V issued a bull depriving
Henry of Navarre of his rights to the succession, and the
following pope, Gregory XIV, did not hesitate to excommuni-
cate all clerics supporting Henry and to send a papal army to
join forces with the League. This aspect of the struggle
clearly reflected the issue between the final authority of the
papacy, through the dominance of religious considerations,
and the independence of the secular authority. Those supporting the legitimate heir and the freedom of kingship from
papal control perceived that their ends might best be gained
through the doctrine of the divine right of kings, for that
theory permitted a double emphasis, which, when carried to
logical conclusions, practically eliminated the pope from national life. First, that doctrine established the direct divine
authorization of the royal power. Kings were established in
their right by God alone and were responsible only to Him.
The pope was ruled out as transmitter of the secular authority
and could claim no right to control its holder, since pope and
king stood on an equal footing under God according to their
separate and independent spheres of authority. And secondly,
the theory went far toward establishing the king as leader of
the religious life of the state. Although the Gallicans did not
attribute to their ruler the capacity to pronounce concerning
spiritual matters, they regarded him as the active head of the
Gallican Church. It was a primary tenet of Gallicanism that
the king held control over the entire ecclesiastical *police*, while
the monarch and the councils of the French clergy, national
and local, were regarded as directing the life and policies of
the ecclesiastical institution. And when it was asserted in
addition that the king represented God on earth and was a
superior being, there remained small place for the pope in
national life. To the claims of the Leaguers based upon the
supreme importance of religion, the proponents of divine-right
sovereignty opposed a theory in which the king was inde-

pendent of the pope both in source of authority and ability to guide all portions of the state.

It was of crucial importance in the evolution of French political thought that the royalist pamphleteers should adopt this position and method of argument. When analyzed in terms of specific contributions, their doctrines appear not as direct innovations but simply as exaggerated statement and recombination of earlier ideas, but such were the principal ingredients from which new conceptions were fashioned. The immediate followers of Bodin had taken the important step of placing his concept of legislative sovereignty upon a basis of divine institution, but, with the exception of Blackwood, himself a pamphleteer,[42] they had hesitated before the more absolutistic implications of their position. However, the supporters of the royal authority in its conflict with the League showed no such hesitation in handling their concepts; they seized upon the theories of sovereignty and divine right and turned them to the best advantage of their cause. The pamphlets of these writers may have been composed hastily and without due consideration for legal distinctions, but they succeeded, in part through sheer bravado, in extending the theory of divine-right sovereignty to new heights of absolutism. And because it was their good fortune to support the party which triumphed at the close of the struggle, the doctrines of these royalists were to play a large part in French political concepts for more than a century. Although later writers provided that logical rigidity necessary to the incorporation of the new ideas into complete legal systems, they were frequently content with reiterating ideas which had been set forth earlier in the militant pamphlets opposing the pretensions of the League.

The literature in which these royalists stated their position is today very scattered and difficult to evaluate, but there are certain works, not anonymous, which may be accepted as

[42] As the title indicates, his work, cited above, was written in answer to George Buchanan's *De iure regni apud Scotos*.

representative. Those of Servin [43] and Belloy [44] are of value
as portions of contemporary controversy, being directed specifically against the League and the policy of the papacy. The
treatise of Le Jay [45] was an elaborate pamphlet published at
Tours in 1589 during the period when that city served as
Henry IV's provisional capital. The book of Jacques Hurault [46] and the speeches of Jacques de La Guesle,[47] the Procureur General, may be regarded as significant expressions of
opinion by members of the royal administration. Through an
examination of these works, remarkably similar in content,
it is possible to evaluate the exact nature of that theory of
the royal authority which was developed in government circles
during the chaotic period of the League.

The general acceptance of Bodin's conception of sovereignty
during the period under discussion is evidenced by the fact
that not only the royalists but the Leaguers as well incorporated it into their political pamphlets.[48] The great Ange-

[43] Louis Servin, *Vindiciae secundum libertatem ecclesiae Gallicanae.* This
work was first published in 1590; our references are to the reprint in Goldast's
Monarchia (Frankfort, 1688), III.

[44] Pierre de Belloy, *Apologie catholique* (1585), *Moyens d'abus, entreprises
et nullitez du rescrit et bulle du pape Sixte V* (1586), *De l'autorité du roy et
crimes de leze majesté, qui se commettent par ligues* (1587). All are without
place of publication.

[45] François Le Jay, *De la dignité des roys* (Tours, 1589).

[46] Jacques Hurault, *Des offices d'estat* (Paris, 1588).

[47] Jacques de La Guesle, *Les Remonstrances* (Paris, 1611).

[48] Le Jay, *op. cit.*, pp. 81b, 187a, 189a; Hurault, *op. cit.*, p. 3a. The acceptance of Bodin's theory by the Leaguers is illustrated by the following
passage from one of their anonymous pamphlets. "Or quand ie parle ainsi du
Prince, i'entende celuy qui a la puissance absolue et souueraine, car ie suis
d'accord auec tous les Politiques, que toutes especes de Royaumes, ausquels le
Roy ne commande point absoluement, ne sont proprement Royautez: celuy est
proprement Roy qui ne recognoist puissance humaine plus grande qui la sienne.
De tel Prince on a accoustumé de dire, qu'il est deslié de la loy: que les loix
regardent seulement ceux qui sont egaux de race et de pouuoir, mais entre le
peuple et le Roy il n'y a point d'egalité: qu'au Prince ne peut estre imposée loy,
estant lui mesme la loy: qu'en tout Royaume souuerain la coustume est, que
tout se dispose selon la volonté et plaisir du Roy, mais tels dires doiuent estre
entendus sainement. Le Prince est la loy, parce que sa bonne vie doit seruir de
patron et d'exemple à tous ses subiects: il est plus grand que la loy, et que celuy
qui donne est plus grand que ce qu'il donne, et ne luy peut estre soubmis comme
moindre: mais cela est entendu de la loy ciuil, non de la diuine et naturelle, de

vin's doctrines concerning the royal authority were such that they were capable of acceptance by both factions at war, and thus the contemporary social upheavals had small influence in retarding the reception of the new concept. The works of Belloy contain perhaps the clearest statement of that doctrine as it was set forth in the royalist pamphlets. Approaching the problem of state organization through the fundamental concept of dual spheres, Belloy attributed very wide authority to the king. As the body was animated by the soul, likewise the social structure was given life by the sovereign authority. Thus the ruler lent life to the laws, justice, and general rules by which society was governed and according to which it lived.[49] From this, Belloy drew the conclusion that the prince was the source of all law and held as sovereign the combined authorities to make law and to bring about its enforcement.[50] Thus Belloy merely followed his predecessors in ascribing to the monarch the capacities to judge, legislate, and to enforce the execution of his enactments. These were the major elements in the rising theory of sovereignty, and all were specifically included in Belloy's interpretation. In this department

laquelle le Prince n'est deslié. . . . Aussi est il astreinct aux lois qui concernent l'estat du Royaume, et l'establissement d'iceluy, d'autant qu'elles sont vnies et annexées à la couronne, et par ainsi il n'y peut aucunement deroger." *De la puissance des roys*, p. 18. The only questions concerning which he disagreed with Bodin were those rendered necessary by the policy of the League, namely, the legitimacy of revolt (p. 15) and the authority of the Estates General. See above, ch. III, pt. B, n. 90.

[49] "La matiere est la Republique en laquelle la forme et Majesté Royalle commande souuerainement. Si bien donc qu'il s'ensuit que les loix, la iustice, et les reigles ordonnees en la Cité, sont l'ame de ce corps ciuil, et le Roy qui commande est l'organe, et la bouche de toute la police, laquelle seroit tousiours muette si le Roy ne l'a fait parler." *Autorité du roy*, p. 21b.

[50] "Ainsi en la Majesté du Roy qui est le chef du corps politicque, reside l'intelligence, c'est à dire les loix, conseils, decrets, constitutions, et puis la volonté et execution faicte par la vertu de la parolle, affin que s'il estoit autrement obserué cest animal ciuil ne s'alterast et corrompist d'inquité, d'iniustice, de confusion et d'impieté, partant la marque, l'Estat et Majesté Royalle contient le droict, le pouuoir et l'authorité de commander seul, comme Monarque et souuerain en sa Republique." *Autorité du roy*, pp. 21b–22a. Belloy repeated Bodin: ". . . le principal charactere du Monarque gist en ce qu'il peut donner la loy à tous en general, et à chacun en particulier, sans le consentement ny volonté d'autre quel qu'il soit." *Ibid.*, p. 24b.

of legal thought, even the royalists found it sufficient to reiterate the ideas of Bodin.

Like the earlier followers of Bodin, the royalist pamphleteers inevitably placed his concept of sovereignty upon a basis of divine authorization. Their emphasis upon the sacrosanct and exalted character of kingship was not equalled by any earlier writings of the century, even those which had appeared under Francis I. A few examples will suffice to illustrate the tenor of their statements. Le Jay held that kings received their authority directly from God and were constantly guided by Him, that they were established for the honor and service of God, and that subjects should obey their ruler as they would a divinity on earth.[51] The same emphasis permeates the works of Belloy.[52] Servin, whose book was one of the most extreme Gallican treatises of the period, practically eliminating the pope from the religious life of the state, wrote of Henry IV who was as yet unconverted to Catholicism: "God is in our king; by Him he lives and flourishes, and by His spirit he is animated."[53] The lengths to which these convinced proponents of divine right might go when combatting ultramontane pretensions is well illustrated by the opening passage of a speech by La Guesle, when seeking from the Parlement the condemnation of a cleric who had upheld the supreme authority of the pope over temporal rulers.[54]

[51] Le Jay, *op. cit., passim.* The title of his first chapter reads: "Que Dieu a constitué les principautez du monde, et preside sur la conduite d'icelles. Qu'il y establit telz Princes qu'il luy plaist, et les oste et change selon sa volonté. Qu'ilz sont establis pour la manutention de l'honneur et seruice de Dieu, et du repos et tranquilité publique. Que le Peuple leur doit honneur, seruice et obeissance, comme estans lieutenans de Dieu: et qu'en leur rendant ce deuoir, Dieu benit et fait prosperer le peuple."

[52] E.g., *Autorité du roy*, pp. 4b–15a; *Moyens d'abus*, pp. 2–3.

[53] *Op. cit.*, p. 205.

[54] "Messieurs, l'authorité des Roys est sacro-sancte, ordonnée de la diuinité, principal ouurage de sa prouidence, chef d'œuvre de ses mains, image de sa sublime Majesté, et proportionnée auec son immense grandeur, entant que peut porter la comparaison de la creature auec le Createur, comme chasque Royaume, et Estat auec l'vniuers, l'admirable harmonie duquel, est representée par l'ordre cy-bas estably: car comme Dieu est par nature le premier Roy et Prince, le Roy l'est par creation, et imitation, Dieu en tout, cestui-cy en la terre, Dieu con-

La Guesle's statement may have been exaggerated to suit the occasion, but it in no sense departed from the ideas of divine right generally accepted by the royalist pamphleteers.

With such ideas of divinely appointed monarchy, it was inevitable that the royalists should regard the king as that individual specifically destined by God for earthly government. The logic of their position forced them increasingly to establish the personal divine right of their ruler, rather than merely that of his office. This tendency appeared in many instances in the pamphlet literature of the period,[55] but as with the earlier followers of Bodin, the efforts of these royalist pamphleteers in that direction ran counter to the strong tradition of fundamental law. Because of the nature of Henry IV's claim to the throne through the Salic Law rather than primogenitary succession, his supporters could not interpret his right as one of personal inheritance according to private law, but were forced to base his claim squarely upon fundamental law regulating the royal succession. As the lines of contemporary controversy unfolded, it became extremely pressing that the royalists establish the indefeasible force of the Salic Law. Such they attempted to do,[56] in spite of the fact that that law, in conferring the sovereign authority upon the prince, implied that he held no personal right to the crown and that it was merely a trust committed to him by law for the dura-

---

sistant en luy seul, et de luy seul, le Roy dependant de Dieu seul, qui l'a façonné sur le patron de sa toute-puissance." *Op. cit.*, p. 409. This is the opening section of a speech which La Guesle delivered before the Parlement in 1595.

[55] For example, the following passage from the *Dialogue d'entre le maheustre et le manant*, stating the positions of the *politiques* and the Leaguers respectively:

Maheustre. Je dis que tel qu'il est, soit heretique, soit Catholique, vous ni moy, ne le pouvons rejetter puis qu'il a pleu à Dieu le faire naistre Roy naturel et legitime. . . .

Manant. Vous revenez tousjours à vos suppositions fausses . . . vous supposez qu'aucun naisse Roy, ou par naissance et nature ait droit au Royaume. . . .

Edition printed in the *Satyre menippée de la vertu du catholicon d'Espagne et de la tenu des états de Paris* (Ratisbon, 1726), III, 381–382.

[56] See above, pp. 91–93.

tion of his reign. However, such legal niceties carried small weight with those pamphleteers who were battling for the life of legitimate monarchy. In spite of the lack of logic in their position, they solved the dilemma simply by representing the king as that divinely appointed monarch who succeeded according to fundamental law.[57] In this fashion, the royalist pamphleteers recognized a personal right of the monarch to the throne and combined the divine right of kings (in the strict sense of the phrase) with the long tradition of fundamental law. The great importance of this development was that while it preserved the Salic Law as a rule of succession to the crown, it went far toward denying the all-important legal conception that the royal authority was a dignity and not an heredity. Through sheer weight of emphasis upon the divine right of their monarch, the royalists had reduced the Salic Law to a mere canon establishing the order of succession and had opened the way for the personal claim of the ruler to the crown. The resulting change in ideas concerning the legal position of the king was of immense importance in the rise of absolutism.

In similar fashion, these proponents of divine-right sovereignty advanced to new frontiers of absolutism in regarding the will of the prince as law. In reaction to the treasonable character of the League and its justification of rebellion as necessary to preserve the faith, the legitimists placed very heavy stress upon the time-honored idea that obedience was a religious duty and that to revolt against the legitimate ruler was to rebel against God's appointed agent in temporal gov-

---

[57] "Car ores que le Royaume, singulierement le nostre, ne soit proprement hereditaire patrimonial ou feudal, si est ce qu'il est successif, acquis au plus proche, non comme heretier du defunct, mais comme plus prochain de sang en ligne masculine: par consequent quel qu'il soit, il est appellé . . . par ce que l'eslection est faicte au ciel dés qu'il est venu au monde: Et encourront l'ire et fureur de Dieu, tous ceux qui feront resistance à celuy qui par succession est legitime Roy. . . ." Belloy, *Apologie*, p. 31b. "Qu'il [Dieu] establit sur chacun peuple et nation, telz Rois et Princes qu'il luy plaist: Et que pas vn d'eux n'y est appellé, selon la loy et coustume du pais, que par son decret ordonnance et volonté." Le Jay, *op. cit.*, p. 11b. Cf. Servin, *op. cit.*, p. 205.

ernment.[58] And when that all-embracing precept was combined with Bodinian sovereignty which attributed to the ruler
the authorities to make laws and to enforce their execution,
there was little to restrain the king's will from assuming the
character of law. Reflecting their general belief that the laws
of the prince were *ipso facto* just because they were promulgated by the divinely appointed sovereign, the writers of this
school repeated on every occasion the amorphism of Plutarch
that justice was the end of law, law the work of the prince,
and the prince the creature of God.[59] In developing this position, Hurault explained that the devout prince was guided by
the hand of God and thus could do no wrong.[60] As lieutenant
of God and guardian of His justice, the ruler appeared before
his subjects not as a man but as justice itself, which he dispensed according to the will of God.[61] Hurault concluded that
the prince *was* the law, but he made the all-important proviso
that in consequence of the ruler's position, his acts must be
just.[62] Thus, although the royalist pamphleteers all but identified their king with law and right, they preserved the fundamental conception that highest justice constituted a body of
principles above and apart from the ruler. The will of the
king was law, but it was of necessity his just will and not
merely his unrestrained pleasure.[63] Like Grimaudet, these

[58] Servin, *op. cit.*, p. 186; Belloy, *Autorité*, pp. 11b–13a, 45a, etc.; Le Jay, *op. cit.*, *passim*.

[59] ". . . la Iustice est la fin de la Loy, la Loy l'ouurage du Prince, et le Prince l'ouurage de Dieu. . . ." Hurault, *op. cit.*, p. 3a. Cf. La Guesle, *op. cit.*, p. 42. Budé and Blackwood, among the strongest absolutists earlier in the century, likewise repeated this maxim. See above, n. 16, and ch. II, n. 54.

[60] ". . . le Prince religieux est guidé de la main de Dieu, de telle sorte qu'il ne peut faillir, qui est cause qu'ils le reuerent et luy obeissent plus aisément." *Op. cit.*, p. 69a.

[61] "Car comme dit sainct Paul, le Roy est lieutenant de Dieu en terre, gardien de sa iustice, et quasi comme Chancellier: tellement que ceux qui luy demandent iustice, ne vont à luy comme à vn homme, mais comme à la iustice mesme, de laquelle il est dispensateur par la volonté de Dieu." *Op. cit.*, p. 105b.

[62] "Le Prince donc estant la loy, il s'ensuit qu'il doit estre iuste, et faire iustice à ses subiets: en quoy faisant le monde reçoit vn grand bien. . . ." *Op. cit.*, p. 106b.

[63] "Il ne faut pas toutefois inferer de ce que nous disons: que les Princes pour estre vrais Roys, doiuent faire en leurs monarchies, toutes choses selon leur

writers were unwilling to abandon the distinction between the will of the prince as a source of law and that justice which was a necessary quality of his acts. However, in spite of that fundamental reservation, the royalists had very nearly exhausted the logical possibilities of their approach. The will of the prince was not law for them in the sense that the prince was master over the final principles governing the universe, but short of that there was little to limit his actions. Their emphasis upon the quasi-divine character of kingship went far toward insuring that the king's acts were invariably assumed to be equitable, and they made it clear that from the point of view of the people, their sovereign's enactments were to be regarded as *ipso facto* just. The absolutists of the following century found little to add except a justification of *raison d'état*.[64]

In conclusion, the attitude of these writers toward the relationships between the king and his subjects should be examined. It is evident that the political concepts set forth by the royalist pamphleteers were dominated by a desire to establish the unqualified dominion of the sovereign and the unquestioning obedience of the people. The emphasis of Hurault was representative when he said that monarchy consisted simply of two points: the just command of the prince and the obedience of the subjects.[65] In regard to the legal rights of the people, these writers merely repeated the generally accepted doctrines subjecting all law of the constitution,

---

plaisir: Et que les peuples soient tenus, dy obeir sans discretion. Car comme nous auons monstré cy dessus, que nostre subiection enuers eux est fondée sur l'amour que nous deuons à Dieu seulement: Aussi l'obeissance que nous leur deuons, c'est en ce qu'ils nous commandent justement, et ne nous enjoignent rien contre Dieu." Le Jay, *op. cit.*, p. 189b.

[64] There is little need to add that these writers without exception denied the doctrine of consent to taxation and attributed to the ruler the right to collect all levies necessary to care for governmental expenditures.

[65] "Tous ceux qui ont escrit de l'estat, disent que royauté bien instituee ne consiste qu'en deux poincts. C'est à sçauoir au iuste commandement du Prince, et en la iuste obeyssance des subiets." *Op. cit.*, p. 6b. Like Budé, Hurault found his model of well established monarchy in the παμβασιλεία of Aristotle. *Ibid.*, p. 6a. See above, ch. II, n. 53.

save the two fundamental laws, to the prince.[66] They devoted little attention to any inviolable rights of the subjects, much less the defense of them against the sovereign. Their primary emphasis was upon obedience; the realm they viewed simply in terms of ruler and ruled, and the hierarchy of subjects according to rights and status was quite lacking from their thought. Furthermore, in reaction to the quasi-democratic ideas of the Leaguers and their policy of appealing to the masses for support, there appeared in these broadsides the first indications of that attitude which was so widespread during the following century: that the populace was by nature highly insubordinate and that it should be kept in place by strong rule from above. The people, said La Guesle in 1590, should be permitted to enjoy only such liberty as the prince sees fit to allow to them; additional liberty is contrary to their best interests and dangerous to the state.[67] It is manifest that such an intellectual atmosphere was entirely unsuited to the maintenance of the traditional legal rights of the people and was sufficient in itself to bring about major changes in constitutional thought. The royalist pamphleteers may have used exaggerated statements because of their strong partisanship and their desire to sway current opinion, but much that they said was to characterize later writings. For the triumph of Henry IV, in spite of his many compromises, was the victory of legitimate monarchy as understood by his immediate partisans, and with him rose into favor those ideas which had been forged in support of his cause.

[66] E.g., Belloy, *Moyens d'abus*, pp. 86–87; Le Jay, *op. cit.*, pp. 174b–175b, 204b.

[67] "Car comme la servitude, aussi la liberté infinie, non bornée d'aucuns limites est vn tres-grand mal, et les peuples doiuent souhaitter auoir autant de liberté qu'il plaist à leurs Princes et seigneurs legitimes leur en departir; l'auantage n'est pas meilleur pour eux. . . . aussi la liberté du peuple meslée et attrempée auec l'auctorité des puissances que Dieu a estably sur luy, est bonne, comme sans ceste attrempance, fort pernicieuse et dangereuse." *Op. cit.*, pp. 916–917.

CHAPTER V

THE POLITICAL THEORY OF GUY COQUILLE

IF the fury of the League and the apparent collapse of the royal authority were forcing many political theorists to alter their opinions in a direction favoring gradual relaxation of the legal bonds upon kingship and an expanded royal discretion, such was not the case generally throughout France. It is a striking characteristic of intellectual currents in the sixteenth century, although not without major exceptions, that the strictest adherents to the traditional theory of state were found in the provinces, away from the influence of the royal court and the jurisprudence of the Parlement of Paris.[1] A strong sense of local autonomy characterized very many provinces of the French state, in itself a recent creation, and it is to be expected that the strongest defenders of strictly constitutional theories would be found in the provincial capitals and in the councils of the remaining feudal dignitaries. The controversy between Du Moulin and d'Argentré earlier in the century exemplified the hostility felt by the provincial legal mind toward doctrines favoring increased royal power. There was no other case so clear-cut during the century, but early in the reign of Henry IV there lived a man whose career and political theories stamp him as one of the greatest defenders of constitutional monarchy to be produced by provincial life.

That man was Guy Coquille, Lord of Romenay. A native of the Nivernais, he passed most of his long life at Nevers, the provincial capital, and always exhibited a strong patriotism for his province.[2] As a youth, he studied the humanities at

---

[1] The greatest exception to this generalization is, of course, the influence of the various provincial universities, in particular that of Toulouse, upon the rising theory of absolutism.

[2] The best contemporary sources for Coquille's biography are his Latin poems

the *Collège de Navarre* in Paris, and later followed the instruction in jurisprudence given by Marianus Socinus the
younger, in Padua. With that introduction to the law, he
returned to Paris and passed several years as secretary to
Guillaume Bourgoing, his maternal uncle and councillor in the
Parlement. Being determined to enter the legal profession
and sensing the need of expert instruction, he subsequently
passed two years at the University of Orleans studying Roman
and Canon law, thus securing the most intensive training of
his career. Returning to Paris in 1551, he attempted with
some success the career of barrister before the Parlement, but
after three years he gave up that exacting profession and
returned to his native Nivernais where he remained, with the
exception of several missions of short duration, during the
remainder of his life.

Coquille's withdrawal to provincial life meant that he had
entered upon that portion of his career in which he was
destined to rise to a place of well-deserved recognition, for
it was in connection with the life of his province that he was
important during his lifetime. The prestige of his family
name and his own real ability caused him to be chosen to
represent the third estate of the local *bailliage* at the Estates
General of 1560, 1576–77, and 1588. During the important
meeting of 1576–77, he was one of the body of twelve appointed to recast the *cahiers* into their final form,[3] but his
experience in the assemblies of the Estates seems to have done
little other than to create in him a complete disgust with the
striving of Henry III toward personal government and with
the corruption of the officials in the central administration.[4]

---

and the short biographical sketch by Guillaume Joly, printed in the second
volume of Coquille's works (Bordeaux, 1703). The best modern works are
Dupin, *La Coutume de Nivernais* (Paris, 1864), and Maumigny, *Etude sur Guy
Coquille* (Paris, 1910).

[3] Picot, *op. cit.*, II, 338.

[4] Concerning the assembly of 1576–77, he wrote:

> Quatuor hic menses desedimus: anxia dum nos
> Cura tenet, populi laesis succurrere rebus.
> Sed dum fiscales rapiendi coeca libido

Much more important, however, was Coquille's activity as officer in the ducal administration. In 1568, he was made first *échevin* of Nevers, and in 1571 Louis de Gonzague, Duke of Nevers, appointed him to the position of Procureur General of the duchy, the highest office in the province other than that held by the duke himself. It was in this capacity that Coquille appears in the environment which certainly influenced his theory of state. For as Procureur General, he not only was assigned heavy administrative duties but was also defender of the duke's rights. That he performed well the latter duty is attested not only by the complete accord between himself and his immediate overlord but also by the surviving documents concerning his administrative activity.[5] His capacity as officer in the ducal administration doubtless accounts, in part, for his hatred toward the encroachments of royal officials and for his very provincial attitude. It must be remembered that the Duchy of Nevers was one of the outstanding remnants of the feudal system in the sixteenth-century French state. With the exception of the House of Bourbon which was soon to ascend the throne, that of Nevers was the last of first magnitude which could claim something resembling feudal origins and consequent dignities. Louis de Gonzague, not a native of France, had acquired the duchy through marriage with Henriette de Clèves, heiress to the lands, and whatever may be the truth concerning his enigmatical character, there is no doubt that throughout the Wars

---

Distinet atque usus licito pro jure probatur
Illusum est nobis, plaebi data verba miscellae:
Non solum non est gravitas relevata tributi,
Sed sub pretextu specioso et legis in umbra
Mille gravandi artes inventae: languida donec
Nil praeter gemitum et tristi suspiria corde
Fundere plebs valuit.

Poemata (Nevers, 1590), pp. 118–119.

[5] The major portion of Coquille's *Mémoire de ce qui est à faire pour le bien du pays de Nivernois* is concerned with the encroachments of royal officers upon the judicial authority of the duke. See also the letter of Coquille to his overlord, written December 28, 1571, printed by Destray, "Notes inédites sur Guy Coquille," *Bulletin de la société nivernaise* (1925), pp. 69–91.

of Religion, the Nivernais was one of the most strongly governed provinces of France. The gradual encroachment of the royal authority upon that of the duke throughout the century took the form of strict definition of rights rather than outright confiscation on the part of the royal agents. Although there was some consequent loss in the spheres of judicial and military affairs, the ducal authority remained very strong and his administration suffered relatively little outside interference.[6] It is of note that Coquille, as holder of a key office in that administration, would be working in an atmosphere distinctly feudal in character.

It is not that we wish to show Coquille as a mere local officer who had a knowledge of law. He was much more than that. On certain occasions, he was consulted on judicial matters by litigants from Paris. His reputation for ability and integrity caused both L'Hospital and Henry IV to offer him positions in the royal administration in the capital, but he declined, preferring to remain in Nevers. The fact to be noted is that although he was among the most capable legists of his day, he stood apart from the great body of legal practitioners associated with the royal administration and the Parlement of Paris.[7] His many works on French law did not form a portion of legal learning in the capital during the period because they remained unpublished until early in the following century.[8] They might have been lost to posterity, had they not been published by Guillaume Joly who had close ties with Coquille through common origin in the Nivernais and family connections.[9] Although he wrote the majority of his

[6] Despois, *Histoire de l'autorité royale dans le comté de Nivernais* (Paris, 1912), section III.

[7] Coquille is not mentioned in Loisel's *Dialogue des avocats* which is a source of much information concerning the Parisian *noblesse de robe* during this period.

[8] The only works of Coquille which were published before 1603, the date of his death, were his Latin poems.

[9] Joly's nephew had married one of Coquille's daughters. Editions of Coquille's works by Joly: *Les Coutumes du pays et duché de Nivernois* (Paris, 1605); *Institution au droit des françois* (Paris, 1608); *Questions et reponses sur les coutumes de France* (Paris, 1611); *Histoire du pays et duché de Nivernois* (Paris, 1612). Our citations are to the *Œuvres* published at Bordeaux in 1703.

many works on French law during the decade between 1585 and 1595,[10] he was essentially uninfluenced by contemporary developments in political theory. His thought represents chiefly a continuation, perhaps an exaggeration, of the more traditional constitutionalism which for him took its inspiration from provincial life. For these reasons, Coquille must be classed apart from those currents of thought which gave rise to the absolutism of the seventeenth century.

If Coquille was very provincial in his outlook, he was also distinctly French, in contrast to Roman, in his predilections concerning the study of law. He had studied Roman law in France and Italy,[11] but his aversion to that body of law is marked throughout his works. In regard to this question, the jurists of the period almost invariably stated that Roman law did not have force in France but might be used as a source of legal science and equitable interpretation. It was called written reason. The very indefiniteness of that interpretation allowed great freedom to the jurists in their use of the Roman system. Their policies ranged from general application of it to legal problems, as in the case of Du Moulin, to the greatest hesitance in following its precepts, as in the works of Coquille. The latter did not deny the value of Roman law as a field of jurisprudence, but he insisted heavily that it should never take the place of provincial custom, the true law of the land.[12]

---

[10] The following dates are given in the preface of the *Œuvres*. *Institution au droit des françois*, 1586 or later; *Discours sur les états de France*, 1588 (during the Estates of Blois); *Commentaires sur la coutume de Nivernois* and *Questions et réponses sur les articles des coutumes*, 1590; *Histoire du pays et duché de Nivernois*, 1595. It is extremely unfortunate that the *Œuvres*, published in 1703, were left incomplete by the editor who apparently feared to include certain works of Coquille on the Estates General because of their extremely constitutional character. In accounting for his action, he said that France had at that time a king who was able to handle all political problems without the aid of the Estates. Today the manuscripts of those missing works have disappeared, but a key to their character may be found in the fragment omitted from Coquille's commentary upon the Ordinance of Blois, *Œuvres*, I, 462. That gloss concerned the character of the Estates General and was discovered and published by Dupin in his edition of Loisel's *Institutes coutumières* (Paris, 1846), I, cxxiii–cxxvi.

[11] Roman law was the only secular system in which it was then possible to receive instruction.

[12] "Les Coûtumes des Provinces de France, qu'on appelle Coûtumiers, sont

This interpretation arose from his fundamental concept that the effective law in any state or territory must be the local law established by the inhabitants of that region. The law must be a part of their life and their own creation. Thus the Roman system automatically became inapplicable because it had arisen in an earlier period and among people varying greatly from those of France. Coquille admitted that Roman law might be followed as a last resort when all categories of French law had proved insufficient, but at most it should be used sparingly and only in those aspects which reflected universal qualities. His hostility to Roman law carried him to the lengths of criticizing the system observed in the *pays de droit écrit* as inherently inferior to that obtaining in the *pays de droit coutumier*.[13] The legal instruction in the universities, he said, was based upon the false assumption that practitioners used Roman law rather than French, and he advocated changing the curricula of all schools of law so as to place equal emphasis upon the French and Roman systems.[14] Through-

---

leur vray Droit Civil, et Commun: et peuvent être appellees Droit écrit celles qui selon le consentement du peuple des trois Ordres (qu'on dit Etat) ont été arrestées, mises par ecrit, et autorisées par les Commissaires que le Roy a déleguez. . . . Pourquoy j'estime que nos Docteurs François se mécomptent quand ils comparent nos Coûtumes aux Statuts, dont les Docteurs ultramontains ont fait tant de decisions intriquées. . . . Car en Italie le Droit Commun c'est le même Droit Civil des Romains. . . . Et nous afin de ne nous rendre serfs imitateurs et admirateurs des étrangers, feront bien de n'infrasquer et embrouiller l'intelligence de nos Coûtumes selon lesdites regles perplexes des Statuts: mêmement parce que nos Coûtumes sont nôtre Droit Civil et Commun, et les Statuts ne sont pas Droit Commun. Doncques le Droit Civil Romain n'est pas nôtre Droit Commun, et n'a force de Loy en France: mais y doit être allegué seulement pour la raison. . . . Qui fait que les Loix faites par les Romains nous doivent semondre à nous en aider, quand les Constitutions et Ordonnances de nos Rois, ou le Droit general François non écrit, ou nos Coûtumes nous défaillent. Nous en aider (dis-je) par bienseance et pour la raison et non par necessité." *Coutumes de Nivernois*, pp. 1, col. 1, to 2, col. 1.

[13] *Questions et reponses*, p. 127, col. 2. In the same paragraph, he said: "Pourquoy il me semble avoir été improprement inscrit un petit livret, Des loix abrogées; J'eusse mieux aimé dire, Des lois des Romains non reçues en France." Although Coquille gave no reference, this is doubtless a criticism of Bugnyon's book, *Legum abrogatarum*, cited above. Coquille and Bugnyon were entirely disagreed concerning the force of Roman law in France, for the latter believed that the Roman system had force as such, although certain portions of it had been abrogated.

[14] *Questions et reponses*, p. 128, col. 1.

out, his statements reflected a conviction that local custom and constitutional law were synonymous.

The fundamentals of Coquille's approach to political problems illustrate well the strength of the monarchical tradition, in feudal form, in the provinces. He accepted completely the contemporary idea that monarchy, the rule of one, was inherently the best form of government, consonant with the natural order of things and finding its likeness in all manifestations of life.[15] Such a conception of the universe as uniting a myriad of greater and lesser values, inherently unequal and capped by a supreme Deity, was part and parcel of the aristocratic attitude of contemporary thinkers, and found its most concrete expression in the field of political thought. It permeates Coquille's ideas concerning the organization of the state and was a vital factor in strengthening his essentially feudal approach to legal problems. And like many other writers of the period, he used the figure comparing the state with a living organism to express his idea of its composition and internal bonds.[16] This idea of the state as a living organism, political and mystical, achieving harmonious existence through the cooperation of its component parts, was upheld by thinkers of every stamp during the century; but in Coquille the theory came much nearer toward realizing its implications than in the works of the absolutists. For if that idea of the social organism as composed of two elemental portions — head and members, or prince and people — were pushed to its logical conclusions, there must be a division of authority and right, not necessarily in government but in the life and functioning of the state. The traditional insistence upon the two spheres of legal right would be maintained

[15] *Institution*, p. 1, col. 1.

[16] "Car le Roy est le Chef, et le peuple des Trois Ordres sont les membres, et tous ensemble sont le corps politique et mystique, dont la liaison et union est individue et inseparable, et ne peut une partie souffrir mal, que le reste ne s'en sente et souffre douleur." *Discours des états*, p. 277, col. 1. See also pp. 281–282 of the same work; *Histoire de Nivernois*, p. 390, col. 1; *Dialogue sur les causes des misères de France*, p. 230, col. 2.

in all its rigor, and any attempt of theorists to attribute to the prince an authority over popular immunities would necessarily destroy the delicate balance. This theory of the two mutually exclusive but interdependent authorities is the key to Coquille's political thought. He may be said to have been the last great jurist of the century to maintain that conception intact, both in its fundamentals and its implications.

Coquille's idea concerning the origin of those twin bodies of legal right was an interesting and significant variant from that usually found in the writings of the jurists. Although extremely Gallican in his ideas concerning the secular and spiritual governments, he did not adhere to that tenet so characteristic of Gallicanism, the direct divine authorization of kingship. Concerning the origin of the state, he upheld the idea which we have frequently noted above, namely, that the people were prior to the ruler and originally held authority of government, and that they had instituted the king over themselves by a transfer of their authority to him.[17] It is easily apparent from the text quoted that Coquille's reasoning was very different from that of the average Parisian legist. In place of the direct divine authorization of king and crown, he recalled the transfer of public power from the people to the king who was thus instituted by popular action. In place of the complete transfer of such authority (which was insisted upon by all others who considered monarchy to have originated in this fashion), Coquille described a partial transfer only, the people retaining a portion of it to be exercised in

---

[17] "Des le commencement le peuple a établi les Rois comme par voie de compromis, pour éviter la confusion qui seroit, si en chacune affaire d'importance il faloit rechercher l'avis de tous, pour deliberer et conclure. Cet établissement autorisé de Dieu, est entretenu par lui-même, qui met és coeurs des sujets la volonté d'obeir aux Rois. Nos prédecesseurs François à ce premier établissement n'ont pas transferé aux Rois indistinctement et incommutablement tout pouvoir: dont nous appercevons aujourd'hui quelque ombre demeurée de reste, qui est de l'assemblée des Etats: avec lesquels de tout temps les Rois avoient accoûtumé de deliberer és affaires, étans de l'essence de la Couronne." *Questions et reponses,* p. 125, col. 1.

the assemblies of the Estates General. The variations were fundamental and far-reaching.

From his theory of dual spheres of right in the state, Coquille developed his concepts in regard to the law of the constitution and the institutions of government. Parallel with the original creation of the state by the people, he elaborated in detail the authority of the Estates General to establish fundamental law. The Estates, he said, were occasionally assembled not in the capacity of mere counsellors but in order to act with full power concerning vital questions of constitutional usage. Specifically, such was the procedure used when it was necessary to settle a disputed succession to the crown or to establish a new fundamental law, and he cited the elevation of the Edict of Union to the position of fundamental law by the Estates of 1588.[18] An assembly of the three estates, with the king in their midst, was the tangible expression of the two great authorities in the state, that of the people and that of the ruler, and Coquille found it but logical that if law were to be created, such should be done by those members of the social organism most concerned. It paralleled closely the establishment of custom by the people and the original institution of the state by popular act. Thus, as far as Coquille troubled himself concerning the exact nature of fundamental law, he regarded it as those regulations laid down originally by the people and later by the king and people jointly. This theory was very widespread in connection with the Estates

---

[18] "En certains autres cas les Etats sont appellez non pas comme simples Conseillers, mais comme ayans plein et entier pouvoir; comme si la Couronne etoit en débat entre deux prétendans . . . auquel cas se faut representer le même tems qui etoit quand les François établirent sur eux un Roy: et de même si le Roy pour le doute du droit de son successeur à venir, vouloit de son vivant y pourvoir, ou s'il convenoit faire une loy du Royaume, qu'on appelle fondamentale, c'est-à-dire, qui sont telle que le Roy et ses successeurs et le peuple y soient obligez, et ne puisse être revoquée par le Roy, auquel rang est la loy Salique, et la prohibition d'aliener le Domaine de la Couronne incommutablement: et comme fut la loy que le Roy Henry III fit avec les Princes et ses Etats à Blois le 18 Octobre l'an 1588. qui le meme jour fut jurée et publiée en pleine seances d'Etats: esquels cas les Etats sont non seulement pour conseil, mais aussi pour déterminer en pouvoir." *Histoire de Nivernois*, p. 445.

of 1588, but Coquille was one of the few who combined it with a complete constitutional system of the strictly traditional type. From his approach, it resulted as a matter of course that such law limited the ruler and conferred upon him an authority in which he held no personal right. The legal essentials of this portion of his system were complete.

Coquille defined the exact content of the royal prerogative in the traditional manner of listing various marks of sovereignty. Among them he included the authorities to administer justice and to make laws and ordinances (which he grouped together as the primary mark), to make war, to succeed to the royal domain, to invest bishops, nominate clerics to benefices and exercise general control over the ecclesiastical *police* according to the Gallican liberties, to coin money, to grant graces, dispensations, legitimations, naturalizations, and other favors contrary to law.[19] It is apparent from this enumeration that Coquille's idea of kingship was largely uninfluenced by contemporary currents making for an increased royal power and a hardening of its lines about a single concept. His ideal king was primarily a judge and an administrator, and the primary duty of the ruler was to preserve the state as it stood. In Coquille's system, there was no trace of a royal authority to change the law, or even a consciousness that such might be necessary. For these reasons, he lacked entirely any theory of legislation similar to that set forth earlier by Bodin. Although he included among the marks of sovereignty the authority to make laws and ordinances, he understood this in the older sense of rendering judgment and authorizing acts of administration, rather than the creation of substantive law. Thus he was able to repeat the earlier idea that the giving of law was but a means of dispensing justice.[20] Actual creation of law he recognized only in the establishment of new fundamental laws by the Estates General and in popular institution of custom. And his isolation from

---

[19] *Institution*, opening section, "Du droit de royauté."
[20] *Institution*, p. 2, col. 1.

Bodin's theory of sovereignty is further illustrated by his much looser use of that word.[21] It is in this department of legal theory that Coquille's separation from contemporary intellectual currents is most apparent.

Perhaps Coquille's most important contribution was in his treatment of customary law. This fundamental tenet of constitutional thought he developed along traditional lines and with greater logic and completeness than any other legist of his time. Customary law, according to Coquille, found its origin and source of authority in the act or tacit consent of the people. It was the established order of society that the people enjoyed many legal rights, and customary law was made by the populace in order to preserve those rights. It was at once the expression of popular legal immunities and their guarantee. Being made by the people of a single locality, it mirrored accurately the life of that territory, and as a body of local usage it appeared almost as a convention between the inhabitants whose will it expressed.[22] Thus for Coquille, customary law was synonymous with the entire body of legal right enjoyed by the people, in contrast to that of the king. The concept provided the basis of his constitutional thought and determined his interpretation of all relevant legal problems.

The more conservative legists did not differ from Coquille concerning the origin and nature of customary law. Rather, it was in connection with the several factors forcing them to consider custom in relation to the royal authority that they

[21] In discussing the specific connotation carried by the word "sovereign," Coquille insisted that there were many sovereigns in the realm: the king was sovereign over his kingdom, the duke over his duchy, the baron over his barony, etc. *Questions et reponses*, pp. 154, col. 2, to 155, col. 1. He also used the word "sovereignty" to denote a territorial unit which recognized no superior. *Ordonnances du roi Henri III*, p. 532. For his idea of the sovereignty of the people to make customary law, see below, p. 284.

[22] "Car les Coûtumes étans fondées sur les consentemens du peuple des trois Ordres, il faut inferer qu'elles obligent *quasi ex contractu*, et par consequent lient les personnes pour tous les biens qui leur appartiennent." *Coutumes de Nivernois*, pp. 1, col. 2, to 2, col. 1. "Coûtume, Province, et peuple correspondent l'un à l'autre." *Histoire de Nivernois*, p. 437, col. 2.

tended to weaken the logic of their systems. One of those factors was the necessity of royal permission for the redaction of the provincial *coutumiers*. Coquille was adamant on this point: the codification of custom in the local estates was a manifestation of the ancient and continued authority of the people to establish law over themselves. The royal letters legalizing such assemblies were merely acts of administration and did not affect the nature of the resulting body of written custom.[23] And in confirming the *coutumier*, the king merely insured its preservation.[24] This was the most that Coquille would admit to the royal authority in relation to the redaction of local custom. Far from changing the basis upon which custom rested, the royal order was merely a necessary administrative measure but without further significance. In contrast to the many legists who placed codified custom upon a basis of royal authority and identified the *coutumiers* with the royal ordinances, Coquille preserved inviolate the older concept recognizing the authority of the people to establish the legal guarantee of their rights.[25]

[23] "L'autre pouvoir des Etats est au fait des Coûtumes, qui tiennent lieu et sont le vray droit Civil des Provinces, en l'accordance desquelles Coûtumes est representée l'ancienne liberté du peuple François, en tant qu'il avoit et a encores aujourd'huy le droit de faire loy sur soy-même. . . . Et par le témoignage, avis et volonté desdits Etats, les anciennes Coûtumes sont rapportées et prouvées, si elles semblent bonnes elles sont confirmées, sinon sont reformées ou autres nouvelles faites: Ce qui fait connoître que la puissance de faire ces loix est originairement és mains du peuple: car les Lettres patentes du Roy ne sont que pour permettre et authoriser cette assemblée." *Histoire de Nivernois*, p. 445, col. 2.
[24] "Le premier mouvement, et la premiere naissance et vie de ce droit civil est en la volonté des Etats des Provinces. Le Roy en autorisant et confirmant ces coûtumes y attribuent la vie exterieure, qui est la manutention et exercice de ce droit." *Qu'en fait d'estats*, p. 286, col. 1. See below, n. 26.
[25] The relation of Coquille's interpretation to that upheld in contemporary legal practice is illustrated by the following passage from an *arrêt* of the Parlement of Paris, 1601. ". . . les Coustumes sont fort differentes selon les diuerses moeurs des peuples, ausquels elles s'accommodent: ces Coustumes estans redigées par des personnes selectes, les uns de chacune prouince, ou Bailliage, prins de chacuns des trois Estats les plus experimentez, qui composent les Coustumes le plus proportionnement à leurs moeurs qu'il leur est possible. . . . De sorte que c'est en effect le peuple luy-mesme qui s'est fait la loy conforme à ses moeurs." Montholon, *Arrêts de la cour* (Paris, 1645), pp. 205–206. This was the argu-

Coquille's insistence upon the popular origin of customary law caused him to make statements in direct contradiction with the contemporary theory of sovereignty. Since custom formed the greater portion of the constitution and was made only by the people, it seemed logical to attribute to the populace the law-making power. In one very remarkable passage, Coquille reiterated that to make law was a mark of sovereignty, but he explicitly attributed that prerogative to the populace. The "supreme sovereignty" of the king was recognized, he said, by the fact that the local estates were assembled under his authorization; but he was none the less definite that the law-making power was in the representatives of the people.[26] Although Coquille's phrase was vaguely reminiscent of Bodin, the two men were poles apart regarding both the nature of customary law and the place of the legislative authority in the state. Coquille's interpretation was not necessarily a reaction against Bodinian thought but represented rather a logically developed position resting upon different fundamentals and thus necessarily arriving at varying conclusions. His statements illustrate at once his isolation from the dominant conception of kingship and the great distance

---

ment of the party that lost the case, for the judges decided not according to the letter of relevant custom but according to the general nature of contracts. It is evident that Coquille's ideas, while of continued importance, were losing ground in the general body of legal practice.

[26] "Le Roi Charles VII . . . ordonna que par l'avis des Etats de chacune Province de son Royaume, les Coûtumes fussent arrêtées et redigées par écrit. Ce qui a été executé en la plûpart des Provinces coûtumieres, et selon que les Etats ont été d'accord, tant à rapporter les anciennes Coûtumes que pour en établir de nouvelles. Ainsi les Commissaires ordonnez par le Roi, pour présider en ces assemblées d'Etats, les ont autorisées, en y inspirant la puissance de loi. Mais en effet, c'est le peuple qui fait la loi: qui est une marque de l'ancien établissement de cette Republique Françoise, mêlée de Democratie, Aristocratie et Monarchie. Car faire loi est droit de souveraineté: qui n'est pas pour déroger à l'autorité et Majesté du Roi, auquel le peuple François a toûjours mieux obei que nulle autre nation du monde: mais le peuple obeit plus volontiers à la loi, que lui même a eu agreable. Puis chacune province a ses moeurs et humeurs diverses: et partant les loix, comme elles ne sont semblables, aussi doivent-elles être faites selon le goût et sens de chacun peuple. Aussi la suprême souveraineté du Roi y est reconnue, en ce que les Etats sont assemblez par l'autorité du Roi et les Commissaires députez par lui y président." *Questions et reponses*, p. 125.

which Bodin had proceeded away from the older theory of the constitution.

In the light of Coquille's heavy insistence upon the independence and self-sufficiency of customary law, it is interesting to examine his attitude toward changes in local custom and toward the question of forming a general, unified body of common law for the French state. Like all jurists, he insisted that the customs of a given territory should be regarded as the local constitution and should be applied in judicial decision. But he did not evince a superstitious reverence for details of custom as such; he was willing to advocate and to secure the abolition of given points of law, even those supporting rights of feudal lords, if he considered such to be required by the best interests of the population.[27] In elucidating details of customary law, he did not hesitate to bring in considerations drawn from customs of other provinces, from Roman law, or from *la raison du sens commun*.[28] With care, he utilized all such materials in an effort to gather together in his *Institution au droit des françois* a well-rounded body of customary law for the whole of France.[29] His works formed an important portion of that long and laborious effort, never entirely completed during the *ancien régime*, to formulate a *droit commun coutumier*. Like Du Moulin, he realized that the only means of achieving that end was to follow precepts broader than those in any single *coutumier*. But unlike his great predecessor, he did not desire to unify customary law because such would create a general body of legal regulations under the authority of the king. On the contrary, Coquille was very hostile to royal interference with custom. His work provides ample evidence that the unification of customary law was not necessarily concomitant with ideals of

---

[27] Concerning his work in securing the suppression of the *bordelages*, see *Plaidoyé, Œuvres*, I, 273; *Mémoire de ce qui est à faire*, p. 269; *Coutumes de Nivernois*, p. 119.

[28] *Institution*, p. 11.

[29] His commentary on the *Coutume de Nivernais* and his *Questions et reponses* were additional works undertaken for this purpose.

royal absolutism. Coquille's sole aim was the better administration of justice.

The hostility of Coquille toward royal control over the
customary law finds its best proof in the complete absence
from his writings of that precept unanimously supported by
the Parisian legists, namely, that the king might abolish individual local customs through royal ordinance. In his refusal
to admit that authority to the king, we believe Coquille to be
unique among the major legists of the century.[30] He included
the constitutions of the king among the categories of law;[31]
and he incorporated into his writings the few royal edicts
directly concerning customary rights, such as the *édit des
secondes noces*,[32] but he did not set forth any royal authority
over customary law as a generally valid maxim. However, a
distinction is necessary in order to explain his position. It
will be recalled that the royal ordinances were chiefly concerned with administrative regulations and rarely touched
private law.[33] Coquille willingly accepted those provisions of
the ordinances dealing with administrative procedure;[34] he
even recognized that in that sphere, royal enactments of a
general nature might abolish local practice.[35] But he never
attributed to the ruler a blanket authority over customary law.
This facet of Coquille's system is graphic illustration of his
strict adherence to the doctrine of two independent and
mutually exclusive spheres of legal right. In this he adhered
more strictly to the logical fundamentals of his thought than
did any other major constitutionalist of the century.

---

[30] The only other writer whom we have found to support this position was
François de Gravelle. See above, ch. III, pt. A, n. 94. However, Gravelle was a
very mediocre writer, without a well developed system. But it is of note that
he was similar to Coquille in writing from the point of view of the provinces.

[31] *Institution*, p. 1, col. 2.

[32] *Institution*, p. 66, col. 2.

[33] See above, pp. 111–113.

[34] *Coutumes de Nivernois*, p. 27, col. 1; p. 51, col. 2; p. 68, col. 1; p. 77, col. 2;
p. 100, col. 2; p. 176, col. 2; p. 270, col. 2; p. 271, col. 2; p. 306, col. 2; p. 321,
col. 2; p. 328, col. 2; p. 334, col. 2.

[35] *Coutumes de Nivernois*, p. 96, col. 1; p. 315, col. 1; p. 331, col. 2.

The crucial test of a theorist's strength of conviction concerning the supremacy of law and the independent legal rights of the people was to be found in his ideas regarding royal taxation. In regard to this question, Coquille was more conservative than any of his contemporaries, in the sense that he drew his theory from the feudal institution of society and regarded as illegal any encroachment by the king upon those rights held by the people under the earlier system. He adhered strictly to the medieval idea that the obligation of each individual to society was limited by custom according to his position in the hierarchical social structure, and he insisted that the tailles were a recent creation, not owed by the third estate during the feudal period.[36] The general rule may have been that each person ought to contribute either his services or his goods,[37] but Coquille was far from using that concept, after the manner of so many others, to establish an unlimited obligation of the people to the ruler. Kings and feudal lords alike, he said, held the right to collect only those levies allowed by custom.[38] The latter did not include the tailles which were extraordinary levies, collected before the time of Charles VII only if granted by the Estates General.[39] This logical reasoning was based upon Coquille's concept of the inviolable property rights of the people according to custom. He concluded that the king was bound by law to observe the ancient liberty of the people, that it was illegal to collect non-customary

[36] ". . . chacun doit service au public ou de sa personne, comme font les nobles à cause de leurs Fiefs, ou de sa bourse, comme les roturiers; car les tailles et autres subsides ne sont ordinaires ni fort anciennes. Et selon cette grande ancienneté, quand les tailles n'étoient point, les Cens ou autres redevances foncieres étoient payées au Roi, ou à ceux qui tiennent en fief du Roi, qui doivent service personnel au Roi, à cause de leurs Fiefs, qui étoit l'aide que chacun faisoit de ses biens au Roi, pour supporter l'entretenement de son Etat." *Institution*, p. 38.

[37] *Coutumes de Nivernois*, p. 120, col. 1.

[38] *Coutumes de Nivernois*, p. 128, col. 2.

[39] "Si on dit que les roturiers contribuent par les tailles et autres subsides, la réponse est, que les tailles ne sont pas revenu ordinaire, et auparavant le Roy Charles VII. elles n'étoient imposées et levées sinon par l'accordance des Etats Generaux." *Coutumes de Nivernois*, p. 120, col. 2.

levies without popular consent accorded by the assemblies of the three estates.[40] Although Coquille thus insisted as heaviiy as Bodin upon the legal requirement of consent to taxation, the reasoning of the two men was quite different. Bodin had attributed to the sovereign an authority over custom and was forced to place property rights and consent to taxation upon a foundation of natural law. But Coquille never allowed to the ruler any discretionary power over customary law because he regarded it as the legal guarantee of popular immunities. Consequently he was able to base the inviolability of property and consent to taxes upon the established custom of the land. And in view of the subsequent distortion of Bodin's ideas, it is clear that this limitation upon kingship found a distinctly more effective form in the theory of Coquille.

Coquille was well aware of the fact that his theory of taxation and consent did not coincide with the policies of the royal government, and he regarded the constant levying of new taxes and the arbitrary increasing of old ones as a major cause of the troubled state of the realm.[41] He gave figures revealing the increase in the tailles since the time of Charles VII,[42] and he repeatedly pointed to the Duchy of Burgundy as a model of constitutional government, for in that province the tailles were granted every three years by the local estates for the limited period between assemblies.[43] He expressed his wrath in no uncertain terms concerning the myriad of royal officers who, through malversation and misuse of funds col-

---

[40] ". . . l'honnête et ancienne liberté du peuple; en ce qu'il n'étoit loisible aux Rois d'imposer Aydes, Tailles, et Subsides nouveaux sur leur peuple, outre les anciens devoirs Domainiaux, sans le consentement et accordance de leurdit peuple, et cetuy est un des cas auquel on avoit accoûtumé de grand ancienneté d'assembler les Etats." *Discours des états*, p. 279, col. 1. Cf. *Institution*, p. 7, col. 2.

[41] *Dialogue sur les causes des misères de France*, pp. 230-231; *Mémoire de ce qui est à faire*, p. 271; *Histoire de Nivernois*, pp. 426, col. 2, 428-429.

[42] *Questions et reponses*, p. 130.

[43] *Institution*, p. 7, col. 2; *Dialogue*, p. 231, col. 1; *Histoire de Nivernois*, p. 428, col. 2.

lected by taxation, waxed rich at the expense of the populace; and he would have allowed the mere appearance of quickly gained riches as sufficient grounds for condemnation.[44] Unlike many constitutionalists who criticized royal policies, he did not confine his abuse to royal officers but attacked the king himself. He specifically pointed to Louis XI and the recent Valois rulers as outstanding examples of misgovernment, particularly in their arbitrary and illegal exactions from the populace.[45] This is decisive evidence that Coquille, as a strict constitutionalist, felt in great measure the ever-increasing

[44] At the Estates of Blois, 1577, Coquille penned the following:

Contra fiscales fures

Haec quae tam paucis patrimonia tanta diebus
Accumulata vides, sine sudore atque periclo,
Nec patriis laribus grates referentia, sed nec
Prudenti donata manu: quaeso vnde parata?
Quam quod versutis sit sacra pecunia fisci
Interuersa modis? Tamen hi quos vesper egentes
Liquerat atque orta sunt visi luce potentes,
Praefectis rationum oculos caligine caeca
Perfudere: etiam nobis imponere tentant,
Qui miserae ex voto tractare negotia plebis
Nitimur: et sceleris causam auctoresque notamus.
Verum cum multis humana scientia subsit
Fraudibus: et modo nos improuidus abstrahat error,
Et speciosa leui mendacia perlita fuco:
Fas sit ab euentu causae momenta probare:
Hosque agitare reos: cum mens male conscia, coram
Non poterit prompta et facili ratione docere
Atque minutatim summasque et tempora certa
Cuiusque augmenti, tanta vnde haec copia census
Prodierit. Quod si in documentis haeserit anceps,
Ipsa peculatus sit plena probatio. Nempe
Natura ingenitus cum pallor inhaereat auro,
Subjacet insidiis. At non occulta solemus
Crimina perspecies coniecturasque probare.

Poemata, pp. 251–252.

[45] Coquille recalled that Louis, as part of his program to place the king *hors de page*, had ". . . abaissé l'autorité des Princes, et aboly le pouvoir des Etats, esquels les nouveaux subsides doivent être accordez, et n'avoit le Roy droit de les imposer autrement. . . ." *Histoire de Nivernois*, p. 389, col. 2. His criticisms of the recent Valois rulers were more serious: ". . . l'oppression du peuple étoit intolerablement excessive, et sembloit qu'on eût cherché toutes les inventions possibles, pour ôter au peuple tous ses moyens, et le rendre nud et languissant." *Dialogue*, p. 233, col. 1. This work is filled with sharp criticisms of royal misgovernment in financial and judicial matters.

effects of personal government, and classes his works as a major outcry against royal policies undermining the traditional constitution. And it accounts for the general tone of much of his writing, an all-pervading pessimism concerning the safety and future of the state. He realized that the king habitually went beyond his rightful sphere of authority and that in consequence the legal bases of the state were greatly endangered, but he found no means of checking the king other than to set forth the traditional limits of law and to counsel the king to abide by them. Concerning the most flagrant abuse, arbitrary taxation, he could merely assert: *"Nos Rois avec la grace de Dieu, pourvoyront au pauvre peuple, s'il leur plait."* [46] His sole recourse was to remonstrate and to hope for a ruler more reverent toward the traditional foundations of the state.

Parallel with his concept of tempered monarchy, Coquille placed great emphasis upon the position and influence of the royal counsellors. He listed as "born" counsellors the princes of the blood and the peers of the realm, and as "made" counsellors the great officers of the crown. [47] As definitely as Bodin did he recognize that the king alone held authority of government, [48] but he insisted that the recognized counsellors should have influence in shaping royal policies. In this connection, he placed especial emphasis upon the counsel of the peers. Under the line of Hugh Capet, he said, the monarchy was not intolerable because the six lay peers acted as controllers of the king's actions in case he deviated from reason. But with the reunion of those peerages with the crown, he added, the kings have exercised untempered authority. [49] And

[46] *Ordonnances du Roy Henri III*, p. 562, col. 1.

[47] *Institution*, p. 2, col. 1.

[48] "Le Roy est Monarque et n'a point de compagnon en sa Majesté Royale." *Institution*, p. 1, col. 2.

[49] "Cette Monarchie du tems de la lignée d'Hugues Capet, n'étoit pas Monarchie intolerable, car quoy que le Roy fût respecté comme Souverain avec tous honneurs qu'un Monarque peut desirer et meriter, si est-ce que les six Pairs de France laiz luy étoient donnez comme Conseillers naiz, et par une cabale occulte non écrite, etoient comme contrôlleurs de ses actions en cas qu'il

Coquille believed that bad counsellors, particularly those who persuaded the king that all property in the realm belonged to him, were responsible for the major ills of the state.[50] Again appears his pessimism resulting from the break from former usage, but as a solution he could only propose a return to the older forms.

Coquille's writings concerning the Estates General were among the most important produced during the century, both because of the high place which he ascribed to that institution and because of his activity in three important assemblies. It will be recalled that he upheld the very unusual doctrine that the original transfer of authority to the king had not been complete, since the people retained a portion of it to be exercised in the Estates.[51] As matters over which the Estates held final authority, Coquille listed the settlement of disputed successions to the crown, the making of fundamental law, and the granting of taxes.[52] Furthermore, he regarded the institution as an important source of counsel for the king. The assembled deputies he believed capable of giving the best possible counsel concerning weighty matters because their opinions were those of the people.[53] Coquille's heavy insistence upon the right of the people to make their law caused him to regard the counsel given by the Estates in a somewhat different manner than did his contemporaries. Like them, he recognized the fact that the assembled deputies acted strictly as representatives of the people and held no authority over matters of government. Thus the *cahiers* were merely counsel and petition, and the decisions of the deputies could not bind the ruler.[54] But if Coquille was thus in strict accord with

---

se detournât de la raison. . . . Ces Pairies abbatues et unies à la Couronne, les Rois ont usé de puissance absolue." *Histoire de Nivernois*, p. 337, col. 1.

[50] *Dialogue*, p. 230, col. 2.   [51] See above, n. 17.

[52] *Discours des états*, pp. 277–280; *Histoire de Nivernois*, p. 445.

[53] ". . . és affaires de tres-grande importance comme sont les affaires pour lesquelles on assemble les Etats Generaux, ils ne peuvent prendre meilleur ny plus asseuré conseil que de leurs sujets mêmes." *Histoire de Nivernois*, p. 444, col. 2.

[54] "En toutes ses assemblées d'Etats, le peuple des trois Ordres n'a prétendu

other writers concerning the relative authorities of king and Estates, he nevertheless would attribute a certain moral weight to the representations of the deputies. Because of his strong conviction that the people ought to be the source of their law, he urged that the ordinances based upon the *cahiers* should be regarded as laws made by the king holding his Estates, and should be irrevocable except in a similar assembly. However, he added that many kings had dispensed with that procedure.[55] Thus, although he did not deny the traditional idea that the king alone held authority to make ordinances, he urged that the people should at least have a voice in the framing of such law. Coquille's statements, when compared with those of his contemporaries, reveal that he was almost alone in attributing such a large measure of active influence to the Estates General. And his reason for such was his fundamental conviction that the will of the people should be a primary factor in shaping the constitution.

---

aucune part ny communication en ce qui est du gouvernement. Seulement en aucuns d'iceux a été dit, que les Etats étans reconnus par le Roy pour Etats, sont Conseillers du Roy, pour la determination de ce qui se traite és Etats. Ce dire quelquefois a été rejetté tout à plat: quelquefois accordé par apparence, et en effet refusé. En ces Etats de present, le Roy par ses deux propositions des Dimanches 16. et Mardy 18. Octobre 1588. a fait entendre de vive voix à ses Etats, qu'il entendoit se resoudre sur le contenu és cahiers, avec l'avis de ses Etats. Certainement semble qu'avec raison se peut dire, que quand le Roy juge qu'il est convenable d'assembler ses Etats, par même moyen il juge que ses Etats sont appellez par luy comme Conseillers de la Couronne, pour le tems que la tenue des Etats dure. . . ." *Discours des états*, p. 276.

[55] "Quand les Rois veulent ordonner loix perpetuelles, importantes à l'Etat du Royaume, ils ont accoûtumé de convoquer les trois Ordres de leur peuple, qu'on appelle Etats. . . . Esdits Etats generaux le Roi propose la cause pour laquelle il a appellé son peuple, et commande aux Deputez de s'assembler, conferer entr'eux, et dresser des cahiers generaux, sur lesquels il promet faire réponse, et ordonner loix salutaires à l'Etat. En cette assemblée d'Etats generaux, le Roy seant en son trône de Majesté Royale, est assisté des Princes, de son sang, des Pairs de France tant Lais qu'Ecclesiastiques, et des Officiers generaux de la Couronne, oit les propositions qui luy sont faites de vive voix par les Orateurs de chacun Ordre, et aprés avoir reçu leurs cahiers, ordonne loix qui sont dites loix faites par le Roy tenant ses Etats, qui sont loix stables et permanentes, et qui par raison sont irrevocables, sinon qu'elles soient changées en pareille ceremonie de convocation d'Estats. Toutefois plusieurs Rois s'en sont dispensez." *Institution*, p. 2. For specific examples of such laws, see *Coutumes de Nivernois*, p. 155, col. 2, and p. 195, col. 2.

Coquille's ideas concerning the Parlement of Paris were in marked contrast with those in regard to the Estates. For him, the Parlement was merely a court of justice exercising the royal prerogative of supreme jurisdiction, but without major significance beyond that sphere. Together, the court in Paris and those in the provinces he regarded as valuable instruments in administering the justice owed by the king to his subjects; he even referred to them as established in virtue of agreements between ruler and people.[56] Likewise, he repeated the accepted doctrine that royal ordinances were binding only if enregistered by the Parlement.[57] However, he was unwilling to regard that procedure as a serious legal check upon the monarch. The Parlements, he said, had been established merely in order to administer justice between subjects, and not to make laws or handle affairs of state. The procedure of enregistering royal enactments should be preserved, but on such occasions, and particularly in the *lits de justice*, it was the authority of the king alone which was concerned. The act of the court in enregistering edicts was merely for the purpose of preserving them, and remonstrances were mere counsel. He would even discard the term "verification" as defining the court's activity, substituting "publication," and he referred to royal ordinances limiting the capacity of the court as proving the validity of his interpretation.[58] Thus, as an effective instrument, Coquille

---

[56] "Ces Parlemens sont établis par forme de contrats faits par le Roy avec le peuple, et pour le soulagement d'iceluy." *Institution*, p. 2, col. 2.

[57] "Les loix et Ordonnances des Rois doivent être publiées et verifiées en Parlement, ou en autre Cour souveraine, selon le sujet de l'affaire; autrement les sujets n'en sont liez; Et quand la Cour ajoûte à l'acte de publication, que ç'a été de l'exprés mandement du Roy, c'est une marque que la Cour n'a pas trouvé l'Edit raisonnable." *Institution*, p. 2, col. 1.

[58] "Car les Parlemens sont établis pour exercer Justice és causes des particuliers, et non pour faire Lois, ny connoître d'affaires d'Etat, ny pour faire provisions autres que de l'administration de Justice. Vray est que le Roy tient esdits Parlemens son lit de justice avec les Pairs de France, et en iceux sont publiez et enregistrez les Edits et Constitutions que les Rois font. Mais és Edits et Arrests le Roy seul parle et reconnoît que la Cour est son Conseil, et ne la reconnoit pas pour compagne en cette puissance d'ordonner et faire loix. Aussi l'ancien stile porte seulement que l'Edit a été lu, publié et enregistrez en Parlement: Quoy que communément on use du mot de verifier. Auparavant l'Edit

regarded the Parlement as little more than a court for the decision of cases between subjects. He summarized its position in connection with edicts and ordinances as to receive, order published, and enregister the laws which the king makes.[59]

This was no accidental omission but an important aspect of Coquille's constitutional system. Comparison with the ideas of other writers is enlightening on this point. It will be recalled that there was considerable variation among the constitutionalists concerning the attributes which they assigned to the Estates General and the Parlement respectively, and that there was even much confusion of those attributes between the two institutions.[60] This variation is to be found in almost every constitutional system outlined during the century; it was with extreme infrequency that there appeared equal emphasis upon the functions of the Estates and the Parlement. Pasquier represents well the very heavy emphasis which many Parisian legists placed upon the court. He attributed to that body a complete authority to evaluate royal edicts and consequently to check the king, but he expressed extreme doubt concerning the value of the Estates General. Conversely, Coquille regarded the Estates as the primary institution in the state but saw in the Parlement little more than a court of justice. Both thinkers upheld the inviolability of private legal rights, but they advocated the defense of those rights in varying fashions. Coquille emphasized the

---

de Roussillon de l'an 1564 lesdites Cours de Parlement, et autres Souveraines, avoient accoûtumé de modification des Edits, qui étoient comme un controlle de la puissance du Roy, car ces modifications étoient tenues pour loy. Mais par ledit Edit leur a été reservé seulement, si aucun Edit se trouve en difficulté, d'en faire humbles remonstrances au Roy." *Discours des états*, p. 281, col. 2. In support of his ideas concerning the Parlement, Coquille recalled the statement which Charles IX made in 1563, to the effect that the court should concern itself solely with judicial affairs. *Dialogue*, p. 215, col. 2.

[59] ". . . il [le Parlement] est pour juger les causes des particuliers, et pour recevoir, faire publier et enregistrer les loix que le Roy fait." *Histoire de Nivernois*, p. 445, col. 2. It is significant that this statement occurs in Coquille's last work, which expressed his mature thought on a multitude of points.

[60] See above, pp. 137–139.

authority of the people to establish customary law, to carry out its reformation unhampered by royal interference, to give consent to taxes, and all these were functions of the Estates. He regarded the Parlement as of secondary importance in defending popular rights because it could not base its actions upon authority independent of the crown. Pasquier, on the other hand, knew from experience that the Estates General had proved of small value, and believed it sufficient to attribute to the court adequate authority to bring royal enactments under the *civilité de la loy*. Both thinkers would place the king under a check of *la police*, but they differed remarkably in regard to the means of bringing that about. This divergence was caused largely by the varying experience of the two men. Coquille, through his work in the provincial administration, was surrounded by problems turning on points of customary law, and it seemed logical that the Estates, as representing the people whose rights were concerned, should take a hand in the defense of those rights. To Pasquier, a very active member of the Parisian *noblesse de robe*, it seemed best to entrust the defense of popular rights and consequent limitation of the royal discretion to that court whose work was the maintenance of the law. Their desire to limit the king was the same, but they varied completely in their choice of institutions to put it into effect. Such divergence exemplifies the great variation of emphasis possible within the extremely complex constitutional system and forming one cause of its eventual collapse.

The traditional rights of the feudal nobility constituted for Coquille a very important legal question to be considered in relation to the royal authority. As might be expected, his works embodied a very strong defense of baronial rights against the encroachments of royal agents. His fundamental criterion in such matters was the order of society which had existed during the Middle Ages. Feudalism had witnessed the growth of those legal rights which continued to form the basis of society, and whose violation necessarily involved partial destruction of the accepted constitution. This approach appears very sharply in his discussion of alodial lands, which stood outside the feudal hierarchy. In spite of the fact that the *Coutume de Nivernais* stated that all inherited lands were assumed to be free and alodial unless it was shown to the contrary,[61] Coquille, by a process of reasoning not entirely consonant with his theories of customary law, discarded that interpretation on the ground that it was not according to the general tenor of feudalism. He proceeded to trace the origins and rise of the French constitution, emphasizing the hierarchical arrangement of the social structure, the gradation of rights, and the resulting varied obligations of all men toward the maintenance of the state. He concluded that all lands should be assumed to be held under noble or base tenure, and that the presumption was therefore in favor of the feudal rather than the alodial.[62] As in so many details of his system, his interpretation was distinctly in favor of the feudal lord. His statements were in absolute contrast with those of Du Moulin and his followers who stressed the value of alodial holdings and sought generally to break down the pyramidal social structure.

The conflicting purposes of Coquille and Du Moulin appeared in their treatments of several other items directly related to this general question. Du Moulin's most significant statement was his definition of a fief as a piece of land, a conception which he utilized to separate personal status and tenurial rights. Coquille upheld the idea, certainly closer to that obtaining in the Middle Ages, that status and tenure were one and the same thing. A man's holding of land auto-

---

[61] *Coutumes de Nivernois*, p. 119, col. 1.

[62] "Du discours cy-dessus, il faut inferer qu'en France tous heritages, ou sont tenus noblement pour faire service de sa personne en la guerre, ou sont tenus roturierement pour en payer prestation annuelle au Roy ou aux Seigneurs qui tiennent en fief du Roy. . . . Pourquoy en concluant, je dis que la presomption est pour les Seigneurs que les heritages de leurs territoires soient tenus d'eux à fief ou à cens, et que c'est la charge du detenteur de prouver qu'ils soient allodiaux, ou par titre, ou par possession immemoriale." *Coutumes de Nivernois*, p. 120. Cf. *Institution*, p. 38; *Questions et reponses*, pp. 171–172.

matically fixed his status in society, since feudal tenure implied a distinct union of real and personal servitudes.[63] For Coquille, the legally constituted and unequal rights of wealth and position provided the foundation of the feudal hierarchy which he desired to maintain. Similarly, he found none of the baseness emphasized by his predecessor in personal servitudes and in feudal dues owed by the serfs to their lords. He upheld them as a matter of course because they formed a vital portion of the legal system, and in discussing them in great detail he maintained them in all their rigor.[64] In the majority of these interpretations, Coquille paralleled closely those of d'Argentré who wrote specifically in order to refute Du Moulin. Together, Coquille and his Breton contemporary exemplify the resistance offered by the outlying portions of the realm to the rising currents of thought extending from the capital.

Coquille included in his conception of baronial rights a large number of those authorities which Parisian jurists had long regarded as strictly regalian. In his conception of the royal authority, Coquille was much closer to the time-honored theory of dominium than to the more recent Bodinian sovereignty. In place of the absolute indivisibility of the royal prerogative insisted upon by Bodin, Coquille reiterated the older concept which attributed merely supreme authority to the ruler and permitted the alienation of rights to be held *utilement* by others.[65] This was his point of departure and permitted him to attribute to the greater barons many public authorities, particularly those falling under the *droit de fisque*

---

[63] "Combien que le service du vassal soit deu, principalement à la personne du Seigneur, toutesfois, il est deu par le vassal à cause du fief servant, et deu au Seigneur à cause du fief dominant, qui fait que le devoir est mêlé de realité et personnalité." *Coutumes de Nivernois*, p. 41, col. 2.

[64] *Coutumes de Nivernois*, pp. 127–142; *Institution*, pp. 41–48. It is interesting to note that Pasquier cited this chapter of the *Coutume de Nivernais* as unusually severe in maintaining personal servitudes. *Recherches*, Liv. IV, p. 378.

[65] "La verité est, que le droit de Souveraineté, qui represente la Majesté Royale, et est le vray droit de la Couronne, est non alienable. Mais ce qui est de la Seigneurie utile pour les profits et honneurs, semble être alienable, pourvû que la directe Seigneurie, la Souveraineté et le ressort demeurent au Roy." *Institution*, p. 3, col. 2.

and the *droit de justice*. Coquille may have accepted the maxim *fief et justice n'ont rien de commun*,[66] but he refused the consequent idea (stressed so heavily by the royal agents against whom he struggled) that all baronial justice had originated through usurpation and belonged by right only to the king. For all practical purposes, he united fief and jurisdiction by legal and historical argument. He recalled that judicial and financial authorities had originally been granted to the dukes and counts for life only, but in time those prerogatives became hereditary possessions, inseparably united with the great feudal holdings.[67] This feature of social organization he believed to have occasioned the success of the medieval French monarchy.[68] His conclusion that feudal jurisdictions were patrimonial properties embodied in the great fiefs [69] was but another way of saying that the nobility enjoyed as firm a right in their judicial authorities as they did in their lands or anything else guaranteed by custom. In answer to

---

[66] *Coutumes de Nivernois*, pp. 43, col. 1, 71, col. 1; *Institution*, pp. 32, col. 2, 44, col. 2.

[67] "Au temps de la grandeur de la maison et lignée de Charlemagne Roy de France, les Duchés et Comtés n'étoient hereditaires, ains étoient dignitez à vie, comme sont aujourd'huy les Gouvernemens en France; ou bien étoient envoyez par les Provinces, pour y exercer leurs charges durant certain temps. Les Ducs et Comtes avoient droit d'administrer Justice, tant en civil que criminel; mais c'étoit sous le nom et autorité du Roy. Comme ladite lignée commença à decliner et s'affoiblir, à l'exemple de ce qui au même temps fut fait en Allemagne, les Duchés et Comtez furent faits hereditaires et patrimoniaux; et leur fut attribué le droit de faire et administrer Justice, qui fut annexé et uni inseparablement auxdits Duchez et Comtez; et par même moyen leur furent attribuez plusieurs droits de Fisque . . . de telle sorte, que à quiconque venoit la proprieté de la Seigneurie fût par hereditê ou acquisition, il avoit le même droit de Justice et de fisque. D'où vient qu'en France on dit, les Jurisdictions et Justices être patrimoniales; ce qui ne s'entend pas pour en tirer profit, comme de son patrimoine . . . mais parce que le droit est hereditaire, comme les autres biens que chacun a en son patrimoine." *Institution*, pp. 8, col. 2, to 9, col. 1. Cf. *Coutumes de Nivernois*, p. 7; *Questions et reponses*, pp. 130–131.

[68] ". . . cette lignée de Hugues Capet, a prosperé par l'occasion de ce que les Rois ont communiqué portion de leur grandeur et autorité hereditairement aux Seigneurs, retenue aux Rois la souveraineté." *Questions et reponses*, p. 130, col. 1.

[69] ". . . ce droit de faire exercer justice est hereditaire et patrimonial, adherent et uny à la Seigneurie et fief inseparablement, en sorte que celuy auquel est transmis le fief, soit par succession ou achat, ou autre titre, a le même droit de justice." *Histoire de Nivernois*, p. 340, col. 2.

the possible argument that such baronial rights were originally but temporary grants and had become hereditary only during a period of chaos, Coquille asserted that the major portion of customary law maintaining the rights of all persons, high and low, had arisen largely since the time of Hugh Capet.[70] In this fashion, Coquille placed baronial jurisdiction upon a basis of customary law and right. Every encroachment by a royal officer seemed to him a direct violation of the accepted constitution. It is easily apparent that his ideas embodied doctrines against which the Parisian jurists had struggled for centuries.

The great variation between Coquille and the legists of the capital concerning those regalian rights allowed to the feudal lords may be illustrated by comparing the treatments of that question given by Coquille and Bacquet. The latter's book may be regarded as representing the thought of the Parisian legal profession on that point. Bacquet denied entirely to the feudal justices such regalian authorities as *droit d'aubain, franc-fief, annoblissement, nouveaux acquêts,* and *amortissement*; and he allowed but a closely limited right in *droit de bâtardise.*[71] Of these, Coquille attributed fully to the feudal justices the *droit d'aubain* and the *droit de bâtardise* on the theory that *biens vacans* came to feudal lords in virtue of their exercise of regalian *droits de fisque.*[72] And he would even attribute the prerogative of *amortissement* to the great nobles.[73] The lengths to which Coquille would go in maintaining the authority of the duke in administrative matters is

---

[70] *Questions et reponses*, p. 334.

[71] *Op. cit.*, Liv. I, pp. 132, 258; Liv. II, pp. 34–35, 95, 125, 158.

[72] *Institution*, pp. 121–122; *Questions et reponses*, pp. 291–292. "Ce droit de biens vacans est un des droits du Fisque appartenant aux Seigneurs hauts-justiciers utilement, comme Procureurs à leur profit (*in rem suam*) du Seigneur souverain." *Coutumes de Nivernois*, p. 15, col. 2. As a general maxim, he would assert: ". . . en France les Seigneurs Justiciers qui ont droit de fisque, ont aussi droit de commander en tout ce qui est du public, et y faire reglement." *Ibid.*, p. 38, col. 2. As usual, he deplored the encroachment of royal officers upon these baronial rights. *Histoire de Nivernois*, p. 343; *Coutumes de Nivernois*, pp. 307, col. 2, to 310, col. 1.

[73] *Institution*, p. 21, col. 2; *Histoire de Nivernois*, p. 343, col. 1.

illustrated by his insistence that it was the duke's prerogative, and not the king's, to assemble the local estates of the province. This he justified through the historical priority of the provinces over the *bailliages* and by the great prerogatives of the peers in the traditional constitution.[74] His ideal feudal magnate appears as little less than a local monarch. These details reflect the circumstances of Coquille's career and his close association with the Duke of Nevers, but they do not lessen the value of his thought as representative of the best in provincial learning.

Such were the main aspects of the constitutional thought of Guy Coquille. His was the most logically conservative theory of state that is to be found during the century. In his fundamental approach through the two independent spheres of legal right, he was at one with the entire body of his contemporaries, but his ideas represented a significant variant from those of writers in the capital. This contrast is immediately apparent in his attitude toward kingship. Far from repeating the idea stressed by many, that the king stood high above the mass of his subjects both in authority and inherent superiority approaching the divine, Coquille retained the concept of the corporate state composed of innumerable pyramided groups with varying rights, the king capping the whole and bound closely to the people by ties of love and fidelity. Far from being exalted high above all other persons in society, the king was but a superior member of the nobility.[75] All men, declared Coquille in a remarkable passage, are subject to similar imperfections; consequently, kings and others in high station should remember that they are not great of themselves but merely through the obedience and respect accorded them by others.[76] Nothing was more pernicious, he said, than

[74] *Discours des états*, p. 282; *Qu'en fait des états*, pp. 286–287; *Histoire de Nivernois*, pp. 436, 444. *Coutumes de Nivernois*, p. 6.

[75] *Ordonnances du roy Henri III*, p. 539, col. 1.

[76] "Les Rois et autres grands doivent penser qu'ils ne sont pas grand d'eux mêmes, ni en eux-mêmes: car ils sont hommes semblables aux autres, mais leur grandeur se montre et entretient en ce que plusieurs autres personnes leur obeis-

the flattery lavished upon the king by base-born royal crea-
tures, for they tended to turn the king's head and to separate
him from his subjects, breaking down the vital unity of the
state.[77]

At the time of Coquille's writing, his system represented
an ideal which was generally regarded as outmoded and was
rapidly disappearing, both in the theory and practice of political life. Although many of his contemporaries accepted
numerous aspects of his thought, the overwhelming current
was making for the abandonment of the traditional political
conceptions which Coquille preserved in somewhat exaggerated
form. The weight of opinion was lifting the king to new
heights above his subjects, and his dominance over popular
rights guaranteed by customary law was accepted by a majority of writers. Coquille stood alone among the major jurists
of his day in refusing to the king authority over custom for
any reason whatsoever. The general emphasis of his thought
was occasioned by his life in the provinces and his isolation
from contemporary developments in political thought. Fundamentally, he was unaffected by the growing conviction among
theorists that the traditional concept of the state was an insufficient theoretical counterpart of a society recognizedly in
rapid evolution. For Coquille, the traditional constitution
stemming from the Middle Ages was the best and the only
possible basis of the state. The only new laws which he recognized were customs made in the local estates and fundamental
laws laid down by the Estates General. He denied to the king
any authority over the law, customary or fundamental; consequently he included in his thought no concept of royal legislation. His ideal monarch was a judge who preserved the state
as it stood, ruling his subjects in paternal but not autocratic
fashion, and always respectful of those limits placed upon his
authority by the law of the land and the rights of his subjects.

---

sent et les respectent; et l'origine est de la bonne volonté de leurs sujets, qui
s'addonnent à cette obeissance." *Questions et reponses*, p. 332, col. 1.

[77] *Histoire de Nivernois*, p. 390, col. 1; *Dialogue*, p. 230, col. 2.

Coquille was well aware that contemporary royal policy was far from his ideal, and he expressed his anger and disappointment in no uncertain terms. But his fundamental approach was such that he could but hope for a ruler who, through superior qualities and strength of purpose, would conform more closely to his pattern. Hence his strong support of Henry IV. If he was unaffected by the rising intellectual currents which were undermining the older constitutionalism, his theory nevertheless embodied doctrines extremely significant in the evolution of political concepts. Coquille represented a dying cause, but his works stand as a monument to much that was best in the constitutional thought of France.

CHAPTER VI

THE THEORY OF ABSOLUTISM

The triumph of Henry IV inaugurated a period of French history during which the monarchy was destined to achieve greatness far surpassing that attained in any earlier period of its existence. If the rule of Francis I and Henry II had been strong to the point of silencing serious opposition among contemporary writers, that of their Bourbon successors was to gain an importance in European affairs far beyond the aspirations of the earlier Valois rulers. The major qualities of seventeenth-century absolutism, both in terms of royal policy and its counterpart in political theory, not only characterized the reign of Henry IV but exhibited a vigor surprising in view of the depths to which the sovereign authority had sunk during the previous reign. Yet it was that degradation of monarchy and threat to the life of the state which caused such swift reaction toward strong control under the first Bourbon. Thinkers of no party during the Wars of Religion seriously challenged the principles upon which monarchy rested, and in the presence of the great political and social disruption concomitant with the religious struggle, those jurists defending legitimate monarchy were willing to attribute to the ruler increased legitimate authority if only in order to preserve the state from collapse. The vital influence of the period of strife and confusion was to prepare the land for absolutism. If the new regime was not always accepted with equanimity, it was regarded as infinitely superior to that disrupted state of affairs which had prevailed during the entire previous generation.

The period of upheaval had witnessed unprecedented disruption of social classes, vested interests, and legal rights of all types, in a word, the specific concern of the jurists and that which they believed to provide the foundations of the state. Although many had been brought to abandon the older, static political conceptions in favor of a dynamic theory of state, their fundamental approach through legality caused them necessarily to view with dismay the great threat to the established constitution. The activities of the Leaguers had appeared especially revolting to these jurists who were overwhelmingly Gallican and *politique*. Not only had the final period of civil war witnessed the disintegration of the realm into a series of local seigneuries and city-states, but the policy of the Leaguers of appealing to popular emotions had in many places caused the lower elements of the population to throw off the dominance of their traditional superiors and to substitute petty tyrannies. Such action ran completely counter to the aristocratic attitude of the age [1] and caused the great majority of legists and intellectuals generally to demand strong rule from above and the restoration of the constitution according to traditional rights. Such was the meaning of Pierre Pithou when he wrote in 1593 that there was a general desire for *"un Roy qui donnera ordre à tout."* [2] The crying need was for the restoration of social stability, and in consequence the jurists sought to reestablish that primary requisite, popular obedience to royal government. The many speeches given by the legal practitioners and members of the royal administration throughout the realm during the last stages of the war invariably placed great emphasis upon the

[1] This reaction to the policies of the League is well illustrated by the following passage from the *Dialogue d'entre le maheustre et le manant*. The *maheustre* (the *politique*), after decrying the rabble-rousing activities of the League's preachers and the popular tyranny of the Sixteen, goes on: "Le peuple ne s'en est pas esloigné, qui comme un animal farouche et sauvage a voulu secouer le joug de la domination Royale, pour acquerir je ne sçay quelle liberté imaginaire, qui a esté à leur grand malheur et confusion changée en une tyrannie la plus cruelle et barbare que jamais ayent enduré les pauvres esclaves des infideles." *Dialogue*, p. 544. Two pages later, he said: ". . . faut que le peuple croye et obeisse à la Noblesse."

[2] *Satyre menippée*, I, 177, in the "Harangue d'Aubray," written by Pierre Pithou. The concluding section of this harangue (pp. 177–192) illustrates well the desire of the *politiques* for strong monarchical rule.

obedience of the subject as the principal need for successful political life and the best interests of the individual. There are seven fundamentals of social life, said Pierre Matthieu when speaking before the people of Lyon in 1593, which require the implicit obedience of all subjects: the law of God, the commands of the Church, the natural order of all things, the subjection required by the King of France because of his divine right and his capacity as vicar of God, the justice inherent in the rule of all French monarchs, the lamentable result of social unrest, and the necessity of preserving the traditional constitution.[3] The greatest liberty and happiness, said Du Vair before the people of Marseilles in 1596, are to be found under the rule of a strong prince, for it is he who is the soul of the social organism and preserves civil society from decay. He is established in that capacity by God, and obedience is due to him both because of his divine authorization and because of his position as guide and preserver of the state.[4] Such was the tone adopted by the jurists and all who sought to bring order to the land. It was the attitude of the entire body of men who wrote or acted in the interests of legitimate monarchy.

As major characteristics of this inevitable reaction, there arose in intellectual life an emphasis upon form, discipline, the virtues of the intellect, strict control from above, a contempt for the common man and his rights, in a word, those qualities which played such a large part in seventeenth-century classicism. Such factors, in themselves but manifestations of an all-embracing attitude, exercised great influence upon contemporary political thought and channeled great portions of legal theory toward an increased royal authority and the

[3] Pierre Matthieu, *Harangue aux consuls et peuple de Lyon: Du deuoir et obeissance des subiects enuers le roy . . . prononcee le xxiii decembre, MDXCIII.* Without place or date of publication.

[4] Guillaume Du Vair, *Remonstrance aux habitans de Marseille, faicte le vingt-troisiesme jour de decembre, 1596,* in Radouant, *op. cit.,* pp. 201–202. These sentiments were, of course, by no means new to the jurists. Loisel had expressed substantially the same opinion in the speeches which he made during the *grands jours* of Guyenne, 1582–84. *La Guyenne* (Paris, 1605), *passim.*

subjection of the populace to highly autocratic rule. The force
of these intellectual currents, even before the restoration of
order to the land, may be illustrated by statements set forth
by Pierre Charron in 1595.[5] In outlining his ideas concerning
royal sovereignty, Charron followed both the sense and the
phraseology used by Bodin, but he lent that concept an autocratic emphasis lacking even in the works of the austere
Angevin. The state, said Charron, using that word in the
narrow sense, is a domination, an ordering involving command
and obedience, and is the foundation, the internal link, and
the guiding spirit of human affairs; it is the bond within
society which cannot exist without it, the vital essence which
brings life to human and natural associations.[6] Grandeur and
sovereignty are coveted by all men; they constitute something beautiful and divine although difficult of achievement,
a vital means of exacting that respect and obedience due from
the people in the interest of peace and quiet.[7] That such was
hardly a fitting intellectual atmosphere in which to preserve
the inviolability of private rights and customary law is illustrated by Charron's statements concerning the same. After
reviewing the differences between the laws of the prince and
the custom of the land, stressing the ability of the ruler to
make or break the latter through royal act, he criticized custom severely as mere arbitrary usage occurring in various
localities because of immediate circumstance. Listing many

[5] Charron's intellectual equipment included law, philosophy, literature, and
religion; consequently, he was better able to record contemporary intellectual
developments than was the average legal practitioner. His main work, *De la
sagesse*, was first published in 1595. Our references are to the edition of Paris,
1604.

[6] "L'état, c'est à dire la domination, ou bien l'ordre certain en commandant
et obeissant, est l'appui, le ciment, et l'ame des choses humaines: c'est le lien de
la societé, qui ne pourroit autrement subsister; c'est l'esprit vital, qui fait
respirer tant de milliers d'hommes, et toute la nature des choses." *Op. cit.*, p. 266.

[7] "La grandeur et souueraineté est tant desirée de tous, c'est pource que tout
le bien qui y est paroit dehors, et tout son mal est au dedans: Aussi que commander aux autres est chose tant belle et diuine, tant grande et difficile. Pour
ces mesmes raisons sont estimés et reuerés pour plus qu'hommes. Cette creance
est vtile pour extorquer des peuples le respect et obeissance nourrice de paix et
de repos." *Op. cit.*, p. 268.

bizarre customs effective in given places, he concluded that customary law might serve as a guide to justice for the common people and the foolish but could never act as such for the wise man.[8] That was the essence of his criticism. Custom could not embody justice because it varied from place to place; it corresponded in no manner with that justice which was the especial virtue and ability of the wise.[9] Far from regarding custom as a major portion of the law, Charron condemned it as a negation of law because a travesty upon justice.[10] His statements reveal the disintegrating influence which extreme emphasis upon intellectual values and the rising veneration of discipline and strict control exercised upon the older constitutionalism. The jurists of the period did not exhibit such complete contempt for customary law, but they were subject to the same intellectual currents that produced Charron.

During the years 1596–98, there appeared a series of short political treatises which set forth in straightforward terms several features of the rising doctrine of absolutism. The

[8] "Quand ce vient à juger de ces coustumes, c'est le bruit et la querelle: le sot populaire et pedant ne s'y trouue point empeché, car tout détroussement il condamne comme barbarie et bestise tout ce qui n'est de son goust, c'est à dire de l'vsage. commun, et coustume de son pays. Car il tient pour regle vnique de verité, iustice, bienseance, la loy et coustume de son pays. . . . Le sage est bien plus retenu. . . ." *Op. cit.*, p. 423.

[9] "Elle fait et desfait, authorise, et desauthorise tout ce qu'il luy plaist, sans rithme ny raison, voire souuent contre toute raison: elle fait valoir, et establit parmy le monde, contre raison et jugement toutes les opinions, religions, creances, obseruances, moeurs, et manieres de viure les plus fantasques et farouches, comme a été touché cy dessus. Et au rebours elle degrade, injurieusement, raualle et desrobe aux choses vrayement grandes et admirables, leur pris, leur estimation, et les rend viles. . . . C'est donc vn tresgrande et puissante chose que la coustume. . . . Elle nous enchante si bien qu'elle nous fait croire, que ce qui est hors de ses gonds, est hors des gonds de raison, et n'y a rien de bon que ce qu'elle approuue. . . . Ceci est tollerable parmy les idiots et populaires, qui n'ayans la suffisance de voir les choses au fonds, juger et trier, font bien de se tenir et arrester à ce qui est communement tenu et reçeu: mais aux sages qui jouent vn autre roolle, c'est chose indigne de se laisser ainsi coiffer à la coustume." *Op. cit.*, pp. 427–428.

[10] Charron did not conclude that custom did not form a part of the constitution and should be ignored; he advised his readers to continue to abide by it, even while judging it according to abstract criteria. *Op. cit.*, pp. 428–429. His attitude and many of his statements are reminiscent of those of Charondas.

authors of these works included such men as Du Rivault,[11] Poisson,[12] Dorleans,[13] and Constant,[14] all mediocre writers but quite capable of recording the dominant intellectual currents of that brief interval. Du Rivault, the ablest of the group, was one of the innumerable clientele of literary hangers-on at the royal court and fairly represented the type. In the flow of political concepts, the opinions of these writers may be regarded as representing a continuation and development of those set forth earlier by the royalist pamphleteers discussed above, rather than those of the more detached legists. For the latter group frequently could not accept the extremely absolutistic statements of this small body of writers whose thought reflected the impact of innumerable factors, intellectual and circumstantial, forcing thinkers to push to the farthest limits their concepts of absolute monarchy. Yet if such ideas were not entirely accepted by all parties, the works in which they were set forth represented the major expressions of opinion during that short period of rapid intellectual movement and must be assigned a place in the history of ideas.

Following the example of earlier writers, these publicists reiterated the fundamental conception — generally accepted before the close of the century — representing kingship as sovereign authority, in the Bodinian sense, exercised by the temporal ruler in virtue of direct divine authorization.[15] Divine right provided, in their eyes, the major foundation of the political power and received corresponding emphasis, even exaggeration, in their systems.[16] Du Rivault believed the

---

[11] David Du Rivault, *Les Etats, esquels il est discouru du prince, du noble et du tiers-état, conformément à nostre temps* (Lyon, 1596).

[12] Pierre Poisson, *Traicté de la maiesté royalle en France* (Paris, 1597).

[13] Regnault Dorleans, *Les Observations de diuerses choses remarquees sur l'estat, couronne et peuple de France, tant ancien que modern recueillies de plusieurs autheurs* (Vennes, 1597).

[14] Pierre Constant, *De l'excellence et dignité des rois* (Paris, 1598).

[15] Du Rivault, *op. cit.*, Discours III; Dorleans, *op. cit.*, ch. VI; Constant, *op. cit.*, Discours VIII; Poisson, *op. cit.*, pp. 7–8.

[16] E.g., Constant: "C'est chose tres-certaine et sans doubte, que toute puissance prouient de là sus, et quiconques y resiste, cela est autant, comme s'opposer aux commandemens et à l'ordonnance de Dieu. . . . i'entends discourir d'vne

person of the king as well as his office to result from divine institution, and represented the ruler as literally a minor god on earth, admonishing him always to bear in mind his capacity as. a lesser divinity and creature of the Deity.[17] Because of the nature of Henry IV's claim to the throne, these writers without exception recognized the validity of the Salic Law, thus preserving a modicum of legality in their conception of kingship. But they reduced that law to a mere rule of succession and placed their major emphasis upon the divine choice and superhuman qualities of the monarch. In order to account for the divine appointment of the ruler, Du Rivault set forth that idea which was to win wide acceptance during the following century: that God had originally chosen the reigning prince by causing him to be born into the family of legitimate rulers, and that at his coronation he was merely confirmed in that divinity which had been a part of his being from the beginning.[18] In this fashion, the extreme absolutists reduced drastically the traditional significance of fundamental law, of the distinction between the king and the crown, and even of the coronation ceremony, and based their fundamental theory of kingship simply upon the personal divine right of the reigning monarch.

In incorporating this conception of the political power into

---

vraye et syncere puissance, qui regne sur nous, par la grace de Dieu, et par vne voye legitime, authentique, et bien receue par les loix et constitutions d'vn Royaume. De telle puissance i'entends parler, puissance, di-ie, encors absolue, et plein pouuoir, fondé sur l'equité des loix diuines, de nature, et ciuiles, digne ornement d'vn vray Roy, fille legitime du Ciel, non mesuree ny subiecte au controlle des hommes. . . ." *Op. cit.*, pp. 29–31. Cf. Dorleans, *op. cit.*, opening section.

[17] "En fin pour conclure ce present discours du Prince qui est le Christ et l'oint de Dieu, il luy seroit tres-utile d'auoir tousiours deuant les yeux, la description qu'Esaie faict du sainct, parfaict et immaculé, Christ, laquelle ne peut estre mal attribué aux Roys, desquels il est escript *Vous estes Dieux et les fils du tres-haut.*" *Op. cit.*, pp. 136–137. "Tout Roy de la terre est Dieu." *Ibid.*, p. 139.

[18] "Or ceste influence diuine tombee en l'homme que Dieu eslit et faict naistre de la race qui legitimement regne, confirme la Maiesté de-ia nee en luy mesme, dés que la succession legitime l'auoit saisi et appellé à la dignité. . . ." *Op. cit.*, pp. 45–46.

their general theory of state, these writers invariably followed
the time-honored approach to that question through public and
private spheres of legal right. But they moulded their interpretation in such fashion that governmental authority completely overshadowed private rights, thereby distorting the
primary meaning of the conception. Through extreme emphasis upon the divinity and all-embracing authority of the
prince, these proponents of absolutism had come to regard the
prince not only as the focal point of the state's existence but
also as the sum and substance of the entire *chose publique.*
The state, wrote Du Rivault, receives its life and vigor from
the king who provides the vitalizing essence within the social
structure. Likewise, it is regulated according to his pleasure,
since he moves all and disposes of all either in person or
through his lieutenants in accordance with his institution on
earth by God.[19] Such a conception did not deny the populace
a place in the life of the social organism, but for all practical
purposes, Du Rivault asserted that the people existed for the
king rather than the king for the people. Any legal rights
remaining to the subjects consequently lost their traditional
inviolability and required a distinctly new definition.

One of the most important considerations resulting from
this conception of divine-right sovereignty was the relationship of the king and the law. Combining the ideas that the
king stood as the divinely appointed legislator and supplied
the animating essence of the state, Constant wrote that the

---

[19] "Car telles Republiques ne prennent leur force et vigueur que du Roy, au
bon plaisir duquel elles sont rapportees, et procedent de luy presque de mesme
façon, que les facultez et puissance de vegeter et sentir, naissent en nous de
l'ame intellectuelle à laquelle on compare volontiers vn Roy semblable à celuy
que nous auons descript. Par ce que le Royaume qu'il possede, est comme vn
Monde, auquel le Roy meut tout, pendant qu'il demeure bien ordonné, faict
tout, dispose de tout, ou donne puissance à ses lieutenans, qui n'ont vigueur en
leurs commandemens que par luy. . . . Bref comme l'homme ne se peut rien
attribuer en la production de l'Ame, et qu'à Dieu seul est rapportee la creation
de ceste forme separable de la masse corporelle: Ainsi les vrais Roys viennent
purement de Dieu, qui les nous donne tels qu'il luy plaist, doux, seueres, sages,
fols, grossiers, subtils, comme son infinie sagesse le delibere et arrest. . . ."
Op. cit., pp. 27–29.

ruler was not only superior to all civil laws and alone lent them vigor,[20] but that such laws found their inviolability in that divinity with which they had been inspired by the king, their maker.[21] And Du Rivault pushed this conception of divinely authorized royal legislation to the fantastic conclusion of identifying royal enactments with divine law itself, both in original source and immediate effect.[22] This was without doubt the most extreme statement made in support of royal absolutism during the reign of Henry IV. In juxtaposition with such concepts, any legal limitations upon the monarch's freedom of action appear quite out of place, yet these writers, even Du Rivault, were unwilling to abandon the doctrine that ultimate justice existed above and apart from the prince, necessarily limiting his rightful discretion. This they maintained, although they specifically dissociated that concept from any constitutional rights of the subjects. In regard to specific legal values, they had but to reiterate the dominant conception representing all law as divine, natural, or civil, and placing the prince under the first two but over the latter.[23] Du Rivault adopted these working categories and made it clear that the

[20] ". . . bien est-il sur le droict positif, sur les loix et police des hommes, aux cas que dessus: de maniere qu'au manquement de la supresme et souueraine autorité du Roy, la loy est sans vigueur, sans lumiere, sans bouche, et comme vn corps perclus de toutes ses parties. Le Roy seul viuifie la Loy. . . ." *Op. cit.*, pp. 69–70.

[21] "Et à dire vray, les loix sont inuiolables, à cause de la diuinité dont elles sont inspirees, à laquelle participe la Majesté et dignité du Roy. . . ." *Op. cit.*, p. 73.

[22] "D'auantage comme Dieu qui est le Roy vniuersel, donne les loix generales et supremes: ainsi le Prince faict les loix de son Estat, ausquelles nul ne peut contreuenir, sans encourir fortune de vie, ou autre punition au poix de l'offence. Et si Dieu remet les peines, et pardonne les pechez: de mesme le Prince donne grace és crimes, et baille la vie à ceux sur lesquelles il luy plaist d'estendre sa clemence. Si bien qu'en comparaison de leurs effects, la loy de Dieu est quelque fois appellee la loy du Roy: comme si l'vne et l'autre portoient d'vne mesme source, et que l'arrest de la puissance humaine ne fust autre, que celuy qui est decreté au plus priué conseil de la volonté diuine. Et par consequent, si les authoritez se ressemblent, et que les noms de dignité suiuent l'authorité, pourquoy le Roy ne seroit-il appellé proprement Dieu?" *Op. cit.*, p. 144.

[23] E.g., Constant, *op. cit.*, p. 69. Fundamental law, of course, constituted a special category apart from these major types and was recognized by all to be inviolable.

royal supremacy over civil law automatically subjected all legal rights of the people to the sovereign to deal with as he would.[24] The populace could hardly claim inviolability of any sort, since in all civil matters the king not only made and changed the law, but his unqualified will, even his error, was law.[25] And by combining this with the idea that all rights had originally been distributed by the divinely authorized sovereign and were held subject to his discretion, Du Rivault concluded that the people held no indefeasible rights of any kind.[26] Thus the movement inaugurated by the separation of customary law and private rights was brought to its logical conclusion, and both were subjected to the royal discretion. With the exception of ultimate truths of eternal law, the prince stood forth quite without bounds to his authority. The doctrine could be developed no further.

It must be emphasized that these extreme ideas of royal absolutism appeared only in the writings of certain persons closely associated with the royal court and that they did not represent either the attitude of the large body of contemporary jurists or the general tenor of royal policy. Such exaggerated statements may provide valuable clues to the intellectual

[24] "Mais en tout autre cas encores indefiny par telles loix [fondamentales], les subiects sont tellement obligez au Roy, qu'ils ne peuuent à proprement parler, se dire offencés de luy à quelque chose qu'il les contraingne. . . ." *Op. cit.*, p. 173.

[25] "D'auantage la volonté du Prince, est la loy mesme: car sans autre texte ou formulaire de droict, son bon plaisir est loy, et faut y obeyr, si tost qu'il le faict cognoistre. . . . C'est pourquoy il est appellé la loy viue, et n'y a loy dans l'Estat qu'autant que sa volonté l'accorde, et l'arreste: tant qu'au changement d'icelle les subiects reçoiuent changement de loix, sans qu'il leur soit loisible de requerir autre fondement de raison. Iusques là mesme que la faute, et erreur du Prince est loy selon les constitutions du droict humain." *Op. cit.*, p. 174.

[26] "Et les subiects possedent leur bien par le droict du Roy, tellement que s'ils viennent à dire lors qu'il demande quelque chose . . . qui a-il entre le Roy et nous? Il leur respondra iustement. Qui a-il entre vous, et les biens que vous auez? Car les droicts des subiects, sont distribuez à la volonté du Seigneur, que Dieu leur a donnée pour loy, et laquelle ils ne peuuent refuser, qu'incontinent ils ne quittent ce qu'ils possedent, et que leurs biens ne soient reunis à la couronne, ou appliquez au fisque. Contre quoy, on ne peut alleguer, que ce qu'il veut n'ait esté faict par ses ancestres, ou qu'il soit inaudit auoir iamais esté demandé ou practiqué auparauant. Car mesme contre les coustumes de la cité, de la prouince ou du Royaume qui ne sont fondamentales de l'Estat entier, le Prince peut innouer des Constitutions. . . ." *Op. cit.*, pp. 174–175.

atmosphere at the royal court and the forces motivating the actions of various royal servants and administrators, but in themselves they necessarily present a distorted picture of Henry's government. The rule of the first Bourbon was characterized by slow and painstaking effort to bring order to the strife-torn land and to reestablish the royal authority over all portions of the state. In the process, Henry was forced to exercise great caution, for if the people felt great relief after the establishment of peace, they were not willing to give up in a moment those liberties which they had won during the period of strife. Often he found it possible to preserve order only by balancing opposing factions one against the other, while maintaining but a precarious control over all. His prudence in dealing with the institutions of government is illustrated by the fact that he resorted to the *lit de justice* only once during his reign, and that at a time when a major crisis threatened the safety of the state. However, it was not because of his great respect for the liberties of the subject that he refrained from violating them but rather because of the patent impossibility of doing so immediately after the restoration of peace. His aim throughout was to eliminate those social factors which might challenge the royal authority, to consolidate his immediate advantages, and to lay the groundwork for strong rule by future members of the dynasty. And in the process, particularly in the later years of his reign, he did not hesitate to resort to high-handed action if circumstances permitted and the concomitant risks were not excessively great.

The uneasiness which Henry's rule inspired in the provinces concerning the continued inviolability of customary rights is illustrated by the work of Jean de Souvert,[27] written in 1605 immediately antecedent to the assembling of the Estates of Burgundy, that body to which Coquille had referred as a

---

[27] Jean de Souvert, *Advis pour messieurs les gens des trois estats du pais et duché de Bourgogne, sur le subject de leur assemblee du mois de may prochain mil six cens cinq.* Without place or date of publication.

model of constitutional procedure. Souvert apparently feared for the life of that institution itself, since he insisted that the right of the local deputies to assemble in their estates was a primary privilege of the province [28] and expressed in veiled form his anxiety lest the assemblies be discontinued.[29] In his criticism of the central administration, he expressed in no uncertain terms his dislike for the evocation of cases from the Parlement of Dijon to that of Paris, the arbitrary acts of the *conseil privé*, and the bad financial administration which habitually dissipated taxes collected in the provinces.[30] In similar vein were his statements concerning the illegality of royal taxation. The ancient procedure, he said, involved simply the levying of that sum which had been accorded by the local estates. But to this had been added a series of extraordinary taxes which had originated through administrative action rather than the vote of the deputies and which were rapidly becoming permanent and increasing in volume.[31] Although these criticisms were distinctly less vehement than those which had assailed the rule of Henry III, they reveal the strong reaction of contemporaries in the face of governmental encroachment upon their traditional liberties. Such apprehension

---

[28] "Suiuant quoy, permettez moy ie vous supplie messieurs, de vous dire, qu'il sera besoin en premier lieu, reprendre vostre ancienne liberté par la conseruation des priuileges de la prouince, entre lesquels celuy portant le pouuoir de s'assembler en corps d'Estats est le plus illustre . . . en la Monarchie Royalle les subiets ne sont reputez comme enfans." *Op. cit.*, p. 9.

[29] ". . . il suffit que les remonstrances des estats tournent en simples supplications, enuers le Roy, en quoy ne gist pas encor peu de gloire et de resolution, veu que tout ainsi que le propre du Tyran, et la façon de gouuerner les nations nouuellement conquises, est d'aneantir toute sorte de colleges, et communautez, afin d'oster au public les moyens d'intelligence et de se recognoistre. . . . De mesmes, la marque d'vn bon Roy est de permettre à ses subjets s'assembler pour le supplier en toute humilité, et d'auctoriser leurs Estats, où se font les plus iustes plaintes. . . ." *Op. cit.*, p. 15.

[30] *Op. cit.*, pp. 26–61.

[31] "L'ancienne imposition qui souloit estre en Bourgongne, estoit seulement de l'octroy ou don gratuit, que les estats à chacune assemblee faisoient au Roy: du depuis a succedé la gabelle du sel, les decimes, le taillon, l'entretenement des garnisons, auec la composition faicte pour l'abolition de la Pancharte; et quelques autres parties qui tournent d'oresnauant en charges ordinaires. Mais outre ce qu'au respect du passé elles sont excessiues, ie treuue que celles qui sont extraordinaires les excedent encores." *Op. cit.*, p. 63.

was not without cause. The spirit as well as the immediate import of Henry's rule were well represented in his answer to a deputation from the same Estates of Burgundy in 1608: *"Vos plus beaux privileges sont quand vous avez les bonnes grâces de vostre Roy."* [32] Although the central government did not take complete advantage of doctrines subjecting popular rights to the royal discretion, the powerful combination of aggressive royal policy and intellectual justification for the same was providing the spearhead of the great social movement pushing forward toward seventeenth-century absolutism.

Although the legists of the period could not accept the extremes of royal autarchy advocated by those writers who moved in the shadow of the royal court, the men of the law were subject to the same currents that influenced all other thinkers and were not far behind their more rabid contemporaries in setting forth doctrines of absolutism. The appearance of such men as William Barclay, Pierre de L'Hommeau, and Charles Loyseau announced the advent of the type of jurist which was to dominate the profession until the period of the Enlightenment. Although these legists of the early seventeenth century embodied in their works major conceptions stemming from the older constitutionalism and frequently evinced reluctance to accept many doctrines concomitant with royal absolutism, they nevertheless incorporated the latter into their intellectual systems, and often added parallel interpretations of great importance to the ultimate success of the seventeenth-century conception of kingship. This was the manner of thought visible in the writings of Loyseau, by far the ablest jurist of the period.[33] The great majority of intellectuals early in the century were entirely convinced concerning

[32] Henri Beaune, "Un discours inédit de Henri IV," *Bulletin du bibliophile* (1862), p. 1390.

[33] In sheer intellectual ability, Loyseau was without doubt the greatest jurist of the entire period covered by this study, superior even to Bodin. Loyseau's influence upon French political thought was not as great as that of Bodin, largely because the major contributions to that field, as it was known during the *ancien régime*, had been made before the early seventeenth century.

the pressing necessity of strong royal government, and the legists were no exception. Their major contribution to the field of political thought was their amalgamation of the more recent conceptual developments with the general body of legal learning, thereby lending the theory of absolutism a rigidity and precision lacking in the works of earlier writers. With the appearance of these complete legal systems embodying the major tenets of royal absolutism, the seventeenth-century conception of kingship may be regarded as having achieved predominance in political thinking.

In their ideas concerning the king and his authority, the jurists of the early seventeenth century were in essential agreement with their more absolutist predecessors. We have observed the manner in which the extreme royalists, through exaggerated emphasis upon divine right, had shifted divine authorization from the authority of the king to his person, thereby assigning to the ruler a personal divine right on the basis of his celestial appointment for secular government. This fundamental change regarding the ultimate basis of the political power was accepted by the majority of later jurists. Although Loyseau made deference to "historical" evidence concerning the early practice of electing the French kings,[34] he insisted that such formed no valid precedent; and throughout his works he upheld the direct divine institution of king and crown alike.[35] Similarly, he followed the path of his predecessors in representing the king as a superior being, born into

---

[34] *Traité des seigneuries* (Paris, 1608), ch. II, no. 24. He cited Hotman as his authority.

[35] On the royal tenure of authority directly from God, see Loyseau's *Cinq Livres du droit des offices*, Liv. I, ch. VI, nos. 4–6; Liv. II, ch. II, nos. 21–24. This work was first published in 1610; we have used the edition of Cologne, 1613. The following passage shows his acceptance of the divine choice of the individual ruler: "Mais sur tout le grand Dieu des armees, par qui les Rois regnent, et les Princes sont maintenus, en a fait la decision, non seulement en establissant nostre inuincible Roy en son throsne, malgré tant d'ennemis et de suiets rebelles, mais le faisant florir et regner aussi paisiblement et heureusement, que iamais aucun de ses predecesseurs ait fait, et outre tout cela luy ayant donné quasi inesperement, vne si belle lignee, *Non haec sine numine Diuum*." *Traité des ordres et simples dignitez* (Cologne, 1613), ch. VII, no. 76. This work is printed with the *Offices*.

a family which necessarily surpassed all others in the excellence of its blood.[36] Among the jurists of the period, there was no significant questioning of Loisel's maxim, *"Le Roy ne tient que de Dieu et de l'espee."* [37]

The divine appointment of each reigning prince according to celestial determination was not found to conflict with the tradition of fundamental law, although it certainly lessened the significance of the latter. If the Salic Law were defined simply as a rule of succession, both that law and divine choice might be interpreted as directing the accession of a given individual and as complementary the one to the other. Largely through the superposition of divergent but not conflicting ideas, the jurists represented the reigning prince as that divinely appointed individual who had acceded according to fundamental law. Thus, the long tradition of legal succession to the crown opposed no effective barrier to newer ideas representing the prince as that person specifically chosen for temporal government by God. The most significant influence of that tradition in seventeenth-century political thought was that it delayed for long the appearance of doctrines ascribing to the king a personal, hereditary title to the crown similar to that of private inheritance according to civil law. The crown was a portion of the nation at large, and royal succession was according to fundamental law, a separate portion of the constitution. Since the recipient of the prerogative was

---

[36] "Ce qui est certainement bien conuenable à l'extreme respect et reuerence, que le peuple de France, plus que tout autre, porte à ses Rois, et à leur sang, en l'excellence duquel on ne doit imaginer aucune souilleure ni corruption, ains au contraire ce sang Royal purifie et ennoblit tout autre sang auec lequel il se mesle. Car il faut aduouer, qu'il est d'estoffe et qualité trop plus noble et auguste, que celuy des autres hommes: veu que Platon au 3. de sa Republ. a dit, que ceux, qui sont nays pour commander, sont composez d'autre metail, que les autres. Et Aristote a dit encor plus à propos, que les Roys sont d'vn genre moyen entre Dieu et le peuple. Comme donc les Poetes appellent les bastards des Dieux, Heroès ou demy-dieux, aussi pouuons nous dire, que les bastards des Roys sont demy-Roys, c'est à dire Princes, qui est la qualité moyenne entre les Roys et les autres hommes." *Traité des ordres*, ch. VII, no. 92.

[37] Antoine Loisel, *Institutes coutumières*, p. 19. This work was first published in 1607 with Coquille's *Institution*. Our references are to the critical edition by Michel Reulos, Paris, 1935.

designated strictly by the provisions of that law, it was logically impossible for him to claim a personal, proprietary right to the authority thus conferred upon him. The continued strength of this concept is illustrated by its explicit reiteration in the works of L'Hommeau who was one of the most abso-lutistic jurists of the period.[38]

However, there were devious means of circumventing this vital corollary of fundamental law and of attributing to the ruler a quasi-proprietary right to his authority. His specific appointment by God, widely accepted during this period, im-plied that he enjoyed a personal right to the crown which was thus assigned to him by divine will. Furthermore, the contemporary idea that authority of any kind might be held as property tended to weaken the concept that kingship was a dignity and not an heredity. Loyseau, through a series of definitions and distinctions, all but represented the prerogative as the personal property of the ruler. As his initial approach to the problem, he defined legal right (seigneury) as authority held as property (*puissance en proprieté*).[39] Both elements were required in true kingship: a royal officer might hold and exercise authority (*puissance*), but it was the ruler's pro-prietary right in the prerogative which distinguished him from his agents and made him a true sovereign.[40] Thus the king was an officer in the sense that he might exercise public authority, but he was also a sovereign (seigneur) in that he held entire proprietary right to the crown.[41] In order to give

---

[38] "Les Rois de France ne sont heritiers ni paternelle, mais legale et statutaire: de sorte que les Rois de France sont simplement successeurs à la couronne, par vertu de la loy et coustume generale de France. . . . le Roy ne vient pas à la succession du Royaume par droict hereditaire: mais par vertu de la loy fonda-mentale du royaume de France, inviolablement gardee depuis l'establissement de la Monarchie Françoise. . . ." Pierre de L'Hommeau, *Les Maximes ge-neralles du droict françois* (Rouen, 1614), pp. 26–27. Although this work was published under Louis XIII, it was written during the reign of Henry IV, as is proved by a reference to that ruler on page 12.

[39] *Seigneuries*, ch. I, no. 25.   [40] *Offices*, Liv. II, ch. II, *passim*.

[41] ". . . le Roy est parfaitement Officier, ayant le parfait exercice de toute puissance publique: et est aussi parfaitement Seigneur, ayant en perfection la proprieté de toute puissance publique." *Offices*, Liv. II, ch. II, no. 21.

this conception an historical sense, Loyseau added that the earliest, elected rulers were no more than princes or officers, merely exercising the authority conferred upon them by the people who retained title to the same.[42] But in time, the kings appropriated to themselves the right to public authority largely through usurpation, a procedure quite capable of creating rightful title in such matters, thereby becoming true sovereigns.[43] It is manifest that Loyseau believed the ruler's proprietary right in his prerogative to form a major requisite of kingship.[44] However, the strong tradition of fundamental law forced Loyseau to qualify his position and to admit that in the final analysis the crown was essentially an office or dignity, rather than a property. Even in those realms where hereditary succession is established, he said, fundamental law confers the crown upon the succeeding rulers who thus receive the same, not in virtue of hereditary, proprietary right, but according to the law of the realm.[45] As corollaries, he repeated

---

[42] "Bien est vray que du commencement ils n'estoient que simples Princes, c'est à dire simples Officiers, n'ayans que l'exercice, et non-pas la proprieté de la souueraineté: ains le peuple, qui les elisoit et preposoit sur soy, demeuroit en sa liberté naturelle tout entiere, sans se submettre ny rendre subiect au Prince, par droicte de seigneurie. . . ." *Offices*, Liv. II, ch. II, no. 26.

[43] "Mais comme la mutation de l'Office en seigneurie est facile, . . . l'Office souuerain est aisé à conuertir en seigneurie souueraine, ny ayant aucun qui l'en empesche. Aussi il y a long temps que tous les Rois de la terre, qui par concession volontaire des peuples, qui par vsurpation antique (laquelle fait loy en matiere de souuerainetez, qui n'en peuuent receuoir d'ailleurs) ont prescrit la proprieté de la puissance souueraine, et l'ont iointe auec l'exercice d'icelle." *Offices*, Liv. II, ch. II, nos. 27, 28. Cf. *Seigneuries*, ch. II, nos. 20-24. Also, see below, n. 67.

[44] In support of the doctrine "the king never dies," Loyseau did not hesitate to utilize the maxim of private legal inheritance, *le mort saisit le vif. Offices*, Liv. I, ch. X, no. 58.

[45] "Et toute-fois ce qu'en plusieurs Monarchies on a admis cette succession, n'a pas esté pour les rendre purement hereditaires et patrimoniales, comme les fiefs, ni en effait pour le profit et aduentage des Monarques: ains seulement, pour le repos du peuple. . . . Ce qui ne s'est peu faire autrement, qu'en destinant, par vne loy Royale et fondamentale, les plus proches de la lignee Royale, à regner successiuement, comme appellez par la loy de l'Estat, laquelle induit vne maniere de substitution graduelle en la famille des Princes du sang. . . . Et ainsi en vsons-nous en France, où il est vray de dire que la corone n'est pas purement hereditaire, ni par testament, ni mesme ab intestat, ains est deferée par la loy du Royaume au premier Prince du sang *iure sanguinis, et citra ius et nomen haeredis.* . . ." *Offices*, Liv. II, ch. II, nos. 32-34.

the orthodox statements that the ruler might not will the realm, divide it, resign, or alienate a portion of the prerogative without the consent of the Estates General or the Parlement. He concluded that monarchies thus partook more of the nature of offices than of seigneuries.[46] Not yet were the jurists willing to attribute to the ruler an unqualified proprietary right to the crown, thereby abandoning the time-honored conception that kingship was a dignity and not an heredity.

Thus it appears that in this department of legal thought, the jurists of the early seventeenth century made little advance beyond the position of their more absolutistic predecessors. Writers of both groups recognized the divine choice of the royal person, thus lessening the parallel significance of fundamental law and reducing the latter essentially to a mere rule of succession. But they refused to abandon the significance of fundamental law altogether by representing the prince as that divinely appointed individual who acceded to the crown according to his private, personal title to the same. Kingship remained a dignity beyond the proprietary right of its immediate holder. Yet if the jurists refused to take the final step toward an absolutism recognizing no distinction between the king and the crown, their works reveal those intellectual currents which were to direct their successors to such a conclusion. The proprietary nature of all true authority, public or private, was a fundamental basis of Loyseau's system, and if he excepted the royal prerogative, the latter nevertheless represented the exception rather than the rule. Furthermore, contemporary ideas placing superabundant emphasis upon the personal divine right of the ruler and his quasi-divinity depicted him as a God-given sovereign, complete in every sense, thereby all but identifying the king and the crown [47] and

---

[46] "Bref de toutes ces raisons il appert, que les monarchies sont plus Offices, que Seigneuries." *Offices*, Liv. II, ch. II, no. 42.

[47] Certain statements of Barclay illustrate the tendency in this direction. Although his principal emphasis was upon the divine authorization of kingship, he asserted that the person of the king was divine and that obligations and obedience were due to the king as an individual rather than to him merely as

eliminating a primary tenet of legal kingship. Fundamental law remained, but it was gradually being replaced by other considerations as the primary factor determining the theory of rulership. If the jurists writing under Henry IV did not extend the doctrines of royal absolutism to their furthest limits, their successors had but to develop the concepts which had previously been set forward.

Although Loyseau refused to define the crown as the private possession of the sovereign, he nevertheless took long strides toward a concept of much greater import in the theory of absolutism: the identity of the king and the state. The idea that the monarch represented and embodied the entire realm was distinctly a seventeenth-century development, entirely lacking to the earlier period examined by this study.[48] True, Bodin and Le Roy had reiterated the Aristotelian idea that the place and character of the supreme authority determined the form and nature of the state, and that in that sense the sovereign was the state.[49] But such did not imply that the monarch summed up in himself and symbolized the entire nation. Loyseau provided the groundwork for this remarkable conclusion, as always, through a complex network of legal distinctions. As subdivisions of legal authority, he listed seigneury *in abstracto* and *in concreto*. The former was property, or authority as such which was held through proprietary right, while the latter signified the land in which that right

---

holder of the prerogative. William Barclay, *De regno et regali potestate adversus Buchananum, Brutum, Boucherium, et reliquos monarchomachos, libri sex* (Paris, 1600), p. 166. Barclay carried his ideas to the lengths of asserting that no ruler with a legitimate title could be a tyrant. For citations on the latter question, see below, n. 79.

[48] This question was very rarely considered by sixteenth-century writers because it was quite foreign to their mode of thought. Their reaction to the proposition, at its infrequent appearances, is illustrated by the following passage from Matharel's answer to Hotman: "Itaque non est cur tantopere Hotomanus miretur illam maiorum nostrorum sapientiam, quam tanquam in speculo contemplandam censet, quos ait, maximam posuisse differentiam, inter Regnum et Regem. Quis enim nescit aliud Regem, aliud Regnum, aliud Pastorem, aliud oues, aliud tutorem, aliud pupillum? Quis vnquam talia in dubium vocauit?" Matharel, *op. cit.*, p. 106.

[49] See above, pp. 227–228.

was held.[50] Seigneury *in concreto*, however, was more than a mere circumscription; it was a fictitious entity formed by the union of public and private seigneury, that is, the justice owned by the overlord and the fief over which he wielded the same. The fief was the matter which was animated by justice, the form, and the two together formed a true seigneury from which no component part could be subtracted without destroying the whole.[51] By applying this reasoning to the state, Loyseau represented the realm as a body politic constituted by the union of public authority (sovereignty) and that territory in which such authority was wielded (*une terre seigneuriale*). Sovereignty, being the animating essence of the state, was quite inseparable from the same; if it were subtracted from the state, the latter would surely disintegrate. Thus, he concluded, sovereignty was the form which gave being to the state, while sovereignty *in concreto* (combining rulership and territory) was synonymous with the state itself.[52] In this fashion, Loyseau was brought to make that celebrated statement which has often been interpreted to mean that the state and governmental authority were synonymous.[53] However, it is evident from the outline of his argument that he

[50] "De sorte que maintenant le mot de *Seigneurie* a deux significations, l'vne de signifier *in abstracto* tout droit de proprieté, ou puissance proprietaire qu'on a en quelque chose, qu'à l'occasion d'icelle on peut dire sienne: L'autre de signifier *in concreto*, vne terre Seigneuriale." *Seigneuries*, ch. I, no. 23.

[51] *Seigneuries*, ch. IV, nos. 17, 29, 31.

[52] "Ceste souueraineté est la propre seigneurie de l'Estat. Car combien que toute seigneurie publique deust demeurer à l'Estat, ce neantmoins les seigneurs particuliers ont vsurpé la suzeraineté: mais la souueraineté est dutout inseparable de l'Estat, duquel si elle estoit ostee, ce ne seroit plus vn Estat, et celuy qui l'auroit, auroit l'Estat entant et pourtant qu'il auroit la seigneurie souueraine, comme quand le Roy François quitta la souueraineté de Flandres, la Flandre fut par consequent distraicte et ostee de l'Estat de France, et deuint vn Estat à part. Car en fin la souueraineté est la forme, qui donne l'estre à l'Estat, mesme l'Estat et la Souueraineté prise *in concreto*, sont synonimes, et l'Estat est ainsi appellé, pource que la Souueraineté est le comble et periode de puissance, ou il faut que l'Estat s'arreste et establisse." *Seigneuries*, ch. II, nos. 4–6.

[53] E.g., Georg Jellinek, *Allgemeine Staatslehre* (Berlin, 1900), pp. 419, 444. Jellinek not only misunderstood Loyseau's meaning but represented this statement as embodying Loyseau's major political conception, thus giving it an emphasis and significance quite lacking to Loyseau. Also André Lemaire, although much less insistent that Jellinek, seems to ascribe undue significance to this state-

never intended to set forth a theory of state sovereignty or even to identify the king and the realm. Although his statements opened the path toward such a conclusion, he did not take the final steps of identifying the king with the crown and the latter with sovereignty *in concreto*. The royal prerogative he defined specifically as a body of public authority adhering to the state [54] and contrasting with private legal right in essence, effect, and place in the social structure.[55] Sovereignty *in concreto* was for him the union of private and public authorities into a mystical whole, either a *seigneurie subalterne* composed of fief and justice, or the realm constituted by the fusion of royal authority and social structure. Thus, his statement that sovereignty taken *in concreto* was synonymous with the state appears as little more than an ingenious reinterpretation of that fundamental and well-established concept which represented the state as a union of public and private spheres of legal right. Loyseau's writings may have given impetus to political concepts which ultimately brought about the identification of the king and the realm, but it was reserved to others to develop to the full that most important basis of absolutism.

It is evident from the above that the more abstract and mystical bases of seventeenth-century absolutism — the identification of the king with the crown and the realm — remained short of full development in the works of those jurists who wrote during the reign of Henry IV. Although they were distinctly feeling their way toward both conclusions, it was not until the full blossoming of seventeenth-century monarchy that writers advanced political systems representing the ruler as the sum and substance of national existence. It was rather in the legal aspects of the rising political doctrine that the jurists before 1610 set forth the chief essentials of abso-

---

ment of Loyseau, although he is quite correct concerning its ultimate implications. *Op. cit.*, pp. 152–153, 285.

[54] *Seigneuries*, ch. II, nos. 7–9. See below, n. 64.

[55] *Seigneuries*, ch. I, nos. 26–85. See below, n. 65.

lutism. Again Loyseau evinced reluctance to abandon the
fundamental principles of the older constitutionalism, but
either because of compulsion or conviction, the superficies of
his thought closely paralleled that of the unqualified royalists.
Together, these writers set forth the major legal elements of
seventeenth-century absolutism.

Throughout the entire period examined by this study, the
jurists conceived of the royal authority as a body of power,
absolute within its sphere but suffering legal limitations whenever the sovereign went beyond the constituted bounds of his
prerogative. The specific activities of the ruler fell into two
distinct categories: acts of authority or *government* proper,
and *jurisdiction* involving administrative and judicial competence over the rights of the subjects. The first comprehended
those matters over which the ruler held absolute authority
(war and peace, appointment of magistrates, coinage, etc.)
and suffered only external limits of law, while the second,
being concerned with rights normally beyond the control of
the prerogative, appeared as little more than definitions of
those rights according to law and consequently embodied inherent legal limitations. This fundamental conception had
been set forth in its essentials by Seyssel at the opening of the
century: while representing the prerogative as a body of
absolute authority, he circumscribed it with limitations of *la
police* (the great body of customary, private rights and the
laws at their basis) and *la justice*, that is, judicial declaration
of those limits inherent in the royal authority of jurisdiction.
But as the century progressed, that delicate balance of public
and private rights suffered a series of reinterpretations, each
involving additional expansion of the legitimate royal discretion, that is, the encroachment of government upon that
sphere formerly reserved to jurisdiction. One very important
step in that process occurred when Bodin broke from the older
idea of kingship as a series of legally defined marks of sovereignty, and substituted his conception of public authority as
a body of natural power summed up in the right to make law.

And subsequent writers took a further step in that direction when they amalgamated Bodin's theory of sovereignty with the divine right of kings. The all-important result of these developments in political thinking appeared in the subordination of popular legal rights to the royal discretion, and it was that portion of seventeenth-century absolutism which received full development at the hands of the jurists here under discussion.

According to the older political conceptions, the law of the constitution provided the most significant limitation upon the king's discretion, and it was precisely that body of law — with the exception of the fundamental laws pertaining specifically to the prerogative — which these jurists subjected to the monarch. The generally accepted doctrine of legislative sovereignty seemed to predicate the ruler's supremacy over established law, and thus it became habitual for the jurists to classify all laws as divine, natural, or positive and to place the prince under the first two categories but over the third.[56] The result was that legal writers not only subjected all customary law to the prince but refused to recognize it as law unless it had his tacit or expressed approval. In pure monarchies, wrote Loyseau, it is the prince alone who has authority to make laws. Although he may permit the people to choose certain customs according to which they wish to live, it is necessary that those customs not only be codified under royal order before his commissioners but also that they be approved and verified by him in his Parlement like his other laws.[57]

---

[56] Loyseau, *Seigneuries*, ch. II, no. 9; ch. III, no. 11. Barclay, *op. cit.*, Bk. III, chs. XIV, XV. L'Hommeau, *Maximes*, p. 5, and the same author's *Deux Livres de la iurisprudence françoise* (Saumur, 1605), p. 10.

[57] "Mais aux pures Monarchies, où les Princes maintiennent mieux leur souueraineté . . . il n'y a que le Roy seul, qui puisse faire des loys. Et combien que sa bonté permette au peuple des Prouinces coustumieres de choisir certaines Coustumes, selon lesquelles il desire viure, si est-ce qu'il faut tousiours que ces Coustumes soient, non seulement arrestées par le mandement du Roy, et pardeuant les Commissaires par luy ordonnez; mais encor qu'elles soient approuuées et verifiées par luy en son Parlement, ainsi que ses autres loix." *Seigneuries*, ch. III, no. 11.

And L'Hommeau stated explicitly that it was not the presence and consent of the three estates of the province which gave force to custom, but the king acting through his commissioners.[58] It is manifest that these jurists not only accepted completely the monarch's dominion over custom but assimilated it with the ordinances and all other types of law emanating from the sovereign. Instead of representing custom as the work of the people and reflecting their authority to establish the legal guarantee of their inviolable rights, this category of law was classed simply as the work of the prince. His authority over such law, instead of being limited to judicial declaration, now included the power to make and break, since custom was classified merely as an additional matter over which he held unlimited discretion. This far-reaching development represents one of the most important among the many encroachments of government upon that sphere of legal right formerly reserved to jurisdiction.

Parallel with the subjection of constitutional law to the monarch, there occurred a sharp diminution of the check of *la justice*. Largely because of established judicial practice, writers continued to recognize the validity of cases tendered against the ruler,[59] but they eliminated enregistering and remonstrance as an effective limitation upon the monarch's authority to make new laws. The predominant attitude toward that procedure seems to have been that the king should obtain the Parlement's approval of his laws in order to observe the established forms and to appear heedful of counsel, but that the court's approbation added nothing to the binding character of the enactments and might well be waived. Barclay represented the enregistering of royal edicts as for no more significant purpose than the recording of them for future reference, and he insisted that the king alone might establish them

---

[58] "Ce n'est pas la presence et consentement des trois estats du pais qui donne force à la coustume, mais le Roy, par les commissaires qu'il depute à cest effect." *Deux Livres*, p. 8.

[59] See above, ch. III, pt. B, n. 36.

in force without the approval of the magistrates.[60] In similar vein, L'Hommeau wrote that judicial verification of royal acts lent them no additional force, that they were binding without the court's endorsement, and that the Parlement should not deliberate concerning royal edicts and ordinances pertaining to affairs of state and should act merely as a court for the administration of justice between subjects.[61] Such statements foreshadowed the policy of Louis XIV who reduced enregistering to an empty formality and dispensed with remonstrances altogether.[62]

As a logical concomitant of the monarch's dominion over customary law, the jurists subjected to him that vast array of private rights whose inviolability had previously been guaranteed by such law. This extension of the royal authority to a position of dominance over the great body of popular rights was of momentous importance in the rise of absolutism and represented perhaps the most significant encroachment of government upon that portion of the constitution formerly

[60] "Regum igitur Franciae edicta, leges, et constitutiones in senatu illo Parisiensi amplissimo nobilissimoque recitari, expendi, et promulgari solent: non quod hoc ordine praetermisso populum non teneant, sed vt regestis et actis publicis mandatae constitutiones singulis facilius innotescant, et ad posteritatis memoriam reseruentur. . . ." *Op. cit.*, pp. 292–293. "Curiam siue Parlementum sine Rege nihil: Regem vero sine Parlemento, quaecunque e Repub. esse viderit, edictis, decretis, legibus, sancire posse: ita vt Curiae perpetuo necessaria sit Regis autoritas, Regi vero Curiae consensus nunquam." *Ibid.*, p. 285. Cf. p. 203.

[61] "Quant à la verification des Edicts du Roy, qui se fait aux Cours souueraines, elle n'authorise et ne donne aucune force aux Edicts du Roy, qui ne laissent de sortir effect, sans la verification des Parlemens: laquelle *non tam necessitatis est, quam humanitatis*, et ne faut pas que les Cours souuerains mettent en deliberation les ordonnances et Edits du Roy, mesmes quand elles concernent les affaires d'Estat. . . ." *Maximes*, p. 23. L'Hommeau repeated the statement made by Charles IX in 1563 that the Parlement should confine itself to judicial matters.

[62] During the reign of Henry IV, there appeared in addition several lesser works which recounted in detail the entire administrative system, including judicial verification of royal enactments. But this was invariably combined with highly absolutistic conceptions, causing such reiteration of the older forms to appear as little more than an empty shell of the earlier constitutionalism. E.g., André Duchene, *Les Antiquitez et recherches de la grandeur et majesté des roys de France* (Paris, 1609), and Jerome Bignon, *De l'excellence des roys, et du royaume de France* (Paris, 1610).

subject only to jurisdiction. It is important to note the specific treatment accorded this question by the jurists of the early seventeenth century, since their approach was followed by the majority of subsequent legal writers during the period of absolutism. The men of the law did not deny the existence of private legal rights by attributing all property solely to the king. On the contrary, they recognized that the people continued to hold such rights, but they placed that entire portion of the state structure under the discretionary power of the prince. The subjects retained a precarious tenure of their traditional properties, but the inviolability of the same was eliminated. It has been noted above that the great majority of sixteenth-century jurists refused to accept this distortion of the traditional constitutionalism. Although many had recognized the ruler's supremacy over customary law, they had insisted that such did not establish his dominion over popular rights. Bodin had solved this dilemma by placing the immunities of the subjects upon a basis of natural law, but such proved to be but a step toward their subjection to the ruler. The persistence of political conceptions analogous to those of Bodin is illustrated by the fact that both L'Hommeau and Loyseau reiterated the Angevin's conceptions of royal and seigneurial monarchy, indicating that the former type of government preserved inviolate the persons and properties of the subjects.[63] Yet neither writer would uphold the crucial test of that doctrine: popular consent to taxation.

It was in regard to this general question that Loyseau showed greatest hesitation to break from the older conceptions, yet the outline of his argument embodied interpretations which were to prove invaluable to the extreme absolutists. His fundamental approach to the question of legal right was in his conception of public and private seigneury. Public seigneury, or sovereignty, he defined as supreme authority over persons or things, while private legal right consisted in

---

[63] Loyseau, *Seigneuries*, ch. II, nos. 52–58; L'Hommeau, *Maximes*, pp. 8–9.

immediate tenure of those things which constituted the properties of the subjects.[64] Significant differences characterized these two types of legal authority: the owner of private possessions might use them as he would, since he held them absolutely and was not bound to respect another man's rights. But the purpose of sovereignty was the protection of free persons and their properties, and thus the ruler could not exercise unlimited authority over the same without usurping private possessions and reducing his subjects to slaves.[65] It is evident that Loyseau followed his predecessors in dividing property rights into two independent and mutually exclusive categories. However, he was forced to admit that established legal practice was far from resembling his ideal. The strict separation of public and private rights was partially obscured because certain public authorities were held by the feudal lords, and, conversely, the king had taken a number of private rights. In accounting for this variation, Loyseau set forth an interpretation with extremely absolutistic potentialities. The ownership of certain jurisdictions, which were public authorities and should be held only by the prince, had been usurped

---

[64] "Quant à sa diuision, la Seigneurie a deux especes, à sçauoir la Seigneurie publique et la priuée. La publique consiste en la superiorité et auctorité qu'on a sur les personnes, ou sur les choses. . . . Quant à la Seigneurie priuée, c'est la vraye proprieté et iouyssance actuelle de quelque chose, et est appellée priuée, pource qu'elle concerne le droict que chacun particulier a en sa chose." *Seigneuries*, ch. I, nos. 26–28.

[65] "Et faut remarquer hardiment, qu'il y a vne difference fort importante en l'vsage de ces deux Seigneuries, à sçauoir qu'on peut vser de la seigneurie priuée à discretion et libre volonté, *quilibet enim est liber moderator et arbiter rei suae*, dit la loy, pource que consistant en ce qui est nostre, il n'eschet gueres, que facions tort à autruy, en quelque façon que nous en vsions: mais pour ce que la seigneurie publique concerne les choses qui sont à autruy, ou les personnes qui sont libres, il en faut vser auec raison et iustice. Et celuy qui en vse à discretion, empiete et vsurpe la seigneurie particuliere qui ne luy appartient pas: si c'est sur les personnes, c'est les tenir pour esclaues: si c'est sur les biens, c'est vsurper les biens d'autruy. . . . Bref ces deux especes de Seigneurie sont entierement differentes quant à l'effect. Car comme la Seigneurie priuée n'induit point de puissance publique, aussi la Seigneurie publique, qui consiste en la Iustice, n'attribue aucune Seigneurie priuée, et ne diminue aucunement la liberté parfaicte du subject ou iusticiable, au contraire l'augmente et la conserue. . . ." *Seigneuries*, ch. I, nos. 33–34.

by feudal lords and continued to be held by them as suze-
rainties, an anomalous element in the constitution.[66] Likewise
the king, by appropriating certain prerogatives originally
lacking to public authority in the strict definition, had acquired
through prescription an increased measure of legitimate discretionary power.[67] The significant feature of these statements
was the varying legal weight which Loyseau assigned to the
encroachments of either party upon the rights of the other.
The public authorities sequestered by the barons might constitute an established portion of the constitution, but their
basis remained mere usurpation.[68] However, the prerogatives
appropriated by the king Loyseau represented as rightfully
adhering to the crown, their illegal origin having been effaced
through prescription. It may be noted that the justification
of royal encroachments upon popular rights simply on the
basis of prescription constituted a very dangerous and far-
reaching doctrine, capable of almost indefinite extension. Because it might be used to justify almost any royal activities
contrary to law, it had been avoided by the great majority of
sixteenth-century jurists;[69] and for the same reason it was a

[66] "Par ainsi outre la Seigneurie priuée concedée à ces Seigneurs tant de terres
de leur distroit, que des personnes des Gaulois, ils ont encor vsurpé vne espece
de Seigneurie publique, c'est à dire vne proprieté de la puissance publique.
Dont s'ensuit qu'en France, et en si peu qu'il y a d'autres pays, où la Iustice et
puissance publique est laissée en proprieté aux particuliers, il y a deux degrez de
Seigneurie publique, à sçauoir celle qui demeure inseparablement par deuers
l'Estat, nonobstant ceste vsurpation; que nous appellons *Souueraineté:* Et celle
qui a esté ainsi vsurpée par les particuliers, pour laquelle exprimer il nous a
fallu forger vn mot expres, et l'appeller *Suzeraineté,* mot qui est aussi estrange,
comme ceste espece de Seigneurie est absurde." *Seigneuries,* ch. I, nos. 81–82.

[67] "Or puisque l'vsurpation estant suiuie par apres d'vne longue iouissance
volontaire et paisible, qui efface son vice, donne loy aux Souuerainetez qui n'ont
aucun en ce monde, dont elles la puissent receuoir, on ne doit reuoquer en
doubte la souueraineté des Roys, qui sont en possession ancienne d'en vser."
Seigneuries, ch. II, no. 87. See above, n. 43.   [68] *Seigneuries,* ch. IV, *passim.*

[69] The only earlier jurists who made significant use of this doctrine, to our
knowledge, were Du Haillan and Blackwood. Du Haillan's emphasis seems to
have resulted from his highly pragmatic approach to political questions. See
above, ch. III, pt. A, n. 18, and pt. B, n. 121. Blackwood, on the other hand,
used prescription in order to support a fundamentally absolutistic conception
of kingship. *Op. cit.,* p. 36. On the use of this doctrine by Du Haillan and
Loyseau, see Lemaire, *op. cit.,* p. 158.

favorite device with the absolutists of the following century. The manner in which Loyseau incorporated prescription into his intellectual system seems to indicate that he found in it a convenient justification for the king's well-known violation of many constitutional immunities. But however that may be, Loyseau's statements served as valuable precedent for later writers. And he himself seems to have valued that highly autocratic regime made possible by the wide authority thus acquired by the king, if only because of the social stability which it engendered.[70]

The acid test of a given jurist's strength of conviction concerning the inviolability of private rights appeared in his statements concerning consent to taxation, and it was in regard to this question that Loyseau's doctrine of prescription proved its potentialities. In accord with his initial approach through dual spheres of legal right, Loyseau insisted that unlimited taxation was not a mark of sovereignty but a seizure of unrightful power,[71] and that the most exacting jurists required popular consent to such levies because they involved the taking of private property, contrary to the purposes of royal monarchy.[72] But after building up this case for consent to taxation, Loyseau reversed himself by stating that it was no

[70] "Et à la verité c'est bien la forme d'Estat la plus stable de toutes, et moins subject à mutation, que celle des Principautez souueraines tout à fait . . . pource que tant qu'il y a quelque manquement à la souueraineté, le Prince ne cesse de remuer, iusques à ce qu'il l'ayt enuahie de tout point. Et si les Estats du pays se trouuent bastans pour luy resister, c'est vne guerre perpetuelle. . . ." *Seigneuries*, ch. II, no. 88.

[71] "Aucuns, et non sans cause, en adioustent vn sixiesme [marque de souueraineté], à sçauoir de leuer deniers sur le peuple: mais les plus retenuz disent, que ce n'est point vn droit, ains vne entreprise et pouuoir desreglé, au moins de faire ces leuées à discretion. . . ." *Seigneuries*, ch. III, no. 7.

[72] "Finalement à l'esgard de faire des leuées de deniers sur le peuple, i'ay dit que les plus retenuz Politiques tiennent, que les Roys n'ont droit de les faire par puissance reglée, sans le consentement du peuple, non plus que prendre le bien d'autruy, pource que la puissance publique, ne s'estend, qu'au commandement et auctorité, et non pas en entreprendre la Seigneurie priuée des biens des particuliers, qui est le poinct, auquel consiste la difference de la Monarchie Seigneuriale, d'auec la pure souueraineté, d'autant que celle-là a la Seigneurie publique et priuée tout ensemble, des personnes et des biens de ses subiects: et celle-cy n'en a que la Seigneurie publique." *Seigneuries*, ch. III, no. 42.

longer necessary to secure popular approval of royal levies because the king had acquired authority over the same through prescription.[73] In this convenient fashion, Loyseau justified royal policies directly contrary to the fundamentals of his constitutional system.[74] However, the majority of his contemporaries evinced no such hesitation in ascribing to the ruler the authority to tax according to the necessities of government. Like the immediate followers of Bodin considered above, the jurists of the early seventeenth century incorporated the right to tax into the crown and made it simply another mark of sovereignty. Such was the emphasis of Barclay, as far as he considered the question,[75] while Loisel asserted as a general maxim of French law: *"au Roy seul appartient de prendre tribut sur les personnes."* [76] The statements of L'Hommeau were particularly revealing in regard to the exact legal connotation which the jurists lent this matter. The right to levy taxes he regarded simply as a manifestation of the royal authority to make law.[77] Thus the entire body of popular proprietary rights was brought under the discretionary power of the prince to dispose of through acts of government. Instead of viewing the social organism as composed of two independent and mutually exclusive spheres of legal right, the jurists sub-

[73] "Mais je croy qu'à present le contraire s'obserue par tout ailleurs: et qu'il n'y a quasi plus d'autres Princes Souuerains, meme de Princes sujets, qui n'ayent prescrit droit de leuer deniers sur le peuple. De sorte qu'à mon avis il ne faut plus douter qu'en France (qui est possible aujourd'huy la plus pure et la plus parfaite Monarchie du monde) nostre Roy n'ayant d'ailleurs presque plus autres fonds de finance, ne puisse faire des leuées de deniers sans le consentement des Estats. . . ." *Seigneuries*, ch. III, no. 46.

[74] It is noteworthy that this was the only mark of sovereignty which Loyseau attributed to the king on the basis of prescription.

[75] *Op. cit.*, pp. 166, 196.

[76] *Institutes*, p. 19. Loisel's immediate intention in framing this statement may have been to deny to the nobles any authority to collect taxes, but it is to be noted that he denied the necessity of popular consent to the tailles. *Ibid.*, Liv. VI, Tit. VI. He apparently attributed taxation to the ruler as a regalian right.

[77] "Celuy qui a puissance de donner la Loy, a aussi puissance de mettre et leuer tailles et imposts sur ses subiets: il n'y a que le Roy, qui puisse donner loy: et consequemment il n'appartient qu'au Roy, à mettre tailles sur ses subiets." *Maximes*, p. 50.

ordinated private legal authority to the public, both in terms
of specific immunities and the laws at their root. The basis
of the interpretation was well summed up by Barclay in his
statement that the king was superior to the entire *populus
universus*.[78] The approach did not deny the existence of
popular legal rights, but it gave rise to a distinctly new definition of the same, because of the elimination of their inviolability. With the subordination of customary law and rights to
the sovereign, the major significance of Seyssel's check of *la
police* may be regarded as eliminated from French political
thought.

Coincident with theories of divine-right sovereignty and the
ruler's supremacy over the rights of his subjects, there appeared the inevitable tendency to regard the will of the king
as law in all civil matters. Not only was the monarch superior
to positive law, the most specific limitation upon acts of government, but his legislative activity suffered no effective
judicial check by the Parlement. And when such ideas were
combined with the prevailing emphasis upon the quasi-divinity
of the ruler and his constant guidance by God, theorists could
but represent his government as *ipso facto* just, in terms of
all criteria determined by constitutional law. The lengths to
which the jurists might extend such ideas is well illustrated
by Barclay's statement that only a usurper might be a tyrant;
the tyranny of a legitimate ruler was a logical impossibility.[79]
It is quite evident that in Barclay's eyes the king could do
no wrong, not because his acts coincided with established law
but because he was above any criteria according to which they
might be evaluated. Bodin's conception of legislative sovereignty had been developed to the point where theorists were
content to regard the mere will of the king as sufficient basis
for law. Such was the meaning widely ascribed to the first
maxim of Loisel's *Institutes: "Qui veut le Roy, si veut la
loy."* [80] In commenting upon this proposition, L'Hommeau

---

[78] *Op. cit.*, p. 172.   [79] *Op. cit.*, pp. 267–268, 483, 494, 496, etc.
[80] *Institutes*, p. 19. The following passage from one of Loisel's earlier works

explained that since the ruler alone might make new laws, what pleased the prince had the force of law; and it is clear that he intended this to mean that the established laws rested solely upon the royal will.[81] Such was made manifest, he said, by the dictum *car tel est nostre plaisir* which was appended to all edicts.[82] Thus the theorists arrived at the conclusion that in all civil matters the pleasure of the king was synonymous with law and *ipso facto* just. The doctrine was of fundamental importance to seventeenth-century absolutism.

Although the jurists regarded the will of the prince as law in all matters pertaining to government, they nevertheless refused to part with the fundamental conception that there existed a final justice over and above all men, including the prince, and that he was bound by such principles. Such a doctrine may have had small influence upon constitutional procedure, but it vitally affected the tenor of political thought throughout the period of absolutism. Specifically, it precluded the substitution of a doctrine of might for that of right. As long as writers adhered to a concept of universals binding all men alike and establishing the criteria of final justice, they could not accept a theory of state which justified all acts of the sovereign simply on the basis of force. This was the vital influence of the jurists' continued adherence to the conceptions of natural and divine law. In consequence, throughout

---

is a valuable commentary upon his maxim: "Tout homme qu'il a pleu à Dieu faire naistre en un estat de Royauté, est tenu d'obeyr à la volonté de son Roy, laquelle il doit tenir pour loy, sans qu'il luy soit loisible d'en demander ny rechercher les raisons; mesmement quand elle luy est declaree par ses Edicts publiez et verifiez és Cours souveraines du Royaume. . . ." *La Guyenne*, p. 71.

[81] "En France il apartient au Roy seul à faire loix, edicts, et ordonnances, *et quod principi placuit legis habet vigorem:* et quand le Roy de France fait des edits il peut dire, *sic volo, sic iubeo, sit pro ratione voluntas:* car la Loy ne depend que du seul Prince souuerain." *Maximes*, pp. 19–20. This passage and that in the following footnote occur in L'Hommeau's book under the heading: "La volonté du Roy, vaut Loy."

[82] ". . . les Rois de France comme souuerains, tiennent leurs authorité et puissance de Dieu seul: et partant peuuent faire loix et ordonnances de leur propre mouuement et franche volonté, ce qui est demonstré par ces mots estans à la fin des Edicts, CAR TEL EST NOSTRE PLAISIR. De maniere que le seul plaisir et volonté du Roy, fait la loy." *Maximes*, p. 21.

the period of absolutism they maintained the moral purpose of monarchy in terms of the aims and ends of human existence. In matters of practical policy, the immediate significance of such conceptions was often neutralized by ideas of *raison d'état*, but contemporary writers rarely sought to justify the same. In the main currents of French political thought, Hobbism was not a significant factor throughout the entire *ancien régime*.

However, that abstract conception of ultimate justice could not fill the place of the older constitutionalism in limiting the king's freedom of action in relation to his subjects. With the establishment of royal dominion over customary law and popular rights, and the elimination of the Estates General and the Parlement of Paris as serious institutional checks upon royal policy, the ruler was essentially released from those limitations imposed upon him by the established constitution. Short of violating the general principles of universal justice, he was free to deal with the populace as he would. In consequence, the older, mutual obligations of king and people underwent a distinct transformation, emerging as little more than duties on the part of the people and prerogative rights on the part of the prince. The two categories of persons in the realm were henceforth simply those of ruler and ruled, with the monarch standing forth as that divinely appointed sovereign who exercised an absolute authority over all other men. The metamorphosis of the realm from feudal community to national state was complete. France had entered upon a new period of her national existence, to be characterized by brilliant achievements in many fields but lacking those stabilizing qualities inherent in the older constitutionalism.

BIBLIOGRAPHY

BIBLIOGRAPHY

I. PRIMARY SOURCES

A. TREATISES AND PAMPHLETS

Anon., *De la puissance des roys, et droict de succession aux royaumes, contre l'vsurpation du tiltre qualité de roy de France, faicte par le roy de Navarre*. Paris, 1590.

—— *Dialogue d'entre le maheustre et le manant*. In *Satyre menippée*. Ratisbon, 1726. III.

—— *La Loy salicque, premiere loy des françois*. Printed with Claude de Seyssel, *La Grande Monarchie de France*. Paris, 1558.

—— *Remonstrance d'vn bon catholique françois, aux trois estats de France, qui s'assembleront à Blois*. 1576. Without place of publication.

—— *Remonstrance aus Parlemens de France, touchant l'obseruation de la paix*. 1581. Without place of publication.

—— *Replique faicte à la responce, que ceux de la ligue ont publiee, contre l'examen qui avoit esté dressé sur leur precedent discours, touchant la loy salique de France*. 1587. Without place of publication.

—— *Responce à vn liure de Belloy plein de faulsetez et de calomnies*. Paris, 1588.

—— *Sommaire Responce à l'examen d'vn heretique, sur vn discours de la loy salique, faussement pretendu contre la maison de France, et la branche de Bourbon*. 1587. Without place of publication.

—— *Traicté de la succession à la couronne de France*. 1588. Without place of publication.

Albon, Claude d', *De la maiesté royalle*. Lyon, 1575.

Angleberme, Jean d' [Pyrrhus], *De lege salica et regni successione*. In *Opuscula*, printed with his *Consuetudines Aurelianenses*. Paris, 1543.

Argentré, Bertrand d', *Commentarii in patrias Britonum leges, seu consuetudines generales antiquissimi ducatus Britanniae*. Paris, 1621.

Aubert, Guillaume, *Mémorial juridique et historique*. Extract from the *Mémoires de la société de l'histoire de Paris et de l'Ile de France*. Paris, 1909. XXXVI.

Ayrault, Pierre, *Opuscules et divers traitez*. Paris, 1598.

Bacquet, Jean, *Les Œuvres*. Geneva, 1625.

Barclay, William, *De regno et regali potestate adversus Buchananum, Brutum, Boucherium, et reliquos monarchomachos, libri sex*. Paris, 1600.

Belleforest, François de, *Les Chroniques et annales de France des Phara-mond, jusqu'au roy Charles neuvieme.* Paris, 1573.

Belloy, Pierre de, *De l'autorité du roy et crimes de leze majesté, qui se commettent par ligues.* 1587. Without place of publication.

—— *Apologie catholique.* 1585. Without place of publication.

—— *Examen du discours publié contre la maison royalle de France, et particulièrement contre la branche de Bourbon.* 1587. Without place of publication.

—— *Moyens d'abus, entreprises et nullitez du rescrit et bulle du pape Sixte V.* 1586. Without place of publication.

[Beza, Théodore de], *Du droit des magistrats sur leurs sujets.* In [Gou-lart], *Mémoires de l'estat de France sous Charles IX.* Meidelbourg, 1578. II.

Bignon, Jerome, *De l'excellence des roys, et du royaume de France.* Paris, 1610.

Blackwood, Adam, *Adversus Georgii Buchanani dialogum, de iure regni apud Scotos, pro regibus apologia.* In *Opera.* Paris, 1644.

Bodin, Jean, *Les Six Livres de la république.* Paris, 1576.

—— *De republica libri sex.* Frankfort, 1622.

—— *Methodus ad facilem historiarum cognitionem.* Paris, 1572.

—— *Relation journalière de tout ce qui s'est negotié en l'assemblée générale des états.* In Mayer, *Des états généraux et autres assemblées nationales.* Paris, 1788. III.

Bourg, Etienne de, *Solium regis christianissimi Franciae in suprema curia parlamenti Parisiensis, tribunal iudicum et cathedra doctorum.* Lyon, 1550.

Breche, Jean, *Manuel royal.* Tours, 1541.

Budé, Guillaume, *Annotationes in quatuor et viginti pandectarum libros.* Basel, 1557.

—— *Forensia.* Printed with the *Annotationes.*

—— *De asse et partibus eius, libri V.* Lyon, 1550.

—— "De l'institution du prince." *Bibliothèque de l'arsenal,* Paris, MS. 5103. Dated 1519.

Bugnyon, Philibert, *Legum abrogatarum et inusitarum in omnibus curiis, terris, jurisdictionibus et dominiis regni Franciae tractatus.* Brussels, 1666.

—— *Commentaire sur les ordonnances faictes par le roy Charles neu-fiesme en la ville de Moulins au mois de feurier, l'an mil cinq cens soixante six.* Lyon, 1567.

—— *Commentaires sur les ordonnances de Blois establies aux estats generaux conuoquez en la ville de Blois, MDLXXIX.* Lyon, 1584.

Charondas Le Caron, Louis, *Pandectes ou digestes du droict françois*. Paris, 1637.

—— *La Claire, ou de la prudence de droit*. Paris, 1554.

—— *Les Dialogues*. Paris, 1556.

—— *Discours philosophiques*. Paris, 1583.

—— *Questions diverses et discours*. Paris, 1579.

—— *Panegyrique ou oraison de louange, au roy Charles VIIII. nostre souuerain seigneur*. Paris, 1566.

—— *Panegyrique II, ou oraison de l'amour du prince et obeissance du peuple envers luy. Au roy Charles VIIII. nostre souuerain seigneur*. Paris, 1567.

—— *Panegyrique III. Du deuoir des magistrats*. Paris, 1567.

—— *Resolutions de plusieurs notables, celebres et illustres questions de droict*. Lyon, 1625.

—— *Responces du droict françois*. Lyon, 1602.

—— *Commentaire sur l'édict des secondes nopces*. Lyon, 1573.

—— *Le Grand Coustumier de France*. Paris, 1598.

Charron, Pierre, *De la sagesse*. Paris, 1604.

Chasseneuz, Barthélemi de, *Catalogus gloriae mundi*. Lyon, 1546.

—— *Consuetudines ducatus Burgundiae*. Paris, 1547.

—— *Consilia*. Lyon, 1588.

Choppin, René, *Œuvres*. 5 vols. Paris, 1643.

Clary, François de, *Philippiques contre les bulles, et autres pratiques de la faction d'Espagne*. Tours, 1592.

Combes, Jean, *Traicté des tailles, et aultres charges, et subsides, tant ordinaires que extraordinaires, qui se leuent en France*. Paris, 1576.

Constant, Pierre, *De l'excellence et dignité des rois*. Paris, 1598.

Coquille, Guy, *Œuvres*. 2 vols. Bordeaux, 1703.

—— *Poemata*. Nevers, 1590.

Dorleans, Regnault, *Les Observations de diuerses choses remarquees sur l'estat, couronne et peuple de France, tant ancien que moderne recueillies de plusieurs autheurs*. Vennes, 1597.

Du Boys, H., *De l'origine et autorité des roys*. Paris, 1604.

Duchene, André, *Les Antiquitez et recherches de la grandeur et maiesté des roys de France*. Paris, 1609.

Du Haillan, Bernard de Girard, *De l'estat et succez des affaires de France*. Paris, 1571.

—— *De l'estat et succez des affaires de France*. Paris, 1580.

—— *De l'estat et succez des affaires de France*. Paris, 1595.

—— *Histoire de France*. 2 vols. Paris, 1585.

Du Moulin, Charles, *Omnia quae extant opera*. 5 vols. Paris, 1681.

—— *Le Grand Coustumier général, contenant toutes les coustumes generalles et particulieres du royaume de France et des Gaulles.* 2 vols. Paris, 1567.

Duret, Jean, *Commentaires aux coustumes du duché de Bourbonnois.* Lyon, 1584.

—— *Harmonie et conference des magistrats romains auec les officiers françois.* Lyon, 1574.

Du Rivault, David, *Les Etats, esquels il est discouru du prince, du noble et du tiers-état, conformément à nostre temps.* Lyon, 1596.

Du Tillet, Jean, *Aduertissement à la noblesse, tant du party du roy, que des rebelles et coniurez.* Lyon, 1558.

—— *Pour la maiorité du roy tres chrestien contre les escrits des rebelles.* Paris, 1560.

—— *Pour l'entiere maiorité du roy tres chrestien.* Paris, 1560.

—— *Recueil des roys de France, leur couronne et maison.* Paris, 1607.

—— *Les Memoires et recherches contenans plusieurs choses memorables pour l'intelligence de l'estat des affaires de France.* Rouen, 1578.

Du Vair, Guillaume, *Œuvres.* 2 vols. Rouen, 1614.

Espence, Claude d', *Institution d'vn prince chrestien.* Paris, 1548.

Fauchet, Claude, *Les Œuvres.* 2 vols. Paris, 1610.

Ferrault, Jean, *Tractatus jura seu privilegia aliqua regni Franciae continens.* In Du Moulin, *Opera.* II.

Figon, Charles de, *Discours des estats et offices tant du gouuernement que de la iustice et des finances de France.* Paris, 1579.

Gousté, Claude, *Traité de la puissance et authorité des roys.* 1561. Without place of publication.

Grassaille, Charles de, *Regalium Franciae, libri duo: jura omnia et dignitates christianissimi Galliae regis continentes.* Lyon, 1538.

Gravelle, François de, *Politiques royales.* Lyon, 1596.

Grégoire, Pierre, *De republica libri sex et viginti.* Lyon, 1609.

—— *Syntagma iuris universi.* Lyon, 1587.

Grimaudet, François, *Les Œuvres.* Paris, 1670.

—— *Remonstrance aux estatz d'Anjou.* Lyon, 1561.

Guyart, Jean, *De l'origine verité et usance de la loy salique fondamentale et conseruatrice de la monarchie françoise.* Tours, 1590.

Heluis, Jean, *Le Mirouer du prince chretien.* Paris, 1566.

Hotman, Antoine, *Traicté de la loy salique.* In *Opuscules françoises des Hotmans.* Paris, 1616.

—— *Traité des droits ecclésiastiques.* In Jean Louis Brunet, *Traitez des droits et libertez de l'église gallicane.* Paris, 1731. I.

Hotman, François, *Francogallia.* Frankfort, 1586.

Hurault, Jacques, *Des offices d'estat*. Paris, 1588.

Imbert, Jean, *La Practique iudiciare*. Paris, 1604.

—— *Enchiridion*. Paris, 1603.

La Boétie, Etienne de, *Discours de la servitude volontaire*. In [Goulart], *Mémoires de l'estat de France sous Charles IX*. Meidelbourg, 1578. III.

L'Alouette, François de, *Des affaires d'état: des finances, du prince, de la noblesse*. Metz, 1597.

—— *Traité des nobles et des vertus dont ils sont formés*. Paris, 1577.

La Loupe, Vincent de, *Commentarii de magistratibus et praefecturis Francorum*. Paris, 1577.

—— *Origine des dignitez, magistratz, offices et estats du royaume de France*. Lyon, 1572.

La Madeleine, Jean de, *Discours de l'estat et office d'vn bon roy, prince ou monarque*. Paris, 1575.

La Perriere, Guillaume de, *Le Miroir politique*. Lyon, 1555.

La Planche, Regnier de, *Histoire de l'estat de France, tant de la république que de la religion, sous le règne de François II*. In Jean Alexandre Buchon (ed.), *Choix de chroniques et mémoires sur l'histoire de France*. Paris, 1836. XIII.

La Popeliniere, Lancelot Voisin, sieur de, *L'Histoire des histoires*. Paris, 1599.

—— *L'Idee de l'histoire accomplie*. Printed with the *Histoire des histoires*.

La Primaudaye, Pierre de, *Academie françoise*. Paris, 1577.

—— *Academie françoise*. Paris, 1579.

La Roche-Flavin, Bernard de, *Treze Livres des Parlemens de France*. Bordeaux, 1617.

Le Jay, François, *De la dignité des roys*. Tours, 1589.

Le Maistre, Gilles, *Les Œuvres*. Paris, 1653.

Le Rouillé, Guillaume, *Le Grant Coustumier du pays et duché de Normandie*. Paris, 1534.

Le Roy, Louis, *De l'origine, antiquité, progres, excellence et vtilité de l'art politique*. Paris, 1567.

—— *Les Politiques d'Aristote*. Paris, 1568.

—— *De l'excellence du gouvernement royal*. Paris, 1575.

—— *De la vicissitude ou variété des choses en l'univers*. Paris, 1575.

—— *Exhortation aux françois pour vivre en concorde et jouir du bien de la paix*. Paris, 1570.

—— *Les Monarchiques*. Paris, 1570.

Leschassier, Jacques, *Œuvres*. Paris, 1649.

L'Hommeau, Pierre de, *Deux Livres de la iurisprudence françoise*. Saumur, 1605.

—— *Les Maximes generalles du droict françois*. Rouen, 1614.

L'Hospital, Michel de, *Œuvres complètes*. P. J. S. Duféy, ed. 5 vols. Paris, 1824–1826.

Loisel, Antoine, *Institutes coutumières*. A. M. J. J. Dupin, ed. 2 vols. Paris, 1846.

—— *Institutes coutumières*. Michel Reulos, ed. Paris, 1935.

—— *Divers Opuscules*. Claude Joly, ed. Paris, 1652.

Loyseau, Charles, *Cinq Livres du droit des offices*. Cologne, 1613.

—— *Traité des seigneuries*. Paris, 1608.

—— *Traité des ordres et simples dignitez*. Printed with the *Offices*.

Masselin, Jean, *Journal des états généraux de France tenus à Tours en 1484 sous le règne de Charles VIII*. A. Bernier, ed. Paris, 1835.

Masuer, Jean, *Practica forensis*. Lyon, 1577.

—— *La Practique de Masuer . . . mise en françois par Antoine Fontanon*. 4th ed. Paris, 1587.

Matharel, Anton, [and Masson, Papire], *Ad Franc. Hotomani Francogalliam Antonii Matharelli, reginae matris a rebus procurandis primarii, responsio*. Paris, 1575.

Matthieu, Pierre, *Histoire des derniers troubles*. 2 vols. Lyon, 1594–1595.

—— *Histoire de France et des choses memorables aduenues aux prouinces estrangeres: durant sept annees de paix du regne de Henry IIII*. Paris, 1605.

—— *Histoire de Louys XI*. Paris, 1610.

Mellier, Guillaume, *Edict du roy Henry II sur les mariages clandestins*. Lyon, 1558.

Miraulmont, Pierre de, *De l'origine et etablissement du Parlement, et autres jurisdictions royalles*. Paris, 1612.

Montaigne, Jean de, *Tractatus de parlamentis et collatione parlamentorum*. In *Tractatus universi juris*. Venice, 1584. XVI.

Pasquier, Etienne, *Œuvres*. 2 vols. Amsterdam, 1723.

—— *L'Interprétation des Institutes de Justinian*. Paris, 1847.

Peleus, Julien, *Histoire de Henry le grand*. 4 vols. Paris, 1614–1616.

—— *Le Premier President du Parlement de France*. Paris, 1611.

—— *Les Œuvres*. Paris, 1638.

Pibrac, Guy du Faur de, *Les Quatrains*. Paris, 1640.

Pithou, Pierre, *Les Coustumes du bailliage de Troyes en Champagne avec annotations sur icelles*. Troyes, 1628.

[Pithou, Gillot, etc.], *Satyre menippée de la vertu du catholicon d'Espagne et de la tenu des états de Paris*. 3 vols. Ratisbon, 1726.

Poisson, Pierre, *Traicté de la maiesté royalle en France*. Paris, 1597.

Postel, Guillaume, *La Loy salique*. Paris, 1552.

—— *Les Raisons de la monarchie*. Paris, 1556.

Ragueau, François, *Indice des droicts royaux et seigneuriaux*. Paris, 1583.

Rebuffi, Pierre, *Commentarii in constitutiones seu ordinationes regias*. 3 vols. 1613. Without place of publication.

—— *Tractatus de consuetudine, usu, et stylo in iudiciis valde frequens, et utilis*. In *Commentarii*, III.

—— *Feudorum declaratio*. In *Tractatus universi juris*. Venice, 1584. X.

—— *Explicatio ad quatuor primos pandectarum libros*. Lyon, 1589.

—— *Tractatus varii*. Lyon, 1600.

—— *De christianissimi atque invictissimi regis Franciae muneribus et eius tractatus*. In *Tractatus varii*.

—— *De regum et principum muneribus ac praerogativis*. In *Tractatus varii*.

[Rolland, Nicolas] *Remonstrances treshumbles au roy de France et de Pologne Henry troisiesme de ce nom, par un sien fidele officier et subiect, sur les desordres et miseres de ce royaume, causes d'icelles, et moyens d'y pouruoir à la gloire de Dieu et repos vniuersel de cet estat*. 1588. Without place of publication.

Rubys, Claude de, *Sommaire explication des articles de la coustume du pays et duché de Bourgongne*. Lyon, 1588.

Savaron, Jean, *Chronologie des estats generaux*. Paris, 1615.

Serres, Jean de, *Inventaire general de l'histoire de France*. Paris, 1597.

Servin, Louis, *Vindiciae secundum libertatem ecclesiae Gallicanae*. In Goldast, *Monarchia*. Frankfort, 1668. III.

Seyssel, Claude de, *La Grande Monarchie de France*. Paris, 1558.

—— *Les Louenges du bon roy de France, Louis XII. de ce nom, dict pere du peuple, et de la felicité de son regne*. Paris, 1615.

—— *La Proposition et harangue faicte et proposée par messire Claude de Seyssel . . . au roy d'Angleterre Henry VII*. Printed with *Les Louenges*.

—— (ed.) *Appian Alexandrin, historian grec, des guerres des romains liures XI*. Paris, 1573.

Sorbin, Arnault, *Le Vray Reveille-matin des calvinistes, et publicains françois: où est amplement discouru de l'auctorité des princes, et du deuoir des suiets enuers iceux*. Paris, 1576.

Souvert, Jean de, *Advis pour messieurs les gens des trois estats du pais et duché de Bourgongne, sur le subject de leur assemblee du mois de may prochain mil six cens cinq*. Without place or date of publication.

Terre Rouge, Jean de, *Contra rebelles suorum regum*. Lyon, 1526.

Tiraqueau, André, *Opera*. 2 vols. Frankfort, 1616.

Zampini, Mathieu, *Des estats de France, et de leur puissance*. Paris, 1588.

B. Speeches

Anon., *Harangues et actions publiques des plus rares esprits de nostre temps*. Paris, 1609.

—— *Premier recueil des publicques actions de l'éloquence françoise contenant trente une remonstrances faictes aux ouvertures des parlements et autres cours de ce royaume*. Lyon, 1604.

—— *Sommaire de toutes les harangues, édits et ordonnances . . . en ses estats tenus à Bloys*. 1588. Without place of publication.

Bauffremont, Claude de, *Proposition pour toute la noblesse . . . en l'assemblee generale des`estats de ce royaume en la ville de Bloys l'an 1577*. Paris, 1577.

Beaune, Renaud de, *La Requeste faite au Roy . . . pour le soulagement de son peuple, et subiects le 25 novembre, 1588*. Paris, 1588.

—— *Declaration ou harangue faicte aux estats tenus à Bloys*. Blois, 1589.

Birague, *La Harangue prononcee . . . à l'ouverture des estatz tenuz en la ville de Bloys, le sixiesme de decembre, 1576*. Paris. Without date of publication.

Epinac, Pierre d', *Harengue prononcée deuant le roy, seant en ses estats generaulx à Bloys . . . au nom de l'estat ecclesiastique de France*. Paris, 1577.

La Guesle, Jacques de, *Les Remonstrances*. Paris, 1611.

Lange, Jean, *La Harangue du peuple et tiers estat de toute la France*. Orleans, 1560.

Loisel, Antoine, *La Guyenne*. Paris, 1605.

Marion, Simon, *Plaidoyez*. Paris, 1609.

Matthieu, Pierre, *Harangue aux consuls et peuple de Lyon: Du deuoir et obeissance des subiects enuers le roy . . . prononcee le xxiii decembre, MDXCIII*. Without place or date of publication.

Montluc, Jean de, *Harangue faicte et prononcee . . . en l'assemblée tenue à Warssauie, pour l'election du nouueau roy*. Paris, 1573.

Poisson, Pierre, *Harangue au peuple de France sur les louanges des anciens françois*. Paris, 1588.

Radouant, René (ed.), *Actions et traictez oratoires*. Paris, 1911.

Servin, Louis, *Plaidoyers*. 1603. Without place of publication.

C. Collections of Documents

Anon., *Extraict des registres du premier chapitre du caier des trois estatz . . . à Blois en janvier, 1589*. Lyon. Without date of publication.

—— *Instruction des gens des troys estats du royaume de France . . . à . . . leurs deputez vers le roy de Nauarre*. Blois, 1577.

Bernard, Auguste (ed.), *Procès-verbaux des états généraux de 1593.* Paris, 1842.

Brisson, Barnabé, *Code du Roy Henry III.* Paris, 1587.

Condé, Louis I de Bourbon, prince de, *Mémoires, ou recueil pour servir à l'histoire de France sous les règnes de François II et Charles IX.* 6 vols. London, 1740.

Fontanon, Antoine, *Les Edicts et ordonnances des roys de France.* 2 vols. Paris, 1580.

Godefroy, Théodore, *Le Cérémonial de France.* 2 vols. Paris, 1619.

Gonzague, Louis de, *Les Memoires de monsieur le duc de Nevers.* 2 vols. Paris, 1665.

[Goulart, Simon], *Mémoires de la ligue.* 6 vols. Amsterdam, 1758.

—— *Mémoires de l'estat de France sous Charles IX.* 3 vols. Meidelbourg, 1578.

Isambert, *Recueil général des anciennes lois françaises.* 28 vols. Paris, 1829.

Le Vest, Barnabé, *CCXXXVII arrêts celebres et mémorables du Parlement de Paris.* Paris, 1612.

Louet, Georges, *Recueil d'aucuns notables arrests donnez en la cour de Parlement de Paris.* Paris, 1612.

Mayer, Ch. J. de, *Des états généraux et autres assemblées nationales.* 18 vols. Paris, 1788.

Montholon, Jacques de, *Arrêts de la cour.* Paris, 1645.

Papon, Jean, *Recueil d'arrêts notables des cours souverains de France.* Paris, 1556.

Robert, Anne, *Rerum judicatarum libri IV.* 1599. Without place of publication.

II. SECONDARY SOURCES [1]

Allen, J. W., *A History of Political Thought in the Sixteenth Century.* London, 1928.

Atkinson, Geoffroy, *Les Nouveaux Horizons de la renaissance française.* Paris, 1935.

Baudrillart, Henri, *Jean Bodin et son temps.* Paris, 1853.

Becker, H., *Louis Le Roy.* Paris, 1896.

Blocaille, *Etude sur François Hotman.* Dijon, 1902.

Brejon, Jacques, *André Tiraqueau.* Paris, 1937.

Brown, John L., *The methodus ad facilem historiarum cognitionem of Jean Bodin: A Critical Study.* Catholic University Press, 1939.

[1] This list does not include all secondary sources consulted, particularly the innumerable short studies on individual theorists. It includes only those works cited above, plus certain others which have proved of value in developing the conclusions embodied in this study.

Carlyle, A. J., and Carlyle, R. W., *A History of Medieval Political Theory in the West.* 6 vols. London, 1909–1936.

Chamberland, Albert, *Le Conflit de 1597 entre Henri IV et le Parlement de Paris.* Paris, 1904.

Chauviré, Roger, *Jean Bodin, auteur de la république.* Paris, 1914.

Chénon, Emile, *Histoire générale du droit français, public et privé, des origines à 1815.* 3 vols. Paris, 1926.

Cougny, Edme, *De la philosophie chez les jurisconsultes du XVIᵉ siècle et en particulier chez Simon Marion.* Paris, 1865.

—— *Un Procès en matière de droits régaliens au XVIᵉ siècle.* Paris, 1864.

Declareuil, J., *Histoire générale du droit français des origines à 1789.* Paris, 1925.

De la Bigne de Villeneuve, Marcel, *Traité général de l'état.* 2 vols. Paris, 1929–1931.

Despois, L., *Histoire de l'autorité royale dans le comté de Nivernais.* Paris, 1912.

Dock, Adolf, *Der Souveränetätsbegriff von Bodin bis zu Friedrich dem Grosse.* Strassburg, 1897.

Dubois, Ernest, *Guillaume Barclay, jurisconsulte écossais.* Nancy, 1872.

Dufayard, Charles, *De Claudii Seisselii vita et operibus.* Paris, 1892.

Dupin, A. M. J. J. (ed.), *La Coutume de Nivernais.* Paris, 1864.

Esmein, A., *Histoire du droit français.* Paris, 1910.

—— *Eléments de droit constitutionnel français et comparé.* 2 vols. Paris, 1921.

Feist, Elisabeth, *Weltbild und Staatsidee bei Jean Bodin.* Halle, 1930.

Ferrari, Giuseppe, *Histoire de la raison d'état.* Paris, 1860.

Figgis, John Neville, *The Divine Right of Kings.* Cambridge, 1914.

—— *From Gerson to Grotius.* Cambridge, 1907.

Filhol, René, *Le Premier Président Christofle de Thou et la réformation des coutumes.* Paris, 1937.

Friedrich, Carl Joachim, *Politica methodice digesta of Johannes Althusius.* Harvard University Press, 1932.

Garosci, A., *Jean Bodin, Politica e dritto nel Rinascimento francese.* Milan, 1934.

Gierke, Otto von, *Das Deutsche Genossenschaftsrecht.* 4 vols. Berlin, 1868–1913.

—— *Natural Law and the Theory of Society, 1500–1800.* 2 vols. Ernest Barker, ed. Cambridge University Press, 1934.

—— *The Development of Political Theory.* Bernard Freyd, ed. New York, 1939.

Gilmore, Myron P., *Argument from Roman Law in Political Thought: 1200–1600.* Harvard University Press, 1941.

Hancke, E., *Bodin, Eine Studie über den Begriff der Souverainetät.* Breslau, 1894.

Hanotaux, Gabriel, *Etudes historiques sur le XVI* et le XVII* siècle en France.* Paris, 1886.

Jellinek, Georg, *Allgemeine Staatslehre.* Berlin, 1900.

Joucla, Edmond, *Les Doctrines politiques de Grégoire de Toulouse.* Toulouse, 1899.

Kan, J. van, *Les Efforts de codification en France.* Paris, 1929.

Lagarde, Georges de, *Recherches sur l'esprit politique de la réforme.* Paris, 1926.

Landmann, Max, *Der Souveränetätsbegriff bei den Französischen Theoretikern, von Jean Bodin bis auf Jean Jacques Rousseau.* Leipzig, 1896.

Lebrun, Auguste, *La Coutume.* Paris, 1932.

Lelong, Jean, *La Vie et les œuvres de Loyseau.* Paris, 1909.

Lemaire, André, *Les Lois fondamentales de la monarchie française d'après les théoriciens de l'ancien régime.* Paris, 1907.

Lewin, Wera R., *Claude de Seyssel.* Heidelberg, 1933.

Martin, Olivier, *see* Olivier-Martin, François.

Maugis, Edouard, *Histoire du Parlement de Paris.* 3 vols. Paris, 1913–1916.

Maumigny, J. de, *Etude sur Guy Coquille.* Paris, 1910.

McIlwain, Charles Howard, *Constitutionalism, Ancient and Modern.* Cornell University Press, 1940.

—— *Constitutionalism and the Changing World.* Cambridge University Press, 1939.

—— *The Growth of Political Thought in the West.* New York, 1932.

Meinecke, Friedrich, *Die Idee der Staatsräson in der Neueren Geschichte.* Munich, 1925.

Mesnard, Pierre, *L'Essor de la philosophie politique au seizième siècle.* Paris, 1936.

[Mey, Claude], *Maximes du droit public françois.* Amsterdam, 1775.

Moreau-Reibel, Jean, *Jean Bodin et le droit public comparé, dans ses rapports avec la philosophie d'histoire.* Paris, 1933.

Olivier-Martin, François, *Histoire de la coutume de la prévoté et vicomté de Paris.* 3 vols. Paris, 1922–1930.

—— *L'Organisation corporative de la France d'ancien régime.* Paris, 1938.

—— *Précis d'histoire du droit français.* Paris, 1934.

Picot, Georges, *Histoire des états généraux.* 4 vols. Paris, 1872.

Rehm, Hermann, *Allgemeine Staatslehre.* Freiburg, 1899.

—— *Geschichte der Staatsrechtswissenschaft.* Freiburg, 1896.

Reynolds, Beatrice, *Proponents of Limited Monarchy in Sixteenth Century France: Francis Hotman and Jean Bodin.* Columbia University Press, 1931.

Ronzy, Pierre, *Un Humaniste italianisant: Papire Masson.* Paris, 1924.

Villers, Robert, *L'Organisation du Parlement de Paris et des conseils supérieurs d'après la réforme de Maupeou.* Paris, 1937.

Viollet, Paul, *Histoire des institutions politiques et administratives de la France.* 3 vols. Paris, 1890–1903.

—— *Précis de l'histoire du droit français.* 3 vols. Paris, 1884.

Weill, Georges, *Les Théories sur le pouvoir royal en France pendant les guerres de religion.* Paris, 1892.

Woolf, Cecil N. Sidney, *Bartolus of Sassoferrato.* Cambridge University Press, 1913.

III. PERIODICAL LITERATURE

Aubépin, "De l'influence de Du Moulin sur la legislation française," *Revue critique de la jurisprudence,* III (1853), 603–625, 778–806; IV (1854), 27–44, 261–300; V (1854), 32–62, 305–332.

Beaune, Henri, "Un discours inédit de Henri IV," *Bulletin du bibliophile* (1862), pp. 1386–1392.

Chauviré, Roger, "La Pensée religieuse de Jean Bodin (d'après des documents nouveaux)," *La Province d'Anjou* (1929), pp. 433–451.

Destray, P., "Notes inédites sur Guy Coquille," *Bulletin de la société nivernaise* (1925), pp. 69–91.

Hitier, J., "La Doctrine de l'absolutisme," *Annales de l'université de Grenoble,* XV (1903), nos. 1, 3.

Jacqueton, G., "Le Trésor de l'épargne sous François I," *Revue historique,* LV (1894), 1–43; LVI, 1–38.

Meynial, Ed., "Etudes sur l'histoire financière du XVIe siècle," *Nouvelle Revue historique de droit français et étranger,* XLIV (1920), 451–515; XLV (1921), 459–583.

Olivier-Martin, François, "Le Roi de France et les mauvaises coutumes au moyen âge," *Zeitschrift der Savigny-Stiftung für Rechtsgeschichte. Germanistische Abteilung,* LVIII (1938), 108–137.

Potter, John Milton, "The Development and Significance of the Salic Law of the French," *English Historical Review,* LII (1937), 235–253.

Shepard, Max Adams, "Sovereignty at the Crossroads: A Study of Bodin," *Political Science Quarterly* (1930), pp. 580–603.

INDEX

INDEX

Absolutism, theory of, 17, 20, 21, 43–73, 179, 307–312, 315–335; origins of theory, 8, 18, 19, 45, 245, 246, 251, 263, 268; result of social developments, 77, 303–305

Administrators, importance in constitutional thought, 5; without title to royal prerogative, 37–39, 52–54, 121–123, 125–127, 130, 188, 189, 237–239; exercise of the prerogative, 39, 40, 52–54, 121–123, 125–127, 130, 188, 189; shared prerogative with the king, 123–125

Allen, J. W., 22, 220

Alodial lands, 183, 184, 239, 296

Angleberme, Jean d', 49, 50

Argentré, Bertrand d', 106–108, 182, 187, 272, 297

Aristotle, 61, 132, 212, 218, 228, 253, 270, 321

Aubert, Guillaume, 153

Bacquet, Jean, 101, 113, 145–147, 299

Baldus, 181, 185, 186

Barclay, William, 20, 132, 133, 315, 320, 321, 325–327, 332, 333

Barker, Ernest, 12

Bartolists, use of Roman law, 9, 10; on tenure of public authority, 52, 56; on legislation, 56, 57, 96; mentioned, 106, 112, 184

Bartolus, 9

Bauffremont, Claude de, 119, 163

Beaumanoir, 127

Beaune, Henri, 315

Beaune, Renaud de, 174

Belleforest, François de, 169, 170

Belloy, Pierre de, 19, 91–93, 246, 264–266, 268, 269, 271

Beza, Théodore de, 14, 123–125

Bignon, Jerome, 327

Blackwood, Adam, position in intellectual currents, 245, 246; on divine right of kings, 247, 248; on the royal succession, 250; denies constitutional limitations, 253, 254; equates justice and royal government, 253, 254; on spheres of legal right, 259, 260; doctrine of prescription, 330; mentioned, 19, 251, 263, 269

Bodin, Jean, position in intellectual currents, 13, 15, 45, 76, 212, 213, 223, 229, 235, 242–247, 254, 255, 264, 265; character and method of thought, 13, 15, 212, 213, 215–217, 219; on universal values, 215–219, 229, 230; on religion in the state, 217, 218; on changes in the constitution, 213–216, 221–223, 230, 231, 236; dynamic conception of the state, 213–216, 221–223, 236; on celestial forces over men and states, 213, 214, 221, 222; on historical study, 215, 216; theory of climate, 216, 217; on corporations, 99, 100; on the family, 99, 220, 223–225; on paternal authority, 220, 223–225; classification of states, 227, 228; on royal and seigneurial monarchy, 225, 231, 232, 239, 257; concept of legitimate government, 220, 231, 232; theory of sovereignty, 212, 216, 220, 222–224, 226–231, 235, 243–245, 250, 251, 264, 265; on royal legislation, 228–230; widens sphere of royal discretion, 222, 225, 227, 230, 235–237; categories of legal values, 229, 230, 232, 233, 236, 237; emphasis upon natural law, 214, 216–221, 223–226, 229, 231–237, 242, 288; on fundamental law, 233; on customary law, 226, 235–237; on contracts, 233, 234; on private property, 225, 226, 231, 234, 235, 240, 288; on consent to taxation, 167, 234, 235, 238, 240, 257, 288; denies authority of Estates General to frame law, 162, 163, 238; on authority of magistrates, 237–239; on Parlement of Paris, 221, 238, 239; on the land